T0319835

Developments in Entrepreneurial Finance and Technology

Edited by

David B. Audretsch

Indiana University, USA and the Department of Innovation Management and Entrepreneurship, University of Klagenfurt, Austria

Maksim Belitski

Henley Business School, University of Reading, UK and ICD Business School of Paris, France

Nada Rejeb

ICD Business School of Paris, France

Rosa Caiazza

Parthenope University of Naples, Italy

Edward Elgar PUBLISHING

Cheltenham, UK • Northampton, MA, USA

Published by
Edward Elgar Publishing Limited
The Lypiatts
15 Lansdown Road
Cheltenham
Glos GL50 2JA
UK

Edward Elgar Publishing, Inc.
William Pratt House
9 Dewey Court
Northampton
Massachusetts 01060
USA

A catalogue record for this book
is available from the British Library

Library of Congress Control Number: 2022938784

This book is available electronically in the **Elgar**online
Business subject collection
http://dx.doi.org/10.4337/9781800884342

ISBN 978 1 80088 433 5 (cased)
ISBN 978 1 80088 434 2 (eBook)

Printed and bound by CPI Group (UK) Ltd, Croydon, CR0 4YY

Contents

Contributors

Daniel Agyare is currently a third-year PhD fellow in Technology, Innovation and Management (TIM) in the Department of Management, Information and Production Engineering and a member of the Center for Young and Family Enterprise (CYFE), both at the University of Bergamo, Italy. He earned his bachelor's and master's degree in International Business Management at the same university. His research primarily focuses on non-accounting drivers and external equity financing in the context of academic spin-offs (ASOs). He believes that these dimensions of ASOs play an important role in the decision making of investors around the world.

Martina Aronica is a research fellow at the University of Palermo, Italy. She holds a MSc in Economic and Financial Analysis and a PhD in Economics and Statistics from the same university. She has been a visiting student at the Pompeu Fabra University in Spain. She received the 9th "Giorgio Rota" Best Paper Award and the AISRe-GSSI Best Paper Award. Her research interests mainly focus on regional science, spatial economics, and innovation studies. She has published in international journals such as *Spatial Economic Analysis*, *Journal of International Trade and Economic Development*, *The World Economy*, and *Papers in Regional Science*.

David B. Audretsch is a Distinguished Professor and the Ameritech Chair of Economic Development at Indiana University, USA, where he also serves as Director of the Institute for Development Strategies. He is an Honorary Professor of Industrial Economics and Entrepreneurship at the WHU-Otto Beisheim School of Management in Germany and a research fellow of the Centre for Economic Policy Research in London, UK. His research has focused on the links between entrepreneurship, government policy, innovation, economic development, and global competitiveness. He is co-author of *The Seven Secrets of Germany*, published by Oxford University Press. He is co-founder and Editor-in-Chief of *Small Business Economics: An Entrepreneurship Journal*. He was awarded the Global Award for Entrepreneurship Research by the Swedish Entrepreneurship Forum (Entreprenörskapsforum) and the Schumpeter Prize from the University of Wuppertal in Germany. He has further received honorary doctorate degrees from the University of Augsburg in Germany and Jonköping University in Sweden.

Maksim Belitski is a Professor in Entrepreneurship and Innovation at Henley Business School, University of Reading, UK, at ICD Business School of Paris, France, and a research fellow at the Institute for Development Strategies, Indiana University Bloomington, USA. He is a field expert in small business economics and the use of digital technologies, contributing to the *Digitally Driven* report for Europe (2021). Previously, he has held appointments at Loughborough University, University College London, and University of Leicester, all in the UK, as well as the University of Economics in Bratislava, Slovakia and Belarusian State University in Belarus. He teaches entrepreneurship, managerial economics, research methods, and digital leadership. He holds a PhD in Social Sciences from the University of Leicester, UK, as well as a PhD in Economics from the University of Milan, Italy. He is a "Trusted" researcher of the Secure Data Service, UK Data Archive and Virtual Microdata Lab of the UK's Office of National Statistics and has been a fellow of the Higher Education Academy since 2013. His research interests lie in the areas of entrepreneurship, innovation and regional economics, and digital competences and skills for SMEs. He is an editor of *Small Business Economics: An Entrepreneurship Journal*, which is a leading journal in the field of small business and entrepreneurship.

Rosa Caiazza, PhD, is Professor of Management at Parthenope University of Naples, Italy, and Visiting Professor at Wharton University of Philadelphia, USA. She has been included in the top 100,000 scientists worldwide across all knowledge areas, according to a study of Stanford University published in PLOS Biology. She has been included in the ICSB's Educator 300, the International Council for Small Business's list of 300 of the world's most renowned professors of small business and entrepreneurship. She serves as an advisory board member for a number of top-tier academic journals. Her research and teaching activity is focused on strategy, corporate governance, entrepreneurship, innovation, and operation management. She has published four books and over a hundred journal articles and book chapters. She has been the chair of many international conferences and has won several awards for excellence.

Wendy Chen is an Assistant Professor at Texas Tech University, USA. She is also a Senior Associate Editor for the *Management Decision* journal, where she bridges management theories and practices. Having worked in media, small businesses, multinational corporations, and nonprofits from around the globe, Wendy's research aims to provide actionable managerial and policy recommendations to improve organizational efficiency and better our communities.

James A. Cunningham is a Professor of Strategic Management at Newcastle Business School, Northumbria University, UK. He has held academic positions at University College Dublin and National University of Ireland Galway (NUI Galway). At NUI Galway he held a variety of leadership positions including Head of Strategic Management group, Executive MBA Programme Director, Director of the Centre of Innovation and Structural Change, and founding Director of the Whitaker Institute. His research focuses on strategy issues with respect to scientists as principal investigators; university technology transfer commercialization; academic, public sector, and technology entrepreneurship; entrepreneurial universities; and business failure.

Hoda El Kolaly is a Visiting Assistant Professor of Management in the School of Business at the American University in Cairo (AUC), Egypt. She earned her PhD in Business and Management from the University of Nottingham, UK, in 2018, and her MBA and BSc from AUC in 2002 and 2006, respectively. She has taught various courses in universities in Egypt and the United Arab Emirates, namely, Misr International University (MIU), the American University of Sharjah (AUS), and the American University of Ras Al Khaimah (AURAK). Her academic experience is coupled with a strong practical experience in the field of marketing and business development. Her primary research interests are in the areas of service research and consumer behavior. Her current interests extend to entrepreneurial marketing in family and non-family businesses, with a special interest in research on women entrepreneurs.

Henry Etzkowitz is CEO of the International Triple Helix Institute in Palo Alto, USA, and President of the Triple Helix Association. He is the author of iconic articles on the entrepreneurial university, the triple helix and women in science, research policy, and technology forecasting and social change. Henry is the author of *MIT and the Rise of Entrepreneurial Science* and co-author of *Triple Helix: University–Industry–Government Innovation and Entrepreneurship* and *Athena Unbound: The Advancement of Women in Science and Technology*.

Maribel Guerrero is Professor of Entrepreneurship in Facultad de Economía y Negocios at Universidad del Desarrollo, Santiago, and at the Global Center for Technology Transfer, School of Public Affairs, Arizona State University, USA. She is also an affiliated member of CIRCLE – Centre for Innovation Research at Lund University, Sweden. Prof. Guerrero holds a PhD and MPhil in Business Economics from the Department of Business of the Autonomous University of Barcelona, Spain. Her main research interests are focused on entrepreneurship, intrapreneurship, ecosystems, and emerging economies. She serves on the board of *The Journal of Technology Transfer* (Associate Editor), *Journal of Small Business* (Associate Editor), *Technology Forecasting* *and Social Change* (Advisory Board), *Entrepreneurship Theory and Practice* (Reviewer Board), and *Small Business Economics* (Reviewer Board). Also, she serves on the AoM Entrepreneurship Division Executive Committee (re-elected treasurer), and is a board member of the Global Entrepreneurship Monitor Association (GERA), Technology Transfer Society, and others.

Davide Hahn is a postdoctoral research fellow in the Department of Management, Information and Production Engineering and in the Center for Young and Family Enterprise (CYFE) at the University of Bergamo, Italy. He obtained his doctoral degree from the PhD Program on Economics and Management of Technology offered jointly by the University of Pavia and the University of Bergamo. His research focuses on entrepreneurship in the context of university. His research has appeared in the *Journal of Management Studies*, *Small Business Economics*, *Entrepreneurship and Regional Development*, *The Journal of Technology Transfer*, and the *International Entrepreneurship and Management Journal*.

Patrick Haslanger works as a Strategy Consultant at the Boston Consulting Group (BCG). He received his PhD from the University of Augsburg, Germany, and holds an MBA from the Purdue Krannert School of Management, Indiana, USA. He further worked as a research fellow at the LMU Munich School of Management, Ludwig Maximilian University of Munich, Germany. His research concentrates on corporate entrepreneurship, especially corporate venture capital and corporate accelerators.

María José Ibáñez is a Business Management Engineer, with a bachelor's degree in Education and a master's degree in Industrial Management. She is currently a PhD candidate in Business Economics at the School of Business Economics, Universidad del Desarrollo, Chile. Her research interests focus on gender issues, entrepreneurship, and sustainable business.

Matthias Menter is a Tenure Track Assistant Professor of Business Dynamics, Innovation, and Economic Change at the Friedrich Schiller University Jena, Germany. He is also a research fellow at the Institute for Development Strategies (IDS) at Indiana University, USA, having earlier been a visiting scholar and adjunct lecturer at the university's School of Public and Environmental Affairs (SPEA). Prior to this he worked as a research fellow at the University of Augsburg, Germany. His research focuses on aspects of entrepreneurial and innovative ecosystems, academic entrepreneurship, university–industry collaborations, and public policy.

Alexander Mikhaylov is a graduate of HSE University, Moscow, Russia, and a PhD student at the Institute of Geography of the Russian Academy of Science (RAS), where he is writing a thesis on the topic of spatial economic structures of Russian urban agglomerations. He is a research fellow in the Centre for Economic Geography and Regional Studies of the Russian Presidential Academy of National Economy and Public Administration (RANEPA). His main research interests include spatial and regional economics, diffusion of innovations, and entrepreneurship studies.

Tommaso Minola is Associate Professor in the Department of Management, Information and Production Engineering (DIGIP) and co-founder and Director of the Center for Young and Family Enterprise (CYFE) at the University of Bergamo, Italy. In his research, he is interested in studying how different dimensions of the enterprising individual (e.g., motivation, cognition, behavior) and of the entrepreneurial firm (e.g., goals and resource allocation) are affected by embeddedness in social contexts, such as the university and the family. He has established several research collaborations, mainly across Europe and the United States. His works have been published in leading academic journals on innovation, entrepreneurship, and small business, such as *Research Policy*, *Journal of Management Studies*, *Entrepreneurship Theory and Practice*, *Strategic Entrepreneurship Journal*, *Small Business Economics*, *Journal of Small Business Management*, *Entrepreneurship and Regional Development*, and *The Journal of Technology Transfer*.

Rita Nasr is a doctoral researcher at Henley Business School, University of Reading, UK. Her research explores the institutional role of middle-level brokers in developing recycling practices. She also explores research themes that involve the role of digital technologies in work practices within organizations pre and post the COVID-19 pandemic. She facilitates learning in the UK higher education sector at various levels and serves as editorial administrator for *Planning Theory*, where she deploys her expertise in spatial transformation for governance in urban design, planning, and sustainable development. Rita holds a BA in Architecture, a master's degree in Urban Planning, and is currently pursuing her PhD at Henley. She participates regularly in international conferences, where she presents on dynamic urban transformations and waste management practices.

Kofi Osei-Frimpong is a Senior Lecturer in Marketing at the University of Professional Studies, Accra (UPSA), Ghana. He is also a research fellow at the Vlerick Business School, Ghent, Belgium. He received his PhD from the University of Strathclyde, Glasgow, UK. His research interests include value co-creation in healthcare service delivery, customer engagement practices, social media use, artificial intelligence voice assistants, online customer support, and service design. He has presented papers at international service research conferences and has published in high-impact academic journals including *Information Technology and People*, *Journal of Business Research*,

Computers in Human Behavior, *Technological Forecasting and Social Change*, and *European Journal of Work and Organizational Psychology*, among others.

Davide Piacentino is Associate Professor of Economic Statistics at the University of Palermo, Italy. He has been a visiting scholar at University of Strathclyde and University of Sussex, both in the UK. He holds a MSc in Economics and Econometrics from the University of Rome Tor Vergata and a PhD in Economic Analysis and Policies for Local Development from the University of Palermo. His research interests focus on regional science, spatial economics, innovation studies, and firm demography. He has published papers in international journals such as *Regional Studies*, *Spatial Economic Analysis*, *Annals of Regional Science*, *Spatial Statistics*, *Economic Modelling*, *Growth and Change*, *Papers in Regional Science*, *Geographical Analysis*, and *Journal of International Trade and Economic Development*.

Pasquale Massimo Picone is Associate Professor of Management at the University of Palermo, Italy. He has worked at the University of Bergamo, Italy, and at the University of Catania, Italy, where he also received his PhD in Business Economics and Management. He has held visiting positions at Texas A&M University, USA and IE Business School in Madrid, Spain. His research interests include the psychological foundations of management and temporary competitive advantages. His research has been published in leading journals, including *Academy of Management Perspectives*, *Corporate Governance: An International Review*, *Family Business Review*, *Global Strategy Journal*, *International Journal of Management Review*, *Business Horizons*, and *Journal of Management and Governance*. He is an active member of the editorial board of *Management Decision* and *Journal of Management and Governance*.

Natalya Radko is a research associate in the Department of Leadership, Organisations and Behaviour, Henley Business School, University of Reading, UK. Natalya's research activity is focused on studying the university as a key stakeholder of entrepreneurial society, as well as the role universities can play in the process of knowledge transfer. Her research interests include the development of entrepreneurial universities, considering different stakeholders for the knowledge spillover of entrepreneurship, with an emphasis on the process by which universities can work together with relevant actors, including authorities and business. She studies entrepreneurial ecosystems around the university, applying both a stakeholder theory approach and the knowledge spillover theory of entrepreneurship. In addition to being a teaching assistant at Henley Business School, Natalya is a manager within the Creative Spark: Higher Education Enterprise Programme. This is a five-year British Council initiative to support partnerships to develop enterprise skills and creative economy across seven countries in Central Asia and the South Caucasus.

Nada Rejeb is Associate Professor in Entrepreneurship and Strategy at ICD Business School of Paris, France. She holds a Visiting Professor position at JAMK School of Business, Finland. Her research interests revolve around entrepreneurship, innovation, knowledge networks, and collaborative relationships, with a specific interest in family firms collaboration and innovation strategies. She is also interested in topical issues in entrepreneurship, such as entrepreneurial entry by disadvantaged minorities.

Mahsa Samsami is a doctoral candidate in the Economics and Business Programme at University of Santiago de Compostela, Spain. She earned her master's degree in Business Administration from Tehran University, Iran. Her academic background is complemented by extensive practical experience in business administration, notably family businesses, entrepreneurship, investor behavior, especially in financial markets and in the digital environment, and marketing communication, especially electronic word of mouth in financial institutions. She has worked as a human resource and executive manager, was a member of the board in a brokerage firm of a stock exchange, and was a teaching assistant at Tehran University.

Deepa Scarrà is a research fellow at Henley Business School, University of Reading, UK, an affiliate researcher at Scuola Superiore Sant'Anna, Italy, and a visiting lecturer at ICD Business School, France. She also works as a consultant for startups. She obtained a PhD in Management from Scuola Superiore Sant'Anna, studying technology transfer and innovation in big science environments. She is passionate about innovation and entrepreneurship.

Thomas Schøtt undertook his doctoral studies at Columbia University, USA, received postdoctoral training at Yale University, USA, held various kinds of professorships across the United States, Denmark, China, Colombia, Morocco, and Iran, and currently sojourns as a Professor at University of Agder, Norway, and as a Distinguished Visiting Professor at the American University in Cairo, Egypt. For some decades he has been working with the Global Entrepreneurship Monitor. His publications have appeared in *Research Policy*, *Small Business Economics*, *Entrepreneurship and Regional Development*, and elsewhere. His current research focuses on entrepreneurial recovery from the pandemic around the world.

Nikolaus Seitz is Deputy Professor for Management at the LMU Munich School of Management, Ludwig Maximilian University of Munich, Germany. He is also Assistant Professor at the University of Augsburg, Germany. Apart from these roles, he coordinates the Augsburg Center for Entrepreneurship at the University of Augsburg. His research aims at developing a better understanding of entrepreneurship-driven development strategies, innovation milieus, and the role of corporate venturing in regional startup ecosystems.

Recent projects focus on the performance of corporate accelerators and entrepreneurship policies.

Lebene Richmond Soga is a Program Director and Lecturer in Entrepreneurship and Leadership at Henley Business School, University of Reading, UK. His research explores a range of themes, including the social aspects of digital technologies in organizational life, entrepreneurship ecosystems, and manager–employee relations. He regularly presents his research at international conferences for business leaders, academics, and policymakers to progress the understanding of various organizational challenges and the implications of new technologies for the practice of leadership. His insights are featured within Business Value Exchange (now Thrive), CIPD, ACCA Global, and Forbes. He has published in leading academic and practitioner outlets, including *Harvard Business Review*, *MIT Sloan Management Review*, *European Journal of Work and Organizational Psychology*, and *Small Business Economics*, among others.

Silvio Vismara is Professor of Corporate Finance at the University of Bergamo, Italy. Silvio is Editor of *Small Business Economics*, Executive Editor of the *Review of Corporate Finance*, Associate Editor of *The Financial Review*, *The Journal of Technology Transfer*, and *Management Review Quarterly*, and an editorial board member for other journals. His research interests are in entrepreneurial finance and focus mainly on IPOs, equity crowdfunding, and ICOs. His research is widely cited in academic publications and has been covered in media outlets around the world, including *The Economist* and *The Financial Times*.

Kayleigh Watson is a Senior Lecturer at Newcastle Business School, Northumbria University, UK. Prior to joining the school, she held the role of Postgraduate Academic Assistant at the University of Sunderland, UK, following completion of her undergraduate and postgraduate degree studies at Newcastle University. Kayleigh also holds a Postgraduate Certificate in Teaching and Learning in Higher Education and is a fellow of the HEA. Her main research area concerns the promotion of startup competitions as an entrepreneurial learning experience. In addition to her core research interests, she is keen to use her practice as an educator to inform research. This has inspired pedagogical research around the embedding of formative feedback within module design and delivery.

Stepan Zemtsov graduated from Lomonosov Moscow State University, Russia, where in 2013 he completed his PhD thesis on the topic "Innovative potential of the Russian regions". He is now the Director of the Centre for Economic Geography and Regional Studies in the Russian Presidential Academy of National Economy and Public Administration (RANEPA). He has authored over 120 publications, including ones in leading Russian and foreign journals and is a permanent expert of professional Russian media. Stepan is a specialist in the field of regional analysis, consulting, and strategic planning and has participated in federal strategies for the development of the SME sector. His main research interests include regional development, entrepreneurship studies, high-tech business in Russia, the geography of innovations, and the influence of geographic conditions on socio-economic development.

Chunyan Zhou, PhD, is Director/Senior Researcher of the International Triple Helix Institute located in the Silicon Valley, USA. Her research interests focus on the university–industry–government triple helix for innovation, especially on government's roles, the entrepreneurial university, and regional innovation policy. Dr. Zhou co-authored the book *The Triple Helix: University–Industry– Government Innovation and Entrepreneurship* (Routledge, 2018) with Henry Etzkowitz; authored *From Science to Technology: The Scientific Basis in the Technological Era* (NEU Press, 2002); co-edited the book *Social Entrepreneurship: Leveraging Economic, Political and Cultural Dimensions* (Springer, 2014); and translated the book *PASTEUR'S QUADRANT: Basic Science and Technological Innovation* (Science Press, 1999) by Donald E. Stokes. Her key contributions include proposing the "triple helix field", "triple helix twins", and "government-pulled triple helix" concepts.

Introduction to entrepreneurial finance and technology

David B. Audretsch, Maksim Belitski, Nada Rejeb, and Rosa Caiazza

Entrepreneurship is one of the fundamental drivers of economic progress (Audretsch and Belitski, 2013). In addition, it is an effective tool for growth in emerging or developed countries (Audretsch et al., 2015), growth that is shaped by quality institutions (Audretsch et al., 2021; Chowdhury et al., 2019). Entrepreneurship is also considered a powerful lever in fighting poverty and deprivation (Bruton et al., 2010; Belitski et al., 2021) and redirecting financial resources to their most productive means (Cumming et al., 2021).

In recent decades, and with the beginning of the global pandemic, we have witnessed a revolution in the world economy driven by dramatic changes in technology and the use of finance. These changes have affected local and global economies, small and medium-sized enterprises (SMEs), and the self-employed. The most commonly used term to describe these changes is digitization. Even though there is no standard definition of this term in the literature, it generally refers to converting information into a digital format that can be processed and handled at platforms and creating tools based on using knowledgeable systems. Along with digitization, the process of alternative financing has started to accelerate. Methods of financing such as venture capital (VC), equity crowdfunding, reward-based crowdfunding, and initial coin offerings (Belitski and Boreiko, 2021) have played a prominent role in the development of new products and services by entrepreneurs.

Despite the importance of digitization and alternative finance, micro- and macroeconomic-level analysis of the role that digitization and new methods of financing play in entrepreneurship and regional development is still lacking. The purpose of this book is to contribute to the discussion on the role of the methods of finance and technology in enhancing entrepreneurship and growing regional economies. The emergence of digital technologies and new methods of finance has proved to be a useful catalyst for the spillover of new ideas and their commercialization through innovation (Audretsch and Belitski, 2022).

1. FINANCING FOR ENTREPRENEURSHIP

Resources such as finance and technology are needed for entrepreneurial activity. This book addresses several aspects of the evolving landscape caused by digitalization, points to new developments in alternative sources of finance in the entrepreneurship and regional development literature, and offers a research agenda for future research.

Securing needed finance is one of the main challenges facing those wanting to start a new business. While corporate finance traditionally focuses on established listed corporations, entrepreneurial finance largely focuses on younger, privately owned firms. Entrepreneurial finance encompasses a variety of finance types from various sources, including VC, private equity, business angel finance, crowdfunding, grants, funding from incubators or accelerators, and support from family and friends (Cosh et al., 2009).

In recent years, entrepreneurial finance has witnessed the emergence of new agents and channels of fundraising for startups. New regulations on alternative funding (AF) in the United States and Europe potentially have significant implications for entrepreneurs and investors (Estrin et al., 2018; Cummings et al., 2020). AF enables entrepreneurs to bypass the conventional financial industry's channels such as banks, public debt, and VC (Block et al., 2018a, 2018b; Hornuf and Schwienbacher, 2017, 2018).

Crowdfunding, a new AF method of funding startups through online portals by collecting contributions from many investors, has become a valid universal tool for financing projects worldwide and is regulated and promoted by many countries (Cumming et al., 2016; Vismara, 2016, 2018). The subsequent development of blockchains and smart contracts embedded in the limited regulatory environment of emerged cryptocurrencies has been conducive to attracting funds from small, dispersed investors. Along with equity crowdfunding (Vismara, 2018), initial coin offering (ICO) has emerged as a novel mechanism for financing entrepreneurial ventures. Through an ICO, a venture offers a stock of specialized crypto tokens for sale, promising that those tokens will operate as the only medium of exchange when accessing the venture's future products (Catalini and Gans, 2018).

Prior research on AF has almost entirely focused on two main strands. The first strand relates to the economics and rationale of using token sales as a financing method (Catalini and Gans, 2018; Howell et al., 2020) and the geography of ICOs (Huang et al., 2020). The second, earlier, and more empirically focused strand relates to the potential regulation of the ICO activity (Rohr and Wright, 2019; Zetsche et al., 2017), with most recent papers studying determinants of ICO funding success (Adhami et al., 2018; Fisch, 2019; Fisch and Momtaz, 2020; Amsden and Schweizer, 2018; Blaseg, 2018; Boreiko and Sahdev, 2018).

Equity crowdfunding has been particularly fast-growing, attracting attention from entrepreneurs and industry (Vismara, 2018). The role of public investors in crowdfunding has been studied by Vismara (2016) for 271 projects listed on UK platforms such as Crowdcube and Seedrs. The author found that campaigns launched by entrepreneurs who sold a smaller fraction of their companies at listing and had more social capital had higher success. Unfortunately, detailed data on equity-crowdfunding investments are not always readily available as very few portals openly share their data and, when they do, they only provide daily aggregates. This data could shed light and provide valuable evidence on the dynamics of overall investment by the crowd, which were, for example, studied in a seminal paper by Hornuf and Schwienbacher (2017). Information plays a crucial role in entrepreneurial equity finance (Vismara, 2018). Initial public offerings (IPOs) with a high level of institutional demand in the first days of book building had higher bids and vice versa. This fact explains why some IPOs typically result in either oversubscription or undersubscription.

Funding new products and services is a central concern of entrepreneurial finance. One issue related to funding innovation concerns information asymmetries between entrepreneurs and finance providers. Extant literature emphasizes important mechanisms investors use to address agency issues, such as negotiating high-powered contracts and active involvement in their portfolio firms (Cumming and binti Johan, 2008). This literature argues that early-stage investors need to specify more detailed information disclosure requirements than investors in listed corporations. Investments at early stages take place over several rounds, conditional on pre-specified progress targets being met, thereby reducing potential agency issues (Yung, 2019). Yet the growing interest in high-tech startups highlights the high uncertainty surrounding those companies and points to the need to consider new criteria that can be used in early-stage equity investments.

2.   DIGITIZATION, TECHNOLOGY, AND ENTREPRENEURSHIP

Technology has been advocated as a source of opportunities for entrepreneurs (Mosey et al., 2017; Beckman et al., 2012), allowing entrepreneurs to experiment and produce new products and services which are intricately related to advances in scientific and technological knowledge. Digital technology has been exceptionally helpful in facilitating scaling up with both startups and incumbents, in particular creating an immediate competitive advantage, independently of firm size and history.

To explain the role of digital technologies in creating a competitive advantage for entrepreneurship, let us appeal to the concept of digital dynamic capabilities, which establish the basis of competitive advantage for firms (Helfat, 2000; Helfat and Peteraf, 2003).

Digitization of dynamic capabilities to quickly redeploy, for example, an R&D capability from one market to another digitally will require three mechanisms (Van Grembergen and De Haes, 2010), with the change happening within three domains: strategic, management, and operational (Tallon and Pinsonneault, 2011; LEAD, 2014).

These three domains do not exist in a vacuum (Santoro et al., 2019). They consist of interrelated elements embedded into three digitization mechanisms that entrepreneurs use to grow and sell. Along with the managerial and operational domain of dynamic capabilities employed across organizational departments, the strategic domain is likely most important for a firm's performance and growth. This domain aims to promote new product creation and strategic alignment of business and IT operations and objectives (Henderson and Venkatraman, 1993), leading to better integration of all digital technologies in the organization. The strategic digital component of dynamic capabilities can also reduce costs by enabling better access to various consumers, thereby enhancing sales and productivity. Higher concentrations of workers with IT-enabled strategic and managerial skills appear to drive firm growth and productivity (LEAD, 2014).

According to the digital dynamic capabilities of entrepreneurial firms, strategy is essential for building up the business and IT infrastructures, for business and IT aligned vision, and for promoting competitive advantage and growth and doing so both internally and externally as advocated by the new open innovation paradigm. SMEs face considerable shortages of resources compared to larger firms, and thus will experience more significant challenges in terms of achieving sufficiently diverse resources and will require applying various combinations of digitization mechanisms to leverage these shortages (Helfat, 1997; Cassiman and Valentini, 2016; Merindol and Versailles, 2020).

Digital entrepreneurship pushed the developments in science or engineering that constitute a core element of the opportunity that enables the emergence of a venture, market, cluster, or industry. Does this raise the fundamental dilemma of which innovation strategy – Market Pull or Technology Push – entrepreneurs should adopt? On the one hand, the diffusion of digital technologies such as artificial intelligence (AI), big data, and cloud computing generates new business models aiming to harness these sophisticated, cutting-edge technologies (Kohli and Melville, 2019; Sorescu, 2017). On the other hand, by enabling direct, frequent, and deep interactions between firms and their consumers, digital innovation is spawning numerous business models that can better identify, analyze, understand, and answer consumer needs (Priem et al., 2018; Wirtz et al., 2010).

The COVID-19 pandemic enabled "digital acceleration" for digitally advanced small and medium-size businesses (SMBs), which were demonstrated to be more prepared to implement digital changes during the pandemic. Indeed, 97 percent of them in the United States have made some digital changes, while only 49 percent of digitally uncertain SMBs implement such changes (Digitally Driven, 2020). Overall, around 80 percent of SMBs have made digital changes during the pandemic in Europe and the United States. This is mainly due to the adoption rate of digitally advanced SMBs and not to a kind of advancement of digitally uncertain SMBs (Digitally Driven, 2020, 2021).

More precisely, higher usage of digital tools in the pre-pandemic period is correlated with "digital acceleration" during the pandemic. In order to embrace digital technologies, the following four pillars of digitization need to be adopted:

- Mindset: recognizing digital tools are more helpful now than pre-pandemic.
- Familiarity: feeling comfortable with digital tools.
- Investment: increased financial investment in digital tools, both in the tools themselves and in employee training.
- Deployment: increased use of at least one digital tool during a pandemic or in crises.

We conclude that the digital gap between less and more advanced SMBs is due to a lack of "digital optimization," which enables SMBs to use certain kinds of digital tools to optimize their use of other tools and their business as a whole. Indeed, the adoption of digital tools has an exponential effect on entrepreneurship growth, opportunity discovery, and innovation. Consequently, policies have to address this digital gap by supporting SMBs leaders in the digital transformation.

3.   THE CONTENTS OF THE BOOK

In summarizing their contribution, we present the book chapters in the sequence in which they appear in the book to allow the reader to plan their reading experience. The first part of the book highlights the importance of technological, cognitive, social, and institutional contexts (Audretsch et al., 2022) in facilitating the adoption of digital technology by entrepreneurs. In the second part of the book, we collected chapters on the role of finance in entrepreneurship, emphasizing the emerging alternative finance route.

In Chapter 1, "The technological dilemma for entrepreneurial leaders: who drives innovation?" by Lebene Richmond Soga, Kofi Osei-Frimpong, and Rita Nasr, the authors review the theories of technological innovation, which they relate to how humans and firms adapt to the new technologies. The authors emphasize that technological innovation in most cases delivers social change and the entrepreneur as a leader drives this change in the pursuit of market profits.

In Chapter 2, "Startups and regional entrepreneurship ecosystems: the Russian case" by Stepan Zemtsov and Alexander Mikhaylov, the authors investigate the role of the entrepreneurial ecosystem in entrepreneurship, focusing on high-tech startups and a new technological revolution. They use empirical data from the Russian regional entrepreneurial ecosystem to show that startup activity was higher in regions with a more educated population and a high density of university students, as young entrepreneurs with a high level of skills create many startups. The authors describe the role of knowledge context for entrepreneurs and the startup activity in regions with scientific and technological knowledge and those generating significant knowledge spillovers for R&D and the productivity of entrepreneurs (Audretsch and Belitski, 2020; Caiazza et al., 2020; Audretsch et al., 2020b). They build on Audretsch and Belitski's (2021c) seminal study in explaining the role of agglomeration economies and industrial structure in European regions and apply the framework to Russian regions.

In Chapter 3, "Women serial high-tech entrepreneurs: a literature review and research agenda" by María José Ibáñez and Maribel Guerrero, the authors continue the discussion of the role of context for entrepreneurs and emphasize how serial entrepreneurs use technology to grow. Serial entrepreneurship has become increasingly visible, and its impact on the economy is substantial. Due to women's different attitude to risk and uncertainty, there are important gender differences in risk-taking behavior, which may prevent women entrepreneurs from entering the technology industry (Belitski and Desai, 2021; Audretsch et al., 2020a). The authors provide an excellent literature review on the features and characteristics of serial entrepreneurship, specifically female serial entrepreneurship. Based on the content analysis of the literature on serial entrepreneurship, some new trends are proposed, including in relation to how serial entrepreneurs make decisions in the digital age.

In Chapter 4, "Big data analytics and internationalisation in Italian firms" by Martina Aronica, Davide Piacentino, and Pasquale Massimo Picone, the authors examine the role of big data in developing firms' international e-commerce. This empirical study is based on 18,900 Italian firms, with most being SMEs. SMEs are characterized by high managerial flexibility, and in turn, such flexibility represents a key driver of digitalization processes. The main research question addressed in this chapter is how do Italian firms take advantage of big data analysis for developing their international e-commerce?

In Chapter 5, "Science, entrepreneurship, and spin-off diversity" by Deepa Scarrà, the author discusses the diversity of university spin-offs coming from science. This type of academic entrepreneurship has different characteristics and needs. It is more likely to adopt a technology-push than a market-pull approach due to the complexity and novelty of the technology used by academic spin-offs. Connecting different theoretical approaches, this study also demonstrates the competitive university strategies of knowledge commercialization (Belitski et al., 2019) and provides a set of conditions on how science-based spin-offs may adopt technology and what it leads to.

In Chapter 6, "Entrepreneurial university stakeholders and their contribution to knowledge and technologies transfer" by Natalya Radko, the author contributes to developing a new conceptual model of the entrepreneurial university applying a stakeholder perspective (Zott et al., 2011; Audretsch and Belitski, 2021a, 2021b). The author considers an entrepreneurial university as a central organization in driving change and technological development in a region, and that stakeholders play an important role in adopting new technologies. The model provided in the chapter represents a first conceptualization of the multi-actor model of the entrepreneurial university to identify various types of stakeholders (e.g., corporate, industry, government, VC, incubators, science parks) and their roles in knowledge creation, transfer, and commercialization within and outside the university (Audretsch and Belitski, 2019).

In Chapter 7, "The invention and diffusion of venture capital: when knowledge married capital" by Henry Etzkowitz, Chunyan Zhou, and Rosa Caiazza, the authors outline the development of a university-based startup strategy for regional development. The strategy focuses on firms, with the university as a subsidiary element, supplying existing knowledge and building connections with the industry to attract investments. The authors demonstrate how university strategy can ensure knowledge transfer to industry. They conclude that there should be a relative balance between two strategies, one strategy focused on firms, the other on universities, with the mutual objective of knowledge diffusion and commercialization.

In Chapter 8, "Public sector entrepreneurship, principal investigators, and entrepreneurial effectuation" by James A. Cunningham, Matthias Menter, and Kayleigh Watson, the authors examine the role and influence of public sector entrepreneurship (PSE) programs designed to advance scientific knowledge and have economic, social, and technological impacts. This chapter demonstrates that an academic environment is likely to create greater value for entrepreneurial ecosystem stakeholders in a region (Audretsch and Belitski, 2017). A fundamental question that this chapter addresses is how publicly funded principal investigators use entrepreneurial effectuation to shape, lead, and deliver on PSE programs.

In Chapter 9, "A systematic literature review of reward-based crowdfunding" by Wendy Chen, the author examines the process of crowdfunding, which is a new type of finance. The chapter aims to benefit scholars interested in crowdfunding research, as well as entrepreneurs, organizations, and policymakers, who can gain insights from the studies reviewed. It starts with a discussion of the methodological approach used to build the database for this systematic literature review and then describes how the reviewed articles contribute to a better understanding of different types of reward-based crowdfunding. The review ends with a discussion of directions for future research and the challenges that such research may encounter.

In Chapter 10, "Business angels' ties with entrepreneurs" by Mahsa Samsami, Hoda El Kolaly, and Thomas Schøtt, the authors analyze the role of business angel investment in entrepreneurship. The business angel may fund someone they are strongly tied to, notably family and relatives, or perhaps someone with whom they have no ties, such as a stranger pitching a good idea. This chapter discusses what influences the business angel to select one type of tie over others for funding. It argues that this selection is embedded in culture, specifically the dimension of traditional versus secular-rational culture. Using a sample of 133,553 business angels in 115 countries obtained from a survey by the Global Entrepreneurship Monitor, the authors applied hierarchical linear modeling for testing hypotheses.

In Chapter 11, "Exploring the landscape of corporate venture capital and corporate accelerators in Germany" by Nikolaus Seitz and Patrick Haslanger, the authors aim to contribute to the literature on external corporate venturing, especially corporate venture capital (CVC) and corporate accelerators (CAs), by providing an overview of the German corporate venturing market and offering new empirical insight into how CVC and CAs work. Using a novel dataset of 765 startups managed by 36 venturing units, this chapter presents findings regarding the setting up, organization, and staffing of corporate venturing units, as well as the characteristics of startups.

Finally, in Chapter 12, "Non-accounting drivers of start-up valuation by early-stage equity investors: literature review and future research agenda" by Daniel Agyare, Davide Hahn, Tommaso Minola, and Silvio Vismara, the authors focus on early-stage equity investors' funding of innovative startups. Early-stage equity investors are equipped to overcome information asymmetries surrounding the financing of innovation. The authors demonstrate how, when choosing which startups to invest in, investors use selection criteria that help them deal with the uncertainty surrounding innovative startups' commercialization of new products and services. To this extent, the contribution of this chapter is in moving from a literature review on the valuation of innovative startups by early-stage equity investors to advancing a theory-informed taxonomy of non-accounting drivers used by early-stage equity investors in the valuation of innovative startups.

REFERENCES

Adhami, S., Giudici, G., and Martinazzi, S. (2018). Why do businesses go crypto? An empirical analysis of initial coin offerings. *Journal of Economics and Business*, *100*, 64–75.

Amsden, R., and Schweizer, D. (2018). Are blockchain crowdsales the new "gold rush"? Success determinants of initial coin offerings. Available at SSRN: https://ssrn .com/abstract=3163849.

Audretsch, D. B., and Belitski, M. (2013). The missing pillar: the creativity theory of knowledge spillover entrepreneurship. *Small Business Economics*, *41*(4), 819–836.

Audretsch, D. B., and Belitski, M. (2017). Entrepreneurial ecosystems in cities: establishing the framework conditions. *Journal of Technology Transfer*, *42*(5), 1030–1051.

Audretsch, D. B., and Belitski, M. (2019). Science parks and business incubation in the United Kingdom: evidence from university spin-offs and staff start-ups. In S. Amoroso, A. N. Link, and M. Wright (eds), *Science and Technology Parks and Regional Economic Development* (pp. 99–122). Cham, Switzerland: Palgrave Macmillan.

Audretsch, D. B., and Belitski, M. (2020). The role of R&D and knowledge spillovers in innovation and productivity. *European Economic Review*, *123*, 103391.

Audretsch, D. B., and Belitski, M. (2021a). A strategic alignment framework for the entrepreneurial university. *Industry and Innovation*, *29*(2), 285–309.

Audretsch, D. B., and Belitski, M. (2021b). Three-ring entrepreneurial university: in search of a new business model. *Studies in Higher Education*, *46*(5), 977–987.

Audretsch, D. B., and Belitski, M. (2021c). Towards an entrepreneurial ecosystem typology for regional economic development: the role of creative class and entrepreneurship. *Regional Studies*, *55*(4), 735–756.

Audretsch, D. B., and Belitski, M. (2022). The limits to open innovation and its impact on innovation performance. *Technovation*, 102519.

Audretsch, D. B., Belitski, M., and Brush, C. (2020a). Innovation in women-led firms: an empirical analysis. *Economics of Innovation and New Technology*, 1–21.

Audretsch, D. B., Belitski, M., Caiazza, R., Günther, C., and Menter, M. (2022). From latent to emergent entrepreneurship: the importance of context. *Technological Forecasting and Social Change*, 121356.

Audretsch, D. B., Belitski, M., Caiazza, R., and Lehmann, E. E. (2020b). Knowledge management and entrepreneurship. *International Entrepreneurship and Management Journal*, *16*(2), 373–385.

Audretsch, D. B., Belitski, M., and Cherkas, N. (2021). Entrepreneurial ecosystems in cities: the role of institutions. *PLOS ONE*, *16*(3), e0247609.

Audretsch, D. B., Belitski, M., and Desai, S. (2015). Entrepreneurship and economic development in cities. *Annals of Regional Science*, *55*(1), 33–60.

Beckman, C., Eisenhardt, K., Kotha, S., Meyer, A., and Rajagopalan, N. (2012). Technology entrepreneurship. *Strategic Entrepreneurship Journal*, *6*(2), 89–93.

Belitski, M., Aginskaja, A., and Marozau, R. (2019). Commercializing university research in transition economies: technology transfer offices or direct industrial funding? *Research Policy*, *48*(3), 601–615.

Belitski, M., and Boreiko, D. (2021). Success factors of initial coin offerings. *Journal of Technology Transfer*, 1–17.

Belitski, M., and Desai, S. (2021). Female ownership, firm age and firm growth: a study of South Asian firms. *Asia Pacific Journal of Management*, *38*, 825–855.

Belitski, M., Desai, S., and Godley, A. (2021). Small business and poverty: evidence from post-Soviet cities. *Regional Studies*, *55*(5), 921–935.

Blaseg, D. (2018). Dynamics of voluntary disclosure in the unregulated market for initial coin offerings. Available at SSRN: https://ssrn.com/abstract=3207641.

Block, J. H., Colombo, M. G., Cumming, D. J., and Vismara, S. (2018a). New players in entrepreneurial finance and why they are there. *Small Business Economics*, *50*(2), 239–250.

Block, J., Hornuf, L., and Moritz, A. (2018b). Which updates during an equity crowd-funding campaign increase crowd participation? *Small Business Economics*, *50*(1), 3–27.

Boreiko, D., and Sahdev, N. K. (2018). To ICO or not to ICO – Empirical analysis of initial coin offerings and token sales. Available at SSRN: https://ssrn.com/abstract=3209180.

Bruton, G. D., Ahlstrom, D., and Li, H. L. (2010). Institutional theory and entre-preneurship: where are we now and where do we need to move in the future? *Entrepreneurship Theory and Practice*, *34*(3), 421–440.

Caiazza, R., Belitski, M., and Audretsch, D. B. (2020). From latent to emergent entre-preneurship: the knowledge spillover construction circle. *Journal of Technology Transfer*, *45*(3), 694–704.

Cassiman, B., and Valentini, G. (2016). Open innovation: are inbound and outbound knowledge flows really complementary? *Strategic Management Journal*, *37*(6), 1034–1046.

Catalini, C., and Gans, J. S. (2018). Initial coin offerings and the value of crypto tokens. National Bureau of Economic Research Working Paper No. w24418.

Chowdhury, F., Audretsch, D. B., and Belitski, M. (2019). Institutions and entre-preneurship quality. *Entrepreneurship Theory and Practice*, *43*(1), 51–81.

Cosh, A., Cumming, D., and Hughes, A. (2009). Outside entrepreneurial capital. *The Economic Journal*, *119*(540), 1494–1533.

Cumming, D., and binti Johan, S. A. (2008). Preplanned exit strategies in venture capital. *European Economic Review*, *52*(7), 1209–1241.

Cumming, D. J., Hornuf, L., Karami, M., and Schweizer, D. (2016). Disentangling crowdfunding from fraudfunding. Max Planck Institute for Innovation and Competition Research Paper No. 16-09. Available at SSRN: https://ssrn.com/abstract=2828919.

Cumming, D., Meoli, M., and Vismara, S. (2021). Does equity crowdfunding democra-tize entrepreneurial finance? *Small Business Economics*, *56*(2), 533–552.

Cummings, M. E., Rawhouser, H., Vismara, S., and Hamilton, E. L. (2020). An equity crowdfunding research agenda: evidence from stakeholder participation in the rule-making process. *Small Business Economics*, *54*(4), 907–932.

Digitally Driven (2020). *U.S. Small Businesses Find a Digital Safety Net during COVID-19*. Report. Connected Commerce Council. Available at: https://connectedcouncil.org/wp-content/uploads/2020/09/Digitally-Driven-Report.pdf.

Digitally Driven (2021). *European Small and Medium-Sized Enterprises (SMEs): Transformation, Innovation, and Resilience during the COVID-19 Pandemic.* Report. Connected Commerce Council. Available at: https://digitallydriven .connectedcouncil.org/europe/wp-content/uploads/sites/2/2021/03/Digitally-Driven -Europe-FINAL-1.pdf.

Estrin, S., Gozman, D., and Khavul, S. (2018). The evolution and adoption of equity crowdfunding: entrepreneur and investor entry into a new market. *Small Business Economics*, *51*, 425–439.

Fisch, C. (2019). Initial coin offerings (ICOs) to finance new ventures. *Journal of Business Venturing*, *34*(1), 1–22.

Fisch, C., and Momtaz, P. P. (2020). Institutional investors and post-ICO performance: an empirical analysis of investor returns in initial coin offerings (ICOs). *Journal of Corporate Finance*, *64*, 101679.

Helfat, C. E. (1997). Know-how and asset complementarity and dynamic capability accumulation: the case of R&D. *Strategic Management Journal*, *18*(5), 339–360.

Helfat, C. E. (2000). Guest editor's introduction to the special issue: the evolution of firm capabilities. *Strategic Management Journal*, *21*(10–11), 955–960.

Helfat, C. E., and Peteraf, M. A. (2003). The dynamic resource-based view: capability lifecycles. *Strategic Management Journal*, *24*, 997–1010.

Henderson, J. C., and Venkatraman, N. (1993). Strategic alignment: leveraging information technology for transforming organizations. *IBM Systems Journal*, *32*(1), 4–16.

Hornuf, L., and Schwienbacher, A. (2017). Should securities regulation promote equity crowdfunding? *Small Business Economics*, *49*(3), 579–593.

Hornuf, L., and Schwienbacher, A. (2018). Market mechanisms and funding dynamics in equity crowdfunding. *Journal of Corporate Finance*, *50*, 556–574.

Howell, S. T., Niessner, M., and Yermack, D. (2020). Initial coin offerings: financing growth with cryptocurrency token sales. *Review of Financial Studies*, *33*(9), 3925–3974.

Huang, W., Meoli, M., and Vismara, S. (2020). The geography of initial coin offerings. *Small Business Economics*, *55*(1), 77–102.

Kohli, R., and Melville, N. P. (2019). Digital innovation: a review and synthesis. *Information Systems Journal*, *29*(1), 200–223.

LEAD (2014). E-leadership skills for small and medium sized enterprises project. European Commission, Directorate-General for Enterprise and Industry. Available at: http://eskills-guide.eu/news/single-view/article/lead-e-leadership-skills-for-small -and-medium-sized-enterprises/.

Merindol, V., and Versailles, D. W. (2020). Boundary spanners in the orchestration of resources: global–local complementarities in action. *European Management Review*, *17*(1), 101–119.

Mosey, S., Guerrero, M., and Greenman, A. (2017). Technology entrepreneurship research opportunities: insights from across Europe. *Journal of Technology Transfer*, *42*(1), 1–9.

Priem, R. L., Wenzel, M., and Koch, J. (2018). Demand-side strategy and business models: putting value creation for consumers center stage. *Long Range Planning*, *51*(1), 22–31.

Rohr, J., and Wright, A. (2019). Blockchain-based token sales, initial coin offerings, and the democratization of public capital markets. *Hastings Law Journal*, *70*, 463–524.

Santoro, G., Thrassou, A., Bresciani, S., and Del Giudice, M. (2019). Do knowledge management and dynamic capabilities affect ambidextrous entrepreneurial intensity and firms' performance? *IEEE Transactions on Engineering Management*, *68*(2), 378–386.

Sorescu, A. (2017). Data-driven business model innovation. *Journal of Product Innovation Management*, *34*(5), 691–696.

Tallon, P. P., and Pinsonneault, A. (2011). Competing perspectives on the link between strategic information technology alignment and organizational agility: insights from a mediation model. *MIS Quarterly*, *35*(2), 463–486.

Van Grembergen, W., and De Haes, S. (2010). A research journey into enterprise governance of IT, business/IT alignment and value creation. *International Journal of IT/Business Alignment and Governance (IJITBAG)*, *1*(1), 1–13.

Vismara, S. (2016). Equity retention and social network theory in equity crowdfunding. *Small Business Economics*, *46*(4), 579–590.

Vismara, S. (2018). Information cascades among investors in equity crowdfunding. *Entrepreneurship Theory and Practice*, *42*(3), 467–497.

Wirtz, B. W., Schilke, O., and Ullrich, S. (2010). Strategic development of business models: implications of the Web 2.0 for creating value on the internet. *Long Range Planning*, *43*(2–3), 272–290.

Yung, C. (2019). Entrepreneurial manipulation with staged financing. *Journal of Banking and Finance*, *100*, 273–282.

Zetsche, B., Heidenreich, M., Mohanraju, P., Fedorova, I., Kneppers, J., DeGennaro, E. M., ... and Zhang, F. (2017). Multiplex gene editing by CRISPR–Cpf1 using a single crRNA array. *Nature Biotechnology*, *35*(1), 31–34.

Zott, C., Amit, R., and Massa, L. (2011). The business model: recent developments and future research. *Journal of Management*, *37*(4), 1019–1042.

PART I

Technology and entrepreneurial context

1. The technological dilemma for entrepreneurial leaders: who drives innovation?

Lebene Richmond Soga, Kofi Osei-Frimpong, and Rita Nasr

INTRODUCTION

Technology is undoubtedly a critical resource for contemporary organisations as it supports significant levels of resources within the organisation (Pearlson et al., 2020). In a world that is increasingly described as digital (Bennis, 2013), one in which technology is ubiquitous (Vodanovich et al., 2010), or as a world of hybrids (Bloomfield, 2001), inter alia, entrepreneurial innovation has thrived by fundamentally changing the way humans organise themselves. While technology has altered how work is organised, and therefore has had corresponding impacts on labour and operational processes, demonstrated in the ubiquity of technological infrastructure in organisations, arguments have been raised as to whether such a role of technology is worth the time and resources committed to those technological undertakings (see for example Marshall, 2006). This dilemma remains for entrepreneurial leaders as they deploy technology, or seek to do so, in order to drive innovation for competitive advantage. But who or what really drives innovation in the organisation? Is it the human deploying technology as a means to an end or is it the technology that 'forces' the desired innovative change? And what consequences emerge from deploying such technology?

In Zuboff's (1988) ethnographic study of the deployment of a technological system at a pulp mill (detailed in her book, *In the Age of the Smart Machine*), she demonstrates the transformative *impact* of technology in organisations. Kallinikos (2011) recognises the importance of Zuboff's work by acknowledging how, even after two decades, Zuboff's (1988) study, 'as perhaps every great work, holds out remarkably' having 'rapidly gained recognition across a wide spectrum of social science disciplines, including management and organization studies, information systems, social psychology, and sociology, and has been debated and quoted extensively' (p. 1). We hold a similar view and take it as a starting point to advance arguments on some of the major debates that this field of study has generated over the years. Even more importantly, it is argued that, despite the era of the publication of Zuboff's work, key insights concerning the impact of technologies on organisations remain useful for the analysis of phenomena such as current technological innovations that were not yet present when she conducted her study (Kallinikos, 2011).

In the Age of the Smart Machine presents us with the argument that technology fundamentally restructures our material world, resists the magnetism of past ways of working, delivers innovative possibilities, and compels new decisions within the organisation (Zuboff, 1988). Being such a revealing study of how individuals felt about the transformation of their work vis-à-vis the technology, as well as the changing dynamics of managerial control, the call for understanding how technology impacts individuals and work could not be any more pressing. However, this is also indicative of how importance is placed on technology creating a path for humans, with little thought on how humans have participated in shaping or constructing this impact of technology on themselves. The study also demonstrates how technology, which is originally intended to automate work, simultaneously generates data that triggers a new set of reflexive processes that inform different managerial behaviours and actions. In other words, technology does not only automate work, but it also reflexively 'informates' managers and elicits corresponding managerial action (Zuboff, 1988). From this school of thought, a passiveness of leadership action in its relationship with technology is implied so that even an unintended consequence of technology determines how leadership is practised within the organisation.

A key question remains for us, that is, what practical and methodological implications unfold when this capacity of technology to 'informate' becomes amplified as entrepreneurial leaders introduce various technological innovations into their organisational practices? Zuboff's (1996) later analysis on the need for a new kind of leadership in the information economy may be instructive. In this later analysis, Zuboff (1996) argues that the *impact* of technology on organisations is not benign. For instance, even though its transformative power in the organisation cannot be overlooked, technology has nonetheless compelled managers to pursue ways of improving organisational efficiency that have become detrimental to the *moral* fabric of the organisation. That is, its 'informating' capacity has engendered an evolutionary mechanism in which low-skilled workers are no longer employable. In a practical sense, exploiting this new 'informated' organisation demands

> opening up the information base of the organization to members at every level, assuring that each level has the knowledge and skills to productively engage with

that information, and endowing all members with the authority to express and ultimately act on what they can know. It implies a new social contract that redefines who people are at work, what they can know, and what they can do. (Zuboff, 1996, p. 16)

The choice of 'who people are' in the 'informated' organisation, the author argues, now becomes a moral burden for managers who must subscribe to a 'kind of moral leadership that can articulate new values' (Zuboff, 1996, p. 17). Opening up of the information base within the organisation may be parallel to today's digital technologies introduced into organisations, but this presents a conundrum when notions of 'morality' are mentioned. Although arguments of morality are out of scope for this chapter, it is still indicative of how power and agency are attributed to technology that it is able to lure humans into such a contested zone. What this 'moral leadership' is is unclear, but the call for *proactive* action by managers in an 'informated' organisation seems contradictory. This is because technology is presented earlier as dictating the pace while at the same time calls are made for managers to be proactive in the changing organisation.

Arguably, these arguments constitute many twists of thought-provoking phenomena especially when juxtaposed with recent developments of technological innovation in entrepreneurial organisations. Whether organisations are passive actors in their relationship with technology or, rather, (pro)active in their connection with technology, the implications for entrepreneurial leaders in the organisation cannot be taken for granted. This is because leadership is attributed to organisational success or failure (Müller and Turner, 2010; Nixon et al., 2012; Pisarski et al., 2011; Turner and Müller, 2005) even though that is itself a contested phenomenon in some cases (Grint, 2005; Yukl, 2010). To deepen our analysis of the arguments around this technological dilemma, we turn to major debates in the literature that overarch the role of technology in organisations. At the core of these debates is the question of who is really in control: is it the human or is it the technology that is deployed in the organisation to drive innovation?

As an overview, this chapter examines the philosophical dimensions associated with technology and its relationship with entrepreneurial innovation. We begin by laying out arguments in technological determinism, which lies at one end of the spectrum. We then discuss the social shaping of technology and, finally, at the other end of the spectrum, raise the debates regarding the social construction of technology. We recognise the weaknesses in these schools of thought and provide one way of examining the arguments raised, using the actor-network perspective. We conclude the chapter by offering what implications these arguments hold for future research and practice.

TECHNOLOGICAL DETERMINISM

Who is in control? Do entrepreneurial organisations have a choice in how they organise or reorganise themselves in the face of their (new) technological innovations? These are questions that potentially undermine or challenge the role of entrepreneurial leaders depending on one's worldview on the subject of technological determinism. Determinism is the idea that there is an inevitable path for progression in society determined by some factor (Smith and Marx, 1998). Philosophically, William James identifies in the old classic, *Essays in Pragmatism*, what the notion of determinism acknowledges. For him, determinism

> professes that those parts of the universe already laid down absolutely appoint and decree what the other parts shall be. The future has no ambiguous possibilities hidden in its womb: the part we call the present is compatible with only one totality. Any other future complement than the one fixed from eternity is impossible. (James, 1948, p. 40)

The philosophical argument here is that the universe, according to determinists, is one complete whole whose many parts must fit into their respective places in order to conform to a predetermined actuality. Here, the direction taken by events becomes an issue of the will (or its imprisonment) thereof; that is, no other possibilities exist except those necessitated by things preceding them; all other possibilities are rendered imaginary and cannot be reified. In Smith and Marx (1998), the possibilities that exist in organisational practices are necessitated by the dictates of technology, which the authors argue dates back to the Industrial Revolution in which scholars believed that technological innovation drove change in society more than any other factor. Smith (1998) for instance provides an analysis of the historical development of the idea of technological innovation driving social progress. In his evaluation, technological innovation assumed a place of dominance in American culture while artists and writers touted technology as a force that could deliver the promise of American life. 'Such technocratic pitches constituted a form of technological determinism that embedded itself deeply in popular culture' (Smith, 1998, p. 14).

While providing detailed documentary evidence for such a claim, what is obvious is Smith's (1998) focus on the wider social *impact* of technology leaving out intra-organisational dimensions. However, in using Mumford's 1964 *The Myth of the Machine* and Ellul's 1967 *The Technological Society* to bolster his analysis, Smith (1998) draws out the strength of technology asserted by these authors and its possible impact in organisations. For instance, Jacques Ellul's classic, *The Technological Society*, is a provocative one that reduces the human to a 'slug inserted into a slot machine' (Ellul, 1967, p. 135). Even though the human is seen as a moral entity able to decide either good or evil, it nonetheless possesses no power over 'technique' – technological advancement. Rather, technology exercises its autonomy by dominating the human with its advancing spheres. The human could only stand aside or become technology's servant, according to Ellul. That is, humans could not have power over technology in the organisation because the organisation must survive by the latter's dictates, eventually behaving like a machine – perhaps becoming mechanistic and non-flexible in its structure like in Burns and Stalker's (1994) characterisation of a 'mechanistic' organisation (although this characterisation may not be a direct implication of technology). Implicitly, what these arguments suggest is that the boundaries between the social and the technological are now blurred or probably non-existent to the extent that technology forces its way into the equation through its imperatives. A logical implication then is that entrepreneurial leaders in organisations are themselves subject to the directives of the technologies they introduce into their organisations.

Even though social constructivists (Bijker, 1995; Pinch and Bijker, 1989) reject the postulates of technological determinism, the questions of technological determinists are still pertinent and therefore must not be overlooked. Drawing from Smith (1998), Lawson (2007) admonishes that technological determinism, although an under-theorised phenomenon, invariably becomes irresistible and researchers will find it difficult to repel its dangerous charm. Perhaps this is because 'the central point is that technology itself is not neutral. Everything is sucked up into the technological process and reduced to the status of a resource that has to be optimised in some way' (Lawson, 2007, p. 35). A methodological implication for this argument is that the technology being used in the organisation must also form part of the unit of analysis.

However, the non-coherence of theories of technological determinism in the literature in itself causes a rethink of its underlying ideologies. For instance, in *Does Technology Drive History?*, a collection of arguments by Smith and Marx (1998) on the dilemma of technological determinism, a close examination reveals two sets of divergent views. First, views of such contributors as Heilbroner and Perdue that connote technology as the instrument dictating change; these contributors are characterised as *hard* technological determinists who would view technological innovation as solely *impacting* the entrepreneurial action inside an organisation in a *specific* manner, which the researcher must investigate. Second, those as presented by Hughes, Bulliet and Marx that introduce an element of the 'social' into the idea of technological determinism. Here, social change or *impact* is as much a product of other factors like economics and social behaviours as it is of technological innovation. In other words, the direction in which events move is not only a matter of the force of technology but also of socio-economic/cultural influences. This therefore suggests that the degree to which agency is attributed to technology must be weighed against the contribution of other social influences (Hughes, 1998). The implication is that the impact of social shaping and construction of technology on the organisation and its entrepreneurial leaders must also be explored. Thus, arguments for *hard* technological determinism seem to be diluted with a *soft* approach on how the phenomenon is or should be construed.

Methodologically, the *soft* account suggests the inclusion of social constructivist perspectives (Hughes, 1998). But this idea of *soft* technological determinism that incorporates social influences is difficult to grasp if technological innovation is to be ascribed any power that drives organisational progress. Bimber (1998) for instance argues that the term *technological* determinism better not be used at all as it is impossible to consider the social as being a component of 'technological' determinism. But even in established organisations like the Massachusetts Institute of Technology (MIT), technology's 'deterministic' drive of progress seems palpable. Williams (2000) highlights 'the irony, and the poignancy, of MIT's history' (p. 645) by revealing that although arguable, her 'MIT colleagues are convinced it [i.e., technological determinism] is simply true' (p. 649). Williams is a historian of technology and a one-time dean of students and undergraduate education at MIT. Her experiences as well as those of others when she was leader make up the core of her argument, probably a good example of a leader's personal frustration with technology. Williams (2000), who narrates the story of technological change at MIT with its corresponding cultural changes, problematises the idea of technological determinism using her own experiences of the tensions created as a result of the introduction of new technologies. These tensions, she admits, were those in which technology usually won when trade-offs needed to be made. Implicit in the narrative is a frustration about the power technological innovation exudes in an organisation such that organisational actors would have to scramble to address the resultant challenges that occur.

Methodologically, Williams's (2000) analysis implies a thorough consideration of the lived experiences of those involved with technology in order to pass any judgement about how their lives have (or have not) been impacted by the technology. This approach may sound contradictory since technological determinists are not so much interested in whom (or what) technology impacts as they are in the technology that causes the impact. Wyatt (2008) expresses similar methodological concerns with arguments of technological determinism raised by Heilbroner (1998) and Edgerton (1999) in which it is not the lived experiences of social actors that matter, but the technologies available to them that are of consequence. In other words, the object of analysis of any research involving technology must be the technology itself (either in use or just available to actors) and not the lived experiences of those using the technology. But it is also clear that we cannot ignore the relevance of technological determinism to real-life experiences, as dismissing it would be akin to ignoring a thundering herd of elephants (Wyatt, 2008). The arguments thus move us to the idea of the social shaping of technology, which to a large extent embraces social elements in the analysis.

SOCIAL SHAPING OF TECHNOLOGY

One divergent view from the idea of technological determinism is the concept of the social shaping of technology (SST; MacKenzie and Wajcman, 1999). As argued earlier, *soft* technological determinism introduces an element of the social by asserting that technology alone cannot be attributed agency when it comes to social change; instead, other factors like culture, politics, economics and so on make up a plethora of influences on the social in addition to technology. SST carries notions similar to those of *soft* technological determinism as recognised by MacKenzie and Wajcman (1999). They argue that technological determinists tend to focus on the *impact* or *effects* of technology and therefore fail to acknowledge how social and organisational processes are themselves constitutive of technology. In other words, technology does not necessarily influence an organisation as some external source but is itself intricately shaped by the organisation. What this assertion generates methodologically is that not only do we need to ask how individuals *adapt* to the technology, but we must also find out how individuals *shape* these technologies either for political or other organisational reasons.

SST argues that in shaping technology, certain political dynamics are deployed, which may make the technology favourable for one group but unsavoury to others whom Winner (1993), for instance, laments become 'irrelevant' social groups. For example, the 1920s to the 1970s saw Robert Moses as the master builder of New York; he was contracted to build roads, bridges, parks and other public places. Moses built overhead bridges across the road to Long Island so low that only car-owning whites of 'upper' and 'comfortable middle' classes could have access (Winner, 1986). The bridges thus excluded the poor racial minority who mainly used public transport buses. On the surface, the bridges were meant to transport vehicles; nonetheless they were also designed and built to serve Moses's racial prejudice. It is however worth noting that this evidence is disputed by Joerges (1999), who refutes any such attribution of racism to Robert Moses by Winner (1986). This example is an indication of controversies about technology and society that technical things possess qualities that have been built into them which reflect the desires of certain groups of individuals.

Technology is thus a dialectical union of the technologically possible and the socially desirable so that there is a translation of certain human intentionality into technological innovations (Rauner et al., 1988). Consequently, one implication of the SST approach is that the adoption of technological innovation by entrepreneurial leaders in an organisation must not be seen as merely a technological input. In other words, the technology also embodies specific forms of power and authority within the organisation (Subašić et al., 2011). However, the notion of inbuilt political intentions in technology or artefacts like Moses's bridges makes the argument problematic. It presupposes that technology is a static object whose inbuilt determinate aims would effect a desired change which others must comply with (Akrich, 1992). This brings one back to technological determinism, only this time with a focus on implicit human commands.

Orlikowski (2000) thus raises epistemological concerns on how the researcher can obtain knowledge of technology's inbuilt politics. She argues that rather than view technology as an embodiment of certain 'structures' – 'rules and resources instantiated in social practice' (p. 406) – it must be considered as an enactment of *emergent* social practices. That is, the 'use of the technology involves a repeatedly experienced, personally ordered and edited version of the technological artifact, being experienced differently by different individuals and differently by the same individuals depending on the time or circumstance' (Orlikowski, 2000, p. 408). The implication is that how individuals deploy the technology within the organisation may be shaped by factors that were not originally anticipated in its adoption.

Moreover, it is only when individuals actually use the technology in the organisation that it can be said to shape their actions, thus raising the idea of 'sociomateriality' – the argument that considers the relationship between individuals and technology as an entanglement rather than a relationship between distinct entities (Orlikowski and Scott, 2008). SST theorists have thus posited technology as not only *impact*ing the organisation but also as constitutive of certain social practices, is politically shaped by some privileged individuals, engenders emergent practices, and is intimately entangled with individuals within the organisation. Methodologically, these arguments suggest that the researcher examines at the 'micro' level how individuals are interacting with the technology in order to understand fully its social shaping effects (Orlikowski, 2000). This shift from a focus on the technology itself to the social gets even more radical with the idea of the social construction of technology, explored next.

SOCIAL CONSTRUCTION OF TECHNOLOGY

Social construction of technology (SCOT) is an argument that rejects the ascription of any organisational *impact* or progress to some technological logic (Bijker, 1995). Instead, SCOT argues for a *construction* of the technological artefact by people within the organisation based on the meanings that the technology has for them (Pinch and Bijker, 1989). Here, it is not just a *shaping* of what technological innovation is already there but a question of *how* and *why* the innovation came to be used and now taken for granted (Latour, 1987). For SCOT proponents, there are 'relevant social groups' that are involved in negotiating the deployment of technological innovation, but these groups of individuals often differ in their views of how the technology may be appropriated, a notion referred to as 'interpretative flexibility' – that is, to one group the technology may be useful in a particular way but to another group unhelpful (Pinch and Bijker, 1989). This lack of uniformity on what a technological innovation means for individuals in an organisation receives 'closure' when a common interpretation becomes agreed upon. The implication is that entrepreneurial leaders who wish to deploy any technological innovation in their organisations would have to be aware of potential conflicts. This is because 'facts' about technology are always a matter of different interpretations by relevant social groups (Bijker, 1995), while other individuals become marginalised or 'irrelevant' (Winner, 1993). This is a limitation of SCOT as it lacks consideration for the wider social, cultural and political milieu within which technological innovation is made possible (Klein and Kleinman, 2002).

Methodologically, what SCOT suggests is that the researcher needs to identify what 'relevant' social groups were involved in the adoption of the technology (Bijker, 1995) as well as seeking to find out what the 'irrelevant' social groups were in the process (Winner, 1993). Understanding what meanings these different groups of individuals attach to the technology may be instructive in appreciating how the technology has influenced their organisational or entre/intrapreneurial practices. However, as Klein and Kleinman (2002) argue, it is problematic to conceptualise society as composed of groups when in reality many different views arise with power asymmetry both between and within groups. To identify these 'relevant social groups' Bijker (1995) suggests a snowball technique, which Klein and Kleinman (2002) find challenging. In a 'snowball' method, 'the researcher interviews a few actors at the start, asking them to identify relevant groups, and in this way eventually builds up the set of all groups' (Klein and Kleinman, 2002, p. 32). It still risks exclusion of other social actors or becoming so big a 'snowball' that it becomes almost impossible for any meaningful analysis (Klein and Kleinman, 2002).

While critiquing Bijker's (1995) methodological propositions in relation to SCOT, Klein and Kleinman (2002) argue a 'structural' approach to conceptualising and investigating 'closure' of a social group's construction of technology. They argue that structures such as the group's political resources, economic resources, culture and so on must be considered as influential indicators in examining how a particular technology came to be socially constructed. However, this wider socio-structural approach seems to be only concerned about the *design* of technology, as also are other social constructionist ideas (see Bijker, 1995; Pinch, 1998; Pinch and Bijker, 1989), and not the *adop-*

tion of the technological innovation into a new or different setting, which is equally relevant for entrepreneurial leaders. This is because entrepreneurial activity in organisations is not only about the creation or design of new ideas (Schumpeter, 1934) but also about the discovery and use of existing ideas (Kirzner, 1973, 1999). Consequently, implications of SCOT in organisational settings are ignored since most organisations tend to *adopt* and not design from scratch the technologies they find useful for their ventures (McCabe, 2007; Saldanha and Krishnan, 2012).

What is common with SCOT scholars, as argued so far, is the shift from the technological innovations alone as the units of analyses to the social dynamics that engendered the final acceptance and use of any particular technology. Winner (1993), who also disagrees with turning to the technologies alone as the objects of analysis (cf. Heilbroner, 1998; Edgerton, 1999), looks for an alternative approach from social constructivists (e.g., Pinch and Bijker, 1989). However, disappointments still remain when we take only a SCOT perspective in that the consequences of technology are seldom a focus of study. This is because 'what the introduction of new artifacts [technology] means for people's sense of self, for the texture of human communities, for qualities of everyday living, and for the broader distribution of power in society [is] not of explicit concern' (Winner, 1993, p. 368). Moreover, the interpretive behaviours of individuals on whether the adoption of certain technologies in an organisation is of value or not cannot be taken for granted (Leonardi, 2009; Orlikowski and Gash, 1994). We also cannot neglect the unintended consequences of the deployment of technology even though SCOT only implicitly alludes to these.

Whereas technology is acclaimed as having the capability to drive change (Grübler, 2003; Zuboff, 1988), shape outcomes in organisational practices (Tushman and Murmann, 2003) and offer flexibility in work processes (Lucas and Olson, 1994; Valcour and Hunter, 2005), where flexibility is defined as the ability to adapt to new and changing requirements from external market forces (Lucas and Olson, 1994), unintended consequences are also identified in organisational studies, with implications for entrepreneurial leaders. For instance, Church et al. (2002) argue that the relevance of technology in organisational development and change initiatives, though evident, engenders an over-reliance on the technology, which in turn increases the potential for unintended consequences.

In a study of PepsiCo's Web-based career management platform, in which the organisation wishes to encourage a new culture of collaboration and open communication, Church et al. (2002) identify that inadequate representation, decreased participation rates of employees, issues about employee confidentiality, lack of faith, and technical hiccups tend to threaten the integrity of the whole developmental process. The authors find that the ability of technology to drive organisational development has at the same time revealed potential threats. This paradox is also observed by Lucas and Olson (1994), who argue that technology in an organisation enhances organisational flexibility by removing constraints on *where* and *when* work is accomplished, accelerating the processing of information thus affecting the pace of work, and allowing the organisation to respond quickly to market demands. They however concede that technology itself is inflexible, that is, it is difficult to change and maintain technological systems for new workflows.

Thus, technology comes along with unanticipated consequences as the organisation becomes dependent on its imperatives. In fact, even almost mundane technologies like electronic mailing (i.e., email), Intranets, and other social technologies that are deployed for communication among individuals in organisations arguably come with their own unintended consequences. Some have argued, for instance, that email can become a symbol of stress for individuals (Barley et al., 2011; Duxbury et al., 2007; Murray and Rostis, 2007). As a technological means for communication and collaboration (Tyran et al., 2003), emailing is largely asynchronous, asynchrony being the idea that the technology allows individuals to send messages anytime without expecting feedback immediately, as would have been the case, for instance, in telephone conversations in which communication is a two-way activity, that is, 'synchronous' (Barley et al., 2011). Nonetheless, email undeniably impacts human interaction and is shown to induce stress.

It is however worth noting that the extent of technology's effects on the human remains disputed, as SCOT perspectives only seek to understand how humans have come to interact with their technologies and not what the technology has 'caused'. For example, the assertion that email can become a source or symbol of stress is refuted elsewhere (Chesley et al., 2003; Phillips and Reddie, 2007; Renaud et al., 2006). Overall, a 'holistic' approach to this technological dilemma demands that methodological approaches that seek to explore the phenomenon would be better served if they considered arguments from these three schools of thought discussed so far. Here, the actor-network theory, we argue, becomes pertinent to the research undertaking in that it acknowledges technology's ability to act on humans, meaning unintended consequences are sometimes inevitable.

AN ACTOR-NETWORK PERSPECTIVE

In the 1970s, French anthropologist and social scientist Bruno Latour and British sociologist Steve Woolgar deployed ethnographic approaches to investigate what scientists did in the laboratory. By examining the production of scientific 'facts' in the laboratory, they observed how non-human companions such as chemicals, petri dishes, mice, graphs and so on were deployed as allies to overcome challenges to the outcomes of their work (Garrety, 2014). The idea that non-human elements in human sociality could be relied upon to play a part in establishing what humans would accept as facts provoked a different way of thinking in sociology. Later in the 1980s, French sociologist Michel Callon and British sociologist John Law, together with Bruno Latour, were the first to use the term 'actor-network theory (ANT)' to represent the array of concepts that emerged from those 'laboratory studies', and subsequently became the main proponents of the theory. These interrelated concepts would later challenge the distinct boundaries between subject and object, nature and culture, essentially what was human and what was non-human (Singleton and Michael, 1993). Key among the ideas raised by ANT is that of non-human agency. That is, the exercise of agency was no longer about human intentionality alone, but simply 'the ability to act and elicit a response either with inherent intentionality in the case of a human agent, or (un)programmed intentionality in the case of a designed artefact' (Soga et al., 2021, p. 646).

ANT outsteps the traditionally held dichotomy of Nature/Society, thus positing the social as materially heterogeneous (Latour, 2005; Law, 1992). Here, both humans and non-humans – things, technology, texts, machines and so on – all constitute the social and therefore are actors (or actants) in the heterogeneous network of relations. The implication is that the various technologies that are deployed in organisations by entrepreneurial leaders in an attempt to remain competitive are as relevant as their human counterparts. This position challenges the nature of what counts as 'social', although it is not without criticism (see Elder-Vass, 2015; Shapin, 1998). However, ANT's approach to sociology, which is also its 'radical and controversial contribution' (van House, 2004, p. 15), is that it helps us re-examine how we understand and research organisations.

For ANT theorists, the character of the organisation – a set of entities brought together – is undetermined (Callon, 1993; Law, 2004). Its undetermined nature means that an organisation is intermeshed with unidentifiable processes that call for constant negotiations from actors within it. The implication is that in order for entrepreneurial actors to maintain their competitive positions they will have to reorder themselves in response to any shifts in the market. This ANT perspective thus conveys the idea that for the entrepreneurial leader, the deployment of technology for competitive advantage can be a strategic move but also a relational one. In the former case, technology becomes an ally to help achieve a strategic objective, whereas in the latter case, technology is as much an actor as the humans in the organisation, working together relationally to respond to external market demands.

Consequently, ANT offers processes (what it calls 'moments') of translation that create and sustain heterogeneous networks of relations (Callon, 1986). Translation is a concept of interrelated approaches that include *problema-*

tisation, interessement, enrolment, and *mobilisation* (placed in this orderly sequence by Vurdubakis (2007) not necessarily for a straightforward stepwise prescription but for simplicity). In *problematisation,* an actor seeks to build or sustain their network of relations by identifying and exploring a problem in terms of a solution that they want to promote. For example, an entrepreneurial leader who seeks to introduce a new technology to drive innovation would first identify what problem the incoming technology would solve, be it process or product innovation. In ANT terms, because the actor wishes to build a network of relations that would support specific objectives, they make themselves or their proposed solutions obligatory passage points (OPPs), that is, indispensable courses of action or necessary centres of activity that are needed to fulfil the objectives (Callon, 1986). For example, the entrepreneurial leader might point to what competitors are already doing as a basis for action.

The next moment of translation is *interessement,* where the actor generates interest by persuading others about how the proposed solution generates collective benefits for the network of relations. For example, the entrepreneurial leader might argue how the new technology would help increase profits or the organisation's reputation or market capitalisation or overall competitiveness and so on. The next moment of translation is *enrolment,* in which various actors are assigned specific roles in the emerging network of relations in order to carry out laid-out objectives. For example, the entrepreneurial leader might identify some individuals in the organisation who would be responsible for the processes of technology adoption and implementation. In the final moment of translation, which is *mobilisation,* the actor mobilises members of the network of relations while sustaining commitment (and also making withdrawal difficult). For example, the entrepreneurial leader might generate buy-ins through training programmes or upskilling of organisational members to enable adequate use of the newly installed technology. In this example, ANT shows how the deployment of a new technology to drive innovation triggers a set of processes in which a network of relations comes to be formed and sustained. This network is one in which technology and humans come to relate together within an organisation in order to achieve a set objective.

The implication of this ANT perspective is that the researcher now considers the technologies deployed by entrepreneurial leaders in any analysis without necessarily being technologically deterministic. This offers a significant shift in the study of how entrepreneurs deploy technology within their ventures for some competitive advantage or simply for enhanced procedural efficiencies. The unit of analysis moves away from the entrepreneurs or entrepreneurial teams alone to what is now *an assemblage of the human individuals and the technologies* they have deployed in their organisation. Law (1992), for instance, asserts Napoleons are no different in kind to commoners. In other words, the technologies must be given equal consideration in much the same way as the human actors. Although this ANT argument attracts criticisms for anthropomorphism (which ANT is not!), the value of this methodological approach 'lies in a more sophisticated appreciation of the fluid and multiple nature of reality, the view of the active role of objects in shaping social relationships, and a theoretically informed approach to guiding sampling and data collection' (Cresswell et al., 2010, p. 10).

Similarly, ANT theorist Callon (1986) establishes the notion of generalised symmetry, which implies that the same descriptive or explanatory framework that is employed for humans must also be applicable for objects, in this case the technologies. He argues that it requires the researcher to be impartial to the voices of all actors. Methodologically, this implies a qualitative undertaking in which the researcher *follows* all actors in the organisation. By following the actors – that is, both entrepreneurial leaders and their technologies – the researcher is able to trace their trajectories in order to establish how innovation has taken place within the organisation or how the technological dilemma this chapter discusses has unfolded. As highlighted earlier, the underpinning argument of the ANT approach is that both humans and the technologies they deploy form a network of heterogeneous relations and they all act on one another within the network (Latour, 2005).

The methodology of ANT is not without weakness, as a result of its ontological assertions, thus making the 'ANT method' sometimes difficult to operationalise. For example, ANT does not make it clear from where we begin tracing actors in a network of relations since the network is unbounded (Latour, 2005). It is easy to assume this means only 'following' the human actors to trace how entrepreneurial leaders deploy new technologies for innovation in their organisations. But this assumption may equally apply to the technology. This is a pragmatic decision for the researcher. How, specifically, a technology could be 'followed' is not made clear in ANT. We suggest applying ethnomethodological techniques. This could involve long-term observations of the interaction between entrepreneurial leaders or organisational members and the technologies they use. ANT is also criticised as being only descriptive, with no explanatory power, so that in tracing actors we are left with describing the context of the actor-to-actor interactions without explaining why both of these, the context and the interactions, are so.

Callon (1991), for instance, argues that 'to describe a skill is thus, at the same time, to describe its context' (Callon, 1991, p. 138) and therefore we might need some other theory to support the analysis. We suggest theories such as cultural historical activity theory, urban ecology theory, and sociomateriality, and other theories of practice could fill some of the gaps highlighted. Theories at the level of structure, like structuration theory or institutional theory, could offer insights at macro levels of analysis, while ANT addresses the more micro-level analysis. The idea of generalised symmetry presents us with not only an ontological challenge as we grapple with technology's non-human membership of an organisation (Collins and Yearley, 1992; Elam, 1999), but also an epistemological challenge as the researcher must give voice to the technology. Cresswell et al. (2010) acknowledge these weaknesses and suggest pragmatic approaches to navigating an ANT study since 'methodology cannot resolve the higher epistemological [and ontological] debate[s]' (p. 9). In the following we explore what implications the ANT approach has for the arguments raised so far with respect to future research and theory.

IMPLICATIONS AND FUTURE RESEARCH

We return to our core question: who is really in control as entrepreneurial leaders deploy technology in order to drive innovation or to remain competitive? From the arguments raised in this chapter, technology's role in human activity does not seem to offer a straightforward answer. Yet the question remains significant for entrepreneurial leaders who wish to engage technology in their entrepreneurial activities, particularly new technologies in order to drive innovation. This is because technology's failure could result in catastrophic outcomes (Keil and Robey, 1999). For example, the once successful healthcare company, FoxMeyer, with 23 distribution centres across the United States, wanted to take advantage of the increasing aging demographic in order to expand market share. This entrepreneurial drive led the organisation to deploy an Enterprise Resource Planning (ERP) software with an expectation of managing inventory efficiently, reducing operating expenses and expanding services. Ultimately, FoxMeyer hoped they could undercut the competition through lower prices as the new technology was estimated to save the company $40 million in annual operating costs (Olson, 2004). With such expectations of cost savings, which ERP systems can achieve (Davenport and Brooks, 2004), FoxMeyer then '… signed large new contracts, underbidding competitors based upon new expected lower costs' (Olson, 2004, p. 6). These new contracts forced changes in system requirements and, coupled with other coordination problems in a web of many other unexpected situations, eventually resulted in colossal losses of over $15 million (Olson, 2004). Finally, FoxMeyer filed for bankruptcy, and a technological input that was expected to be revolutionary for the business became a nightmare.

Several studies show various levels of failure as a result of the implementation of new technological systems (Keil and Robey, 1999; Majed and Abdullah, 2003; Reel, 1999; Robertson and Williams, 2006). In fact, even with successful technological implementations in organisations, 'previously simple procedures may become complicated and local flexibility constrained' (Marshall, 2006, p. 1). As a result, the implications that new technological implementations carry for entrepreneurial leaders are those that potentially have existential ramifications for their business ventures. The question of 'who is in control?' is thus paramount to our understanding when it comes to practice, methodology and theory. From a technological deterministic perspective, the entrepreneurial leader is hopeless in their attempt to lead their business venture in the competitive market. From the perspectives of SST and those of SCOT, the entrepreneurial leader must work collaboratively with various social factors or observe how these factors come to create the organisation they desire to build.

A passive approach could result in undesired outcomes as the social factors would have been left to construct or shape unintended outcomes. ANT's ontological argument means that the entrepreneurial leader who is now an actor (among other actants) in the heterogeneous network of relations must actively deploy strategies to be in control. What those specific strategies are remain elusive and this offers opportunities for future research. For instance, FoxMeyer blamed its bankruptcy on its new ERP system implementation, and it went on to be acquired by McKesson, also a major drug company, which ironically reported success with the same ERP technology (Olson, 2004). The strategies deployed by McKesson that meant it reported success instead of failure as a result of the technology could offer insights for entrepreneurial leaders. Policy could also address some of the challenges entrepreneurial leaders face in their network of heterogeneous relations. To foster entrepreneurial activity, policy could support access to technology, knowledge spillover, entrepreneurial networking and entrepreneurial finance. This would remove some of the obstacles entrepreneurial leaders are faced with as they navigate their heterogeneous networks.

CONCLUSION

This chapter acknowledges technology as an important actor in the decisions made by entrepreneurial leaders for their business ventures. However, we find that the deployment of technology within the organisation raises a dilemma for all actors involved and could sometimes threaten the business venture itself. The singular lens of a technological deterministic view or arguments of social shaping of technology or social constructivist positions alone do not adequately address the challenges posed when new technologies are introduced. This deployment of technology to gain competitive advantage through innovation also raises the question of who is really in charge of the process. The significance of this question is in the intended outcome for implementing the technology in the first place. If the intended outcome is to be ahead of the competition, answering this question becomes key to remaining ahead. Accordingly, we have argued for the use of a 'new' theoretical lens, the actor-network theory, one that is neither solely technologically deterministic nor socially constructivist. That is, a theory that accepts technology as a non-human actor and acknowledges it as being in a heterogeneous network of relations with the humans deploying it. Such a theory must avoid placing an overemphasis on the agency of only the human actors or on only the techno-logical actants for any meaningful analysis.

REFERENCES

Akrich, M. (1992). The description of technical objects. In W. E. Bijker and J. Law (Eds), *Shaping Technology/Building Society: Studies in Sociotechnological Change* (pp. 205–224). MIT Press.

Barley, S. R., Meyerson, D. E., and Grodal, S. (2011). E-mail as a source and symbol of stress. *Organization Science*, *22*(4), 887–906. https://doi.org/10.1287/orsc.1100.0573

Bennis, W. (2013). Leadership in a digital world: Embracing transparency and adaptive capacity. *MIS Quarterly*, *37*(2), 635–636.

Bijker, W. E. (1995). *Of Bicycles, Bakelites, and Bulbs: Towards a Theory of Sociotechnical Change*. MIT Press.

Bimber, B. (1998). Three faces of technological determinism. In M. R. Smith and L. Marx (Eds), *Does Technology Drive History? The Dilemma of Technological Determinism* (pp. 79–100). MIT Press.

Bloomfield, B. (2001). In the right place at the right time: Electronic tagging and prob-lems of social order/disorder. *Sociological Review*, *49*(2), 174–201.

Burns, T., and Stalker, G. M. (1994). *The Management of Innovation*. Oxford University Press.

Callon, M. (1986). Some elements of a sociology of translation: Domestication of the scallops and the fishermen of St Brieuc Bay. In J. Law (Ed.), *Power, Action and Belief* (pp. 196–233). Routledge.

Callon, M. (1991). Techno-economic networks and irreversibility. In J. Law (Ed.), *A Sociology of Monsters: Essays on Power, Technology and Domination* (pp. 132–161). Routledge.

Callon, M. (1993). Variety and irreversibility in networks of technique conception and adoption. In D. Foray and C. Freeman (Eds), *Technology and the Wealth of Nations: Dynamics of Constructed Advantage* (pp. 232–268). Pinter.

Chesley, N., Moen, P., and Shore, R. P. (2003). The new technology climate. In P. Moen (Ed.), *It's About Time: Couples and Careers* (pp. 220–241). Cornell University Press.

Church, A. H., Gilbert, M., Oliver, D. H., Paquet, K., and Surface, C. (2002). The role of technology in organization development and change. *Advances in Developing Human Resources*, *4*(4), 493–511. https://doi.org/10.1177/152342202237525

Collins, H. M., and Yearley, S. (1992). Epistemological chicken. In A. Pickering (Ed.), *Science as Practice and Culture* (pp. 301–326). Chicago University Press.

Cresswell, K. M., Worth, A., and Sheikh, A. (2010). Actor-network theory and its role in understanding the implementation of information technology developments in healthcare. *BMC Medical Informatics and Decision Making*, *10*(67), 1–11. https://doi.org/10.1186/1472-6947-10-67

Davenport, T. H., and Brooks, J. D. (2004). Enterprise systems and the supply chain. *Journal of Enterprise Information Management*, *17*(1), 8–19. https://doi.org/10.1108/09576050410510917

Duxbury, L. E., Towers, I., Higgins, C., and Thomas, J. A. (2007). From 9 to 5 to 24/7: How technology has redefined the workday. In W. Law (Ed.), *Information Resources Management: Global Challenges* (pp. 305–332). IGI Global.

Edgerton, D. (1999). From innovation to use: Ten eclectic theses on the historiography of technology. *History and Technology*, *16*(1), 111–136.

Elam, M. (1999). Living dangerously with Bruno Latour in a hybrid world. *Theory, Culture and Society*, *16*(4), 1–24. https://doi.org/10.1177/02632769922050692

Elder-Vass, D. (2015). Disassembling actor-network theory. *Philosophy of the Social Sciences*, *45*(1), 100–121. https://doi.org/10.1177/0048393114525858

Ellul, J. (1967). *The Technological Society with an Introduction by Robert K. Merton* (J. Wilkinson, Trans.). Vintage Books.

Garrety, K. (2014). Actor network theory. In H. Hasan (Ed.), *Being Practical with Theory: A Window into Business Research* (pp. 15–19). THEORI. http://tinyurl.com/o5xhx93

Grint, K. (2005). Problems, problems, problems: The social construction of 'leadership'. *Human Relations*, *58*(11), 1467–1494.

Grübler, A. (2003). *Technology and Global Change*. Cambridge University Press.

Heilbroner, R. (1998). Do machines make history? In M. R. Smith and L. Marx (Eds), *Does Technology Drive History?: The Dilemma of Technological Determinism* (pp. 53–66). MIT Press.

Hughes, T. P. (1998). Technological momentum. In M. R. Smith and L. Marx (Eds), *Does Technology Drive History?: The Dilemma of Technological Determinism* (pp. 101–114). MIT Press.

James, W. (1948). *Essays in Pragmatism*. Hafner Publishing Co.

Joerges, B. (1999). Do politics have artefacts? *Social Studies of Science*, *29*(3), 411–431.

Kallinikos, J. (2011). *The 'Age of Smart Machine': A 21st Century View*. http://personal.lse.ac.uk/kallinik/new/IntheAgeof_the_SmartmachineFinal.pdf

Keil, M., and Robey, D. (1999). Turning around troubled software projects: An exploratory study of the deescalation of commitment to failing courses of action. *Journal of Management Information Systems*, *15*(4), 63–87. https://doi.org/10.1080/07421222.1999.11518222

Kirzner, I. M. (1973). *Competition and Entrepreneurship*. University of Chicago Press.

Kirzner, I. M. (1999). Creativity and/or alertness: A reconsideration of the Schumpeterian entrepreneur. *Review of Austrian Economics*, *11*(1/2), 5–17. https://doi.org/10.1023/A:1007719905868

Klein, H. K., and Kleinman, D. L. (2002). The social construction of technology: Structural considerations. *Science, Technology, and Human Values*, *27*(1), 28–52. https://doi.org/10.1177/016224390202700102

Latour, B. (1987). *Science in Action: How to Follow Scientists and Engineers through Society*. Harvard University Press.

Latour, B. (2005). *Reassembling the Social: An Introduction to Actor-Network Theory*. Oxford University Press.

Law, J. (1992). Notes on the theory of the actor-network: Ordering, strategy, and heterogeneity. *Systems Practice*, *5*(4), 379–393. https://doi.org/10.1007/BF01059830

Law, J. (2004). *After Method: Mess in Social Science Research*. Routledge.

Lawson, C. (2007). Technology, technological determinism and the transformational model of technical activity. In C. Lawson, J. S. Latsis, and N. M. O. Martins (Eds), *Contributions to Social Ontology* (pp. 32–49). Routledge.

Leonardi, P. M. (2009). Why do people reject new technologies and stymie organizational changes of which they are in favor? Exploring misalignments between social interactions and materiality. *Human Communication Research*, *35*(3), 407–441.

Lucas, H. C., Jr, and Olson, M. (1994). The impact of information technology on organizational flexibility. *Journal of Organizational Computing*, *4*(2), 155–176. https://doi.org/10.1080/10919399409540221

MacKenzie, D. A., and Wajcman, J. (Eds). (1999). *The Social Shaping of Technology* (2nd edn). Open University Press.

Majed, A., and Abdullah, A. (2003). ERP implementation: Lessons from a case study. *Information Technology and People*, *16*(1), 21–33. https://doi.org/10.1108/09593840310463005

Marshall, J. P. (2006, 27 September). Information technology, disruption and disorder: Australian customs and IT. *Seventh Association of Internet Researchers Conference*. Association of Internet Researchers Annual Conference, Brisbane.

McCabe, D. (2007). *Power at Work: How Employees Reproduce the Corporate Machine*. Routledge.

Müller, R., and Turner, R. (2010). Leadership competency profiles of successful project managers. *International Journal of Project Management*, *28*(5), 437–448.

Murray, W. C., and Rostis, A. (2007). Who's running the machine? A theoretical exploration of work, stress and burnout of technologically tethered workers. *Journal of Individual Employment Rights*, *12*(3), 249–263.

Nixon, P., Harrington, M., and Parker, D. (2012). Leadership performance is significant to project success or failure: A critical analysis. *International Journal of Productivity and Performance Management*, *61*(2), 204–216.

Olson, D. L. (2004). *Managerial Issues of Enterprise Resource Planning Systems*. McGraw-Hill.

Orlikowski, W. J. (2000). Using technology and constituting structures: A practical lens for studying technology in organizations. *Organization Science*, *11*(4), 404–428.

Orlikowski, W. J., and Gash, D. C. (1994). Technological frames: Making sense of information technology in organizations. *ACM Transactions on Information Systems*, *12*(2), 174–207.

Orlikowski, W. J., and Scott, S. V. (2008). The entanglement of technology and work in organizations. Information Systems and Innovation Group, Department of Management, LSE, Working Paper Series, No. 168. http://eprints.lse.ac.uk/33898/1/wp168.pdf

Pearlson, K. E., Saunders, C. S., and Galletta, D. F. (2020). *Managing and Using Information Systems: A Strategic Approach* (7th edn). Wiley.

Phillips, J. G., and Reddie, L. (2007). Decisional style and self-reported email use in the workplace. *Computers in Human Behavior*, *23*(5), 2414–2428.

Pinch, T. J. (1998). The social construction of technology: A review. In R. Fox (Ed.), *Technological Change* (pp. 17–36). Routledge.

Pinch, T. J., and Bijker, W. E. (1989). The social construction of facts and artifacts: Or how the sociology of science and the sociology of technology might benefit each other. In W. E. Bijker, T. P. Hughes, and T. J. Pinch (Eds), *The Social Construction of Technological Systems: New Directions in the Sociology and History of Technology* (pp. 17–50). MIT Press.

Pisarski, A., Chang, A., Ashkanasy, N., Zolin, R., Mazur, A., Jordan, P., and Hatcher, C. A. (2011). The contribution of leadership attributes to large scale complex project success. *Academy of Management Annual Meeting Proceedings*. Academy of Management, San Antonio, Texas. http://eprints.qut.edu.au/46801/

Rauner, F., Rasmussen, L., and Corbett, J. M. (1988). The social shaping of technology and work: Human centred CIM systems. *AI and Society*, *2*(1), 47–61.

Reel, J. S. (1999). Critical success factors in software projects. *IEEE Software*, *16*(3), 18–23. https://doi.org/10.1109/52.765782

Renaud, K., Ramsay, J., and Hair, M. (2006). 'You've got email!'… Shall I deal with it now? Electronic mail from the recipient's perspective. *International Journal of Human–Computer Interaction*, *21*(3), 313–332.

Robertson, S., and Williams, T. (2006). Understanding project failure: Using cognitive mapping in an insurance project. *Project Management Journal*, *37*(4), 55–71. https://doi.org/10.1177/875697280603700406

Saldanha, T. J. V., and Krishnan, M. S. (2012). Organizational adoption of Web 2.0 technologies: An empirical analysis. *Journal of Organizational Computing and Electronic Commerce*, *22*(4), 301–333.

Schumpeter, J. A. (1934). *The Theory of Economic Development: An Inquiry into Profits, Capital, Credit, Interest and the Business Cycle*. Oxford University Press.

Shapin, S. (1998). Placing the view from nowhere: Historical and sociological problems in the location of science. *Transactions of the Institute of British Geographers*, *23*(1), 5–12. https://doi.org/10.1111/j.0020-2754.1998.00005.x

Singleton, V., and Michael, M. (1993). Actor-networks and ambivalence: General practitioners in the UK cervical screening programme. *Social Studies of Science*, *23*(2), 227–264.

Smith, M. R. (1998). Technological determinism in American culture. In M. R. Smith and L. Marx (Eds), *Does Technology Drive History?: The Dilemma of Technological Determinism* (pp. 1–36). MIT Press.

Smith, M. R., and Marx, L. (Eds). (1998). *Does Technology Drive History?: The Dilemma of Technological Determinism*. MIT Press.

Soga, L. R., Vogel, B., Graça, A. M., and Osei-Frimpong, K. (2021). Web 2.0-enabled team relationships: An actor-network perspective. *European Journal of Work and Organizational Psychology*, *30*(5), 639–652. https://doi.org/10.1080/1359432X.2020.1847183

Subašić, E., Reynolds, K. J., Turner, J. C., Veenstra, K. E., and Haslam, S. A. (2011). Leadership, power and the use of surveillance: Implications of shared social identity for leaders' capacity to influence. *The Leadership Quarterly*, *22*(1), 170–181. https://doi.org/10.1016/j.leaqua.2010.12.014

Turner, R., and Müller, R. (2005). The project manager's leadership style as a success factor on projects: A literature review. *Project Management Journal*, *36*(2), 49–61.

Tushman, M. L., and Murmann, J. P. (2003). Dominant designs, technology cycles, and organizational outcomes. In R. Garud, A. Kumaraswamy, and R. N. Langlois (Eds), *Managing in the Modular Age: Architectures, Networks, and Organizations* (pp. 316–347). Blackwell.

Tyran, K. L., Tyran, C. K., and Shepherd, M. (2003). Exploring emerging leadership in virtual teams. In C. Gibson and S. Cohen (Eds), *Virtual Teams that Work: Creating Conditions for Virtual Team Effectiveness* (pp. 183–195). Jossey-Bass.

Valcour, P. M., and Hunter, L. W. (2005). Technology, organizations and work–life integration. In E. E. Kossek and S. J. Lambert (Eds), *Work and Life Integration:*

Organizational, Cultural, and Individual Perspectives (pp. 61–84). Lawrence Erlbaum.

van House, A. N. (2004). Science and technology studies and information studies. *Annual Review of Information Science and Technology*, *38*(1), 3–86. https://doi.org/10.1002/aris.1440380102

Vodanovich, S., Sundaram, D., and Myers, M. (2010). Digital natives and ubiquitous information systems. *Information Systems Research*, *21*(4), 711–723. https://doi.org/10.1287/isre.1100.0324

Vurdubakis, T. (2007). Technology. In D. Knights and H. Willmott (Eds), *Introducing Organizational Behaviour and Management* (pp. 405–438). Thomson.

Williams, R. (2000). 'All that is solid melts into air': Historians of technology in the information revolution. *Technology and Culture*, *41*(4), 641–668.

Winner, L. (1986). *The Whale and the Reactor: A Search for Limits in an Age of High Technology*. University of Chicago Press.

Winner, L. (1993). Upon opening the black box and finding it empty: Social constructivism and the philosophy of technology. *Science, Technology and Human Values*, *18*(3), 362–378.

Wyatt, S. (2008). Technological determinism is dead; long live technological determinism. In E. J. Hackett, O. Amsterdamska, M. Lynch, and J. Wajcman (Eds), *The Handbook of Science and Technology* (3rd edn, pp. 165–180). MIT Press.

Yukl, G. (2010). *Leadership in Organizations* (7th edn). Pearson.

Zuboff, S. (1988). *In the Age of the Smart Machine: The Future of Work and Power*. Basic Books.

Zuboff, S. (1996). The emperor's new information economy. In W. J. Orlikowski, G. Walsham, M. R. Jones, and J. I. DeGross (Eds), *Information Technology and Changes in Organizational Work* (pp. 13–17). Chapman and Hall.

2. Startups and regional entrepreneurial ecosystems: the Russian case

Stepan Zemtsov and Alexander Mikhaylov

INTRODUCTION

Startups play a significant role in job creation, innovation and long-term growth (Fritsch and Mueller, 2008; OECD, 2020). A new industrial revolution (Schwab, 2017) and the coronavirus pandemic have become major socio-economic challenges; technological entrepreneurship may help to adapt to them (Zemtsov, 2020; Fossen and Sorgner, 2021). There is an expansion of entering markets opportunities for new firms due to digital platforms and new markets (Antonova et al., 2020). New opportunities have opened up for startups that are introducing radical innovations in telemedicine, remote personal care, medical equipment, home delivery, food processing, teleworking, online learning, contact tracing and so on.

Entrepreneurial activity in Russia, especially in high-tech sectors, is relatively low. In 2020, less than 7 per cent of residents had their own business (Antonova et al., 2020). The number of new high-tech companies has been steadily decreasing every year since the mid-2010s. According to estimates for Russia (Zemtsov and Smelov, 2018), a decrease in the density of entrepreneurial activity by 1 per cent leads to a decrease in gross regional product (GRP) by 0.22–0.67 per cent. The current decline may exacerbate long-term downward trends in business activity in many countries, including Russia. The innovative activity of already existing companies is also quite low in Russia; for example, in 2018, about 5.2 per cent of small firms introduced technological innovations.

The regional environment differs significantly for small businesses and new companies (Zemtsov and Tsareva, 2018). It is commonly called an entrepreneurial ecosystem (Audretsch and Belitski, 2021). These differences are often underestimated in political decision making. Previously, no work was carried out to investigate the differences between regions in Russia in the density and dynamics of technology startups.

The main purpose of this work is to determine the factors influencing the creation of new firms in high-tech industries in the Russian regions.

LITERATURE REVIEW

Nowadays, the use of the term 'startup' is relatively widespread; nevertheless, it has no single definition. Generally, it refers to a newly created (up to one year) firm, largely controlled by its founders, presenting a new product to the market and having intellectual property rights to it (Robehmed, 2013). High growth potential and increased risks are also important features of a startup (Evers, 2003). More than 80 per cent of such companies do not survive the so-called 'valley of death', when external financing is especially required but the investors are not ready to finance the project because of the risk levels. For a long period of time, no surveys have been conducted covering all technology startups in Russia, although there are examples of sample surveys.

Generally, researchers specify the internal and external factors of startup activity. The internal ones include the specialized skills of entrepreneurs and their personal characteristics (Stuetzer et al., 2013), usually labelled the 'entrepreneurial capital' (Erikson, 2002). The external ones usually depend on the context of the overall socio-economic situation and form 'entrepreneurial ecosystems' (Isenberg, 2011; Zemtsov and Baburin, 2019). Publications in Russia concentrate on examining the inner traits of startup founders and rarely consider external (regional) conditions. Obviously, for a large country, geography matters.

External factors can be divided into those affecting the supply and those affecting the demand of new businesses (Verheul et al., 2002). The supply depends on the characteristics of human capital, as well as the structural and institutional specifics of the local economy, while the demand for entrepreneurial activity depends on incomes and the accessibility of the new markets (Del Bosco et al., 2021).

The concentration of human capital plays the important role in the startup activity (Lee et al., 2004; Audretsch and Lehmann, 2005; Lasch et al., 2013; Belitski and Desai, 2016; Audretsch et al., 2015). Universities, research centres and research departments of large companies, which require highly qualified personnel, are often places of birth for new firms (Novotny, 2008; Qian et al., 2013). Universities are the locus of new-knowledge generation, knowledge that can potentially become the basis for a new company. Despite some of these factors of startup activity in universities still being disputable (Motoyama and Bell-Masterson, 2014), the overall role of education and human capital is considered to be significant. For the Russian case, such an influence of universities and research centres is not obvious and not supported for small businesses in general (Barinova et al., 2018). Russian universities mainly perform educational functions (Eremkin et al., 2015). Russian science is poorly connected with the real sector of the economy (Zemtsov and Kotsemir, 2019), research results are rarely implemented in finished products, so R&D cannot always serve as a basis for creating startups.

Startups are particularly sensitive to formal and informal institutions and norms (Aparicio et al., 2016; Fuentelsaz et al., 2015; Barinova et al., 2018). The unit transaction costs of small businesses are higher than those of large companies or budgetary organizations, so the development of formal institutions is more important for them. Some researchers highlight the unfavourable institutional environment of developing countries (Calá, 2014). The formal norms generally refer to the conditions for registering new firms and for obtaining external financing, along with the regulatory environment (Barinova et al., 2018; Partridge et al., 2019). The growth of informal employment is associated with the inability to conduct legal business due to high taxes, high administrative burden, corruption and other institutional factors (Marlow et al., 2017). The informal sector limits the opening of new businesses, and it can be particularly detrimental to tech entrepreneurship, although it is rarely considered in relevant studies.

The presence of specialized programmes of state financial support and infrastructure for stimulating startup activity may have some beneficial effects (Audretsch et al., 2002; Breitenecker, 2007; Dvouletý et al., 2021), although government support is often ineffective, especially in countries with weak public control. In Russia, the share of the public sector is high. Substantial funding is allocated through specialized development institutions (RUSnano, Russian Venture Company, Innovation Support Fund, Industrial Development Fund, etc.) and federal programmes (cluster initiatives, creation of technology parks, etc.). The question of their effectiveness is highly relevant, but not discussed in the scientific literature in terms of creating startups.

Agglomeration effects are often considered an important group of factors for startups (Audretsch and Fritsch, 1994; Rosenthal and Strange, 2004; Delgado et al., 2010; Audretsch and Lehmann, 2005; Audretsch and Belitski, 2020), emphasizing that agglomerations create large and diverse markets for goods, services, personnel and finance, and the high density of economic agents creates conditions for an intensive exchange and flow of knowledge. In other words, in large agglomerations and near them, startup activity should be higher. In Russia, similar patterns are confirmed for small businesses in general (Barinova et al., 2018), but there is little evidence for the tech sector (Lavrinenko et al., 2019).

Until recently, the scientific literature has rarely given an assessment of the impact of digitalization on entrepreneurship. Nambisan (2017) highlighted digital technologies as one of the factors of startup activity. Digitalization of businesses and access to the Internet may even increase entrepreneurial entry over time (von Briel et al., 2018; Fossen and Sorgner, 2021). The Internet creates new market niches and provides access to consumers all over the world. For example, Alibaba's platform, which allows firms from different countries to sell their products worldwide, has spurred the creation of millions of new firms worldwide. However, estimates are most often given for the IT industry in developed countries, while we were interested in the impact on all technology startups.

The sectoral structures of the regional economy strongly influence the levels of 'demand' and 'supply' of startup activity (Audretsch and Vivarelli, 1996; Armington and Acs, 2002). For instance, the industries producing raw materials create a relatively weak demand for startup activity. Fritsch and Wyrwich (2018) show that in Germany the number of startups has historically always been lower in regions specializing in coal mining. This phenomenon may relate to the 'resource curse' (Guriev and Sonin, 2008), when capital and personnel in these types of regions flow into the most profitable resource sector. This process can have a negative impact on local institutions and entrepreneurship conditions, which are significantly important for new firms.

The case of Russia is rarely considered in startups research, since the country is rather weakly represented in the world's technology markets. Nevertheless, a fairly large number of new technology companies are being created in Russia, and the government is striving to diversify the economy. Many conclusions that are obvious for developed economies may be poorly applicable for Russia due to the Soviet legacy, high interregional diversification, government actions and other factors.

RESEARCH METHODOLOGY

We proposed several variables to test the below hypotheses which we formulated on the basis of our literature review.

First, concentration of human capital and R&D activity can boost the number of new high-tech companies. This is not obvious for Russia, where universities do not perform innovative functions (Eremkin et al., 2015) and the results of scientific research are rarely commercialized (Zemtsov and Kotsemir, 2019).

Second, the unfavourable business environment, such as the high share of the informal sector and lower access to credits, may restrict the formation of new firms (Barinova et al., 2018). General institutional conditions may not affect startups, which are often created in special economic zones and in technology parks at universities; and bank capital is not the main source of growth for them.

Third, government support helps startups survive, and accordingly their density increases. Venture capital investments are underdeveloped in Russia, so the state seeks to replace them with public funds. However, these funds can be ineffective at creating startups.

Fourth, the proximity and accessibility of large markets encourages the emergence of new firms due to the diversity of market niches. The entire world market is open for technological startups, especially in the field of information technology, so the influence of geographical distance to the largest markets or size of the local market may be insignificant.

Fifth, higher Internet access allows more startups to grow. The Internet provides an opportunity to access the global market. But the level of Internet coverage is already quite high, so it can be insignificant as a regional factor.

The generalized equation of the econometric model has the following form:

$$startup_{i,t} = const + \beta_1 \times education_{i,t} + \beta_2 \times rndpot_{i,t} + \beta_3 \times inst_{i,t}$$
$$+ \beta_4 \times support_{i,t} + \beta_5 \times infr_{i,t} + \beta_6 \times market_{i,t} + \beta_7 \times economy_{i,t} + \varepsilon_{i,t}$$

where:

- i – 83 Russian regions;
- t – years: 2010–2015;
- *startup* – the number of new high-tech companies for ten thousand work-force participants;
- *education* – the level of education (human capital);
- *rndpot* – scientific and technical potential;
- *inst* – characteristics of the institutional environment;
- *support* – characteristics of state support;
- *infr* – level of infrastructure development;
- *market* – market access;
- *economy* – economic structure;
- ε – error.

Each of the selected factors included one or two variables, depending on the results of the analysis of paired correlations. The list of variables is presented in Table 2.1.

According to our analysis, the dynamics of new high-tech companies in recent years can hardly be called favourable. Since the mid-2010s, the number of such firms in Russia has been steadily decreasing – from 17.5 thousand units in 2015 to 11.6 thousand units in 2019. The sectoral structure of the distribution of startup activity is shown in Figure 2.1. About half of the Russian startups can be classified as knowledge-intensive services in the business-to-consumer (B2C) and business-to-business (B2B) categories. In contrast, the manufacturing sector accounts for less than 12 per cent of new high-tech companies (the number being derived from the sum of several codes

Table 2.1   List of used factors and variables

Factor	Variable
Educational level	Average number of years of education per person
(education)	Number of students per one thousand people population, people
Scientific and	Share of R&D expenditures in GRP, %
technical potential	Innovative Development Index as arithmetic mean of normalized values: share of
(rndpot)	R&D expenditures in GRP, share of employed in R&D and patent activity
Institutional	Share of employed in the informal sector, %
environment *(inst)*	Aggregate index of banking services, units (Bank of Russia)
State support of	The level of state financial support for startups by development institutions for ten
startup activity	thousand employed people (Semenova et al., 2019)
(support)	
Information and	Share of organizations using high-speed Internet, %
communication	Share of persons (households) with access to the Internet, %
infrastructure *(infr)*	
Market access	Income minus the subsistence minimum per month per person, rubles
(market)	The sum of incomes minus the subsistence minimum, mln rubles
	Population of the regional centre, thousand people
Economy structure	Share of high-tech sector in GRP, %
(economy)	Share of crop production in GRP, %
	Share of mining industry production in GRP, %
	The average size of a high-tech firm (average number of employees in the firms of
	the high-tech sector, people)

Source: Authors' calculations based on Rosstat data.

from the groups of mechanical engineering, pharmaceuticals and medical instrument production, and chemical industry), although its share in the total revenue of Russian startups exceeds 45 per cent. The information technology sector accounts for slightly less than a fifth of the total number of all startups, and about 8 per cent of the total revenue.

RESULTS AND DISCUSSION

Startup activity is extremely unevenly distributed in the regional context as it is in many large countries (the United States, China, Brazil, etc.). About every fourth new high-tech company is created in Moscow. Moscow, St Petersburg and the Moscow region together concentrate about 40 per cent of such firms, and ten leading regions in terms of startup activity (the Sverdlovsk region, Novosibirsk region, Tomsk region, Nizhny Novgorod region, the Republic of Tatarstan, etc.) concentrate about 58 per cent of such companies.

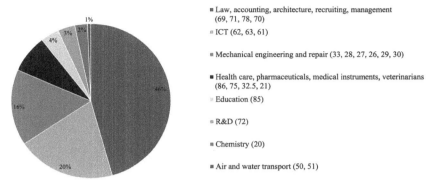

Source: Authors' calculations based on Spark-Interfax and RUSLANA data.

Figure 2.1   Sectoral structure of the Russian startups (OKVED – Russian classification of economic activities)

The largest urban agglomerations (Moscow, St Petersburg, Samara, Kazan (Tatarstan), Yekaterinburg), research and educational centres (Novosibirsk, Tomsk regions) and manufacturing centres (Vologda, Kaliningrad, Perm, Ryazan, Krasnoyarsk regions) have the highest number of high-tech startups per unit of workforce.

For verification of our hypotheses we used models with fixed and random effects (see Table 2.2). Some factors were strongly related to each other, therefore we evaluated the potential multicollinearity and did not use strongly correlated variables in the models.

Empirical models make it possible to partially confirm the first hypothesis. The regions with the highest concentration of human capital (large universities and research centres) are distinguished by relatively high amounts of startup activity: Moscow, Tomsk, Novosibirsk and Samara regions, the Republic of Tatarstan, and some others. Moreover, in regions with a high density of university students, the number of startups was higher. Despite their low efficiency in the creation of startup activity in Russia, the scientific and technological potential also turned out to be significant both in terms of the density of startups and in terms of their dynamics (models 1 and 3). This is consistent with the literature review and results in developed countries (Lee et al., 2004; Audretsch and Lehmann, 2005; Lasch et al., 2013; Belitski and Desai, 2016). In our opinion, this is due to the fact that universities and research centres are important not only as sources of academic startups, but as sources of knowledge spillovers from the academic to the real sector.

The second hypothesis is also supported by the empirical models 1 and 3. A higher share of employment in the informal economy leads to a decrease in the density and dynamics of new high-tech companies. A high share of the informal sector indicates a potentially unfavourable business environment, as was previously stated in the literature (Marlow et al., 2017). Unlike the results of previous works (Sutaria and Hicks, 2004), access to credit capital is not significant in any of the models. Most Russian tech startups use their own funds for development, without resorting to lending. At the same time, it is an important factor for the development of small businesses in general (Barinova et al., 2018).

Public support from development institutions turned out to be insignificant, which does not support the third hypothesis. Many development institutions and federal programmes were not focused on supporting startups, and most of the funding went to large projects (Semenova et al., 2019). Public–private co-financing has been found to be more successful than support from public funds (Cumming et al., 2017).

The fourth hypothesis was confirmed. The purchasing power of the region's residents (sum of all personal incomes minus the living wage) is a significant factor of startup activity as most young Russian high-tech firms create services and products for local large businesses and private households. If the economic situation deteriorates, the number of new tech firms decreases; we can observe this during the coronavirus crisis. A large and growing city creates new market niches and opportunities for cooperation, and, accordingly, the density of start-ups grows in it. The results are in line with those previously found in developed countries (Lee et al., 2004; Audretsch and Keilbach, 2008; Plummer, 2010; Goel and Saunoris, 2017), which emphasized the role of agglomeration effects and market access.

In confirming the fifth hypothesis, that better access to high-speed Internet increases startup activity, we showed the importance of the infrastructure component (Audretsch and Belitski, 2017). This may be due to the fact that digital technologies are expanding markets for young companies. Furthermore, many new companies are connected in one way or another with information technology. Most startups are focused on entering Internet markets, and business digitalization is creating new markets for startups. This factor was especially important during the pandemic.

The average size of high-tech firms is negatively interrelated with startup activity, since this may be an indirect indicator of barriers to entry into a market dominated by larger players. In these regions, there is a low density of small businesses and, accordingly, a poorly developed entrepreneurial ecosystem. This is also confirmed for developed countries (Lee et al., 2004; Plummer, 2010).

Table 2.2   *Factors explaining regional differences in startup activity and its dynamics*

Factors	Variables	Number of new high-tech firms per ten thousand people (labour force)		Annual increase of the dependent variable, %	
Dependent variable		random effects	fixed effects	random effects	fixed effects
Estimation method		1	2	3	4
	Constant	3*** (0.31)	−6.62*** (1.82)	0.98*** (0.28)	1.52*** (0.22)
Human capital	Average number of years of study		0.35*** (0.16)		
	Number of students per 100 people	0.226*** (0.03)		0.06*** (0.02)	
Innovation potential	Share of R&D expenditures in GRP, %	0.085*** (0.013)			
	Innovative Development Index			0.04** (0.02)	
Institutions	Employed in the informal sector as a % of the total number of employed	−0.167*** (0.056)		−0.05** (0.02)	
Infrastructure	Share of organizations using high-speed Internet access	0.205*** (0.05)		0.05* (0.03)	
Market potential and agglomeration effects	The sum of incomes minus the subsistence minimum, mln rubles	0.087*** (0.021)		0.03** (0.01)	0.27*** (0.06)
	Average monthly income minus the subsistence minimum per capita, rubles		0.78*** (0.19)		
	Increase in average monthly income minus the cost of living, %				0.97*** (0.17)
	Growth in the number of residents of the central city in the region, %			1.27*** (0.27)	
Economic structure	The average size of a high-tech firm	−0.515*** (0.05)	−0.38*** (0.04)	−0.17*** (0.05)	−0.24*** (0.07)
	Share of extractive industries in GRP, %	−0.062*** (0.019)			
	Share of crop production in GRP, %		−0.11** (0.05)		
Base level	The number of startups per unit of workforce a year earlier			−0.26*** (0.05)	−0.84*** (0.08)

Dependent variable		Number of new high-tech firms per ten thousand people (labour force)		Annual increase of the dependent variable, %	
	Estimation method	random effects	fixed effects	random effects	fixed effects
LSDV R^2			0.9		0.56
Within R^2			0.13		0.54

Notes: *p-value<0.1; **p-value<0.05; ***p-value<0.01. All variables are logarithmic. Robust standard errors.

In general, startup activity is lower in regions where the extraction of minerals and agriculture plays an important role. In resource regions, this may be due to the manifestation of the so-called 'resource curse': when investment and employment moves to the extractive sector of the economy. A similar result was obtained for German coal-mining regions (Fritsch and Wyrwich, 2018). For the first time, we have traced this impact for Russian tech startups. Rural regions have a lower level of education, more conservative communities and a low demand for new technologies, which is consistent with the literature review.

Most of the identified patterns are common across the country (models with random effects), and only the level of education, market access and average firm size explain the differences between regions (models 2 and 4).

RECOMMENDATIONS

Taking into consideration the identified factors, the following recommendations can be proposed:

1. Wide implementation of the concept of 'entrepreneurial universities'
    It is essential to promote an increase in the share of commercialized patents and other R&D results of universities and scientific organizations by:
    *   Implementing entrepreneurship training courses (Dukhon et al., 2018; Alvarez-Torres et al., 2019).
    *   Expanding opportunities for interaction between universities and business, in particular by facilitating the organization of business-oriented departments, personal scholarships and open lectures by famous entrepreneurs (Alvarez-Torres et al., 2019).
    *   Identifying universities with entrepreneurial potential and providing them with special support (Alvarez-Torres et al., 2019). One of the potentially most effective areas could be the further expansion of the

'Startup as a Diploma' programme, which allows students to defend a project to create a company instead of their final qualifying work.

- Formation of a university entrepreneurship ecosystem in the most promising universities (Alvarez-Torres et al., 2019) by introducing individual courses, MBAs, entrepreneurship centres, business incubators, technology valleys, associated grants and innovation vouchers, patenting and commercialization centres, and so on.

2. Attraction of highly qualified specialists

Decisions related to attracting and retaining highly qualified personnel in Russia (Barinova et al., 2022), such as increasing the number of students in key areas, are especially relevant. Additional measures are needed to improve housing conditions for young entrepreneurs; for example, in the Republic of Tatarstan, a programme is being implemented to provide preferential mortgages and rental housing for founders of startups who will move from other regions. A similar programme may be relevant for attracting entrepreneurs from neighbouring countries.

3. Improving access to funding

Another way to accelerate the pace of emergence of new high-tech firms may be to increase the availability of financial resources.

- Partnership programmes of public and private venture funds are significant (Cumming et al., 2017). Redistribution of state funds to the most demanded technological areas will be required. Currently, Russia is carrying out an initiative of the Central Bank to attract funds from non-profit pension funds to the venture capital sector.
- Promoting practice and increasing funding for innovation vouchers and associated grants (Cornet et al., 2006). In the first case, startups are issued certificates for the implementation of R&D in large universities and research centres, which stimulates the interaction of startups with educational and scientific organizations. In the second case, budget funds are allocated to universities and research centres only, with additional funding from the private sector.
- Formation of information support and consulting centres ('soft services').
- Expanding the practice of creating corporate venture funds and stimulating intrapreneurship (internal entrepreneurship) in state-owned companies.

4. Expanding accessibility of markets

Expanding the accessibility of markets will require wider involvement of the population in the digital economy and the expansion of digital infrastructure (OECD, 2019):

- Allocation of additional funds for training in the basics of digital literacy, training entrepreneurs to work in a digital environment.

- Initiation of a separate programme to support the digitalization of state-owned companies, which in turn will create a market for startups.
- Reduction of the digital divide in Internet access and digital skills. The expansion of ICT infrastructure (including broadband Internet, 5G) will create conditions for the formation of new industries: 3D printing, augmented and virtual reality technologies, telemedicine, the Internet of Things, and so on. Bridging the digital divide for online learning in schools is especially relevant.

Supporting digital ecosystems for startups can be an effective tool (Jin and Hurd, 2018) as well as digitalization of all government services.

CONCLUSION

The results made it possible to verify most of the hypotheses and identify key regional factors that determine startup activity in Russia: concentration of human capital and R&D, quality of the business and institutional environment, market and Internet access, and sectoral economic specialization.

These factors are not obvious for Russia. Thus, the level of education strongly depends on its quality, which has decreased in the post-Soviet period, and only one Russian university is included in the top 100 world ratings. Most of the universities do not create any startups. However, regions with higher education levels and student density have higher startup activity. Young graduates want to start new businesses (Shirokova et al., 2016). The low commercialization of most research results hinders the creation of startups; however, in more innovative regions, startup activity is higher. Institutional conditions are important for small businesses, but very specific institutions are important for technology startups (protection of intellectual property, venture capital, etc.). Nevertheless, in regions with a high share of the informal sector, the level of corruption and pressure on business is so high that it limits the development of any businesses. In Russia, the state spends significant funds on direct financial support for innovation projects, but no connection with the growth of tech startups has been found. This raises the questions of whether the corresponding programmes and development institutions are efficient, and whether they need to change their focus from large-scale projects to small, more technological ones. Household incomes, size of local market and geographic proximity to large markets significantly affect the development of small businesses, but tech startups create products with high added value and could target global markets regardless of their distance. However, the rise or fall of the local market is important for most of the new high-tech companies. Digitalization and increased access to the Internet contribute to the development of technological entrepreneurship by increasing access to other users and contractors, and facilitating the emergence of new market niches. Previously, there were no assessments in the literature of the impact of the 'resource curse' on the number of startups, but there are indeed fewer new technological companies in the resource regions.

Each of the factors make it possible to formulate certain directions and propose tools for entrepreneurial policy. For example, optimizing human capital requires measures to attract highly qualified specialists as well as students, and the development of global universities. The role of scientific potential justifies the need to increase R&D costs, especially in the private sector, and expand the interaction between universities and business. The importance of the institutional environment confirms the need to improve the business climate. The results substantiate the need to increase ties with external markets, to promote export and to develop the Internet sphere. Our results can also be helpful in understanding the mechanism of the resource curse. Resource-based regional economies are actually not able to diversify their economies themselves due to oppressed startup activity, and therefore require the attention of the federal government despite their high budgetary self-sufficiency.

We have no reason to assert that startup activity in Russia will grow sharply in the future, since the main factors have a negative trend: incomes and market access are decreasing, R&D share in GDP is not increasing. However, on a more positive note, the formal conditions for doing business are improving and digitalization has accelerated following the pandemic, which gives some hope.

REFERENCES

Alvarez-Torres, F. J., Lopez-Torres, G. C., and Schiuma, G. (2019). Linking entrepreneurial orientation to SMEs' performance: Implications for entrepreneurship universities. *Management Decision*, 12(57), 3364–3386. https://doi.org/10.1108/MD-11-2018-1234

Antonova, M. P., Barinova, V. A., Gromov, V. V., Zemtsov, S. P., Krasnoselskikh, A. N., Milogolov, N. S., and Tsareva, Y. V. (2020). *Development of Small and Medium-Sized Entrepreneurship in Russia in the Context of the Implementation of the National Project*. Publishing House 'Delo' RANEPA.

Aparicio, S., Urbano, D., and Audretsch, D. (2016). Institutional factors, opportunity entrepreneurship and economic growth: Panel data evidence. *Technological Forecasting and Social Change*, 102, 45–61.

Armington, C., and Acs, Z. J. (2002). The determinants of regional variation in new firm formation. *Regional Studies*, 36(1), 33–45.

Audretsch, D. B., and Belitski, M. (2017). Entrepreneurial ecosystems in cities: Establishing the framework conditions. *Journal of Technology Transfer*, 42(5), 1030–1051.

Audretsch, D. B., and Belitski, M. (2020). The role of R&D and knowledge spillovers in innovation and productivity. *European Economic Review*, 123, 103391.

Audretsch, D. B., and Belitski, M. (2021). Towards an entrepreneurial ecosystem typology for regional economic development: The role of creative class and entrepreneurship. *Regional Studies*, 55(4), 735–756.

Audretsch, D. B., and Fritsch, M. (1994). The geography of firm births in Germany. *Regional Studies*, 28(4), 359–365.

Audretsch, D. B., and Keilbach, M. (2008). Resolving the knowledge paradox: Knowledge-spillover entrepreneurship and economic growth. *Research Policy*, 37(10), 1697–1705.

Audretsch, D. B., and Lehmann, E. E. (2005). Does the knowledge spillover theory of entrepreneurship hold for regions? *Research Policy*, 34(8), 1191–1202.

Audretsch, D. B., Lehmann, E. E., and Paleari, S. (2015). Academic policy and entrepreneurship: A European perspective. *Journal of Technology Transfer*, 40(3), 363–368.

Audretsch, D. B., Thurik, R., Verheul, I., and Wennekers, S. (Eds). (2002). *Entrepreneurship: Determinants and Policy in a European–US Comparison*. Economics of Science, Technology and Innovation (ESTI, volume 27). Boston, MA: Springer.

Audretsch, D. B., and Vivarelli, M. (1996). Determinants of new-firm startups in Italy. *Empirica*, 23(1), 91–105.

Barinova, V., Rochhia, S., and Zemtsov, S. (2022). Attracting highly skilled migrants to the Russian regions. *Regional Science Policy and Practice*, 1(14), 147–173. https://doi.org/10.1111/rsp3.12467

Barinova, V. A., Zemtsov, S. P., and Tsareva, Y. V. (2018). Entrepreneurship and institutions: Does the relationship exist at the regional level in Russia. *Voprosy ekonomiki*, 6, 92–116.

Belitski, M., and Desai, S. (2016). What drives ICT clustering in European cities? *Journal of Technology Transfer*, 41(3), 430–450.

Breitenecker, R. J. (2007). Analysing regional firm startup activity using geographically weighted regression: The case of Austria. Presentation at *15th European Young Statisticians Meeting*, Castro Urdiales, Spain, 10–14 September.

Calá, C. D. (2014). *Regional Issues on Firm Entry and Exit in Argentina: Core and Peripheral Regions*. Doctoral dissertation, Universitat Rovira i Virgili.

Cornet, M., Vroomen, B., and Van der Steeg, M. (2006). *Do Innovation Vouchers Help SMEs to Cross the Bridge towards Science?* CPB Discussion Paper, no. 58.

Cumming, D. J., Grilli, L., and Murtinu, S. (2017). Governmental and independent venture capital investments in Europe: A firm-level performance analysis. *Journal of Corporate Finance*, 42, 439–459.

Del Bosco, B., Mazzucchelli, A., Chierici, R., and Di Gregorio, A. (2021). Innovative startup creation: The effect of local factors and demographic characteristics of entrepreneurs. *International Entrepreneurship and Management Journal*, 17(1), 145–164.

Delgado, M., Porter, M. E., and Stern, S. (2010). Clusters and entrepreneurship. *Journal of Economic Geography*, 10(4), 495–518.

Dukhon, A. B., Zinkovsky, K. V., Obraztsova, O. I., and Chepurenko, A. Y. (2018). The impact of entrepreneurial education programs on small business development in Russia: An empirical experience in a regional context. *Voprosy obrazovaniya*, 2, 139–172 (in Russian).

Dvoulety, O., Blažková, I., and Potluka, O. (2021). Estimating the effects of public subsidies on the performance of supported enterprises across firm sizes. *Research Evaluation*, 30(3), 290–313.

Eremkin, V., Barinova, V., and Zemtsov, S. (2015). Factors of attractiveness of the leading Russian universities: Overview of literature and econometric analysis of the leading universities. *Voprosy obrazovaniya*, 4, 201–233.

Erikson, T. (2002). Entrepreneurial capital: The emerging venture's most important asset and competitive advantage. *Journal of Business Venturing*, 17(3), 275–290.

Evers, N. (2003). The process and problems of business start-ups. *The ITB Journal*, 4(1), 3.

Fossen, F., and Sorgner, A. (2021). Digitalization of work and entry into entrepreneurship. *Journal of Business Research*, 125, 548–563. https://doi.org/10.1016/j.jbusres.2019.09.019

Fritsch, M., and Mueller, P. (2008). The effect of new business formation on regional development over time: The case of Germany. *Small Business Economics*, 30(1), 15–29.

Fritsch, M., and Wyrwich, M. (2018). Regional knowledge, entrepreneurial culture, and innovative start-ups over time and space – an empirical investigation. *Small Business Economics*, 51(2), 337–353.

Fuentelsaz, L., González, C., Maícas, J. P., and Montero, J. (2015). How different formal institutions affect opportunity and necessity entrepreneurship. *BRQ Business Research Quarterly*, 18(4), 246–258.

Goel, R. K., and Saunoris, J. W. (2017). Dynamics of knowledge spillovers from patents to entrepreneurship: Evidence across entrepreneurship types. *Contemporary Economic Policy*, 35(4), 700–715.

Guriev, S., and Sonin, K. (2008). Economics of the resource curse. *Voprosy ekonomiki*, 4, 61–74.

Isenberg, D. (2011). The entrepreneurship ecosystem strategy as a new paradigm for economic policy: Principles for cultivating entrepreneurship. Presentation at the Institute of International and European Affairs, Dublin, Ireland, 12 May.

Jin, H., and Hurd, F. (2018). Exploring the impact of digital platforms on SME internationalization: New Zealand SMEs use of the Alibaba platform for Chinese market entry. *Journal of Asia-Pacific Business*, 19(2), 72–95.

Lasch, F., Robert, F., and Le Roy, F. (2013). Regional determinants of ICT new firm formation. *Small Business Economics*, 40(3), 671–686.

Lavrinenko, P. A., Mikhailova, T. N., Romashina, A. A., and Chistyakov, P. A. (2019). Agglomeration effect as a tool of regional development. *Studies on Russian Economic Development*, 30(3), 268–274.

Lee, S. Y., Florida, R., and Acs, Z. (2004). Creativity and entrepreneurship: A regional analysis of new firm formation. *Regional Studies*, 38(8), 879–891.

Marlow, S., Swail, J., and Williams, C. C. (2017). *Entrepreneurship in the Informal Sector: An Institutional Perspective*. New York: Routledge.

Motoyama, Y., and Bell-Masterson, J. (2014). *Beyond Metropolitan Startup Rates: Regional Factors Associated with Startup Growth*. Ewing Marion Kauffman Foundation.

Nambisan, S. (2017). Digital entrepreneurship: Toward a digital technology perspective of entrepreneurship. *Entrepreneurship Theory and Practice*, 41(6), 1029–1055.

Novotny, Á. (2008). Academic entrepreneurship in Hungary: Can the Bayh–Dole model of university technology transfer work in an Eastern European context? *Periodica Polytechnica Social and Management Sciences*, 16(2), 71–80.

OECD. (2019). *Going Digital: Shaping Policies, Improving Lives*. Paris: OECD Publishing.

OECD. (2020). *Covid-19 SME Policy Responses.* https://read.oecd-ilibrary.org/view/
?ref=119_119680-di6h3qgi4x&title=Covid-19_SME_Policy_Responses
Partridge, M., Tsvetkova, A., Schreiner, S., and Patrick, C. (2019). The effects of
state and local economic incentives on business start-ups in the US: County-level
evidence. Andrew Young School of Policy Studies Research Paper Series (19-02).
Plummer, L. A. (2010). Spatial dependence in entrepreneurship research: Challenges
and methods. *Organizational Research Methods*, 13(1), 146–175.
Qian, H., Acs, Z. J., and Stough, R. R. (2013). Regional systems of entrepreneurship: The nexus of human capital, knowledge and new firm formation. *Journal of
Economic Geography*, 13(4), 559–587.
Robehmed, N. (2013). What is a startup. *Forbes*, 16 December. https://www.forbes
.com/sites/natalierobehmed/%202013/12/16/what-is-a-startup/
Rosenthal, S. S., and Strange, W. C. (2004). Evidence on the nature and sources of
agglomeration economies. In J. V. Henderson and J.-F. Thisse (Eds), *Handbook
of Regional and Urban Economics* (Vol. 4, pp. 2119–2171). Amsterdam: Elsevier.
Schwab, K. (2017). *The Fourth Industrial Revolution*. New York: Currency.
Semenova, R., Barinova, V., and Zemtsov, S. (2019). State support of high technologies and innovations in Russia. *Innovatsii*, 3(245), 33–44 (in Russian).
Shirokova, G., Osiyevskyy, O., and Bogatyreva, K. (2016). Exploring the intention–
behavior link in student entrepreneurship: Moderating effects of individual and
environmental characteristics. *European Management Journal*, 34(4), 386–399.
Stuetzer, M., Obschonka, M., and Schmitt-Rodermund, E. (2013). Balanced skills
among nascent entrepreneurs. *Small Business Economics*, 41(1), 93–114.
Sutaria, V., and Hicks, D. A. (2004). New firm formation: Dynamics and determinants.
Annals of Regional Science, 38(2), 241–262.
Verheul, I., Wennekers, S., Audretsch, D., and Thurik, R. (2002). An eclectic theory
of entrepreneurship: Policies, institutions and culture. In D. Audretsch, R. Thurik,
I. Verheul and S. Wennekers (Eds), *Entrepreneurship: Determinants and Policy in
a European–US Comparison* (pp. 11–81). Economics of Science, Technology and
Innovation (ESTI, volume 27). Boston, MA: Springer.
von Briel, F., Davidsson, P., and Recker, J. (2018). Digital technologies as external
enablers of new venture creation in the IT hardware sector. *Entrepreneurship Theory
and Practice*, 42(1), 47–69.
Zemtsov, S. (2020). New technologies, potential unemployment and 'nescience
economy' during and after the 2020 economic crisis. *Regional Science Policy and
Practice*, 12(4), 723–743.
Zemtsov, S. P., and Baburin, V. L. (2019). Entrepreneurial ecosystems in Russian
regions. *Regional Researches*, 2, 4–14 (in Russian).
Zemtsov, S., and Kotsemir, M. (2019). An assessment of regional innovation system
efficiency in Russia: The application of the DEA approach. *Scientometrics*, 120(2),
375–404.
Zemtsov, S., and Smelov, Y. (2018). Factors of regional development in Russia:
Geography, human capital and regional policies. *Journal of the New Economic
Association*, 40(4), 84–108 (in Russian).
Zemtsov, S. P., and Tsareva, Y. V. (2018). Entrepreneurial activity in the Russian
regions: How spatial and temporal effects determine the development of small business. *Journal of the New Economic Association*, 1(37), 118–134.

3. Women serial high-tech entrepreneurs: a literature review and research agenda

María José Ibáñez and Maribel Guerrero

INTRODUCTION

Serial entrepreneurship has received less close attention in research, considering the development of other areas of study in entrepreneurship. Serial entrepreneurship is a widespread phenomenon but challenging to detect since the study of entrepreneurship focuses mainly on the nascent venture (Lafontaine and Shaw, 2016; Plehn-Dujowich, 2010; Ropega, 2020; Shaw and Sørensen, 2019). The literature on serial entrepreneurship moves in several directions, and although theories have been proposed to explain this phenomenon, it has not been possible to group this line of research under a common umbrella (Plehn-Dujowich, 2010; Sarasvathy et al., 2013; Shaw and Sørensen, 2019).

So far, the presence of women in serial entrepreneurship has not been explored. In general, research on serial entrepreneurship does not distinguish individuals by gender, which means there is a massive gap in the literature considering the female entrepreneurial process's unique nature. It has been shown that business opportunities in industries are different for men and women (Davidsson et al., 2020; Kalnins and Williams, 2014; Sullivan and Meek, 2012). High-performance and high-growth entrepreneurial activity is associated with male stereotyping; women establish businesses in low-performance sectors with high competition and low growth expectations (Gupta et al., 2019; Hundley, 2001; Klapper and Parker, 2010). This persistent reasoning in research on female entrepreneurship, in general, assumes that women's participation in serial entrepreneurship may have the same characteristics.

This literature review is based on 83 research articles on serial entrepreneurship, published between 2010 and 2020 and listed on the Scopus and Web of Science platforms. A content analysis of the selected articles is conducted to identify serial entrepreneurship's main concepts and build a conceptual framework to describe the serial entrepreneurial process. A definition of serial entrepreneurship is proposed to unify the different perspectives developed in this research field. Four categories of serial entrepreneurs were identified: portfolio entrepreneur, intermittent entrepreneur, second-chance entrepreneur, and corporate entrepreneur. We use serial women entrepreneurs' participation in the technology industry as a context to analyze the results of this study in the gender domain. Since the literature on female serial entrepreneurship is underdeveloped, aspects of female entrepreneurship, in general, have been related to proposing future lines of research in this area.

The conceptual framework proposed in this literature review contributes to the theory of serial entrepreneurship, describing the serial entrepreneurial process and identifying the main categories of entrepreneurs in this field. Unlike other reviews, this chapter has proposed a unified definition of serial entrepreneurship to develop this research field under a common umbrella. Finally, new directions are proposed to study female serial entrepreneurship, linking advances in serial entrepreneurship literature with the gender approach in entrepreneurship theory and the context of the high-growth male-dominated industry.

METHODOLOGY

This research has been designed as a systematic review of the literature (Tranfield et al., 2003), whose objective is to identify, analyze, and combine evidence from previous studies in the field of serial entrepreneurship and women serial entrepreneurs. By interpreting the most relevant findings, a conceptual framework is proposed to synthesize the serial entrepreneurial process, identify the main categories in this entrepreneurial activity type, and explore the current topics on female serial entrepreneurship. In the Scopus and Web of Science databases, peer-reviewed academic publications were reviewed from 2010 to 2020. The search used the key concepts of "serial entrepreneurship," "portfolio entrepreneurship," "corporate entrepreneurship," "re-entry after failure," and "female serial entrepreneurship," among other related emerging concepts. The first level of analysis is the overall literature on serial entrepreneurship. In the second level, we retrieved the studies on women serial entrepreneurs for establishing the current state of research on this specific topic.

The search articles' titles and keywords were examined in the first stage, and those not focused on serial entrepreneurship were discarded. In the second stage, the summaries of the works preserved in the first stage were reviewed. Those that best fit the objectives of the research were selected. One hundred articles were obtained for review and in-depth analysis. The documents were subject to an open coding process to detect emerging concepts to find similarities and differences between the papers. The next step was the articles' axial codification to reduce the first-order concepts and build second-order themes

Table 3.1   *Distribution of the literature on serial entrepreneurship by topic of interest*

Topic	Study
Portfolio entrepreneurship	Baert et al. (2016); Carbonara et al. (2020); Chandra et al. (2015); Cruz and Justo (2017); Kerr et al. (2017); Morris et al. (2015); Parker (2014); Sarasvathy et al. (2013); Sieger et al. (2011); Sigfusson and Harris (2013); Tihula and Huovinen (2010); Yin et al. (2020)
Intermittent entrepreneurship	Amaral et al. (2011); Fu et al. (2018); Gottschalk et al. (2017); Holland and Garrett (2015); Hsu et al. (2017); Iacobucci and Rosa (2010); Lin et al. (2019); Nielsen and Sarasvathy (2016); Podoynitsyna et al. (2012); Robson et al. (2013); Ropega (2020); Spivack et al. (2014); Thorgren and Wincent (2015)
Second-chance entrepreneurship	Amankwah-Amoah et al. (2019); Baù et al. (2017); Corner et al. (2017); Eggers and Song (2015); Espinoza-Benavides and Díaz (2019); Franco et al. (2020); Guerrero and Espinoza-Benavides (2020); Guerrero and Peña-Legazkue (2019); Jenkins et al. (2014); Lafuente et al. (2019); Lin and Wang (2019); Nahata (2019); Simmons et al. (2014, 2019); Singh et al. (2015, 2016); Ucbasaran et al. (2010); Wakkee and Moser (2016); Yamakawa and Cardon (2015)
Corporate entrepreneurship	Behrens and Patzelt (2016); Bengtsson (2013); Corradini et al. (2016); Farinós et al. (2011); Lerner (2013); Matusik and Fitza (2012); Nason et al. (2015); Sun et al. (2014); Terjesen et al. (2011)
Gender entrepreneurship	Baù et al. (2017); Cruz and Justo (2017); Shaw and Sørensen (2019); Simmons et al. (2019)
Literature review	Korber and McNaughton (2018); Lattacher and Wdowiak (2020); Tipu (2020); Yamakawa et al. (2015)
Venture capital, crowdfunding, innovation, and other issues	Alves et al. (2019); Butticè et al. (2017); Chen (2013); Lahiri and Wadhwa (2020); Lee and Chiravuri (2019); Santana et al. (2017); Shang et al. (2020); Vaillant and Lafuente (2019a, 2019b); Yun et al. (2019)

(Gioia et al., 2013). Finally, the aggregate dimensions obtained constitute the core of the definition of serial entrepreneurship proposed in this chapter. The data structure obtained is the basis for the proposed conceptual framework. The data were triangulated with academic articles from other disciplines to contrast and validate the proposed construct's findings. In Table 3.1, the selected articles' classification detail is shown considering the type of serial enterprise on which they are focused.

The number of studies published per year, between 2010 and 2020, has not followed a regular trend. The year in which the largest number of articles in this review were published was 2019, with 15 publications. Figure 3.1 shows the evolution over time of the documents selected for this review. More than 60 percent of the studies analyzed offer quantitative methodological approaches, and only 12 percent used purely qualitative methods for researching serial entrepreneurship. Four studies were identified that mention the influence of gender in serial entrepreneurship, two in 2017 and two in 2019. To develop the section describing women's presence in serial entrepreneurship, it was necessary to triangulate these studies' findings with the literature on women's entrepreneurship and entrepreneurship in general.

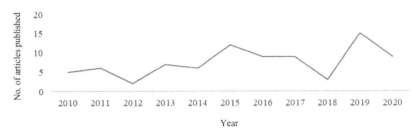

Source: Scopus and Web of Science, 2020.

Figure 3.1   *Time evolution of serial entrepreneurship research,*
                 2010–2020

THE PROCESS OF SERIAL ENTREPRENEURSHIP

According to the literature review, a conceptual framework to describe the serial entrepreneurship process is proposed in Figure 3.2. The serial entrepreneurial process begins with the individual's decision to become an entrepreneur or enter the job market (Fu et al., 2018; Plehn-Dujowich, 2010; Vereshchagina and Hopenhayn, 2009). Salaried workers can become nascent entrepreneurs at any time, represented by the punctuated arrow leading from the labor market to entrepreneurship (Stenard and Sauermann, 2016). Once potential entrepreneurs begin their business activity, they can choose to focus on a single business to achieve established company status, become serial entrepreneurs, or withdraw from business activity during the start-up period (Carbonara et al., 2020). Early-stage entrepreneurs can become serial entrepreneurs at any time; this is indicated by the dotted arrow that goes from early-stage entrepreneurship to serial entrepreneurship.

   Serial entrepreneurship can be of four types – portfolio entrepreneurship (Baert et al., 2016; Parker, 2014; Sarasvathy et al., 2013), corporate entrepreneurship (Behrens and Patzelt, 2016; Lerner, 2013; Ren and Guo, 2011), intermittent entrepreneurship (Parker, 2013; Ucbasaran et al., 2003; Westhead et al., 2009), or second-chance entrepreneurship (Hessels et al., 2011; Ucbasaran

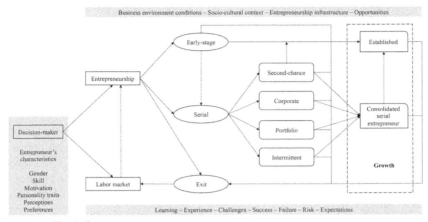

Figure 3.2   *Conceptual framework for the serial entrepreneurial process*

et al., 2010; Wakkee and Sleebos, 2015) – depending on the outcome of the novice venture and the entrepreneur's preferences (Malmström et al., 2015). Regardless of the success or failure of the business considered in serial entrepreneurship, if the overall result allows the serial entrepreneur to remain in operation, the entrepreneur can move to the consolidated serial entrepreneur status (Rocha et al., 2015). The second-chance entrepreneur can operate a single venture and be part of the early-stage entrepreneurs who seek to move towards an established company (Carbonara et al., 2020; Hessels et al., 2011). Something similar occurs with consolidated serial entrepreneurs, who can keep only one of their ventures and operate as an established company.

At any stage of the serial entrepreneurial process, entrepreneurs have the option of leaving, regardless of the type of entrepreneur (Cumming et al., 2016; Fu et al., 2018; Plehn-Dujowich, 2010). The serial entrepreneurial process is influenced by the conditions of the business environment and other exogenous elements that can affect the enterprise's survival and growth (Amankwah-Amoah, 2018; Fu et al., 2018; Guerrero and Espinoza-Benavides, 2020). When entering a venture of any kind, the decision-maker is exposed to any risk (Roussanov, 2010; Ucbasaran et al., 2009; Vereshchagina and Hopenhayn, 2009; Yin et al., 2020). However, business failure in this context can benefit an entrepreneur's business skills through learning and experience (Carbonara et al., 2020; Espinoza-Benavides and Díaz, 2019). Individuals' motivation and expectations also influence decisions to enter, exit, re-enter, and stay in a venture of any kind.

Men and women have the same options in developing the serial entrepreneurial process. However, they can face different context conditions and value the risks, opportunities, learning, and experiences of success or failure of the entrepreneurial activity differently (Arauzo-Carod and Segarra-Blasco, 2005; Hasan and Almubarak, 2016; Saridakis et al., 2014). Decisions to enter, exit, re-enter, and stay in a venture may depend on various factors depending on the gender of the entrepreneur (Klapper and Parker, 2010; Swail and Marlow, 2018). Another aspect to consider in differentiating men's and women's choices in a venture is their characteristics. In this sense, the stereotype of the male entrepreneur can influence women to adopt behaviors and attitudes related to male attributes (Byrne et al., 2019; Javadian and Singh, 2012). Some women may view male entrepreneurship as a role model for better business performance and for achieving their business growth expectations (Barragan et al., 2018; Miller, 2004). These environmental influences on gendered social constructions may lead women serial entrepreneurs to adopt an alternative identity to the female stereotype to achieve business success (Barragan et al., 2018).

Understanding the serial entrepreneurial process is necessary to define what serial entrepreneurship is and how each type of serial entrepreneur transits through the different stages proposed. Every serial entrepreneur has different motivations, expectations, and preferences; therefore, determining each type's unique characteristics is critical to exploring the serial entrepreneurs' behavior. Also, the categorization of serial entrepreneurs is the starting point for measuring wide phenomena since the sample characteristics depend on the specific type of serial entrepreneur being analyzed. On the other hand, the increasing activity of women in serial entrepreneurship calls for the exploration of the particular attitudes and behaviors related to women's serial entrepreneurs' decision processes. In this vein, there is a need to understand the implications of stereotypes in male-dominated sectors (such as the technology industry) for searching for and selecting opportunities for growth by women entrepreneurs. The following sections develop these themes (definition, measurement, and gender) in more depth.

DEFINING SERIAL ENTREPRENEURSHIP

Plehn-Dujowich (2010) proposed a theory of serial entrepreneurship, identifying serial entrepreneurs as those who launch and subsequently close companies until they find a sufficiently profitable business. Furthermore, it suggests that serial and portfolio ventures are part of a broader category, called regular ventures. Other studies have used simplified definitions to refer to the serial entrepreneur as one who opens multiple businesses (Shaw and Sørensen, 2019), a person who enters and leaves the enterprise repeatedly (Hyytinen and

Ilmakunnas, 2007; Lafuente et al., 2019), and individuals with multiple entrepreneurial experiences (Amaral et al., 2011), among others. Different serial entrepreneurship definitions make its operationalization difficult and prevent research results from being generalizable (Westhead and Wright, 2015).

Several articles have studied the relationship between business failure and serial entrepreneurship (Nahata, 2019; Sarasvathy et al., 2013). This recurring association incorporates other typologies of serial entrepreneurs such as renascent entrepreneur (Wakkee and Sleebos, 2015), resilient entrepreneur (Korber and McNaughton, 2018), and experienced entrepreneur (Fu et al., 2018). These categories relate to the entrepreneur's ability to overcome business failure and re-enter entrepreneurship (Corner et al., 2017; Tipu, 2020; Ucbasaran et al., 2009, 2010). Another type of serial entrepreneur identified in the literature is corporate entrepreneurs, who seek entrepreneurial opportunities to incorporate them into their business units for strategic purposes (Lerner, 2013). The emergence of these superimposed dimensions makes it even more challenging to characterize serial entrepreneurship and highlights the different paths taken in parallel in serial entrepreneurship. To broaden the field of research on serial entrepreneurship and discuss women's role in this context, it is necessary to start from a unified definition and identify its main dimensions.

Human behavior is influenced by serial decision-making: past decisions affect the choices that set the context for selecting future options (Abzug and Sommer, 2018b). In the behavioral sciences, the study of serial decision-making represents the core of the study of learning and the sequential behavioral process (Abzug and Sommer, 2018a, 2018b; Lenow et al., 2017; St. John-Saaltink et al., 2016; Török et al., 2017). Although the association between serial entrepreneurship and serial decision-making seems evident, no research was found that makes a direct link between the two in the way proposed here. In this sense, the theoretical development of serial decision-making in behavioral sciences allows a unified definition of serial entrepreneurship. By integrating the literature on the serial decision-making process and serial entrepreneurship, we define serial entrepreneurship as an:

> entrepreneurial process in which an individual, group of people, or established owners create or invest in more than one early-stage venture simultaneously, sequentially, or intermittently, considering past experiences to select between various alternatives for present and future business.

Unlike the novice entrepreneur, the serial entrepreneur already has previous ventures that can succeed or fail. In serial entrepreneurship research, subtypes of entrepreneurship have been identified. These categories depend on the number of entrepreneurs involved in the venture (individual, group, or established business), the motivations for start-up, the time of entry (sequential, simultaneous, intermittent), and the method of opportunity seeking. The most common types used to classify serial entrepreneurship are portfolio, intermittent, second chance, and corporate. In the following, we provide a definition of these categories.

Portfolio Entrepreneurship

This is when an individual, group of individuals, or established company creates and operates more than one venture simultaneously (Parker, 2014; Sarasvathy et al., 2013). Over time, the portfolio entrepreneur adds more new companies to their portfolio sequentially (Baert et al., 2016; Sarasvathy et al., 2013). As the entrepreneur evaluates their ongoing businesses, those with low performance are closed and those that are scalable are continued until they are transformed into established companies (Behrens and Patzelt, 2016). The portfolio's ventures can be located in various sectors. Portfolio diversification allows this type of serial entrepreneur to reduce the risk in their entrepreneurial activity (Yin et al., 2020).

Intermittent Entrepreneurship

This involves opening and closing businesses repeatedly at various points in time, either due to previous companies' failures or due to the exploitation of contingent or short-term business opportunities (Parker, 2013; Ucbasaran et al., 2003; Westhead et al., 2009). In this case, the entrepreneur can constantly move between the enterprise and salaried work, according to their preferences at a given time (Cumming et al., 2016; Fu et al., 2018; Plehn-Dujowich, 2010).

Second-Chance Entrepreneurship

Entrepreneurs who, as newcomers, failed to develop their first business and decide to try again, are in this group (Ucbasaran et al., 2010). This second opportunity can lead them to become established entrepreneurs, portfolio entrepreneurs, intermittent entrepreneurs, or salaried workers if the second attempt fails (Carbonara et al., 2020; Hessels et al., 2011). Second-chance entrepreneurship is challenging since entrepreneurs must overcome the adverse effects of business failure (social, economic, and emotional) to start over (Korber and McNaughton, 2018; Shepherd et al., 2009, 2011; Simmons et al., 2016).

Corporate Entrepreneurship

Established companies looking to diversify their business areas by seeking new investment opportunities are in this group (Ren and Guo, 2011; Sun et al.,

2014). Unlike portfolio entrepreneurship, corporate entrepreneurship refers to companies that seek to start or invest in new businesses for strategic reasons (Farinós et al., 2011; Lerner, 2013; Nason et al., 2015) – for example, international diversification for export, horizontal or vertical integration, complementary investments in the stock market, launching new products or services, and innovation needs. Although a portfolio structure is produced in this type of venture, the objective of the portfolio is to create synergy between existing and new businesses to maximize the value of the principal or leading company (Baert et al., 2016; Behrens and Patzelt, 2016; Birkinshaw et al., 2005; Farinós et al., 2011).

MEASURING SERIAL ENTREPRENEURSHIP

Empirical studies on serial entrepreneurship have addressed various issues, for example performance (Paik, 2014), innovation (Lahiri and Wadhwa, 2020), probability of becoming a serial entrepreneur (Carbonara et al., 2020), business failure (Amankwah-Amoah et al., 2019), internationalization (Chandra et al., 2015), and learning and experience (Vaillant and Lafuente, 2019b). The most commonly used variables to operationalize serial entrepreneurship in empirical studies are entrepreneurs who own more than one business (Lafontaine and Shaw, 2016; Parker, 2014; Shaw and Sørensen, 2019), entrepreneurs who started one or more enterprises after business failure (Lin and Wang, 2019; Nielsen and Sarasvathy, 2016; Rocha et al., 2015; Simmons et al., 2019; Wakkee and Moser, 2016), an entrepreneur who has experience in a previous business (Cumming et al., 2016; Gottschalk et al., 2017; Hsu et al., 2017), and an entrepreneur who has failed in an earlier business with or without the intention of re-entering (Baù et al., 2017; Jenkins et al., 2014; Simmons et al., 2014).

Thorgren and Wincent (2015) suggest that serial entrepreneurs experience a higher passion for entrepreneurial activity than other entrepreneurs. Paik (2014) found that serial entrepreneurs' companies perform better than those of novice entrepreneurs, regardless of previous business failure or success. In the same vein, Shaw and Sørensen (2019) confirm that serial entrepreneurs have higher sales and greater productivity than novice entrepreneurs. As for the profile of the serial entrepreneur, interesting studies have also been developed. Lin and Wang (2019) point out that the older the serial entrepreneur is, the longer it takes to restart a company. Several studies have found a positive relationship between entrepreneurs' human capital (e.g., experience, skills, knowledge, social networks) and the likelihood of becoming serial entrepreneurs (Carbonara et al., 2020; Espinoza-Benavides and Díaz, 2019). Other research has explored what happens to entrepreneurs after a business failure and how this experience affects their future entrepreneurial activities (Corner et al., 2017; Singh et al., 2016). In this context, the findings relate primarily to the value of learning from failed entrepreneurship for re-entry into business (Amaral et al., 2011; Guerrero and Peña-Legazkue, 2019; Yamakawa and Cardon, 2015) and the ability of entrepreneurs to overcome business failure (Franco et al., 2020; Jenkins et al., 2014; Yamakawa et al., 2015).

Several studies describe how serial entrepreneurs access resources and financial capital and the valuation that the financial system makes of them compared to novice entrepreneurs. Bengtsson (2013) explored the relationship between serial entrepreneurs and the venture capital (VC) companies that have financed their previous ventures. She concluded that information preservation is an essential motivation for relationship funding when detection and monitoring costs are high and that these relationships can be disrupted if VC companies specialize in a particular type of business. Nahata (2019) found that start-ups founded by successful serial entrepreneurs obtain higher valuations in VC financing than start-ups founded by newly initiated entrepreneurs. Also, serial entrepreneurs, even if they have failed in the past, get better financing terms from venture capitalists than novice entrepreneurs. In general, evidence shows that serial entrepreneurs have better prospects for financing than novice entrepreneurs (Robson et al., 2013). The business experience and learning of serial entrepreneurs are attributes that financial institutions value and give experienced entrepreneurs a significant advantage over novice entrepreneurs (J. Zhang, 2011; L. Zhang, 2019).

It has been shown that environmental conditions also influence serial entrepreneurship. Amankwah-Amoah (2018) identified factors such as the stigmatization of business failure, the fear of failure, the mistrust of governments towards the private sector, and the lack of clear national policies as barriers to serial entrepreneurship development. Guerrero and Espinoza-Benavides (2020) propose that the decision to re-enter entrepreneurship is positively related to support, mentoring, and training programs; the positive evaluation of the experience of failure by the financial system; and social norms that do not stigmatize business failure. Labor market conditions, such as regulations and employability, also influence decisions to re-enter entrepreneurship after failure and the likelihood of individuals becoming serial entrepreneurs (Fu et al., 2018).

Measuring the women's serial entrepreneurship phenomenon involves adding unique topics to those described above, especially in analyzing entry options in specific sectors and growth opportunities (Ellemers and Nadal, 2018; Gupta et al., 2019; Hundley, 2001). The persistent gender stereotypes in business may discourage women from participating in the male-dominated industries and affect their performance in these sectors. In fields such as technology, construction, mining, and finance the business owners are primarily men, and businesswomen represent a minor share of owners in these sectors

(Collins, 2014; Rocha and Praag, 2020). However, women serial entrepreneurs may feel more confident in entering male-dominated industries, since they have the experience and entrepreneurial skills to face challenging business environments. The following section describes the current state of the literature on women serial entrepreneurs and identifies the main topics associated with the discussion around this theme.

UNCOVERING FEMALE SERIAL ENTREPRENEURSHIP

The process, definition, and measurement of serial entrepreneurship also extend to women's serial entrepreneurship research, taking into account the differences between male and female behavior. The above themes presented in this chapter may improve the research on women's serial entrepreneurship, considering the nascency of the field. In research on serial entrepreneurship, women's participation has been unexplored. In general, gender has been included in serial entrepreneurship studies as a control variable, moderator, or mediator to explain other serial entrepreneurship phenomena. Baù et al. (2017) suggested that the gender of the failed entrepreneur moderates the relationship between age and likelihood of re-entry into the business throughout the entrepreneur's career. Amaral et al. (2011) found that men and older people tend to re-enter entrepreneurship more quickly than women and younger people. In the same vein, Simmons et al. (2019) conclude that the probabilities of re-entry after a recent business failure are significantly lower for women than for men; this relationship reflects the gender gap in the initial entry.

There is much material to analyze female serial entrepreneurship in all the typologies described in previous sections. For example, in *Forbes'* America's Richest Self-Made Women ranking, five of the ten wealthiest women entrepreneurs can be considered serial entrepreneurs (Forbes, 2020). Meg Whitman, Marian Ilitch, Lynda Resnick, Thai Lee, Oprah Winfrey, and Doris Fisher are the world's most wealthy serial entrepreneurs, together accounting for $21.5 billion by 2020. There are more successful cases of women serial entrepreneurs worldwide in business activities of various sizes and different sectors (Forbes, 2020; Mujer Entrepreneur, 2020). Women have even succeeded as serial entrepreneurs in traditionally male-dominated industries. One such case is Caterina Fake, co-founder of Flickr, Hunch, and Findery, who has a successful entrepreneurial career in the digital world (Fake, 2020). Many of these women also share experiences of business failure but have managed to overcome it and re-enter entrepreneurship.

The Technology Industry as a Context for High-Growth Female Serial Entrepreneurship

The technology industry is a male-dominated business field; therefore, the presence of women entrepreneurs in this sector is low (Kuschel et al., 2017; Ozkazanc-Pan and Clark Muntean, 2018; Rocha and Praag, 2020; Women in Tech, 2020). The performance of technology-based ventures led by women is considered lower than that of male-owned companies; but this paradigm is changing (Demartini, 2018). However, women entrepreneurs in the technology sector face gender-related barriers to business development (Kuschel et al., 2017). Joshi et al. (2018) found that, in state technology and innovation funding programs, women are less likely to be awarded these funds. Xie and Lv (2018) suggest that the lack of reputation of women's technology ventures has a negative effect on the performance of their businesses. These challenges faced by women entrepreneurs operating a single business may very well extend to serial entrepreneurs in the technology sector.

Since academic research has not considered female serial entrepreneurship in the technology industry, there is no evidence regarding the entrepreneurial process of women starting multiple businesses in this industry. At the practitioner level, there are quite a few cases of women serial entrepreneurs operating technology-based businesses, suggesting that the phenomenon of female serial technology entrepreneurship exists and is having an increasing impact on the business world (Forbes, 2020; SVBJ Staff, 2019). Therefore, it is worthwhile developing research in this area in order to learn more about the reality of serial women entrepreneurs in the technology sector.

The absence of a gender perspective in serial entrepreneurship research represents a limitation in serial entrepreneurship theory (Ahl, 2006). It has been demonstrated that women's entrepreneurial process can differ from men's (Hasan and Almubarak, 2016). It has also been established that men and women think differently in valuing entrepreneurship opportunities and motivations (Arauzo-Carod and Segarra-Blasco, 2005; Saridakis et al., 2014). The past and current discussion regarding gender in entrepreneurship insist on putting women at a disadvantage compared to male entrepreneurs (Ahl, 2006; Hechavarria and Ingram, 2016; Marlow and Swail, 2014). However, little is known about successful women entrepreneurs' investment preferences or the processes involved in choosing entrepreneurship as a desirable career. Balachandra and colleagues (2017) suggest that women entrepreneurs do not experience bias because they are women, but rather when they show strong female stereotypical behaviors. Thus, women are at a disadvantage when it comes to entrepreneurship unless they recognize and subscribe to a masculinized discourse (Ahl and Marlow, 2012; Ellemers and Nadal, 2018). In male-dominated cultural contexts, women entrepreneurs build an alternative identity to the female one to be successful in business (Barragan et al., 2018). Women in male-dominated environments, such as entrepreneurship, often adapt to the dominant male culture rather than attempt to change it in any way (Miller, 2004).

DISCUSSION AND FUTURE RESEARCH AGENDA

Implications for the Theory about Serial Entrepreneurship

Being in only its early stages, research on serial entrepreneurship can lead to novel findings that can help develop serial entrepreneurship theory (Tipu, 2020). The abundant literature on early entrepreneurship has provided a robust foundation for application to other research directions (Plehn-Dujowich, 2010). According to the literature review in this chapter, twice as many articles were published between 2015 and 2020 than were published between 2010 and 2014. Therefore, the interest in this research field has increased in the last six years (Tipu, 2020). As in other nascent academic fields, there is still no agreement on some fundamental aspects of serial entrepreneurship. For example, there is still no unified definition of serial entrepreneurship, and this concept has been used interchangeably to refer to different types of entrepreneurship (e.g., portfolio, second chance, habitual, corporate, persistent). Consequently, there are various ways to operationalize this variable, which prevents the generalization of the findings of empirical studies.

This review proposes a general definition for serial entrepreneurship and a classification of each type of serial entrepreneur. With these it is possible to operationalize variables for each category of serial entrepreneur and to distinguish the results for each type. Another pending issue is the description of the serial entrepreneurial process. As in entrepreneurship, it is necessary to have a conceptual framework to map the findings and propose models to build serial entrepreneurship theory. This research suggests a process of serial entrepreneurship, drawing together the most outstanding aspects found in the literature to frame future research and complement the findings in previous studies. What is currently known about serial entrepreneurship comes mainly from quantitative studies. It is necessary to strengthen qualitative research in this field of investigation since qualitative methods allow the construction of theory by creating constructs that can later be tested empirically (Dougherty, 2017; Gioia et al., 2013; Murphy et al., 2017).

One of the most evident weaknesses in serial entrepreneurship research is the lack of attention paid to female serial entrepreneurship. Few studies have focused on this topic, so very little is known about women's serial entrepreneurship. In general entrepreneurship, research on women's entrepreneurial activity began much later than research on most other issues (Ahl, 2006;

Lavoie, 1985). Because of this, in serial entrepreneurship, the gender approach can be included in the initial stage of the research field and then can grow at the same time as other topics that are also of interest. The study with a gender focus is not only about including the gender variable as a control, moderator, or mediator; rather, it is essential to go deeper into the distinctive aspects of the female entrepreneurial process in all its dimensions. This chapter proposes a future research agenda in female serial entrepreneurship; however, the literature gaps in this field allow researchers to identify many more interesting research questions.

Implications for the Theory about Female Serial Entrepreneurship

The presence of women in entrepreneurial activity is increasing (Bosma et al., 2020). Although barriers and challenges to women entrepreneurs in relation to gender gaps and male dominance in business have been documented (Klapper and Parker, 2010; Saridakis et al., 2014; Swail and Marlow, 2018), women have managed to infiltrate serial entrepreneurship and achieve business success (Forbes, 2020; Mujer Entrepreneur, 2020). It has been recognized that the motivations for entrepreneurship and the evaluation of business success are different for men and women (Gonzalez-Alvarez and Solis-Rodriguez, 2011). Also, the opportunities available are different according to the gender of the entrepreneur (Ahl, 2006; Kalnins and Williams, 2014; Murzacheva et al., 2019). The entrepreneurial process of women has unique characteristics that determine women's rapid rise in current business activity.

How do women become serial entrepreneurs?
The process of moving from a novice to a serial entrepreneur for women has not received attention in the literature. Even the transition process between the nascent and established entrepreneur has not been deeply explored in entrepreneurship in general. Although some authors have shown that women are less likely to become serial entrepreneurs (Amaral et al., 2011; Simmons et al., 2019), it is necessary to investigate the conditions under which this likelihood can be reversed. Depending on the economic, social, and cultural context, women entrepreneurs may be more willing to pursue a career as serial entrepreneurs. Based on successful and unsuccessful women serial entrepreneurs' experiences, it is possible to understand how gendered social dynamics influence women's entrepreneurship and what factors influence women entrepreneurs' perception of success.

What are the determinants of the choice of serial female entrepreneurs to enter the technology industry?

The entrepreneurship literature has widely described that women choose business opportunities in industries with low performance, high competition, and limited growth (Gupta et al., 2009; Hundley, 2001; Neill et al., 2015). In general, the industries with the highest expectations of profitability are traditionally dominated by men (Ahl and Marlow, 2012; Panda, 2018). However, it is increasingly common for women to enter these latter industries, either as novice entrepreneurs or as serial entrepreneurs. Women entrepreneurs may have preferences for certain types of industries, either by affinity or because of experience, perception of opportunities, social expectations, and cultural conditions, among other reasons (Hundley, 2001). The literature on serial entrepreneurship has not studied how women's ambition, love of risk, or competitive spirit can lead them to develop high-performing serial ventures by forming superior performance business portfolios. The perception of attractive opportunities can lead women entrepreneurs to enter different industries regardless of the gender domain.

How do women's risk preferences influence the configuration of an entrepreneurial portfolio?

Evidence indicates that women are more averse to risk than men (Dawson and Henley, 2015). Women's conservative behavior has been used to explain why they undertake less than men. Women entrepreneurs' aversion to risk also explains women-led businesses' lower performance compared to that of their male counterparts. However, women's risk preferences may not be consistent, that is, women entrepreneurs may be more conservative in certain situations and less conservative in others. For serial entrepreneurs, considerations regarding risk preferences cannot be generalized since they face different risk levels in each venture they operate. On the other hand, it is contradictory that more risk-averse entrepreneurs decide to run a single venture since by managing a portfolio as serial entrepreneurs they can reduce the overall risk of their business (Yin et al., 2020).

What strategic objectives do female corporate entrepreneurs seek to achieve?

Established entrepreneurs can also become serial entrepreneurs by seeking business opportunities to complement their existing businesses for strategic reasons (Lerner, 2013). Since women evaluate business success differently than men, it is interesting to identify the strategic objectives that women entrepreneurs pursue with diversification (Gonzalez-Alvarez and Solis-Rodriguez, 2011). For women entrepreneurs, business success is not only measured by financial indicators: some consider that having a high number of workers or being socially recognized represents a measure of the success of their business. Therefore, it is necessary to understand how female corporate entrepreneurs' success measures are aligned with the strategic objectives they hope to achieve through diversification.

How do women deal with business failure and the process of re-entry into entrepreneurship?

Since historically it has been established that women's ventures perform less well than those owned by men, it follows that women are more likely to fail. However, recent evidence suggests that this underperformance hypothesis is a myth and that companies run by women are no less profitable than those run by their male counterparts (Watson, 2020). Therefore, men and women are equally likely to fail because of poor business performance. In second-chance entrepreneurship, it has been shown that women are less willing to re-enter a venture after failure and take longer to do so than men (Simmons et al., 2019). Thus, individuals may process business failure differently depending on gender, and these cognitive differences may explain women's lower likelihood of re-entry.

Implications for Practice

Individuals can benefit from the strength derived from serial entrepreneurship for their businesses' growth and for seeking business opportunities. Risk reduction through entrepreneurial portfolios can motivate nascent entrepreneurs to get involved in this type of venture (Yin et al., 2020). The experience and learning gained from previous successful or unsuccessful ventures increase entrepreneurs' human and social capital (Amaral et al., 2011; Vaillant and Lafuente, 2019b), for example by strengthening their business skills and social networks. The experience and learning are useful for the re-entry to entrepreneurship or serial entrepreneurship; they also contribute to the professional career of the entrepreneurs who decide to retire and work in the labor market. Serial entrepreneurship is an attractive business activity since the entrepreneurs can get better financing conditions while accumulating wealth from the overall positive performance in running multiple businesses (Nahata, 2019; Robson et al., 2013).

Women's participation in serial entrepreneurship is increasing and gaining more visibility. Those women are more willing to enter sectors traditionally dominated by men since they have more experience and entrepreneurial skills than novice female entrepreneurs. In this vein, the greater visibility of female serial entrepreneurs may provide a role model to others and raise women's entrepreneurial activity. Furthermore, through mentoring, more experienced female entrepreneurs can guide other women and build strong social and business networks that enable women entrepreneurs to access knowledge and resources of all kinds. Women entrepreneurs can take advantage of their business experience to search for opportunities in high-growth industries (e.g., the technology sector) and spread the risk across various entrepreneurial activities.

Established companies can gain important competitive advantages from corporate entrepreneurship (Baert et al., 2016; Birkinshaw et al., 2005). The diversification of a company's business following strategic objectives contributes to obtaining knowledge, synergy, economies of scale, and other valuable resources (Farinós et al., 2011; Lerner, 2013; Nason et al., 2015). Also, corporate entrepreneurship can reduce transaction costs for established businesses through governance structures that mitigate the risk of their overall operations (Gibbons, 2010; Mayer and Argyres, 2004). Corporate entrepreneurs can encourage their own employees' entrepreneurial spirit to develop business ideas that take advantage of attractive business opportunities for the company (Garud et al., 2002; Mayer and Argyres, 2004). For example, the innovation and development departments are liaison units between companies and market opportunities (Bustinza et al., 2019; Reuer and Lahiri, 2013). The experiences of success and failure in corporate entrepreneurship provide companies with new organizational capabilities to improve their performance. The organizational climate that considers the workers' entrepreneurial spirit generates greater employee commitment to the company. Workers may feel more motivated to develop their business ideas through the company rather than venture out independently (Garud et al., 2002).

Serial entrepreneurs are becoming more prevalent; therefore, their activities in the economy are increasing. To encourage failed entrepreneurs to try again, it is necessary to develop policies and business conditions that favor second-chance entrepreneurship. Following Guerrero and Espinoza-Benavides's (2020) findings, some recommendations for motivating re-entry into entrepreneurship after failure are the implementation of mentoring and training programs, the positive evaluation of business failure by the financial system, and encouraging social norms that do not stigmatize business failure. In the case of successful serial entrepreneurs, programs and incentives can be aimed at growing their businesses and establishing their permanence over time. Since serial entrepreneurs have better-developed business skills and operate higher-performing enterprises than novice entrepreneurs, the financial system can benefit through the reduction of the risk of loans and investments related to them (Bengtsson, 2013). Other companies and business partners could also benefit from serial entrepreneurship through collaborations; serial entrepreneurs have a range of organizational capabilities that are more difficult for sole proprietors to develop (Yström and Agogué, 2020). Thus, cooperation between serial entrepreneurs and sole proprietors can lead to the transfer of knowledge and skills between firms to create value.

Advancing research on female serial entrepreneurship has cultural, social, and economic implications. This segment of serial entrepreneurship can generate opportunities for various stakeholders. The dissemination of success stories of women serial entrepreneurs can motivate other women entrepreneurs to take up multiple business opportunities to improve their growth expectations. For example, women who have more than one ongoing business can venture into riskier industries with better profitability and higher growth expectations that are traditionally dominated by men. Likewise, serial entrepreneurship, successful or unsuccessful, can increase women entrepreneurs' social and human capital and lead them to better business or labor performance.

CONCLUSIONS

The literature on serial entrepreneurship is still in an early stage of development. Therefore, this topic is fertile ground for research on serial entrepreneurship with a gender focus. Ahl (2006) proposed that research on women's entrepreneurship should take new directions; serial entrepreneurship is an exciting opportunity to extend the understanding of women entrepreneurship's unique nature. Research on serial entrepreneurship with a gender focus opens up the possibility of leaving behind the masculinized discourse of entrepreneurship and changing the perspective towards the positive aspects of women's entry into entrepreneurship. Beyond estimating the difference in the probability of men and women becoming serial entrepreneurs, this literature review has proposed some new avenues that can be explored in female serial entrepreneurship research.

This research contributes to serial entrepreneurship theory, describing the serial entrepreneurial process and identifying the main categories of entrepreneurs in this field. Unlike other reviews, this chapter has proposed a unified definition of serial entrepreneurship to contribute to the development of this field of research under a common umbrella. Finally, new directions have been proposed for studying female serial entrepreneurship, linking advances in the serial entrepreneurship literature with the gender approach in entrepreneurship theory. The current literature gap on women's serial entrepreneurship represents an excellent opportunity to expand research in this field and open the discussion about new trends in women's business participation.

This study has some limitations. Just two specific sources of information have been used (Scopus and Web of Science) and therefore other sources could complement this research's findings. By incorporating, for example, information from the specialized press, articles indexed in local databases, government and global reports, and similar resources, a better understanding of the phenomenon of serial entrepreneurship along different dimensions could be obtained. Since the literature on serial entrepreneurship is in its early stages, the information available is still limited, especially concerning women's serial entrepreneurship. Little is known about women's serial entrepreneurship process. Elements of serial entrepreneurship form part of other general entrepreneurship phenomena also, as a control variable, moderator, or mediator; therefore, it is difficult to identify these studies to incorporate their contributions to this literature. A broader triangulation is needed between serial enterprise research and other research areas. Several aspects of serial entrepreneurship are scattered across other fields outside of entrepreneurship, for example psychology, economics, law, and finance. Multidisciplinary research will increase the knowledge in this area and establish better foundations for constructing serial entrepreneurship theory.

ACKNOWLEDGMENTS

María José Ibáñez acknowledges the financial support provided during her Ph.D. studies by the Universidad del Desarrollo (UDD) and the Agencia Nacional de Investigación y Desarrollo (ANID), Chile.

REFERENCES

Abzug, Z., and Sommer, M. (2018a). Serial decision-making in monkeys during an oculomotor task. *Journal of Experimental Psychology: Animal Learning and Cognition*, 44(1), 95–102. https://doi.org/10.1037/xan0000154

Abzug, Z., and Sommer, M. (2018b). Neuronal correlates of serial decision-making in the supplementary eye field. *Journal of Neuroscience*, 38(33), 7280–7292. https://doi.org/10.1523/JNEUROSCI.3643-17.2018

Ahl, H. (2006). Why research on women entrepeneurs needs new directions. *Entrepreneurship Theory and Practice*, 30(5), 595–621.

Ahl, H., and Marlow, S. (2012). Exploring the dynamics of gender, feminism and entrepreneurship: advancing debate to escape a dead end? *Organization*, 19(5), 543–562. https://doi.org/10.1177/1350508412448695

Alves, A., Fischer, B., Schaeffer, P., and Queiroz, S. (2019). Determinants of student entrepreneurship. *Innovation and Management Review*, 16(2), 96–117. https://doi.org/10.1108/INMR-02-2018-0002

Amankwah-Amoah, J. (2018). Revitalising serial entrepreneurship in sub-Saharan Africa: insights from a newly emerging economy. *Technology Analysis and Strategic Management*, 30(5), 499–511. https://doi.org/10.1080/09537325.2017.1313403

Amankwah-Amoah, J., Hinson, R., Honyenuga, B., and Lu, Y. (2019). Accounting for the transitions after entrepreneurial business failure: an emerging market perspective. *Structural Change and Economic Dynamics*, 50, 148–158. https://doi.org/10.1016/j.strueco.2019.06.011

Amaral, A., Baptista, R., and Lima, F. (2011). Serial entrepreneurship: impact of human capital on time to re-entry. *Small Business Economics*, 37(1), 1–21. https://doi.org/10.1007/s11187-009-9232-4

Arauzo-Carod, J.-M., and Segarra-Blasco, A. (2005). The determinants of entry are not independent of start-up size: some evidence from Spanish manufacturing. *Review of Industrial Organization*, 27(2), 147–165. https://doi.org/10.1007/s11151-005-8321-z

Baert, C., Meuleman, M., Debruyne, M., and Wright, M. (2016). Portfolio entrepreneurship and resource orchestration. *Strategic Entrepreneurship Journal*, 10(4), 346–370. https://doi.org/10.1002/sej.1227

Balachandra, L., Briggs, T., Eddleston, K., and Brush, C. (2017). Don't pitch like a girl!: how gender stereotypes influence investor decisions. *Entrepreneurship Theory and Practice*, 43(1), 116–137. https://doi.org/10.1177/1042258717728028

Barragan, S., Erogul, M., and Essers, C. (2018). "Strategic (dis)obedience": female entrepreneurs reflecting on and acting upon patriarchal practices. *Gender, Work and Organization*, 25(5), 575–592. https://doi.org/10.1111/gwao.12258

Baù, M., Sieger, P., Eddleston, K., and Chirico, F. (2017). Fail but try again? The effects of age, gender, and multiple-owner experience on failed entrepreneurs' reentry. *Entrepreneurship Theory and Practice*, 41(6), 909–941.

Behrens, J., and Patzelt, H. (2016). Corporate entrepreneurship managers' project terminations: integrating portfolio-level, individual-level, and firm-level effects. *Entrepreneurship Theory and Practice*, 40(4), 815–842. https://doi.org/10.1111/etap.12147

Bengtsson, O. (2013). Relational venture capital financing of serial founders. *Journal of Financial Intermediation*, 22(3), 308–334. https://doi.org/10.1016/j.jfi.2013.04.002

Birkinshaw, J., Hood, N., and Young, S. (2005). Subsidiary entrepreneurship, internal and external competitive forces, and subsidiary performance. *International Business Review*, 14(2), 227–248. https://doi.org/10.1016/j.ibusrev.2004.04.010

Bosma, N., Hill, S., Ionescu-Somers, A., Kelley, D., Levie, J., and Tarnawa, A. (2020). *Global Entrepreneurship Monitor 2019/2020 Global Report*. https://www.gemconsortium.org/file/open?fileId=50443

Bustinza, O., Gomes, E., Vendrell-Herrero, F., and Baines, T. (2019). Product–service innovation and performance: the role of collaborative partnerships and R&D intensity. *R&D Management*, 49(1), 33–45. https://doi.org/10.1111/radm.12269

Butticè, V., Colombo, M., and Wright, M. (2017). Serial crowdfunding, social capital, and project success. *Entrepreneurship Theory and Practice*, 41(2), 183–207. https://doi.org/10.1111/etap.12271

Byrne, J., Fattoum, S., and Diaz, M. (2019). Role models and women entrepreneurs: entrepreneurial superwoman has her say. *Journal of Small Business Management*, 57(1), 154–184. https://doi.org/10.1111/jsbm.12426

Carbonara, E., Tran, H., and Santarelli, E. (2020). Determinants of novice, portfolio, and serial entrepreneurship: an occupational choice approach. *Small Business Economics*, 55(1), 123–151. https://doi.org/10.1007/s11187-019-00138-9

Chandra, Y., Styles, C., and Wilkinson, I. (2015). Opportunity portfolio: moving beyond single opportunity explanations in international entrepreneurship research. *Asia Pacific Journal of Management*, 32(1), 199–228. https://doi.org/10.1007/s10490-014-9400-1

Chen, J. (2013). Selection and serial entrepreneurs. *Journal of Economics and Management Strategy*, 22(2), 281–311. https://doi.org/10.1111/jems.12016

Collins, J. (2014). Characteristics of "masculinized" industries. *Human Resource Development Review*, 14(4), 415–441. https://doi.org/10.1177/1534484314559930

Corner, P., Singh, S., and Pavlovich, K. (2017). Entrepreneurial resilience and venture failure. *International Small Business Journal*, 35(6), 687–708. https://doi.org/10.1177/0266242616685604

Corradini, C., Demirel, P., and Battisti, G. (2016). Technological diversification within UK's small serial innovators. *Small Business Economics*, 47(1), 163–177. https://doi .org/10.1007/s11187-015-9698-1

Cruz, C., and Justo, R. (2017). Portfolio entrepreneurship as a mixed gamble: a winning bet for family entrepreneurs in SMEs. *Journal of Small Business Management*, 55(4), 571–593. https://doi.org/10.1111/jsbm.12341

Cumming, D., Walz, U., and Werth, J. (2016). Entrepreneurial spawning: experience, education, and exit. *Financial Review*, 51(4), 507–525. https://doi.org/10.1111/fire .12109

Davidsson, P., Recker, J., and von Briel, F. (2020). External enablement of new venture creation: a framework. *Academy of Management Perspectives*, 34(3), 311–332. https://doi.org/10.5465/amp.2017.0163

Dawson, C., and Henley, A. (2015). Gender, risk, and venture creation intentions. *Journal of Small Business Management*, 53(2), 501–515. https://doi.org/10.1111/ jsbm.12080

Demartini, P. (2018). Innovative female-led startups. Do women in business under-perform? *Administrative Sciences*, 8(4), 70. https://doi.org/10.3390/admsci8040070

Dougherty, D. (2017). Grounded theory research methods. In J. A. C. Baum (ed.), *The Blackwell Companion to Organizations* (pp. 849–866). Oxford: Blackwell. https:// doi.org/10.1002/9781405164061.ch37

Eggers, J., and Song, L. (2015). Dealing with failure: serial entrepreneurs and the costs of changing industries between ventures. *Academy of Management Journal*, 58(6), 1785–1803.

Ellemers, N., and Nadal, K. (2018). Gender stereotypes. *Annual Review of Psychology*, 69(1), 275–298. https://doi.org/10.1146/annurev-psych-122216-011719

Espinoza-Benavides, J., and Díaz, D. (2019). The entrepreneurial profile after failure. *International Journal of Entrepreneurial Behavior and Research*, 25(8), 1634–1651. https://doi.org/10.1108/IJEBR-04-2018-0242

Fake, C. (2020). About. Caterina.Net. https://caterina.net/

Farinós, J., Herrero, B., and Latorre, M. (2011). Corporate entrepreneurship and acquisitions: creating firm wealth. *International Entrepreneurship and Management Journal*, 7(3), 325–339. https://doi.org/10.1007/s11365-011-0201-4

Forbes. (2020). America's richest self-made women. *Forbes List*. https://www.forbes .com/self-made-women/

Franco, M., Haase, H., and António, D. (2020). Influence of failure factors on entrepreneurial resilience in Angolan micro, small and medium-sized enterprises. *International Journal of Organizational Analysis*. https://doi.org/10.1108/IJOA-07 -2019-1829

Fu, K., Larsson, A.-S., and Wennberg, K. (2018). Habitual entrepreneurs in the making: how labour market rigidity and employment affects entrepreneurial re-entry. *Small Business Economics*, 51(2), 465–482. https://doi.org/10.1007/s11187-018-0011-y

Garud, R., Jain, S., and Kumaraswamy, A. (2002). Institutional entrepreneurship in the sponsorship of common technological standards: the case of Sun Microsystems and Java. *Academy of Management Journal*, 45(1), 196–214. https://doi.org/10.2307/ 3069292

Gibbons, R. (2010). Transaction-cost economics: past, present, and future? *Scandinavian Journal of Economics*, 112(2), 263–288. https://doi.org/10.1111/j.1467-9442.2010 .01609.x

Gioia, D., Corley, K., and Hamilton, A. (2013). Seeking qualitative rigor in inductive research. *Organizational Research Methods*, 16(1), 15–31. https://doi.org/10.1177/1094428112452151

Gonzalez-Alvarez, N., and Solis-Rodriguez, V. (2011). Discovery of entrepreneurial opportunities: a gender perspective. *Industrial Management and Data Systems*, 111(5), 755–775. https://doi.org/10.1108/02635571111137296

Gottschalk, S., Greene, F., and Müller, B. (2017). The impact of habitual entrepreneurial experience on new firm closure outcomes. *Small Business Economics*, 48(2), 303–321. https://doi.org/10.1007/s11187-016-9780-3

Guerrero, M., and Espinoza-Benavides, J. (2020). Does entrepreneurship ecosystem influence business re-entries after failure? *International Entrepreneurship and Management Journal*. https://doi.org/10.1007/s11365-020-00694-7

Guerrero, M., and Peña-Legazkue, I. (2019). Renascence after post-mortem: the choice of accelerated repeat entrepreneurship. *Small Business Economics*, 52(1), 47–65.

Gupta, V., Turban, D., Wasti, S., and Sikdar, A. (2009). The role of gender stereotypes in perceptions of entrepreneurs and intentions to become an entrepreneur. *Entrepreneurship Theory and Practice*, 33(2), 397–417. https://doi.org/10.1111/j.1540-6520.2009.00296.x

Gupta, V., Wieland, A., and Turban, D. (2019). Gender characterizations in entrepreneurship: a multi-level investigation of sex-role stereotypes about high-growth, commercial, and social entrepreneurs. *Journal of Small Business Management*, 57(1), 131–153. https://doi.org/10.1111/jsbm.12495

Hasan, F., and Almubarak, M. (2016). Factors influencing women entrepreneurs' performance in SMEs. *World Journal of Entrepreneurship, Management and Sustainable Development*, 12(2), 82–101. https://doi.org/10.1108/WJEMSD-09-2015-0037

Hechavarria, D., and Ingram, A. (2016). The entrepreneurial gender divide. *International Journal of Gender and Entrepreneurship*, 8(3), 242–281. https://doi.org/10.1108/IJGE-09-2014-0029

Hessels, J., Grilo, I., Thurik, R., and van der Zwan, P. (2011). Entrepreneurial exit and entrepreneurial engagement. *Journal of Evolutionary Economics*, 21(3), 447–471. https://doi.org/10.1007/s00191-010-0190-4

Holland, D., and Garrett, R. (2015). Entrepreneur start-up versus persistence decisions: a critical evaluation of expectancy and value. *International Small Business Journal: Researching Entrepreneurship*, 33(2), 194–215. https://doi.org/10.1177/0266242613480375

Hsu, D., Shinnar, R., Powell, B., and Coffey, B. (2017). Intentions to reenter venture creation: the effect of entrepreneurial experience and organizational climate. *International Small Business Journal*, 35(8), 928–948.

Hundley, G. (2001). Why women earn less than men in self-employment. *Journal of Labor Research*, 22(4), 817–829. https://doi.org/10.1007/s12122-001-1054-3

Hyytinen, A., and Ilmakunnas, P. (2007). What distinguishes a serial entrepreneur? *Industrial and Corporate Change*, 16(5), 793–821. https://doi.org/10.1093/icc/dtm024

Iacobucci, D., and Rosa, P. (2010). The growth of business groups by habitual entrepreneurs: the role of entrepreneurial teams. *Entrepreneurship Theory and Practice*, 34(2), 351–377. https://doi.org/10.1111/j.1540-6520.2010.00378.x

Javadian, G., and Singh, R. (2012). Examining successful Iranian women entrepreneurs: an exploratory study. *Gender in Management: An International Journal*, 27(3), 148–164. https://doi.org/10.1108/17542411211221259

Jenkins, A., Wiklund, J., and Brundin, E. (2014). Individual responses to firm failure: appraisals, grief, and the influence of prior failure experience. *Journal of Business Venturing*, 29(1), 17–33. https://doi.org/10.1016/j.jbusvent.2012.10.006

Joshi, A., Inouye, T., and Robinson, J. (2018). How does agency workforce diversity influence Federal R&D funding of minority and women technology entrepreneurs? An analysis of the SBIR and STTR programs, 2001–2011. *Small Business Economics*, 50(3), 499–519. https://doi.org/10.1007/s11187-017-9882-6

Kalnins, A., and Williams, M. (2014). When do female-owned businesses out-survive male-owned businesses? A disaggregated approach by industry and geography. *Journal of Business Venturing*, 29(6), 822–835. https://doi.org/10.1016/j.jbusvent.2013.12.001

Kerr, G., Schlosser, F., and Golob, M. (2017). Leisure activities and social capital development by immigrant serial/portfolio and lifestyle entrepreneurs. *Journal of Developmental Entrepreneurship*, 22(4), 1750026. https://doi.org/10.1142/S10849 46717500261

Klapper, L., and Parker, S. (2010). Gender and the business environment for new firm creation. *The World Bank Research Observer*, 26(2), 237–257. https://doi.org/10.1093/wbro/lkp032

Korber, S., and McNaughton, R. (2018). Resilience and entrepreneurship: a systematic literature review. *International Journal of Entrepreneurial Behavior and Research*, 24(7), 1129–1154. https://doi.org/10.1108/IJEBR-10-2016-0356

Kuschel, K., Lepeley, M.-T., Espinosa, F., and Gutiérrez, S. (2017). Funding challenges of Latin American women start-up founders in the technology industry. *Cross Cultural and Strategic Management*, 24(2), 310–331. https://doi.org/10.1108/CCSM-03-2016-0072

Lafontaine, F., and Shaw, K. (2016). Serial entrepreneurship: learning by doing? *Journal of Labor Economics*, 34(S2), S217–S254.

Lafuente, E., Vaillant, Y., Vendrell-Herrero, F., and Gomes, E. (2019). Bouncing back from failure: entrepreneurial resilience and the internationalisation of subsequent ventures created by serial entrepreneurs. *Applied Psychology*, 68(4), 658–694. https://doi.org/10.1111/apps.12175

Lahiri, A., and Wadhwa, A. (2020). When do serial entrepreneurs found innovative ventures? Evidence from patent data. *Small Business Economics*. https://doi.org/10.1007/s11187-020-00390-4

Lattacher, W., and Wdowiak, M. A. (2020). Entrepreneurial learning from failure. A systematic review. *International Journal of Entrepreneurial Behavior and Research*, 26(5), 1093–1131. https://doi.org/10.1108/IJEBR-02-2019-0085

Lavoie, D. (1985). A new era for female entrepreneurship in the 80's. *Journal of Small Business – Canada*, 2(3), 34–43. https://doi.org/10.1080/0820957X.1985.10600603

Lee, C., and Chiravuri, A. (2019). Dealing with initial success versus failure in crowdfunding market. *Internet Research*, 29(5), 1190–1212. https://doi.org/10.1108/INTR -03-2018-0132

Lenow, J., Constantino, S., Daw, N., and Phelps, E. (2017). Chronic and acute stress promote overexploitation in serial decision making. *Journal of Neuroscience*, 37(23), 5681–5689. https://doi.org/10.1523/JNEUROSCI.3618-16.2017

Lerner, J. (2013). Corporate venturing. *Harvard Business Review*, 91(10), 86–94.

Lin, S., and Wang, S. (2019). How does the age of serial entrepreneurs influence their re-venture speed after a business failure? *Small Business Economics*, 52(3), 651–666. https://doi.org/10.1007/s11187-017-9977-0

Lin, S., Yamakawa, Y., and Li, J. (2019). Emergent learning and change in strategy: empirical study of Chinese serial entrepreneurs with failure experience. *International Entrepreneurship and Management Journal*, 15(3), 773–792. https://doi.org/10.1007/s11365-018-0554-z

Malmström, M., Johansson, J., and Wincent, J. (2015). Cognitive constructions of low-profit and high-profit business models: a repertory grid study of serial entrepreneurs. *Entrepreneurship Theory and Practice*, 39(5), 1083–1109. https://doi.org/10.1111/etap.12096

Marlow, S., and Swail, J. (2014). Gender, risk and finance: why can't a woman be more like a man? *Entrepreneurship and Regional Development*, 26(1–2), 80–96. https://doi.org/10.1080/08985626.2013.860484

Matusik, S., and Fitza, M. (2012). Diversification in the venture capital industry: leveraging knowledge under uncertainty. *Strategic Management Journal*, 33(4), 407–426. https://doi.org/10.1002/smj.1942

Mayer, K., and Argyres, N. (2004). Learning to contract: evidence from the personal computer industry. *Organization Science*, 15(4), 394–410. https://doi.org/10.1287/orsc.1040.0074

Miller, G. (2004). Frontier masculinity in the oil industry: the experience of women engineers. *Gender, Work and Organization*, 11(1), 47–73. https://doi.org/10.1111/j.1468-0432.2004.00220.x

Morris, M., Neumeyer, X., and Kuratko, D. (2015). A portfolio perspective on entrepreneurship and economic development. *Small Business Economics*, 45(4), 713–728. https://doi.org/10.1007/s11187-015-9678-5

Mujer Entrepreneur. (2020). 14 women entrepreneurs who made their millionaire fortunes without help. https://www.entrepreneur.com/article/268199

Murphy, C., Klotz, A., and Kreiner, G. (2017). Blue skies and black boxes: the promise (and practice) of grounded theory in human resource management research. *Human Resource Management Review*, 27(2), 291–305. https://doi.org/10.1016/j.hrmr.2016.08.006

Murzacheva, E., Sahasranamam, S., and Levie, J. (2019). Doubly disadvantaged: gender, spatially concentrated deprivation and nascent entrepreneurial activity. *European Management Review*. https://doi.org/10.1111/emre.12370

Nahata, R. (2019). Success is good but failure is not so bad either: serial entrepreneurs and venture capital contracting. *Journal of Corporate Finance*, 58, 624–649. https://doi.org/10.1016/j.jcorpfin.2019.07.006

Nason, R., McKelvie, A., and Lumpkin, G. (2015). The role of organizational size in the heterogeneous nature of corporate entrepreneurship. *Small Business Economics*, 45(2), 279–304. https://doi.org/10.1007/s11187-015-9632-6

Neill, S., Metcalf, L., and York, J. (2015). Seeing what others miss: a study of women entrepreneurs in high-growth startups. *Entrepreneurship Research Journal*, 5(4), 293–322. https://doi.org/10.1515/erj-2014-0009

Nielsen, K., and Sarasvathy, S. (2016). A market for lemons in serial entrepreneurship? Exploring Type I and Type II errors in the restart decision. *Academy of Management Discoveries*, 2(3), 247–271. https://doi.org/10.5465/amd.2014.0108

Ozkazanc-Pan, B., and Clark Muntean, S. (2018). Networking towards (in)equality: women entrepreneurs in technology. *Gender, Work and Organization*, 25(4), 379–400. https://doi.org/10.1111/gwao.12225

Paik, Y. (2014). Serial entrepreneurs and venture survival: evidence from U.S. venture-capital-financed semiconductor firms. *Strategic Entrepreneurship Journal*, 8(3), 254–268. https://doi.org/10.1002/sej.1161

Panda, S. (2018). Constraints faced by women entrepreneurs in developing countries: review and ranking. *Gender in Management*, 33(4), 315–331. https://doi.org/10.1108/GM-01-2017-0003

Parker, S. (2013). Do serial entrepreneurs run successively better-performing businesses? *Journal of Business Venturing*, 28(5), 652–666. https://doi.org/10.1016/j.jbusvent.2012.08.001

Parker, S. (2014). Who become serial and portfolio entrepreneurs? *Small Business Economics*, 43(4), 887–898. https://doi.org/10.1007/s11187-014-9576-2

Plehn-Dujowich, J. (2010). A theory of serial entrepreneurship. *Small Business Economics*, 35(4), 377–398. https://doi.org/10.1007/s11187-008-9171-5

Podoynitsyna, K., Van der Bij, H., and Song, M. (2012). The role of mixed emotions in the risk perception of novice and serial entrepreneurs. *Entrepreneurship Theory and Practice*, 36(1), 115–140. https://doi.org/10.1111/j.1540-6520.2011.00476.x

Ren, C., and Guo, C. (2011). Middle managers' strategic role in the corporate entrepreneurial process: attention-based effects. *Journal of Management*, 37(6), 1586–1610. https://doi.org/10.1177/0149206310397769

Reuer, J., and Lahiri, N. (2013). Searching for alliance partners: effects of geographic distance on the formation of R&D collaborations. *Organization Science*, 25(1), 283–298. https://doi.org/10.1287/orsc.1120.0805

Robson, P., Akuetteh, C., Stone, I., Westhead, P., and Wright, M. (2013). Credit-rationing and entrepreneurial experience: evidence from a resource deficit context. *Entrepreneurship and Regional Development*, 25(5–6), 349–370. https://doi.org/10.1080/08985626.2012.729091

Rocha, V., Carneiro, A., and Amorim, C. (2015). Serial entrepreneurship, learning by doing and self-selection. *International Journal of Industrial Organization*, 40, 91–106. https://doi.org/10.1016/j.ijindorg.2015.04.001

Rocha, V., and Praag, M. (2020). Mind the gap: the role of gender in entrepreneurial career choice and social influence by founders. *Strategic Management Journal*, 41(5), 841–866. https://doi.org/10.1002/smj.3135

Ropega, J. (2020). Novice and habitual entrepreneurs and external business support exploitation. *Interdisciplinary Description of Complex Systems*, 18(2-B), 271–285. https://doi.org/10.7906/indecs.18.2.14

Roussanov, N. (2010). Diversification and its discontents: idiosyncratic and entrepreneurial risk in the quest for social status. *Journal of Finance*, 65(5), 1755–1788. https://doi.org/10.1111/j.1540-6261.2010.01593.x

Santana, J., Hoover, R., and Vengadasubbu, M. (2017). Investor commitment to serial entrepreneurs: a multilayer network analysis. *Social Networks*, 48, 256–269. https://doi.org/10.1016/j.socnet.2016.10.002

Sarasvathy, S., Menon, A., and Kuechle, G. (2013). Failing firms and successful entrepreneurs: serial entrepreneurship as a temporal portfolio. *Small Business Economics*, 40(2), 417–434. https://doi.org/10.1007/s11187-011-9412-x

Saridakis, G., Marlow, S., and Storey, D. (2014). Do different factors explain male and female self-employment rates? *Journal of Business Venturing*, 29(3), 345–362. https://doi.org/10.1016/j.jbusvent.2013.04.004

Shang, Y., Yu, H., and Ma, Z. (2020). Venture investors' monitoring and product innovation performance in serial crowdfunding projects: an empirical test. *The Chinese Economy*, 53(3), 300–314. https://doi.org/10.1080/10971475.2020.1721045

Shaw, K., and Sørensen, A. (2019). The productivity advantage of serial entrepreneurs. *ILR Review*, 72(5), 1225–1261.

Shepherd, D., Patzelt, H., and Wolfe, M. (2011). Moving forward from project failure: negative emotions, affective commitment, and learning from the experience. *Academy of Management Journal*, 54(6), 1229–1259.

Shepherd, D., Wiklund, J., and Haynie, J. (2009). Moving forward: balancing the financial and emotional costs of business failure. *Journal of Business Venturing*, 24(2), 134–148.

Sieger, P., Zellweger, T., Nason, R., and Clinton, E. (2011). Portfolio entrepreneurship in family firms: a resource-based perspective. *Strategic Entrepreneurship Journal*, 5(4), 327–351. https://doi.org/10.1002/sej.120

Sigfusson, T., and Harris, S. (2013). Domestic market context and international entrepreneurs' relationship portfolios. *International Business Review*, 22(1), 243–258. https://doi.org/10.1016/j.ibusrev.2012.04.008

Simmons, S., Carr, J., Hsu, D., and Shu, C. (2016). The regulatory fit of serial entrepreneurship intentions. *Applied Psychology*, 65(3), 605–627.

Simmons, S., Wiklund, J., and Levie, J. (2014). Stigma and business failure: implications for entrepreneurs' career choices. *Small Business Economics*, 42(3), 485–505.

Simmons, S., Wiklund, J., Levie, J., Bradley, S., and Sunny, S. (2019). Gender gaps and reentry into entrepreneurial ecosystems after business failure. *Small Business Economics*, 53(2), 517–531. https://doi.org/10.1007/s11187-018-9998-3

Singh, S., Corner, P., and Pavlovich, K. (2015). Failed, not finished: a narrative approach to understanding venture failure stigmatization. *Journal of Business Venturing*, 30(1), 150–166. https://doi.org/10.1016/j.jbusvent.2014.07.005

Singh, S., Corner, P., and Pavlovich, K. (2016). Spirituality and entrepreneurial failure. *Journal of Management, Spirituality and Religion*, 13(1), 24–49. https://doi.org/10.1080/14766086.2015.1029961

Spivack, A., McKelvie, A., and Haynie, J. (2014). Habitual entrepreneurs: possible cases of entrepreneurship addiction? *Journal of Business Venturing*, 29(5), 651–667. https://doi.org/10.1016/j.jbusvent.2013.11.002

St. John-Saaltink, E., Kok, P., Lau, H., and de Lange, F. (2016). Serial dependence in perceptual decisions is reflected in activity patterns in primary visual cortex. *Journal of Neuroscience*, 36(23), 6186–6192. https://doi.org/10.1523/JNEUROSCI.4390-15.2016

Stenard, B., and Sauermann, H. (2016). Educational mismatch, work outcomes, and entry into entrepreneurship. *Organization Science*, 27(4), 801–824. https://doi.org/10.1287/orsc.2016.1071

Sullivan, D., and Meek, W. (2012). Gender and entrepreneurship: a review and process model. *Journal of Managerial Psychology*, 27(5), 428–458. https://doi.org/10.1108/02683941211235373.

Sun, S., Yang, X., and Li, W. (2014). Variance-enhancing corporate entrepreneurship under deregulation: an option portfolio approach. *Asia Pacific Journal of Management*, 31(3), 733–761. https://doi.org/10.1007/s10490-014-9379-7

SVBJ Staff. (2019). Women who lead: Silicon Valley founders and entrepreneurs share advice on starting and scaling a business. *Silicon Valley Business Journal*. https://www.bizjournals.com/sanjose/news/2019/09/16/women-who-lead-silicon-valley-founders-and.html

Swail, J., and Marlow, S. (2018). "Embrace the masculine; attenuate the feminine" – gender, identity work and entrepreneurial legitimation in the nascent context. *Entrepreneurship and Regional Development*, 30(1–2), 256–282. https://doi.org/10.1080/08985626.2017.1406539

Terjesen, S., Patel, P., and Covin, J. (2011). Alliance diversity, environmental context and the value of manufacturing capabilities among new high technology ventures. *Journal of Operations Management*, 29(1–2), 105–115. https://doi.org/10.1016/j.jom.2010.07.004

Thorgren, S., and Wincent, J. (2015). Passion and habitual entrepreneurship. *International Small Business Journal: Researching Entrepreneurship*, 33(2), 216–227. https://doi.org/10.1177/0266242613487085

Tihula, S., and Huovinen, J. (2010). Incidence of teams in the firms owned by serial, portfolio and first-time entrepreneurs. *International Entrepreneurship and Management Journal*, 6(3), 249–260. https://doi.org/10.1007/s11365-008-0101-4

Tipu, S. (2020). Entrepreneurial reentry after failure: a review and future research agenda. *Journal of Strategy and Management*, 13(2), 198–220. https://doi.org/10.1108/JSMA-08-2019-0157

Török, B., Janacsek, K., Nagy, D., Orbán, G., and Nemeth, D. (2017). Measuring and filtering reactive inhibition is essential for assessing serial decision making and learning. *Journal of Experimental Psychology: General*, 146(4), 529–542. https://doi.org/10.1037/xge0000288

Tranfield, D., Denyer, D., and Smart, P. (2003). Towards a methodology for developing evidence-informed management knowledge by means of systematic review. *British Journal of Management*, 14(3), 207–222.

Ucbasaran, D., Westhead, P., and Wright, M. (2009). The extent and nature of opportunity identification by experienced entrepreneurs. *Journal of Business Venturing*, 24(2), 99–115. https://doi.org/10.1016/j.jbusvent.2008.01.008

Ucbasaran, D., Westhead, P., Wright, M., and Flores, M. (2010). The nature of entrepreneurial experience, business failure and comparative optimism. *Journal of Business Venturing*, 25(6), 541–555. https://doi.org/10.1016/j.jbusvent.2009.04.001

Ucbasaran, D., Wright, M., and Westhead, P. (2003). A longitudinal study of habitual entrepreneurs: starters and acquirers. *Entrepreneurship and Regional Development*, 15(3), 207–228. https://doi.org/10.1080/08985620210145009

Vaillant, Y., and Lafuente, E. (2019a). The increased international propensity of serial entrepreneurs demonstrating ambidextrous strategic agility. *International Marketing Review*, 36(2), 239–259. https://doi.org/10.1108/IMR-01-2018-0015

Vaillant, Y., and Lafuente, E. (2019b). Entrepreneurial experience and the innovativeness of serial entrepreneurs. *Management Decision*, 57(11), 2869–2889. https://doi.org/10.1108/MD-06-2017-0592

Vereshchagina, G., and Hopenhayn, H. (2009). Risk taking by entrepreneurs. *American Economic Association*, 99(5), 1808–1830.

Wakkee, I., and Moser, C. (2016). Enduring effects or business as usual? Entrepreneurship after bankruptcy. *International Journal of Business Environment*, 8(3), 217–241. https://doi.org/10.1504/IJBE.2016.10000546

Wakkee, I., and Sleebos, E. (2015). Giving second chances: the impact of personal attitudes of bankers on their willingness to provide credit to renascent entrepreneurs. *International Entrepreneurship and Management Journal*, 11(4), 719–742. https://doi.org/10.1007/s11365-014-0300-0

Watson, J. (2020). Exposing/correcting SME underperformance myths. *International Journal of Gender and Entrepreneurship*, 12(1), 77–88. https://doi.org/10.1108/IJGE-04-2019-0086

Westhead, P., Ucbasaran, D., and Wright, M. (2009). Information search and opportunity identification. *International Small Business Journal: Researching Entrepreneurship*, 27(6), 659–680. https://doi.org/10.1177/0266242609344255

Westhead, P., and Wright, M. (2015). The habitual entrepreneur phenomenon. *International Small Business Journal*, 1–16.

Women in Tech. (2020). "Yes, women can!" Women working in heavy asset industries. https://women-in-tech.org/yes-women-can-women-working-in-heavy-asset -industries/

Xie, X., and Lv, J. (2018). Female technology entrepreneurs: resource shortages and reputation challenges – a view of institutional support. *International Entrepreneurship and Management Journal*, 14(2), 379–403. https://doi.org/10.1007/s11365-017 -0450-y

Yamakawa, Y., and Cardon, M. (2015). Causal ascriptions and perceived learning from entrepreneurial failure. *Small Business Economics*, 44(4), 797–820. https://doi.org/ 10.1007/s11187-014-9623-z

Yamakawa, Y., Peng, M., and Deeds, D. (2015). Rising from the ashes: cognitive determinants of venture growth after entrepreneurial failure. *Entrepreneurship Theory and Practice*, 39(2), 209–236. https://doi.org/10.1111/etap.12047

Yin, L., Liu, Y., and Wang, Z. (2020). Model for design of portfolio venture investment contract when taking moral hazards into account. *Scientific Programming*, 2020, 1–6. https://doi.org/10.1155/2020/8821371

Yström, A., and Agogué, M. (2020). Exploring practices in collaborative innovation: unpacking dynamics, relations, and enactment in in-between spaces. *Creativity and Innovation Management*, 29(1), 141–145. https://doi.org/10.1111/caim.12360

Yun, J., Lee, M., Park, K., and Zhao, X. (2019). Open innovation and serial entrepreneurs. *Sustainability*, 11(18), 5055. https://doi.org/10.3390/su11185055

Zhang, J. (2011). The advantage of experienced start-up founders in venture capital acquisition: evidence from serial entrepreneurs. *Small Business Economics*, 36(2), 187–208. https://doi.org/10.1007/s11187-009-9216-4

Zhang, L. (2019). Founders matter! Serial entrepreneurs and venture capital syndicate formation. *Entrepreneurship Theory and Practice*, 43(5), 974–998. https://doi.org/ 10.1177/1042258718758641

4. Big data analytics and internationalisation in Italian firms

Martina Aronica, Davide Piacentino, and Pasquale Massimo Picone

1.   DIGITALISATION AND INTERNATIONALISATION: A CLOSER LOOK

Two of the most important macro-trends in the current competitive setting are business digitalisation (Bharadwaj et al., 2013; Gray and Rumpe, 2015; Kuusisto, 2017; Parviainen et al., 2017) – which is commonly considered the basis of the fourth industrial revolution (Björkdahl, 2020) – and firms' internationalisation (Volberda et al., 2011; Bergamaschi et al., 2020). *Digitalisation* leads to the technological transformation of firm processes from analogue to digital (Legner et al., 2017). Such processes are configured and reoriented around digital technologies and media structures (Brennen and Kreiss, 2016). Digitalisation does not only involve a technical dimension, but also is the outcome of a socio-technological process (Legner et al., 2017) through which firms redefine their organisational design and strategy (Kohtamäki et al., 2020; Kretschmer and Khashabi, 2020) and entrepreneurial processes (Cennamo et al., 2020). *Internationalisation* is an effective growth strategy that allows firms to exploit market imperfections and/or take full advantage of the potential of their valuable, rare, inimitable and organisational resources (i.e., VRIO resources) in many countries (Hitt et al., 2006). It is a growth strategy alternative to vertical integration and product diversification (Hitt et al., 2006).

Some scholars have tried to research links between a firm's digitalisation and its internationalisation (for a review, see Bergamaschi et al., 2020; Autio et al., 2021). For instance, a large segment of literature posits that digitalisation supports internationalisation through a 'reduction in transaction costs, improvement of coordination, reduction in distance, and reconfiguration of the supply chain' (Bergamaschi et al., 2020, p. 7).

Arguably, digitalisation is a multifaceted phenomenon that includes artificial intelligence, Internet of Things, machine learning and big data (Parida et al., 2019; Aronica et al., 2021a). We expect that not all digitalisation aspects have the same impact on business internationalisation. Similarly, firms can implement an international strategy in multiple ways, such as e-commerce, exportations, joint ventures and business combinations (Malhotra et al., 2003; Aronica et al., 2021b). Accordingly, all modes of internationalisation might not be driven equally by a firm's digitalisation.

This study focuses on the role of big data in developing firms' international e-commerce. We offer a quantitative investigation based on a large sample of Italian firms (about 18,900 firms). As is known, most Italian firms are small and medium sized (SMEs) (Fazio and Piacentino, 2010). On the one hand, they may suffer from the lack of specific expertise and a limited endowment of resources to invest in digitalisation (Schivardi and Schmitz, 2020). On the other hand, SMEs are characterised by high managerial flexibility, and in turn, such flexibility represents a key driver of digitalisation processes (Eller et al., 2020). Definitively, we address the following research question: how do Italian firms take advantage of big data analysis for developing their international e-commerce?

To tackle the above-mentioned question, we explore the effect of three different types of big data approaches on the probability of firms entering international markets via web sales. Specifically, we consider the following approaches: (a) use of big data managed by internal firm staff; (b) use of big data managed by specialised consulting firms; and (c) use of big data jointly managed by internal firm staff and specialised consultant firms. Although the cross-sectional nature of the data does not allow us to talk about causality but only of possible association, our empirical investigation shows some interesting findings. In particular, big data are positively associated with the probability that a firm enters international markets via e-commerce. Remarkably, this effect is even larger when firms combine internal and external resources and knowledge (i.e., the third approach) and even triple in the case of large firms. Then, we contribute to a resource-based view of internationalisation (Hitt et al., 2006; Peng, 2001) by showing the importance of combining internal and external resources and knowledge to exploit the benefits of big data analytics.

This chapter is structured as follows. In Section 2 we develop our hypotheses. Sections 3 and 4 illustrate methodological choice and empirical findings, respectively. Then, we summarise the theoretical and managerial implication of our study in Section 5.

2.   THEORY DEVELOPMENT AND HYPOTHESES

According to Alharthi et al. (2017, p. 286), 'The term big data is used to describe the massive volume of digital data produced by human activity that is very difficult to manage using conventional data analysis tools.' Arguably, big data support the 'fast development of networking, data storage, and the data collection capacity' (Wu et al., 2013, p. 97). Thus, big data at least potentially impact supply chain management, operations, business-to-business (B2B) and customer relations and experiences (Lee, 2017; Hallikainen et al., 2020; Khanra et al., 2020; Caputo et al., 2021). In general terms, big data impact all the activities of Porter's value chain that the firm performs under the high uncertainty conditions (Amado et al., 2018) that characterise today's competitive context (Dagnino et al., 2021). However, some traps related to digitalisation are recognised (Nell et al., 2021).

Even if there is a progressive interconnection between country markets, the world is not globalised, but semi-globalised (Ghemawat, 2003). This means that international decisions are taken under high uncertainty conditions and with cultural distance, and firms may exploit the benefits of managing big data, mainly to acquire knowledge about their markets and customers (Beugelsdijk et al., 2018).

Drawing on three characteristics of big data (i.e., infinite volume, real-time velocity and unstructured variety) reported by Laney (2001) and Alharthi et al. (2017), we argue that using big data effectively sustains the development of international e-commerce for three main reasons. First, cultural distance is one of the most critical constraints of a firm's ability to internationalise (Beugelsdijk et al., 2018). The analysis of large volumes of data enriches a firm's understanding of foreign markets. Managing a volume of digital data that is practically infinite reduces the firm's perception of cultural distance and increases its propensity to offer products to foreign customers. Second, managing big data supports a firm's capability to capture market trends and customers' needs in a timely manner (Efraim et al., 2016; Sharda and Kalgotra, 2018; Sharda et al., 2020). Third, the analysis of various data supports an acceptable segmentation of demand, identifying interesting market niches (Verhoef et al., 2016; Wamba et al., 2015). By exploiting this information, firms can recognise customers' needs and effectively meet them (Verhoef et al., 2016). The arguments mentioned above lead to the following hypothesis:

H1: Big data are positively associated with the development of international e-commerce.

Extant literature argues that digitalisation is more than mere access to a large amount of data (Alharthi et al., 2017). Specifically, the combination of investments in information and communication technologies, workers' technical expertise and digital strategy allows firms to exploit the benefits of real-time information, and the possibility of timely understanding of customers' needs and speedily responding to new ongoing trends (Raguseo, 2018; Eller et al., 2020). Then, as a specification of H1, we argue that using big data managed by internal staff supports the rapid expansion of international e-commerce.

Internal staff leverages the benefits of information and knowledge that big data analysis provides to perform international e-commerce (Correani et al., 2020). Therefore, we formulate the following hypothesis:

H2: Use of big data managed by internal staff is positively associated with the development of international e-commerce.

To use big data effectively, firms may face technological barriers related to infrastructure readiness and complexity of data and lack of skills (Alharthi et al., 2017). For this reason, firms frequently decide to acquire the services of specialised consulting firms to manage big data (Sunscrapers, 2019).

Consulting firms' business models allow them to achieve economies of scale for digital investments. Therefore, consulting firms can make available technologies that are always specialised, updated and powerful. Moreover, frequently acquiring the management of big data from specialised consulting firms is cheaper than internal solutions.

In developing H1, we argue that using big data offers a set of advantages that supports international e-commerce. Likely, this set of advantages may also be obtained by entrusting big data management to specialised consulting firms. Firms will opt for interacting with consulting firms whether or not, with the same level of cost, consulting firms would offer better management of large volumes of data with cutting-edge technologies than internal solutions would. This argument leads to the following hypothesis:

H3: Use of big data managed by specialised consulting firms is positively associated with the development of international e-commerce.

Despite the benefits of using big data managed by specialised consulting firms, there is a negative aspect. First, given a lack of familiarity with big data, firm managers might not fully understand the benefits of using big data in international e-commerce. Second, while consulting firms offer cutting-edge technologies, it is possible that inefficiencies of communication processes between a firm and consulting firm might slow down the success of using the data (Sunscrapers, 2019).

Considering the arguments mentioned above, we argue that the hybrid choice of insourcing–outsourcing to manage big data supports the development of international e-commerce more effectively than the alternative of insourcing or outsourcing by itself. On the one hand, the insourcing–outsourcing management of big data allows the firm to take advantage of professional technical resources and specialised consultants. On the other hand, internal staff can independently navigate data and directly activate new paths of interest for analyses. In addition, the insourcing–outsourcing management of big data creates a common base of knowledge that, in turn, improves the communication processes between the firm and the consulting firm. This supports the timely and effective use of data in internationalisation processes. Accordingly, we formulate the following hypothesis:

H4: Use of big data jointly managed by internal firm staff and specialised consultant firms is positively associated with the development of international e-commerce.

3.   DATA AND METHODS

As discussed above, this chapter aims to investigate whether the use of big data increases the likelihood that a firm enters international markets via e-commerce. To this aim, our analysis exploits data from the *Survey on Information and Communication Technology (ICT) Usage* in Italian enterprises sourced by ISTAT (2016). Data are collected using stratified random sampling techniques on the population of firms with more than ten employees, the final sample amounting to 18,978 firms.[1] This dataset provides information on a large range of aspects such as ICT human resources and their training activities, ICT equipment, and some basic firm characteristics (e.g., size, sector and location), besides, of course, the use of big data with different approaches (e.g., internal, external or combined resources).

Table 4.1 reports the full list of variables employed here and their definition. As a dependent variable, we use a dummy assuming a value equal to 1 if the firm realises web sales outside Italy and 0 if the firm has no e-commerce activities or only e-commerce activities limited to the domestic market (*Web Export*). Among the independent variables, the most interesting ones for our ends are obviously those referring to the use of big data. In this respect, we first focus on the use of big data in general (*Big Data*); then, we look at the approach adopted by firms (*Big Data Combination*). This last variable is categorical and assumes the following values: 0 if the firm does not use big data; 1 if the firm uses big data by exploiting internal resources; 2 if the firm uses big data by exploiting external resources; 3 if the firm uses big data combining internal and external resources.

The other independent variables allow controlling for firms' endowment of ICT equipment and human resources, as well as other main characteristics of firms. Specifically, we include two variables measuring the ICT equipment: (a) the use of a mobile internet connection for business (*Mobile*); (b) the use of broadband at different download speed connections (*Broadband*). Then, we use a binary variable to account for the presence of ICT specialists (*ICT specialists*) and two binary variables on the training activities for employees: (a) training activities for ICT specialists (*Training 1*); (b) training activities for all the other employees (*Training 2*). These are used with the aim of measuring both human capital and management quality that a firm may exploit. Training is a strategic factor for a firm, especially in technological activities, and this is well known by high-quality management. As regards other control variables, we include a qualitative measure of firm size based on four categories:[2] small (10–49 employees); medium-small (50–99 employees); medium-large (100–249 employees); large (>250 employees). Finally, we control for both the sector of activity where the firm operates, as well as for its geographical location at the NUTS2 level.

Table 4.2 shows some summary statistics. In our sample, 1,176 out of 18,978 firms enter international markets via e-commerce (6 per cent); 2,782 use big data (15 per cent) and most of them by exploiting exclusively internal resources (10 per cent), while only 1 per cent do so by exploiting external resources and 3 per cent do so by combining internal and external resources. Most of the firms use mobile internet connections (76 per cent) and broadband connections at an intermediate speed (30 per cent *Broadband 2* and 15 per cent *Broadband 3*). Only 13 per cent and 17 per cent of firms provide training activities to their employees at specialised and general levels, respectively, while in general 32 per cent of the firms employ ICT specialists. The share of small firms is predominant (63 per cent), while only 14 per cent of firms are large sized. Finally, firms mostly operate in *Retail* (30 per cent), *Manufacturing* (25 per cent) and *Services* (25 per cent).

Our first research hypothesis (H1) can be assessed by estimating the following probit model:

$$\Pr(Web\ Export = 1) = \alpha\ Big\_Data + \beta X + \varepsilon \qquad (4.1)$$

In short, the probability a firm enters international markets via e-commerce (*Web Export*) may be associated with the use of big data in general (*Big Data*) and with the set of control variables introduced above (*X*), besides on the usual random term (ε). A more focused goal is pursued by decomposing *Big Data* with respect to the approach adopted by firms as in the following specification:

$$\Pr(Web\ Export = 1) = \alpha_1\ BDC\_1 + \alpha_2\ BDC\_2 + \alpha_3\ BDC\_3 + \beta X + \varepsilon \qquad (4.2)$$

In this case, the probability a firm enters international markets depends on the approach adopted in using big data (*Big Data Combination*). Specifically, we compare firms who do not use big data (*Big Data Combination 0*) with firms that use them by exploiting internal resources (*Big Data Combination 1, BDC_1*), external resources (*Big Data Combination 2, BDC_2*) and, finally, a combination of internal and external resources (*Big Data Combination 3, BDC_3*). This specification allows us to assess hypotheses H2 to H4. We expect firms combining both internal and external resources may have higher

Table 4.1   *List of variables*

Dependent variable	Web Export	Dummy variable equals 1 if the firm realises web sales outside Italy; 0 otherwise
Independent variables	Big Data	Dummy variable equals 1 if the firm uses big data; 0 otherwise
	Big Data Combination	Categorical variable assuming a value equal to 0 if the firm does not use big data (reference category); 1 if the firm uses big data by exploiting internal resources (*Big Data Combination 1*); 2 if the firm uses big data by exploiting external resources (*Big Data Combination 2*); 3 if the firm uses big data combining internal and external resources (*Big Data Combination 3*)
	ICT specialist	Dummy variable equals 1 if the firm employs ICT specialists; 0 otherwise
	Mobile	Dummy variable equals 1 if the firm exploits mobile internet connections; 0 otherwise
	Broadband	Categorical variable assuming a value equal to 0 if the firm exploits a broadband internet connection with a less than 2 Mbit/s download speed (reference category); 1 if the broadband connection is at least 2 but less than 10 Mbit/s (*Broadband 1*); 2 if the broadband connection is at least 10 but less than 30 Mbit/s (*Broadband 2*); 3 if the broadband connection is at least 30 but less than 100 Mbit/s (*Broadband 3*); 4 if the broadband connection is at least 100 Mbit/s (*Broadband 4*)
	Training 1	Dummy variable equals 1 if the firm realises training for ICT specialists; 0 otherwise
	Training 2	Dummy variable equals 1 if the firm realises training for all the other employees; 0 otherwise
	Size	Categorical variable assuming a value equal to 0 if the firm has 10–49 employees (*Small*, reference category); 1 if the firm has 50–99 employees (*Medium-Small*); 2 if the firm has 100–249 employees (*Medium-Large*); 3 if the firm has >250 employees (*Large*)
	Sector	Categorical variable assuming a value equal to 0 if the firm operates in *Manufacturing* (reference category); 1 if the firm operates in *Public Utilities*; 2 if the firm operates in *Building*; 3 if the firm operates in *Retail*; 4 if the firm operates in *Services*
	Region	Dummy variables indicating the NUTS2 region where the firm is located

Source: ISTAT (2016).

Table 4.2   *Summary statistics*

Variables	Observations	# Yes	% Yes
Web Export	18,978	1,176	6
Big Data	18,978	2,782	15
Big Data Combination 0	18,978	16,196	85
Big Data Combination 1	18,978	1,844	10
Big Data Combination 2	18,978	275	1
Big Data Combination 3	18,978	663	3
ICT specialist	18,978	6,115	32
Mobile	18,886	14,346	76
Broadband 0	18,118	841	5
Broadband 1	18,118	7,305	40
Broadband 2	18,118	5,467	30
Broadband 3	18,118	2,705	15
Broadband 4	18,118	1,800	10
Training 1	18,978	2,467	13
Training 2	18,978	3,276	17
Small	18,978	11,888	63
Medium-Small	18,978	2,026	11
Medium-Large	18,978	2,369	12
Large	18,978	2,695	14
Manufacturing	18,978	4,741	25
Public Utilities	18,978	1,272	7
Building	18,978	2,531	13
Retail	18,978	5,783	30
Services	18,978	4,651	25

Note: The % of Yes on broadband connection and mobile is computed excluding missing values that consist of 860 and 92 observations respectively, as reflected in the 'Observations' column.

returns in terms of internationalisation due to the potential absorptive capacity and spillover effects.

4.   EMPIRICAL FINDINGS

The results from the estimation of equations 4.1 and 4.2 are reported in Table 4.3. Specifically, column 1 reports the average marginal effects from equation 4.1; and column 2, those from equation 4.2. Columns 3 and 4 display the results from equation 4.2 but on the sub-samples of small and large firms, respectively.

Starting from column 1, there emerges a positive and statistically significant effect of *Big Data* on the probability a firm enters international markets via e-commerce (*Web Export*). More specifically, this probability approximatively increases, on average, by 5.5 per cent when a firm uses big data in general. Obviously, this effect is independent of the approach adopted by a firm (i.e., using big data by internal, external or combined resources).

Looking at the control variables, we observe that the presence of ICT specialists, broadband connection and training activities for the employees play a role. Specifically, a firm should have access to a speed connection of at least level 2 (10 to 30 Mbit/s) to significantly impact the probability of entering international markets via e-commerce. We do not find significant effects for *Mobile* and *Training 1*. However, this lack of evidence may seriously depend on the qualitative nature of the variables. In other words, some aspects need to be quantitatively measured to manifest a significant impact; this could be, for example, the case of investment in training activities. Finally, we observe that the largest firms (*Large*), as well as those operating in *Services*, have higher probabilities of entering international markets via e-commerce, independently of the fact of using big data.

Several interesting findings emerge when we consider that a firm may adopt different approaches for using big data (*Big Data Combination*). In column 2, we observe that exploiting internal resources (*Big Data Combination 1*) is positively associated with internationalisation via e-commerce. In particular, the probability a firm enters international markets increases, on average, by 4.5 per cent, while this increases by 4.5 per cent and 11.1 per cent in the case of external (*Big Data Combination 2*) and combined resources (*Big Data Combination 3*), respectively. These findings seem to be very interesting since they point out that combining resources may generate returns in terms of internationalisation more than double compared to the case of exploiting only internal resources. Finally, the effects of the other variables confirm the previous findings.

Since firm size may affect the effectiveness of organisational processes related to digitalisation, we replicate our regression analysis to explore whether the impact of big data on internationalisation may differ between small and large firms. To this end, we estimate equation 4.2 by considering the following stratification: (a) the sub-sample composed of small and medium-small firms (column 3); (b) the sub-sample composed of medium-large and large firms (column 4).

In columns 3 and 4, we observe that small and large firms have positive returns from using internal staff for big data analyses (*Big Data Combination 1*), that is, the probability of entering international markets via e-commerce increases approximatively by 3 per cent and 6 per cent, respectively. Important

Table 4.3   Empirical results (Probit model)

Variables	Pr(WebExport) Full sample	Pr(WebExport) Full sample	Pr(WebExport) Small firms	Pr(WebExport) Large firms
	(1)	(2)	(3)	(4)
Big Data	0.0545***			
	(0.00599)			
Big Data Combination 1		0.0447***	0.0360***	0.0629***
		(0.00838)	(0.0108)	(0.0145)
Big Data Combination 2		0.0450**	0.0578**	0.0334
		(0.0211)	(0.0249)	(0.0443)
Big Data Combination 3		0.111***	0.105***	0.124***
		(0.0150)	(0.0218)	(0.0227)
ICT specialist	0.0519***	0.0520***	0.0450***	0.0841***
	(0.00611)	(0.00611)	(0.00683)	(0.0139)
Mobile	0.0105	0.0105*	0.0111*	0.0613**
	(0.00638)	(0.00637)	(0.00597)	(0.0254)
Broadband 1	0.0139	0.0137	0.0115	0.0288
	(0.0112)	(0.0112)	(0.0111)	(0.0329)
Broadband 2	0.0362***	0.0361***	0.0294**	0.0694**
	(0.0115)	(0.0115)	(0.0115)	(0.0331)
Broadband 3	0.0561***	0.0551***	0.0403***	0.106***
	(0.0125)	(0.0125)	(0.0130)	(0.0337)
Broadband 4	0.0568***	0.0554***	0.0132	0.140***
	(0.0134)	(0.0134)	(0.0141)	(0.0347)
Training 1	−0.00826	−0.00834	−0.0290**	0.00304
	(0.00776)	(0.00776)	(0.0113)	(0.0134)
Training 2	0.0218***	0.0212***	0.0224***	0.0193
	(0.00660)	(0.00660)	(0.00809)	(0.0123)
Medium-Small	0.0191**	0.0186**		
	(0.00815)	(0.00814)		
Medium-Large	0.00152	0.00112		
	(0.00731)	(0.00731)		
Large	0.0357***	0.0345***		
	(0.00784)	(0.00784)		
Public Utilities	−0.0659***	−0.0659***	−0.0481***	−0.106***
	(0.00658)	(0.00658)	(0.00711)	(0.0156)
Building	−0.0802***	−0.0800***	−0.0608***	−0.137***

Variables	Pr(WebExport) Full sample	Pr(WebExport) Full sample	Pr(WebExport) Small firms	Pr(WebExport) Large firms
	(1)	(2)	(3)	(4)
	(0.00528)	(0.00528)	(0.00564)	(0.0133)
Retail	0.0865***	0.0865***	0.0710***	0.160***
	(0.00703)	(0.00703)	(0.00744)	(0.0171)
Services	0.0526***	0.0529***	0.0810***	0.0167
	(0.00682)	(0.00682)	(0.00878)	(0.0127)
Regional Dummies	YES	YES	YES	YES
Observations	18,118	18,118	13,159	4,897

Notes: Coefficients are the average marginal effects. Columns 3 and 4 report the average marginal effects for small firms (small and medium-small were grouped) and large firms (medium-large and large companies were grouped), respectively. Estimates are run on a sample of 18,118 since during the estimation procedure missing observations are dropped. Standard errors in parenthesis. *** p<0.01, ** p<0.05, * p<0.1.

differences emerge, instead, when we consider the outsourcing approach. If external resources are exclusively used (*Big Data Combination 2*) only the small firms may benefit in terms of internationalisation; differently, when external resources are combined with internal ones (*Big Data Combination 3*) both small and large firms may have advantages. Moreover, we observe that in the case of combined resources, the effect of big data is even double for large firms (about 12 per cent). Other differences between small and large firms emerge when looking at the control variables. Large firms may have higher returns in terms of internationalisation than small firms from the presence of ICT specialists and broadband connection. For example, a large firm that uses a broadband connection at level 2 (10 to 30 Mbit/s) or 3 (30 to 100 Mbit/s) may increase, on average, the probability of entering international markets by 7 per cent and 11 per cent, while a small firm only by 3 per cent and 4 per cent, respectively. Within the group of large firms, those operating in *Manufacturing* and in *Retail* have the highest probability of internationalisation, while within the group of small firms, the highest probabilities are recorded for those operating in *Retail* and in *Services*.

5.   CONCLUSION AND IMPLICATIONS

Digitalisation and internationalisation are commonly considered two of the most important trends in today's competitive arena (Dagnino et al., 2021). This observation has motivated some scholars to explore the interplay between them (Bergamaschi et al., 2020). In approaching this topic, we argue that both digitalisation and internationalisation are multifaced constructs and we recognise the importance of focusing on specific aspects. Therefore, we address this challenge by focusing on the role of big data in the development of international e-commerce.

Empirically, we find that the use of big data managed by internal staff or by specialised consulting firms is positively associated with the development of international e-commerce but with important differences in relation to the firm size. Small firms benefit more from specialised consulting firms, while large firms benefit more from using internal staff. However, both types of firms have the maximum of benefits when combining external and internal resources. More specifically, compared to the case of using exclusively internal staff, combining internal and external resources may double the returns in terms of internationalisation for large firms and even triple them for small firms.

From a conceptual perspective, our chapter contributes to the resource-based view of internationalisation by showing the importance of orchestrating internal and external resources and capabilities (Hitt et al., 2006; Peng, 2001). While we focus on the relationship between the use of big data (managed by internal staff or by specialised consulting firms) and international e-commerce, we call for further investigations that link different big data management modes and other international modes. Similarly, scholars should consider how other aspects of digitalisation (Parida et al., 2019) affect international modes.

From a managerial perspective, our study suggests that firms will exploit the maximum of benefits related to big data in international e-commerce by combining internal and external resources and capabilities. We shed light on the factors that shape the 'real' contribution of consulting firms to the firm's success and call attention to a common base of knowledge that, in turn, improves the communication processes between the firm and the consulting firm.

NOTES

1. The whole population extracted from Italian Business Registers consists of approximately 182,000 firms. The sample size was fixed by ISTAT at approximately 30,000 units extracted with probabilistic stratified random sampling techniques, where the sector of activity, size of the firms and the NUTS2 regions were used as strata. This sampling design guarantees full representativeness of the final sample, with a response rate of about 60 per cent.
2. We use the grouping criterion adopted by ISTAT in this survey. We cannot operate any modification of this grouping because the quantitative information is not available.

REFERENCES

Alharthi, A., Krotov, V., and Bowman, M. (2017). Addressing Barriers to Big Data. *Business Horizons*, *60*(3), 285–292.

Amado, A., Cortez, P., Rita, P., and Moro, S. (2018). Research Trends on Big Data in Marketing: A Text Mining and Topic Modeling Based Literature Analysis. *European Research on Management and Business Economics*, *24*(1), 1–7.

Aronica, M., Bonfanti, R. C., and Piacentino, D. (2021a). Social Media Adoption in Italian Firms: Opportunities and Challenges for Lagging Regions. *Papers in Regional Science*, *100*(4), 959–978.

Aronica, M., Fazio, G., and Piacentino, D. (2021b). SMEs' Heterogeneity at the Extensive Margin and within the Intensive Margin of Trade. *Journal of International Trade and Economic Development*, *30*(3), 439–467.

Autio, E., Mudambi, R., and Yoo, Y. (2021). Digitalization and Globalization in a Turbulent World: Centrifugal and Centripetal Forces. *Global Strategy Journal*, *11*(1), 3–16.

Bergamaschi, M., Bettinelli, C., Lissana, E., and Picone, P. M. (2020). Past, Ongoing, and Future Debate on the Interplay between Internationalization and Digitalization. *Journal of Management and Governance*, 1–50. https://doi.org/10.1007/s10997-020 -09544-8

Beugelsdijk, S., Kostova, T., Kunst, V. E., Spadafora, E., and Van Essen, M. (2018). Cultural Distance and Firm Internationalization: A Meta-Analytical Review and Theoretical Implications. *Journal of Management*, *44*(1), 89–130.

Bharadwaj, A., El Sawy, O. A., Pavlou, P. A., and Venkatraman, N. (2013). Digital Business Strategy: Toward a Next Generation of Insights. *MIS Quarterly*, *37*(2), 471–482.

Björkdahl, J. (2020). Strategies for Digitalization in Manufacturing Firms. *California Management Review*, *62*(4), 17–36.

Brennen, J. S., and Kreiss, D. (2016). Digitalization. In *International Encyclopedia of Communication Theory and Philosophy*, 1–11. John Wiley & Sons.

Caputo, A., Pizzi, S., Pellegrini, M. M., and Dabić, M. (2021). Digitalization and Business Models: Where Are We Going? A Science Map of the Field. *Journal of Business Research*, *123*, 489–501.

Cennamo, C., Dagnino, G. B., Di Minin, A., and Lanzolla, G. (2020). Managing Digital Transformation: Scope of Transformation and Modalities of Value Co-Generation and Delivery. *California Management Review*, *62*(4), 5–16.

Correani, A., De Massis, A., Frattini, F., Petruzzelli, A. M., and Natalicchio, A. (2020). Implementing a Digital Strategy: Learning from the Experience of Three Digital Transformation Projects. *California Management Review*, *62*(4), 37–56.

Dagnino, G. B., Picone, P. M., and Ferrigno, G. (2021). Temporary Competitive Advantage: A State-of-the-Art Literature Review and Research Directions. *International Journal of Management Reviews*, *23*(1), 85–115.

Efraim, T., Sharda, R., and Delen, D. (2016). *Business Intelligence and Analytics: Systems for Decision Support*. Pearson.

Eller, R., Alford, P., Kallmünzer, A., and Peters, M. (2020). Antecedents, Consequences, and Challenges of Small and Medium-Sized Enterprise Digitalization. *Journal of Business Research*, *112*, 119–127.

Fazio, G., and Piacentino, D. (2010). A Spatial Multilevel Analysis of Italian SMEs' Productivity. *Spatial Economic Analysis*, *5*(3), 299–316.

Ghemawat, P. (2003). Semiglobalization and International Business Strategy. *Journal of International Business Studies*, *34*(2), 138–152.

Gray, J., and Rumpe, B. (2015). Models for Digitalization. *Software and Systems Modeling*, *14*, 1319–1320.

Hallikainen, H., Savimäki, E., and Laukkanen, T. (2020). Fostering B2B Sales with Customer Big Data Analytics. *Industrial Marketing Management, 86*, 90–98.

Hitt, M. A., Tihanyi, L., Miller, T., and Connelly, B. (2006). International Diversification: Antecedents, Outcomes, and Moderators. *Journal of Management, 32*(6), 831–867.

ISTAT. (2016). *Survey on Information and Communication Technology (ICT) Usage in Enterprise.*

Khanra, S., Dhir, A., and Mäntymäki, M. (2020). Big Data Analytics and Enterprises: A Bibliometric Synthesis of the Literature. *Enterprise Information Systems, 14*(6), 737–768.

Kohtamäki, M., Parida, V., Patel, P. C., and Gebauer, H. (2020). The Relationship between Digitalization and Servitization: The Role of Servitization in Capturing the Financial Potential of Digitalization. *Technological Forecasting and Social Change, 151*, 119804.

Kretschmer, T., and Khashabi, P. (2020). Digital Transformation and Organization Design: An Integrated Approach. *California Management Review, 62*(4), 86–104.

Kuusisto, M. (2017). Organizational Effects of Digitalization: A Literature Review. *International Journal of Organization Theory and Behavior, 20*(3), 341–362.

Laney, D. (2001). 3D Data Management: Controlling Data Volume, Velocity and Variety. *META Group Research Note, 6*(70), 1.

Lee, I. (2017). Big Data: Dimensions, Evolution, Impacts, and Challenges. *Business Horizons, 60*(3), 293–303.

Legner, C., Eymann, T., Hess, T., Matt, C., Böhmann, T., Drews, P., Mädche, A., Urbach, N., and Ahlemann, F. (2017). Digitalization: Opportunity and Challenge for the Business and Information Systems Engineering Community. *Business and Information Systems Engineering, 59*(4), 301–308.

Malhotra, N. K., Agarwal, J., and Ulgado, F. M. (2003). Internationalization and Entry Modes: A Multitheoretical Framework and Research Propositions. *Journal of International Marketing, 11*(4), 1–31.

Nell, P. C., Foss, N. J., Klein, P. G., and Schmitt, J. (2021). Avoiding Digitalization Traps: Tools for Top Managers. *Business Horizons, 64*(2), 163–169.

Parida, V., Sjödin, D., and Reim, W. (2019). Reviewing Literature on Digitalization, Business Model Innovation, and Sustainable Industry: Past Achievements and Future Promises. *Sustainability, 11*(2), 391–409.

Parviainen, P., Tihinen, M., Kääriäinen, J., and Teppola, S. (2017). Tackling the Digitalization Challenge: How to Benefit from Digitalization in Practice. *International Journal of Information Systems and Project Management, 5*(1), 63–77.

Peng, M. W. (2001). The Resource-Based View and International Business. *Journal of Management, 27*(6), 803–829.

Raguseo, E. (2018). Big Data Technologies: An Empirical Investigation on Their Adoption, Benefits and Risks for Companies. *International Journal of Information Management, 38*(1), 187–195.

Schivardi, F., and Schmitz, T. (2020). The IT Revolution and Southern Europe's Two Lost Decades. *Journal of European Economic Association, 18*(5), 2441–2486.

Sharda, R., Dursun, D., and Turban, E. (2020). *Analytics, Data Science, and Artificial Intelligence: Systems for Decision Support.* Pearson.

Sharda, R., and Kalgotra, P. (2018). The Blossoming Analytics Talent Pool: An Overview of the Analytics Ecosystem. In J. J. Cochran (ed.), *INFORMS Analytics Body of Knowledge*, 311–326. Wiley.

Sunscrapers (2019). Data Science Outsourcing: Key Risks and Benefits, 27 September, available online at https://sunscrapers.com/blog/data-science-outsourcing-key-risks -and-benefits/ (accessed 7 March 2021).

Verhoef, P., Kooge, E., and Walk, N. (2016). *Creating Value with Big Data Analytics: Making Smarter Marketing Decisions*. Routledge.

Volberda, H. W., Morgan, R. E., Reinmoeller, P., Hitt, M. A., Ireland, R. D., and Hoskisson, R. E. (2011). *Strategic Management: Competitiveness and Globalization (Concepts and Cases)*. Cengage Learning.

Wamba, S. F., Akter, S., Edwards, A., Chopin, G., and Gnanzou, D. (2015). How 'Big Data' Can Make Big Impact: Findings from a Systematic Review and a Longitudinal Case Study. *International Journal of Production Economics*, *165*, 234–246.

Wu, X., Zhu, X., Wu, G. Q., and Ding, W. (2013). Data Mining with Big Data. *IEEE Transactions on Knowledge and Data Engineering*, *26*(1), 97–107.

5. Science, entrepreneurship, and spin-off diversity

Deepa Scarrà

1. INTRODUCTION

Academic entrepreneurship is recognized as a driver for economic growth and science advancement (Audretsch and Caiazza, 2016) as well as being a way of transferring knowledge from public research to the market and a valuable means of research valorization, especially in science-intensive sectors (Bekkers and Bodas Freitas, 2008). Therefore, the support provided to academic startups plays a key role among technology transfer activities.

Scholars have extensively analyzed this phenomenon from different perspectives and considered different dimensions; nevertheless, studies that consider the differences among spin-offs are still lacking.

In fact, as highlighted by Druilhe and Garnsey (2004), the extant literature does not consider spin-off diversity despite the spin-offs' heterogeneity, leading to an inaccurate standardization of the phenomenon and a too-general technology transfer approach (Druilhe and Garnsey, 2004). Therefore, the support provided for entrepreneurship tends to be quite standardized, while it should be more customized, at least from a science-field perspective. Indeed, in the case of science-based spin-offs, a differentiated approach is needed that takes into account the field of origin, because firms from different fields of science might present different characteristics and require a particular type of support.

Empirical studies that investigate spin-off diversity and the characteristics and needs of spin-offs from specific fields of science would help in understanding what they require and in establishing how to better support them in terms of technology transfer activities. To this end, this chapter proposes a framework, exploring these issues through the lens of the resource-based and business model perspectives (Druilhe and Garnsey, 2004; Chiesa and Piccaluga, 2000; Heirman and Clarysse, 2004) together with the effectuation theory (Sarasvathy, 2001; Chandler et al., 2011).

In particular, it would be interesting to investigate the characteristics of startups from specific fields of science, in terms of their resources, business model, and decision-making approach. With regard to resources, it is crucial to take into consideration that they evolve over time. Vohora and colleagues (2004) proposed a framework that can be adopted to explore resource configuration along the different stages of the entrepreneurial process. In addition, by understanding the resources of spin-offs and their method of making decisions, it would be possible to identify the most appropriate ways to support them in terms of technology transfer.

Empirical studies that investigate these issues can hopefully be useful from a practical point of view in giving insights both to technology transfer professionals – with the purpose of better supporting the creation and development of this type of new venture – and to academic entrepreneurs. From a theoretical point of view, bringing together the effectuation theory and the resource-based and business model perspectives might provide a framework for looking at spin-off diversity, comparing spin-offs from different fields of science.

2. THEORETICAL FRAMEWORK

The path of academic spin-offs from lab to market is characterized by different stages, and the resource configuration of the companies changes along the entrepreneurial journey (Druilhe and Garnsey, 2004). As introduced, the framework proposed by Vohora and colleagues (2004) is very useful for considering modifications in the resource base in the different stages of development. This framework recognizes five phases: research, opportunity framing, pre-organization, re-orientation, and sustainable returns (Vohora et al., 2004). The first phase consists of research with traditional academic purposes, in which commercial opportunities arise; in the second phase the opportunity is evaluated in order to understand whether to set up a company to grasp opportunities. The pre-organization phase involves making decisions about the resources and gaining the knowledge needed to go to market: this stage is crucial, and, indeed, it seems to greatly influence future success. The re-orientation phase entails the reconfiguration of resources to deliver a value proposition to customers. The final phase concerns obtaining sustainable returns.

Exploring the resource base of the firms during the phases of the entrepreneurial process described above (Vohora et al., 2004), along with their business model, type of activity, and decision-making approach, might provide an overview of the characteristics and needs of spin-offs from specific fields of science.

2.1   Characteristics of the Academic Spin-Offs

As reviewed by Mustar and colleagues (2006), only a relatively small group of studies on academic spin-offs focuses on firm resources as a means to explain differences among spin-offs or to identify which resources are important in predicting growth; another group focuses on business models by looking at the kind of activity exploited by the firm (Chiesa and Piccaluga, 2000), linking the business model to growth (Heirman and Clarysse, 2004), or highlighting a way to exploit commercial value from knowledge (Druilhe and Garnsey, 2004). That review (Mustar et al., 2006, p. 290) underlined the "growing recognition of the heterogeneity of high-tech ventures" and claimed the need to integrate different perspectives that characterized previous studies, identifying the partial view on the phenomenon as a gap in the research.

The business model and the resource configuration needed by a startup depend on its technological regime (Heirman and Clarysse, 2004); thus, it is reasonable to suppose that the field of origin also plays a role in the configuration of resources and business model design.

To identify the characteristics of the firms, we first consider the *type of activity and the business model of the company.* Autio (1997) highlighted the differences between "science-based firms" that produce basic and broad technologies from scientific knowledge in a technology-push approach, and "engineering-based firms" that turn basic technologies into specific products and applications defined on the basis of specific customer needs, in a logic driven by the market-pull. This distinction, however, might be more blurred, since these transformations can be produced by the same company that, starting from scientific knowledge, generates basic technologies which are then turned into one or more specific technological applications. A distinction that considers this balance between technology and product as output is made also by Pries and Guild (2007). They differentiate between academic spin-offs that operate in product markets, making a product with their technology, and those that operate in markets for technology, licensing or selling their technology to product firms.

Another study (Pirnay et al., 2003) identified four types of academic spin-offs on the basis of two dimensions acknowledged as key factors that divide them: the nature of the knowledge transferred (codified or tacit), and the status of the founders (students or researchers). They characterized each type by considering the entrepreneur, the business opportunity, and the required resources.

Clausen and Rasmussen (2013) looked at the heterogeneity in the business models of academic spin-offs in relation to their innovativeness, analyzing a sample of spin-offs from Norway. Based on evolutionary theories, they supposed and confirmed that different kinds of business models are associated with different levels of innovation performance, and that spin-offs that adopt more than one business model in parallel are more innovative than others. They considered the classification proposed by Druilhe and Garnsey (2004), who analyzed a sample of spin-offs from Cambridge and identified the following types of spin-off firms: consulting companies, which conduct technical consultancy and research activities; development companies that work on immature technologies; product-based companies, which typically produce prototypes or small volumes and often operate in niche markets; and software companies. In a similar manner, Chiesa and Piccaluga (2000) distinguished between spin-off companies that operate in manufacturing, those operating in the service industry, those in consultancy, and those in research. In this distinction, the service companies carry out outsourced activities as part of the value chain of the clients, while consultancy companies perform only pure consultancy services.

These different categorizations can be adopted according to the purposes of the investigation and the peculiarities of the sample. For instance it would be possible to adopt the following revised classification that considers those proposed by prior studies (Druilhe and Garnsey, 2004; Chiesa and Piccaluga, 2000): consultancy and research, product companies, service companies, software companies.

The second element to consider is the *resource base of the firm*. Heirman and Clarysse (2004) looked at spin-off diversity by considering the distinct configurations of financial, technological, and human resources. They studied how heterogeneity in environmental factors such as technological domain, organizational origin, and industry can lead to variations in resource configuration. With reference to technological resources, they thought about whether the innovativeness of the core technology of the company, the stage of the product/technology development at the time of the company's founding, and the scope of the product/technology distinguishes whether the company develops a specific product or a platform to make more than one product. They also considered human resources such as the size of the team; the education, previous experience, and knowledge of the specific sector of the team members; and the capacity to attract experienced managers during the first year. With regard to financial resources, they took under consideration the amount of starting resources and their source, differentiating between companies which received investments from Venture Capitalists (VCs) and those which did not. This last distinction is due to the assumption that VCs provide expertise and knowledge. However, it is important to consider that other kinds of investors are also able to deliver know-how and experience, as is the case with industrial partners.

The types of resources considered by Heirman and Clarysse (2004) are the same as those recognized in the review of Mustar and colleagues (2006). The review, based on prior studies (Brush et al., 2001; Lee et al., 2001), also identified the role of social resources, understood as the network of the company, especially in industry and finance. Expanding the classification of Heirman and Clarysse (2004) by adding social resources in terms of networks, as done by prior studies, distinguishing between networks in industrial, research, or financial environments, provides an overall view about resources. Instead of taking into consideration the start of the company, it would be useful to look at resource configuration at different stages of the entrepreneurial process (Vohora et al., 2004).

2.2   Decision-Making Approach

To start a new venture implies the exploitation of an entrepreneurial opportunity (Shane and Venkataraman, 2000); thus, the entrepreneurial process deals with discovering opportunities and making decisions in order to exploit them.

Sarasvathy (2001) pointed out the difference between two modes of decision-making: effectuation and causation. These modes represent two distinct approaches to setting up a new company (Chandler et al., 2011). In an effectuation mode, the entrepreneur makes decisions based on a given set of means, in this case the existent resources, by considering the possible effects that could be created by that set of means and choosing among them, all the while contemplating the affordable losses, acceptable risks, and the related opportunities and contingencies. The causation mode entails choosing between different means to achieve a given goal, such as the maximization of final returns. Chandler and colleagues (2011) state that the more uncertain the future, the more the entrepreneurs make decisions following the effectuation logic. Considering that academic spin-offs operate in an uncertain environment and often develop cutting-edge technologies that might have several applications, creating opportunities that are not necessarily automatically recognized, it is interesting to test their attitude in making decisions following an effectuation logic. While causation is related to opportunity recognition and strategic plans (Chandler et al., 2011), according to Maine and colleagues (2015, p. 55) "effectuation is associated with a moving spectrum of opportunity creation, rather than detecting and recognizing opportunities with the highest expected returns." Thus, it is reasonable to suppose that the effectuation decision-making approach will be found to be prevalent. In sum, causation is about predicting the future and planning for it, while effectuation is more about controlling an unforeseeable future. Another study (Dew et al., 2009) provides evidence about the prevalence of effectual logic in expert entrepreneurs, while novice entrepreneurs are more driven by causation logic that follows a predictive approach. Maine and colleagues (2015) looked at scientist-entrepreneurs in the biotechnological sector, which is characterized by long decision processes, and confirmed the presence of effectual logic in the case of high levels of uncertainty, especially in the first phases of the entrepreneurial process; however, the effectuation mode can be employed in combination with causation, especially due to environmental factors. According to Lingelbach and colleagues (2015), the blend of effectuation and causation depends on resource constraints; the authors, analyzing innovation processes in emerging countries, found a strong presence of pre-commitment, shared between the two logics, but a weak presence of flexibility.

Chandler and colleagues (2011) developed and validated measures of both the modes of decision-making – causation and effectuation – and also tested the assumptions of Sarasvathy (2001) related to levels of uncertainty. For effectuation, Chandler and colleagues acknowledged a range of sub-dimensions such as experimentation, flexibility, affordable losses, and pre-commitment. In particular, under uncertainty, the entrepreneurs make decisions by evaluating different potential choices that lead to potential returns, testing alternatives through experimentation and selecting them in a way that keeps potential losses affordable. In order to operate in this way, entrepreneurs use the commitment of different actors – suppliers, customers, partners – as leverage. Each sub-dimension is described by different variables. The last dimension, "pre-commitment," is present in both the effectuation and causation modes, even if with a different rationale. In fact, in the effectuation mode it helps to cope with uncertainty, preserving flexibility and reducing risks and losses; while in the causation mode it is a means for following strategic plans and gathering resources (Chandler et al., 2011). The authors provide evidence about the positive relationship between effectuation and uncertainty and the negative relationship between causation and uncertainty. The variables developed in that study, focused on new venture creation, can be usefully adopted in order to empirically test the scientist-entrepreneurs' approach to decision-making.

As mentioned previously, it would be interesting to adopt a mixed methodology, including carrying out quantitative analyses and multiple explanatory case studies. Table 5.1 summarizes variables that could be used to estimate the model.

3.   CONCLUSION

Conducting empirical studies focused on spin-off diversity might provide evidence about the particularities and developmental trajectories of academic spin-offs related to specific fields of science. In this sense, it would be interesting to compare academic spin-offs from different science fields, eventually including cases from different countries in order to better generalize findings. Findings could have practical implications, since the spin-offs require specific support to get from one phase to the next.

Table 5.1   Variables recommended to study spin-off diversity

Dimensions	Variables	References
Resources	Financial	Heirman and Clarysse (2004); Mustar et al. (2006);
	Technological	Brush et al. (2001); Lee et al. (2001)
	Human	
	Social	
Type of company/ business model	Consultancy and research	Druilhe and Garnsey (2004); Chiesa and Piccaluga
	Product companies	(2000)
	Service companies	
	Software companies	
Decision-making approach	Effectuation	Chandler et al. (2011)
	Causation	

Understanding the characteristics of spin-offs from a specific field of origin, as well as the resource configuration across the entrepreneurial process and the decision-making logic, could help in defining policies and support in terms of technology transfer. Thus, different resource configurations and modes of logic in decision-making lead to different needs, which can in turn lead to differentiated support in terms of technology transfer activities. In fact, different resources and types of logic in making decisions imply the need for different support.

From a practical point of view, empirical research on this topic can give useful insights to technology transfer professionals and academic entrepreneurs, while from a theoretical point of view it can bring together different perspectives.

REFERENCES

Audretsch, D., and R. Caiazza (2016). "Technology transfer and entrepreneurship: cross-national analysis." *Journal of Technology Transfer*, 41(6): 1247–1259.

Autio, Erkko (1997). "New, technology-based firms in innovation networks symplectic and generative impacts." *Research Policy*, 26(3): 263–281.

Bekkers, Rudi, and Isabel Maria Bodas Freitas (2008). "Analysing knowledge transfer channels between universities and industry: to what degree do sectors also matter?" *Research Policy*, 37(10): 1837–1853.

Brush, Candida G., Patricia G. Greene, and Myra M. Hart (2001). "From initial idea to unique advantage: the entrepreneurial challenge of constructing a resource base." *Academy of Management Perspectives*, 15(1): 64–78.

Chandler, Gaylen N., Dawn R. DeTienne, Alexander McKelvie, and Troy V. Mumford (2011). "Causation and effectuation processes: a validation study." *Journal of Business Venturing*, 26(3): 375–390.

Chiesa, Vittorio, and Andrea Piccaluga (2000). "Exploitation and diffusion of public research: the case of academic spin-off companies in Italy." *R&D Management*, 30(4): 329–340.

Clausen, Tommy H., and Einar Rasmussen (2013). "Parallel business models and the innovativeness of research-based spin-off ventures." *Journal of Technology Transfer*, 38(6): 836–849.

Dew, Nicholas, Stuart Read, Saras D. Sarasvathy, and Robert Wiltbank (2009). "Effectual versus predictive logics in entrepreneurial decision-making: differences between experts and novices." *Journal of Business Venturing*, 24(4): 287–309.

Druilhe, Céline, and Elizabeth Garnsey (2004). "Do academic spin-outs differ and does it matter?" *Journal of Technology Transfer*, 29(3–4): 269–285.

Heirman, Ans, and Bart Clarysse (2004). "How and why do research-based start-ups differ at founding? A resource-based configurational perspective." *Journal of Technology Transfer*, 29(3–4): 247–268.

Lee, Choonwoo, Kyungmook Lee, and Johannes M. Pennings (2001). "Internal capabilities, external networks, and performance: a study on technology-based ventures." *Strategic Management Journal*, 22(6–7): 615–640.

Lingelbach, David, Ven Sriram, Tigineh Mersha, and Kojo Saffu (2015). "The innovation process in emerging economies: an effectuation perspective." *International Journal of Entrepreneurship and Innovation*, 16(1): 5–17.

Maine, Elicia, Pek-Hooi Soh, and Nancy Dos Santos (2015). "The role of entrepreneurial decision-making in opportunity creation and recognition." *Technovation*, 39: 53–72.

Mustar, Philippe, Marie Renault, Massimo G. Colombo, Evila Pivab et al. (2006). "Conceptualising the heterogeneity of research-based spin-offs: a multi-dimensional taxonomy." *Research Policy*, 35(2): 289–308.

Pirnay, Fabrice, Bernard Surlemont, and Frederic Nlemvo (2003). "Toward a typology of university spin-offs." *Small Business Economics*, 21(4): 355–369.

Pries, Fred, and Paul Guild (2007). "Commercial exploitation of new technologies arising from university research: start-ups and markets for technology." *R&D Management*, 37(4): 319–328.

Sarasvathy, S. D. (2001). "Causation and effectuation: toward a theoretical shift from economic inevitability to entrepreneurial contingency." *Academy of Management Review*, 26(2): 243–263.

Shane, Scott, and Sankaran Venkataraman (2000). "The promise of entrepreneurship as a field of research." *Academy of Management Review*, 25(1): 217–226.

Vohora, Ajay, Mike Wright, and Andy Lockett (2004). "Critical junctures in the development of university high-tech spinout companies." *Research Policy*, 33(1): 147–175.

6. Entrepreneurial university stakeholders and their contribution to knowledge and technologies transfer

Natalya Radko

1. UNIVERSITY BUSINESS MODEL AND INTERACTION WITH STAKEHOLDERS

As a unit of analysis, the business model is an emerging phenomenon (Zott et al., 2011) despite being explored for around a century (Osterwalder et al., 2005). At the simplest level of understanding, a business model is defined as a tool that describes the rationale of how an organisation creates, delivers and captures value (Osterwalder and Pigneur, 2010).

When it comes to universities, the business model of academia is in a transition state where knowledge and technologies transfer is evolving into an open innovation process (Chesbrough, 2010) via commercialisation. The open innovation process requires the collaboration of multiple stakeholders, both internal and external to the university, such as companies (absorbing new technologies), technology transfer offices (protection of intellectual rights for inventions), government (political incentives and financial support to facilitate new technologies development), venture capital firms (initial financing of new firms creation based on the invention) and so on, who are having an influence on the achievement of university goals (Alsos et al., 2011).

Universities are considered as a source of technological advances for industry through their development and transfer of innovations (Bercovitz and Feldman, 2006). Thus, universities have shifted their business models from pure knowledge disseminators to key intermediaries in transferring technologies (Etzkowitz et al., 2000). The transfer of technologies between the suppliers of innovations (e.g., university faculty) and those who can commercialise them (e.g., companies) is not a direct process per se, where universities establish and/or collaborate with diverse stakeholders (e.g., technology transfer and intellectual property offices, science parks, business incubators) (Miller et al., 2014).

New knowledge generated in university labs can be transferred via licensed technologies, but also through establishing new firms (e.g., spin-offs or start-ups) (Powers and McDougall, 2005). These early-stage ventures play a key role in the knowledge-based economy; however, they often suffer from financial constraints (Brown and Earle, 2015). Thus, new players such as venture capitalists, business angels, and crowdfunding platforms have entered the arena (Block et al., 2018), helping such new ventures to grow.

The university business model can be defined as an outline of actions (Zott and Amit, 2010), where its value proposition is dependent on the different activities of multiple stakeholders of the university (Zott et al., 2011). Zott and Amit (2010) stated that there is a need for studies to investigate the ways in which different actors around academia shape the structure, content and administration of the organisational business model and how the transactional and social dimensions of the business model stakeholders can affect the design of the business model.

The role that stakeholders play in the development of business activities is well researched. However, what impact they have on university activity is a not sufficiently studied area (Miller et al., 2014). This chapter will discuss different areas of research that have considered the diverse stakeholders of a university.

2. THE STAKEHOLDER APPROACH TO THE ENTREPRENEURIAL UNIVERSITY

The identification of the main groups of stakeholders is not necessarily simple (Jongbloed et al., 2008). Bartell (2003) emphasised the particular complexity of the university as an organisation with a variety of external and internal stakeholders. However, different customers and employees can have diverse forms of influence on organisations. A stakeholder framework applied to management may be a useful instrument that assists organisational actors when dealing with technologies transfer (Freeman, 1984). The stakeholder approach assists one in recognising 'who or what really counts' and evaluating the extent to which managers pay attention to stakeholders around their organisation.

A commonly used definition of who or what stakeholders are was introduced by Freeman (1984), who defined stakeholders as 'any group or individual who can affect or is affected by the achievement of the firm's objectives' (p. 16). According to Freeman, any business organisation should be concerned about what its stakeholders' interest is when making a strategic decision or choice.

Based on the work of Burrows (1999), university stakeholders are divided into specific groups that are accepted as having an influence on the universities' behaviour, policy and actions.

Stakeholder theory characterises stakeholders from three different perspectives: the normative (why the interests of stakeholders should be considered), the instrumental (the effect that stakeholders have on organisational performance) and the descriptive (whether stakeholder interests are considered by a firm) (Alsos et al., 2011).

The instrumental understanding of stakeholders is linked to their contribution to the creation of entrepreneurial value by the university (San-Jose et al., 2017). The instrumental parts of the theory are applied to identify the connection between stakeholders and their contribution to the achievement of the university's goals (e.g., transfer of technologies via selling intellectual property (IP) rights or setting up a spin-off company). This approach has a prescriptive nature and it categorises stakeholders as a tool to increase the efficiency of technologies transfer from universities. Following Donaldson and Preston (1995), the instrumental approach helps to examine, *ceteris paribus*, the connection and is hypothetical. It helps to find a solution to the following statement: 'if you want to achieve particular result X then adopt (or don't) practice Y'. Applying this logic to the entrepreneurial university concept, we might come up with: 'If a university wants to achieve particular entrepreneurial results, it should collaborate (or not) with a certain set of stakeholders who facilitate or inhibit the process of knowledge creation and dissemination.'

Thus, from the stakeholder perspective, the entrepreneurial university intentionally develops a network of contacts that helps to obtain resources and later assists to convert these resources for added value (Redford and Fayolle, 2014). Based on the entrepreneurial viewpoint, the factors used to determine the relevance of a stakeholder are vital in a practical sense since entrepreneurs have to decide which group they need to deal with at any given stage during the knowledge transfer (Redford and Fayolle, 2014). Thus, from a theoretical perspective it is vital to analyse the literature and conceptualise a framework for application to this task (Redford and Fayolle, 2014). In particular, classification makes conceptualisation possible (Bailey, 1994).

Expanding the stakeholder categorisation proposed by Yusef (2008) and aligning it with the entrepreneurial university model (Audretsch, 2014), we propose to distinguish four categories of entrepreneurial university stakeholders:

1. knowledge enablers: organisations and individuals that facilitate new knowledge manipulation (industry and government) (Jaziri-Bouagina and Jamil, 2017);
2. knowledge providers: organisations and individuals that produce and spillover knowledge and technologies within the entrepreneurial university (university students and faculty) (O'Gorman et al., 2008);

3. knowledge codifiers: organisations and individuals that actively seek new channels and forms of knowledge and technologies transfer, and facilitate knowledge spillovers outside the university (technology transfer and intellectual property offices);
4. knowledge facilitators: organisations that facilitate entrepreneurial incentives (Fayolle and Linan, 2014) and encourage knowledge spillovers and technologies transfer within the university and into the ecosystem (research and science parks, business incubators, accelerators) (Link and Scott, 2006; Autio et al., 2014). These stakeholders may also raise finance (e.g., venture capitalists, angel investors, crowd investors, banks and financial groups).

Based on the categorisation presented above, we identified that while some papers on the entrepreneurial university have analysed one category of stakeholder engagement (e.g., knowledge providers), others addressed several categories, for instance examining the links between two, three or four of these categories (e.g., knowledge enablers, providers and codifiers) (Table 6.1).

Papers that explore empirically the connection between universities and industry and mechanisms for knowledge spillover have advanced significantly since the mid-1990s (see Appendix 6A). The more the phenomenon has been developed, the more robust the measures and sophisticated the methods that have been used to explore it. As an example, the unit of analysis has been expanded from a single case study (Chrisman et al., 1995) to a regional (Guerrero et al., 2015) or ecosystem approach (Miller and Acs, 2017), as well as to multi-country studies (Bischoff et al., 2018). The focus of the majority of previous research was mostly university–industry collaboration, with almost no papers exploring knowledge spillover from university applying the ecosystem approach. Previous studies have been focused on the different means and outputs of collaboration with stakeholders and the effect of other factors in facilitating this collaboration (the role of management and university strategy in developing collaboration with others (Kalar and Antoncic, 2015); the impact of university–industry collaboration on research for knowledge commercialisation (Banal-Estanol et al., 2015); mechanisms for knowledge transfer and engagement with stakeholders (Bramwell and Wolfe, 2008); the role of technology transfer offices (Hu, 2009); and so on).

Table 6.1   *Four distinct types of entrepreneurial university stakeholders*

No	Stakeholders categorisation	Stakeholders	Literature
1	Knowledge enablers	Government Industry	Keast, 1995; Chrisman et al., 1995; Ryu, 1998; Schmoch, 1999; Klofsten and Jones-Evans, 2000; Bernasconi, 2005; de Zilwa, 2005; Lazzeretti and Tavoletti, 2005; Kirby, 2006; Wong et al., 2007; Bramwell and Wolfe, 2008; Hu, 2009; Guerrero and Urbano, 2012; Culkin and Mallick, 2011; Goddard et al., 2012; Hewitt-Dundas, 2012; Sterzi, 2013; Miller et al., 2014; Graham, 2014; Banal-Estanol et al., 2015; Guerrero et al., 2015; Czarnitzki and Delanote, 2015; Bischoff et al., 2018; Miller and Acs, 2017; Fuller et al., 2017; Etzkowitz et al., 2019; Fuster et al., 2019
2	Knowledge providers	Teaching staff Research staff Students	Keast, 1995; Chrisman et al., 1995; Ryu, 1998; Schmoch, 1999; Klofsten and Jones-Evans, 2000; Jacob et al., 2003; Bernasconi, 2005; de Zilwa, 2005; Lazzeretti and Tavoletti, 2005; Kirby, 2006; Wong et al., 2007; Bramwell and Wolfe, 2008; Hu, 2009; Guerrero and Urbano, 2012; Goddard et al., 2012; Hewitt-Dundas, 2012; Sterzi, 2013; Graham, 2014; Miller et al., 2014; Kalar and Antoncic, 2015; Banal-Estanol et al., 2015; Guerrero et al., 2015; Czarnitzki and Delanote, 2015; Bischoff et al., 2018; Fuller et al., 2017; Miller and Acs, 2017; Etzkowitz et al., 2019; Fuster et al., 2019
3	Knowledge codifiers	Technology transfer office (TTO) Patenting office	Keast, 1995; Chrisman et al., 1995; Schmoch, 1999; Klofsten and Jones-Evans, 2000; Jacob et al., 2003; de Zilwa, 2005; Lazzeretti and Tavoletti, 2005; Wong et al., 2007; Bramwell and Wolfe, 2008; Hu, 2009; Guerrero and Urbano, 2012; Hewitt-Dundas, 2012; Sterzi, 2013; Graham, 2014; Miller et al., 2014; Banal-Estanol et al., 2015; Guerrero et al., 2015; Bischoff et al., 2018; Fuller et al., 2017; Etzkowitz et al., 2019; Fuster et al., 2019
4	Knowledge facilitators	Science or technology parks Venture capitalists Accelerators Business incubators	Ryu, 1998; Jacob et al., 2003; Lazzeretti and Tavoletti, 2005; Kirby, 2006; Wong et al., 2007; Guerrero and Urbano, 2012; Hewitt-Dundas, 2012; Graham, 2014; Guerrero et al., 2015; Bischoff et al., 2018; Fuller et al., 2017; Miller and Acs, 2017; Etzkowitz et al., 2019; Fuster et al., 2019

3. STAKEHOLDERS CLASSIFICATION AND CONCEPTUALISATION WITHIN THE ECOSYSTEM OF THE ENTREPRENEURIAL UNIVERSITY

The classification of stakeholders at various levels of the university could help to identify the impact stakeholders have on the performance of the entrepreneurial university (Rowley, 1997). In addition, it shows configurations of stakeholders that represent an entrepreneurial university. Furthermore, classification of stakeholders makes conceptualisation of the university possible (Bailey, 1994). Below we provide a detailed explanation for the classification of stakeholders presented in the previous section.

3.1 Types of University Stakeholders (Knowledge Enablers; Knowledge Providers; Knowledge Codifiers; Knowledge Facilitators)

3.1.1 Knowledge enablers

Government
Government as an external stakeholder facilitates the technology transfer process. Initially, government develops appropriate policies and is the most common funding source for facilitating new knowledge development. Government's explicit policy is directed at increasing the responsibility of academia for ensuing funding for research and its commercialisation (Guerrero et al., 2016).

Collaborative research forms a relationship between two stakeholders and is a knowledge transfer channel. In addition, collaborative research contributes to the increasing awareness of the commercial exploitation of research results and promotes a better understanding of market needs, facilitating academics' engagement with commercialisation (Siegel et al., 2003).

Government also provides the political incentives that encourage entrepreneurship in universities that are focused on either research or teaching. It does this by enacting legislation designed to stimulate R&D-based entrepreneurial activities (e.g., tax incentives) in teaching-led universities and the patenting of own research in research-oriented universities (e.g., knowledge transfer partnership programme). One of the most prominent political instruments is the 1980 Bayh–Dole Act, which became law in the United States with the purpose of facilitating the commercialisation of research outputs.

Additionally, in the Lisbon Strategy, an action plan launched in the European Union in 2000, a lot of attention has been paid to incentives and government policies that encourage universities to pursue technologies commercialisation and entrepreneurship, thereby facilitating the innovative capacity of the region (Guerrero et al., 2015). Thus, government is among the most vital stakeholders enabling technologies transfer from universities.

Industry
When it comes to external stakeholders, besides government, universities also engage with industry. By providing funding for research, industry is considered a significant catalyst for ideas generation and development. The parties form relationships through contract research, which is considered an effective tool or channel for transferring knowledge (Cohen et al., 2002). Contracts with industry positively affect the direct commercialisation of research outputs from universities and encourage the involvement of academics in entrepreneurial activities as well as build an entrepreneurial culture at the university (Powers and McDougall, 2005). Furthermore, contract research facilitates the creation of spin-offs, complements other knowledge exchange activities and offers benefits to regions.

Through the outputs of academic research, academia provides different services to industry in return for funding. Such services are known as knowledge transfer channels and can be in the form of additional trainings for business (Ferreira and Ramos, 2015) or consultancy (Perkmann et al., 2013). As for consultancy, it is driven by the motive of learning together with industry and helping industries to solve their problems (Druckman, 2000). When it comes to training, this channel helps to transfer tacit knowledge and build skills (Ferreira and Ramos, 2015). Both channels represent a potential stream of revenues for academia that can help universities to follow their business model.

Thus, the engagement of knowledge enablers can be summarised as follows. Government holds a responsibility to set up formal rules and policy that regulate the higher education sector. In addition, it provides funding to support research and stimulate links with industry (e.g., Innovate UK programme in the UK). This facilitates the creation of an entrepreneurial environment as well as infrastructure to promote technology transfer. Collaboration with industry and business provides financial support to university researchers, thus boosting R&D, patents and licensing activities and facilitating knowledge exchange via direct knowledge transfer.

3.1.2   Knowledge providers

Researchers
Scholars represent an important group of internal stakeholders. Academics are the core of any scientific production (Jongbloed et al., 2008), the internal

nucleus without which the higher education establishment is not able to function properly.

According to Belitski and Heron (2017), academics are the main driver of knowledge transfer (e.g., via selling IP rights as well as creating both spin-offs and start-ups based on research outputs), who establish the interaction with other stakeholders. Much of this transfer of knowledge and technologies originates in a local region and within the community, linked to the academia.

Academic researchers are pivotal for the university, as owning or having access to new technology facilitates the partnership with other stakeholders (including government and business) to launch a new company as a form of technology commercialisation, thus enabling the monetisation of new technology (Audretsch et al., 2006).

Nelles and Vorley (2010) pointed to 'star scientists' as being crucial leaders for the entrepreneurial turn. Prominent researchers are key to attracting quality faculty able to win competitive research grants, produce and transfer new technologies, and receive entrepreneurial finance for new company development.

Students

Students are another key stakeholder for the university. According to Rothschild and White (1995), education is a customer-input service. Students as customers of universities are a pivotal input into the teaching (Jongbloed et al., 2008). In classes students are educated not only via lectures or professors, but also through ideas or experience sharing as well as the interaction with other students.

Additionally, students play a pivotal role while engaging with the external community (Jongbloed et al., 2008) and are considered one of the vital spillover mechanisms to facilitate new ventures creation (spin-offs and start-ups) (Acosta et al., 2011). They also serve as a measure of the demand for labour (Qian and Acs, 2013). As for the research activities, university students, especially PhD and postdoctoral researchers, are important participants of research projects, producing new knowledge which is then codified in the form of patents and sold as IP rights. This knowledge is used for academic spin-off (Hayter et al., 2018) or identifying market opportunities (Belitski and Heron, 2017). After graduation students become either job seekers or, in the case of setting up a start-up company, job creators. To develop new companies, students need access to entrepreneurial finance that universities can offer based on collaboration with venture capitalists or business angels.

Both university academics and students are thus able to generate new knowledge by expanding upon existing knowledge and acting on market opportunities. These stakeholders are vital for identifying opportunities and experimenting with new ideas in order to commercialise knowledge and technologies and/or create new ventures to address market needs.

Before being transferred to the economy, the knowledge produced by academia might follow either traditional (licensing) or alternative (non-linear; e.g., new ventures creation) routes of commercialisation (Bradley et al., 2013). The former process requires the invention to be codified and protected via technology transfer offices (hereafter TTOs), or any relevant department, and intellectual property offices (hereafter IP offices). The latter involves science parks and/or business incubators. Stakeholders involved in both traditional and alternative routes of commercialisation might be either internal or external to the university.

3.1.3   Knowledge codifiers

TTOs and IP offices
To ensure appropriate protection of the research invention (IP rights, including patents, copyright, trademarks and designs), universities usually work with IP offices.

Patents and licences serve as a codified visible method and channel to transfer knowledge via the traditional route of research commercialisation (Fisch et al., 2016). They facilitate the commercialisation of university inventions which later contribute to the creation of new ventures (e.g., spin-offs), thus contributing to the entrepreneurial mission of the university. They also contribute to start-ups raising external funding (Farre-Mensa et al., 2015). Patenting serves as a strong, robust, research-based predictor of academics participating in the setting up of a firm (Stuart and Ding, 2006). Thus, patents are a promising starting point for entrepreneurial activities by academics, or an initial step for technologies transfer via the traditional way.

Since universities have seen that IP rights can bring commercial wealth, they become more aggressive on the knowledge market (Jongbloed et al., 2008) and establish new structures that connect universities with industry. Universities started to establish TTOs or IP offices to professionally govern their IP rights (Jongbloed et al., 2008). TTOs are at the centre of the research as they act as a key transaction point and foster the link between the academia and business to transfer technologies following the university business model (Perkmann et al., 2013).

TTOs support knowledge spillover via spin-offs from universities and their laboratories (Siegel, 2018). In such a way, TTOs act as 'technology intermediaries' through facilitating the expansion of research results to industry while commercialising new knowledge from research and business ideas via supporting start-ups.

Along with TTOs, IP offices can also help to bridge the gap between research commercialisation at the university and industry development, through issuing patents. TTOs, on the other hand, are intermediaries, gap-fillers as it were, in the process of research commercialisation. In addition, engaging in patenting activities enables researchers to delegate the function of searching for commercialisation opportunities with industry to TTOs and knowledge protection to IP offices, allowing them to focus mainly on developing new ideas or the transferred technology (Aldridge and Audretsch, 2010). Summing up, TTOs and IP offices are essential for codifying new knowledge and are an important conduit to bridge the information asymmetry between university and industry.

3.1.4 Knowledge facilitators

Science parks and business incubators
In cases where knowledge created by academia is not formally commercialised through a TTO, it might instead be used for the creation of new companies. The creation of new ventures requires a supportive infrastructure and stakeholders who can facilitate knowledge spillover outside the university, contributing to local economic development and helping academia to follow the university business model. Within the entrepreneurial university ecosystem, science parks and business incubators play a role of knowledge facilitation (Audretsch and Belitski, 2019).

The initial goal of science parks and business incubators is to facilitate transfers of knowledge from university and research institutions and provide support to create new companies (Hayter, 2016). They also act as boundary spanners and network platforms between academia and industry (Audretsch et al., 2016). Such an approach works very well for research-oriented universities because by collocating with other companies new research-based start-ups can benefit from the localised knowledge spillovers for innovation and production.

According to the International Association of Science Parks (IASP, 2002), Science and Technology Parks (STP) are institutions that aim to facilitate and manage the technology and knowledge flows between academia, companies, markets and R&D institutions and stimulate the formation and growth of new ventures based on innovations through incubation and spin-offs.

In practice, there are a variety of university patents, stakeholders and founders of science parks (Phan et al., 2005), which has facilitated the creation of very heterogeneous organisations (Westhead, 1997), with the academia having a prominent role. Thus, for example, all the STPs in the UK are the initiatives of universities (Siegel et al., 2003), while in other countries – the US (Link and Scott, 2007), China (Wright et al., 2008), Australia (Phillimore, 1999), Spain and Italy (Albahari et al., 2013), Japan (Fukugawa, 2006), Portugal (Ratinho and Henriques, 2010), France (Chordá, 1996) – the degree to which universities are involved in STPs is varied. According to Jongbloed et al. (2008), science parks facilitate the establishment of start-ups and licensees of university patents.

The main idea behind science parks is to develop the infrastructure for, and provide administrative, technical and logistic help to, new companies including those driven by university research (e.g., creating spin-offs utilising IP rights). This is more effective for the research-led universities (Hayter et al., 2018) as new start-ups can participate in joint R&D projects and develop innovation clusters for knowledge commercialisation. Newly established companies need this support to compete with established companies in the market. The debate about the effectiveness of science parks in supporting new firms (Hobbs et al., 2017) suggests that locating new ventures in science parks has a positive effect on company employment and sales.

According to Murphy and Dyrenfurth (2019), the support provided by incubators helps people to conceptualise their ideas (based on, e.g., teaching outcomes and entrepreneurship initiatives) and launch businesses successfully. For the same reasons as for spin-offs from research-based universities, new firms from teaching-based universities seeking to explore market opportunities may enrich their ideas using the solid knowledge background and technologies of other firms co-located in science parks and incubators (Audretsch and Belitski, 2019). Such support to new firms may include workshops, mentorship, access to investors and access to networks of entrepreneurs (Abduh et al., 2007). In addition, business incubators offer support services in the form of equipment, such as fax machines, photocopiers and computers, facilities (office space), as well as knowledge and management support (Hobbs et al., 2017).

Venture capitalists and business angels (entrepreneurial finance)
The availability of entrepreneurial finance is vital to the success of a new company, including spin-offs and start-ups. Under conditions of resource constraints at universities with regard to creating successful new ventures, venture capitalists (VCs) and business angels (BAs) are considered an important source of funding. Universities which are research active and able to commercialise knowledge by starting new firms and acquiring property rights on the inventions will be more successful in securing entrepreneurial finance. Venture capital is the second-most important funding channel in the UK (after government support through University Challenge Funding) (Wright et al., 2006). In addition to financial capital, VCs provide academic entrepreneurs with managerial and technical advice on running a business and allow access to their business networks (Bock et al., 2018). VCs and BAs also add credibility to a start-up and provide connections to markets and industry. Universities in many countries understand the role of entrepreneurial finance in achieving entrepreneurial outcomes and are therefore trying to set up their own VCs or BAs or develop tight links with these stakeholders within their regions.

To summarise, science parks and business incubators along with venture capitalists and business angels are mechanisms that help to facilitate the creation of knowledge-based spin-offs (including via utilisation of IP rights) and university-based start-ups, the former more often for research-oriented institutions and the latter more often for teaching-oriented institutions. Science parks are characterised as a traditional supply-side tool that provides infrastructure and promotes networking among academic and business actors. Business incubators are organisations that are involved at all stages of company development from idea generation to launching an enterprise, and are used as tools to facilitate knowledge transfer in universities of both types. Finally, for every new venture, to survive and grow requires entrepreneurial finance, and this can be acquired from venture capitalists and business angels.

4.   CONCLUSIONS

This chapter contributes to the development of a new conceptual model of the entrepreneurial university applying a stakeholder prospective (Zott et al., 2011). We considered the university as a central organisation and tried to explain the role stakeholders play in facilitating technology transfer and helping academia to follow its business model. Universities are knowledge hubs by their nature and require access to entrepreneurial finance to make the transfer of new knowledge (e.g., business ideas) and technologies possible.

This chapter has provided a first conceptualisation of the multi-actor model of the entrepreneurial university to identify various types of stakeholders (corporate, industry, government, VC) and their roles in knowledge transfer within and outside the university.

Use of stakeholder constructs could help university managers identify the impact multiple actors have on the development and functioning of the entrepreneurial university from new technologies production to its spillover into the ecosystem.

Future research is needed to test the conceptual model and the effects of different stakeholders on technologies transfer within different university business models (e.g., research- (transfer of IP rights, patents) vs teaching- (facilitating new ideas formation and start-ups creation via education activities) oriented entrepreneurial university). Access to entrepreneurial finance is crucial for both teaching- and research-oriented entrepreneurial universities as both types of universities can contribute to the innovative development of the region (e.g., via selling IP rights or creating new companies). In this vein more research is needed to explore whether those providing entrepreneurial finance are among the most vital stakeholders and thus whether universities should try to find a way of bringing more of these stakeholders onboard.

REFERENCES

Abduh, M., D'Souza, C., Quazi, A., and Burley, H. (2007), 'Investigating and classifying clients' satisfaction with business incubator services', *Managing Service Quality: An International Journal*, 17 (1), 74–91. https://doi.org/10.1108/09604520710720683

Acosta, M., Coronado, D., and Flores, E. (2011), 'University spillovers and new business location in high-technology sectors: Spanish evidence', *Small Business Economics*, 36 (3), 365–376.

Albahari, A., Catalano, G., and Landoni, P. (2013), 'Evaluation of national science park systems: A theoretical framework and its application to the Italian and Spanish systems', *Technology Analysis and Strategic Management*, 25 (5), 599–614.

Aldridge, T., and Audretsch, D. B. (2010), 'Does policy influence the commercialization route? Evidence from National Institutes of Health funded scientists', *Research Policy*, 39 (5), 583–588.

Alsos, G., Carter, S., Ljunggren, E., and Welter, F. (2011), 'Introduction: Researching entrepreneurship in agriculture and rural development', in G. Alsos, S. Carter, E. Ljunggren and F. Welter (eds), *The Handbook of Research on Entrepreneurship in Agriculture and Rural Development* (pp. 1–20). Cheltenham, UK and Northampton, MA, USA: Edward Elgar Publishing.

Audretsch, D. B. (2014), 'From the entrepreneurial university to the university for the entrepreneurial society', *Journal of Technology Transfer*, 39 (3), 313–321.

Audretsch, D. B., and Belitski, M. (2019), 'Science parks and business incubation in the United Kingdom: Evidence from university spin-offs and staff start-ups', in S. Amoroso, A. N. Link and M. Wright (eds), *Science and Technology Parks and Regional Economic Development* (pp. 99–122). Cham, Switzerland: Palgrave Macmillan.

Audretsch, D. B., Keilbach, M. C., and Lehmann, E. E. (2006), *Entrepreneurship and Economic Growth*. Oxford: Oxford University Press.

Audretsch, D. B., Kuratko, D. F., and Link, A. N. (2016), 'Dynamic entrepreneurship and technology-based innovation', *Journal of Evolutionary Economics*, 26, 603–620.

Autio, E., Kenney, M., Mustar, P., Siegel, D., and Wright, M. (2014), 'Entrepreneurial innovation ecosystems and context', *Research Policy*, 43 (7), 1097–1108.

Bae, T. J., Qian, S., Miao, C., and Fiet, J. O. (2014), 'The relationship between entrepreneurship education and entrepreneurial intentions: A meta-analytic review', *Entrepreneurship Theory Practice*, 38, 217–254. https://doi.org/10.1111/etap.12095

Bailey, K. D. (1994), *Typologies and Taxonomies: An Introduction to Classification Techniques*. Quantitative Applications in the Social Sciences (Vol. 102), Thousand Oaks, CA: Sage.

Banal-Estanol, A., Jofre-Boneta, M., and Lawson, C. (2015), 'The double-edged sword of industry collaboration: Evidence from engineering academics in the UK', *Research Policy*, 44 (6), 1160–1175.

Bartell, M. (2003), 'Internationalization of universities: A university culture-based framework', *Higher Education*, 45 (1), 43–70.

Belitski, M., and Heron, K. (2017), 'Expanding entrepreneurship education ecosystems', *Journal of Management Development*, 36 (2), 163–177. https://doi.org/10.1108/JMD-06-2016-0121

Bercovitz, J., and Feldman, M. P. (2006), 'Entrepreneurial universities and technology transfer: A conceptual framework for understanding knowledge-based economic development', *Journal of Technology Transfer*, 31, 175–188.

Bernasconi, A. (2005), 'University entrepreneurship in a developing country: The case of the P. Universidad Católica de Chile, 1985–2000', *Higher Education*, 50, 247–274. https://doi.org/10.1007/s10734-004-6353-1

Bischoff, K., Volkmann, C. K., and Audretsch, D. B. (2018), 'Stakeholder collaboration in entrepreneurship education: An analysis of the entrepreneurial ecosystems of European higher educational institutions', *Journal of Technology Transfer*, 43, 20–46. https://doi.org/10.1007/s10961-017-9581-0

Block, J. H., Colombo, M. G., Cumming, D. J., and Vismara, S. (2018), 'New players in entrepreneurial finance and why they are there', *Small Business Economics*, 50, 239–250. https://doi.org/10.1007/s11187-016-9826-6

Bock, C., Huber, A., and Jarchow, S. (2018), 'Growth factors of research-based spin-offs and the role of venture capital investing', *Journal of Technology Transfer*, 43 (5), 1375–1409.

Bradley, S., Hayter, C. S., and Link, A. N. (2013), 'Models and methods of university technology transfer', *Foundations and Trends in Entrepreneurship*, 9 (6), 571–650.

Bramwell, A., and Wolfe, D. A. (2008), 'Universities and regional economic development: The entrepreneurial University of Waterloo', *Research Policy*, 37 (8), 1175–1187.

Brown, J. D., and Earle, J. S. (2015), 'Finance and growth at the firm level: Evidence from SBA loans', IZA Working Paper No. 9267.

Burrows, P. (1999), 'Combining regulation and legal liability for the control of external costs', *International Review of Law and Economics*, 19 (2), 227–244.

Chesbrough, H. (2010), 'Business model innovation: Opportunities and barriers', *Long Range Planning*, 43 (2–3), 354–363.

Chordá, I. M. (1996), 'Towards the maturity stage: An insight into the performance of French technopoles', *Technovation*, 16 (3), 143–152.

Chrisman, J. J., Hynes, T., and Fraser, S. (1995), 'Faculty entrepreneurship and economic development: The case of the University of Calgary', *Journal Business Venturing*, 10 (4), 267–281.

Clark, B. (1998), *Creating Entrepreneurial Universities: Organizational Pathways of Transformation*. Oxford: IAU Press/Pergamon.

Cohen, W. M., Nelson, R. R., and Walsh, J. P. (2002), 'Links and impacts: The influence of public research on industrial R&D', *Management Science*, 48 (1), 1–23.

Culkin, N., and Mallick, S. (2011), 'Producing work-ready graduates: The role of the entrepreneurial university', *International Journal of Market Research*, 53 (3), 347–368.

Czarnitzki, D., and Delanote, J. (2015), 'R&D policies for young SMEs: Input and output effects', *Small Business Economics*, 45, 465–485. https://doi.org/10.1007/s11187-015-9661-1

de Zilwa, D. (2005), 'Using entrepreneurial activities as a means of survival: Investigating the processes used by Australian universities to diversify their revenue streams', *Higher Education*, 50 (3), 387–411.

Donaldson, T., and Preston, L. E. (1995), 'The stakeholder theory of the corporation: Concepts, evidence, and implications', *Academy of Management Review*, 20 (1), 65–91.

Druckman, D. (2000), 'Frameworks, techniques, and theory: Contributions of research consulting in social science', *American Behavioral Scientist*, 43 (10), 1635–1666.

Etzkowitz, H., Germain-Alamartine, E., Keel, J., Kumar, C., Smith, K. N., and Albats, E. (2019), 'Entrepreneurial university dynamics: Structured ambivalence, relative deprivation and institution-formation in the Stanford innovation system', *Technological Forecasting and Social Change*, 141, 159–171.

Etzkowitz, H., Webster, A., Gebhardt, C., and Cantisano Terra, B. R. (2000), 'The future of the university and the university of the future: Evolution of ivory tower to entrepreneurial paradigm', *Research Policy*, 29, 313–330.

Farre-Mensa, J., Hegde, D., and Ljungqvist, A. (2015), 'The bright side of patents', NBER Working Paper No. 21959.

Fayolle, A., and Linan, F. (2014), 'The future of research on entrepreneurial intentions', *Journal of Business Research*, 67 (5), 663–666.

Ferreira, M. L. A., and Ramos, R. R. (2015), 'Making university–industry technological partnerships work: A case study in the Brazilian oil innovation system', *Journal of Technology Management and Innovation*, 10 (1), 173–187.

Fisch, C. O., Block, J. H., and Sandner, P. G. (2016), 'Chinese university patents: Quantity, quality, and the role of subsidy programs', *Journal of Technology Transfer*, 41, 60–84. https://doi.org/10.1007/s10961-014-9383-6

Freeman, R. E. (1984), *Strategic Management: A Stakeholder Approach*. Boston, MA: Pitman.

Fukugawa, N. (2006), 'Science parks in Japan and their value-added contributions to new technology-based firms', *International Journal of Industrial Organization*, 24 (2), 381–400.

Fuller, D., Beynon, M., and Pickernell, D. (2017), 'Indexing third stream activities in UK universities: Exploring the entrepreneurial/enterprising university', *Studies in Higher Education*, 44 (1), 1–25.

Fuster, E., Padilla-Melendez, A., Lockett, N., and del-Águila-Obra, A. R. (2019), 'The emerging role of university spin-off companies in developing regional entrepreneurial university ecosystems: The case of Andalusia', *Technological Forecasting and Social Change*, 141, 219–231.

Goddard, J., Robertson, D., and Vallance, P. (2012), 'Universities, Technology and Innovation Centres and regional development: The case of the North-East of England', *Cambridge Journal of Economics*, 36 (3), 609–627.

Graham, R. (2014), 'Creating university-based entrepreneurial ecosystems evidence from emerging world leaders', MIT Scoltech Initiative, Massachusetts Institute of Technology.

Guerrero, M., Cunningham, J. A., and Urbano, D. (2015), 'Economic impact of entrepreneurial universities' activities: An exploratory study of the United Kingdom', *Research Policy*, 44 (3), 748–764.

Guerrero, M., and Urbano, D. (2012), 'The development of an entrepreneurial university', *Journal of Technology Transfer*, 37 (1), 43–74. http://doi.org/10.1007/s10961-010-9171-x

Guerrero, M., and Urbano, D. (2014), 'Academics' start-up intentions and knowledge filters: An individual perspective of the knowledge spillover theory of entrepreneurship', *Small Business Economics*, 43, 57–74. https://doi.org/10.1007/s11187-013-9526-4

Guerrero, M., Urbano, D., and Fayolle, A. (2016), 'Entrepreneurial activity and regional competitiveness: Evidence from European entrepreneurial universities', *Journal of Technology Transfer*, 41 (1), 105–131.

Hayter, C. (2016), 'A trajectory of early-stage spin-offs success: The role of knowledge intermediaries within an entrepreneurial university ecosystem', *Small Business Economics*, 47 (3), 633–656.

Hayter, C. S., Nelson, A. J., Zayed, S., and O'Connor, Alan C. (2018), 'Conceptualizing academic entrepreneurship ecosystems: A review, analysis and extension of the literature', *Journal of Technology Transfer*, 43, 1039–1082. https://doi.org/10.1007/s10961-018-9657-5

Hewitt-Dundas, N. (2012), 'Research intensity and knowledge transfer activity in UK universities', *Research Policy*, 41 (2), 262–275.

Hobbs, K. G., Link, A. N., and Scott, J. T. (2017), 'Science and technology parks: An annotated and analytical literature review', *Journal of Technology Transfer*, 42 (4), 957–976.

Hu, M. C. (2009), 'Developing entrepreneurial universities in Taiwan: The effects of research funding sources', *Science, Technology and Society*, 14 (1), 35–57.

International Association of Science Parks (IASP) (2002), *Definitions*. https://www.iasp.ws/our-industry/definitions

Jacob, M., Lundqvist, M., and Hellsmark, H. (2003), 'Entrepreneurial transformations in the Swedish university system: The case of Chalmers University of Technology', *Research Policy*, 32 (9), 1555–1568.

Jaziri-Bouagina, D., and Jamil, G. L. (2017), *Handbook of Research on Tacit Knowledge Management for Organizational Success*. Hershey, PA: IGI Global.

Jongbloed, B., Enders, J., and Salerno, C. (2008), 'Higher education and its communities: Interconnections, interdependencies and a research agenda', *Higher Education*, 56, 303–324.

Kalar, B., and Antoncic, B. (2015), 'The entrepreneurial university, academic activities and technology and knowledge transfer in four European countries', *Technovation*, 36, 1–11.

Keast, D. (1995), 'Entrepreneurship in universities: Definitions, practices and implications', *Higher Education Quarterly*, 49 (3), 248–266.

Kirby, D. (2006), 'Creating entrepreneurial universities in the UK: Applying entrepreneurship theory in practice', *Journal of Technology Transfer*, 31, 599–603.

Klofsten, M., and Jones-Evans, D. (2000), 'Comparing academic entrepreneurship in Europe – the case of Sweden and Ireland', *Small Business Economics*, 14, 299–309. https://doi.org/10.1023/A:1008184601282

Lazzeretti, L., and Tavoletti, E. (2005), 'Higher education excellence and local economic development: The case of the entrepreneurial University of Twente', *European Planning Studies*, 13 (3), 475–493. https://doi.org/10.1080/09654310500089779

Link, A. N., and Scott, J. T. (2006), 'U.S. university research parks', *Journal of Productivity Analysis*, 25, 43–55.

Link, A. N., and Scott, J. T. (2007), 'The economics of university research parks', *Oxford Review of Economic Policy*, 23 (4), 661–674.

Meyer, M. (2006), 'Academic inventiveness and entrepreneurship: On the importance of start-up companies in commercializing academic patents', *Journal of Technology Transfer*, 31, 501–510. https://doi.org/10.1007/s10961-006-0010-z

Miller, D. J., and Acs, Z. J. (2017), 'The campus as entrepreneurial ecosystem: The University of Chicago', *Small Business Economics*, 49, 75–95. https://doi.org/10.1007/s11187-017-9868-4

Miller, K., McAdam, M., and McAdam, R. (2014), 'The changing university business model: A stakeholder perspective', *R&D Management*, 44 (3), 265–287. http://dx.doi.org/10.1111/radm.12064

Murphy, M., and Dyrenfurth, M. (2019), 'The expanding business of the entrepreneurial university: Job creation', in S. H. Christensen, B. Delahousse, C. Didier, M. Meganck and M. Murphy (eds), *The Engineering–Business Nexus* (pp. 201–230). Philosophy of Engineering and Technology, Vol. 32. Cham, Switzerland: Springer.

Nelles, J., and Vorley, T. (2010), 'From policy to practice: Engaging and embedding the third mission in contemporary universities', *International Journal of Sociology and Social Policy*, 30 (7/8), 341–353.

O'Gorman, C., Byrne, O., and Pandya, D. (2008), 'How scientists commercialise new knowledge via entrepreneurship', *Journal of Technology Transfer*, 33, 23–43.

Osterwalder, A., and Pigneur, Y. (2010), *Business Model Generation: A Handbook for Visionaries, Game Changers, and Challengers*. Hoboken, NJ: John Wiley & Sons.

Osterwalder, A. P., Pigneur, Y., and Tucci, C. L. (2005), 'Clarifying business models: Origins, present, and future of the concept', *Communications of the Association for Information Systems*, 15, 1–25.

Perkmann, M., Tartari, V., McKelvey, M., Autio, E., Brostrom, A., D'Este, P., and Krabel, S. (2013), 'Academic engagement and commercialisation: A review of the literature on university–industry relations', *Research Policy*, 42 (2), 423–442.

Phan, P., Siegel, D. S., and Wright, M. (2005), 'Science parks and incubators: Observations, synthesis and future research', *Journal of Business Venturing*, 20 (2), 165–182.

Phillimore, J. (1999), 'Beyond the linear view of innovation in science park evaluation: An analysis of Western Australian Technology Park', *Technovation*, 19 (11), 673–680.

Powers, J. B., and McDougall, P. P. (2005), 'University start-up formation and technology licensing with firms that go public: A resource-based view of academic entrepreneurship', *Journal of Business Venturing*, 20 (3), 291–311.

Qian, H., and Acs, Z. J. (2013), 'An absorptive capacity theory of knowledge spillover entrepreneurship', *Small Business Economics*, 40 (2), 185–197.

Ratinho, T., and Henriques, E. (2010), 'The role of science parks and business incubators in converging countries: Evidence from Portugal', *Technovation*, 30 (4), 278–290.

Redford, D. T., and Fayolle, A. (2014), 'Stakeholder management and the entrepreneurial university', in A. Fayolle and D. T. Redford (eds), *Handbook on the Entrepreneurial University* (pp. 11–24). Cheltenham, UK and Northampton, MA, USA: Edward Elgar Publishing.

Rothschild, M., and White, L. J. (1995), 'The analytics of the pricing of higher education and other services in which the customers are inputs', *Journal of Political Economy*, 103 (3), 573–586. http://www.jstor.org/stable/2138699

Rowley, T. J. (1997), 'Moving beyond dyadic ties: A network theory of stakeholder influences', *Academy of Management Review*, 22, 887–910.

Ryu, M. (1998), 'A muted voice in academe: The Korean version of entrepreneurial scholarship', *Higher Education*, 35 (1), 9–26.

San-Jose, L., Retolaza, J. L., and Freeman, R. E. (2017), 'Stakeholder engagement at Extanobe: A case study of the new story of business', in R. Freeman, J. Kujala and S. Sachs (eds), *Stakeholder Engagement: Clinical Research* (pp. 285–310). Issues in Business Ethics, Vol. 46. Cham, Switzerland: Springer. https://doi.org/10.1007/978-3-319-62785-4_13

Schmoch, U. (1999), 'Interaction of universities and industrial enterprises in Germany and the United States – a comparison', *Industry and Innovation*, 6, 51–68.

Siegel, D. S. (2018), 'Academic entrepreneurship: Lessons learned for technology transfer personnel and university administrators', in *World Scientific Reference on Innovation* (pp. 1–21). World Scientific.

Siegel, D. S., Westhead, P., and Wright, M. (2003), 'Assessing the impact of science parks on the research productivity of firms: Exploratory evidence from the United Kingdom', *International Journal of Industrial Organization*, 21 (9), 1357–1369.

Sterzi, V., (2013), 'Patent quality and ownership: An analysis of UK faculty patenting', *Research Policy*, 42, 564–576.

Stuart, T. E., and Ding, W. W. (2006), 'When do scientists become entrepreneurs? The social structural antecedents of commercial activity in the academic life sciences', *American Journal of Sociology*, 112 (1), 97–144.

Westhead, P. (1997), 'R&D "inputs" and "outputs" of technology-based firms located in and off science parks', *R&D Management*, 27 (1), 45–62.

Wong, P., Ho, Y., and Singh, A. (2007), 'Towards an "entrepreneurial university" model to support knowledge-based economic development: The case of the National University of Singapore', *World Development*, 35 (6), 941–958.

Wright, M., Clarysse, B., Lockett, A., and Knockaert, M. (2008), 'Mid-range universities' linkages with industry: Knowledge types and the role of intermediaries', *Research Policy*, 37 (8), 1205–1223.

Wright, M., Lockett, A., Clarysse, B., and Binks, M. (2006), 'University spin-out companies and venture capital', *Research Policy*, 35 (4), 481–501.

Yusef, S. (2008), 'Intermediating knowledge exchange between universities and businesses', *Research Policy*, 37 (8), 1167–1174.

Zhao, F. (2004), 'Academic entrepreneurship: Case study of Australian universities', *International Journal of Entrepreneurship and Innovation*, 5 (2), 91–97. https://doi .org/10.5367/000000004773863246

Zott, C., and Amit, R. (2010), 'Business model design: An activity system perspective', *Long Range Planning*, 43, 216–226.

Zott, C., Amit, R., and Massa, L. (2011), 'The business model: Recent developments and future research', *Journal of Management*, 37, 1019–1042.

APPENDIX 6A

Table 6A.1   Cases studied: entrepreneurial university and collaboration with stakeholders

Author(s), publication year	Unit of analysis	Theoretical framework	Data	Methodology	Findings	Stakeholders covered	Research focus
Keast, 1995	University of Alberta, Canada	Entrepreneurship	Interviews with the vice president and director of research	Description of differences between university and business	Entrepreneurship and associated activities or initiatives are becoming increasingly important to administrators.	Academic entrepreneurs, government, industry, patenting office, TTO	Entrepreneurship and administrators
Kirby, 2006	University of Surrey	The theories of entrepreneurship and intrapreneurship development		Case study	Theory proposes the formulation of a high-level strategy that demonstrates the university's intent, makes it clear that the university encourages this form of behaviour, provides the university's staff with the knowledge and support to start their own businesses and creates an environment that reduces the risk involved.	Incubator, technopark, education programmes, Higher Education Innovation Fund (HEIF), research centre (pre-incubator), venture capital fund	University strategy, supportive environment

Author(s), publication year	Unit of analysis	Theoretical framework	Data	Methodology	Findings	Stakeholders covered	Research focus
Kalar and Antoncic, 2015	University of Amsterdam, University of Antwerp, University of Ljubljana and the University of Oxford		Survey of 1300 academics from different disciplines	Descriptive analysis, cross-tabulation	Academics perceiving their university department as being highly entrepreneurially oriented are less likely to believe that engagement in technology and knowledge transfer can be harmful to academic science.	Academic departments and university faculty	Academics and departmental orientation
Banal-Estanol et al., 2015	40 UK universities: 24 Russell Group and 16 other (engineering departments)		Individual characteristics, publications, patents, research funds Publications in SSCI	Generalised least squares method with fixed effects estimators	The formation of links with the private sector may boost research output (provide new ideas and additional funding), but high degrees of collaboration can also damage research output (low value of research ideas, time-consuming).	Patenting office, government, academic entrepreneurs	University–industry research collaboration
Miller et al., 2014	One UK university	Stakeholder theory	Multi-level semi-structured interviews with stakeholders' representatives	Case study, observation analysis, coding of interviews (Nvivo 10)	Conflicting objectives between each of the stakeholder groups have led to the university business model evolving not as a process of co-creation but rather in a series of transitions whereby multiple stakeholders are continually shaping the university business model through strategies that are dependent upon their salience.	Academic entrepreneurs, TTO, patenting office, government	The changing university business model–stakeholder relationship

Author(s), publication year	Unit of analysis	Theoretical framework	Data	Methodology	Findings	Stakeholders covered	Research focus
Bramwell and Wolfe, 2008	University of Waterloo		96 in-depth interviews with firms, associations, and knowledge institutions	Case study	Beyond generating commercialisable knowledge and qualified research scientists, universities produce other mechanisms of knowledge transfer, such as generating and attracting talent to the local economy and collaborating with local industry by providing formal and informal technical support.	Government, patenting office, academic entrepreneurs, TTO, industry	Mechanisms of knowledge transfer
Guerrero et al., 2015	147 public universities in the UK in 74 NUTS-3 regions (2005–2007)	The endogenous growth theory	Secondary data, Higher Education Business and Community Interaction Survey (HEBCIS)	Structural equation modelling (SEM), exploratory (EFA) and confirmatory factor analysis (CFA)	The economic impact of the control group (UK universities that are not part of the Russell Group) is evident on research, teaching, and entrepreneurial activities, with the highest impact associated with research and knowledge transfer.	Government, patenting office, academic entrepreneurs, TTO, industry	The impact of universities on economic development
Guerrero and Urbano, 2014	Public entrepreneurial universities in Spain (academic period 2008–2009)	The knowledge spillover theory of entrepreneurship The planned behaviour theory	207 online questionnaires with academics enrolled in business economics and engineering areas	Structural equation modelling (SEM), confirmatory factor analysis (CFA)	Partially find support for their hypotheses that academics' motivational factors, subjective norms and entrepreneurial university policies have a knowledge filter effect on academics' start-up intentions.	Entrepreneurial intentions and economic growth	Knowledge spillover process by level of analysis
Hu, 2009	Feng Chia University, Taiwan		149 answers from 435 questionnaires	Structural equation modelling (SEM)	Industry–university links are strengthened by private and public research funding, while there was no evidence that establishing technology licensing and business incubation may reinforce those links.	Academic entrepreneurs, TTO, patenting office, incubators, industry, government	Stakeholders and university–industry collaboration

Author(s), publication year	Unit of analysis	Theoretical framework	Data	Methodology	Findings	Stakeholders covered	Research focus
Goddard et al., 2012	North-east of England: Newcastle University (1998–2008)		In-depth interviews with key decision makers (government) and academics	Description of interviews	The relationships between regional firms and technology and innovation centres in the north-east of England to be limited due to poor matching between a strong academic research base and limited absorptive capacity.	Academic entrepreneurs, government, industry	The relationships between regional firms and technology centres
Meyer, 2006	A small set of European countries (UK, Germany, Belgium)		Publications (Science Citation Index) and patents (US patents)	Description, categorisation	The minority of inventor-authors, that is researchers with high numbers of patents, also tends to publish and be cited over-proportionally.	Patenting office, academic entrepreneurs	The relationship between scientific publication and patenting activity
Sterzi, 2013	UK universities		1376 patent applications at the European Patent Office (EPO) and invented by academic scientists in the UK	A cross-sectional analysis	We find a quality premium for academic patents owned by business companies (corporate patents) in the short and medium term (till 6 years after the patent priority year) with respect to academic patents owned by universities (university patents).	Industry, human capital, patenting office	The quality of patents (academia and business)
Culkin and Mallick, 2011	University of Hertfordshire		Analysis of university strategy and policy	Case study	Delivering employment-ready graduates ignores the demands of a radically altered world of work in the face of the government's response to the latest economic crisis.	Students and industry	University graduates and changed demands

Author(s), publication year	Unit of analysis	Theoretical framework	Data	Methodology	Findings	Stakeholders covered	Research focus
Guerrero and Urbano, 2012	13 Spanish universities	Institutional theory	Spanish Entrepreneurial University Scoreboard (SEUS) (secondary information from 50 universities); e-mail questionnaires with academics	Structural equation modelling (SEM)	Each university community is unique and its attitudes towards entrepreneurship are defined by a combination of factors, such as entrepreneurship education, teaching methodologies, role models and reward systems.	Incubators, science parks, human capital, government, TTO, patenting office	Entrepreneurship education, teaching methodologies, role models and reward systems as factors that explain the attitude towards entrepreneurship at university
Bischoff et al., 2018	20 different higher education establishments from 19 European countries	Stakeholder theory	Interviews and validation through peer groups	An exploratory cross-case analysis of all 20 case studies was conducted on the basis of a context analysis	The findings of this study indicate that none of the examined 20 HEIs possesses an explicit, verbalised strategy for the management of its external stakeholder relations in the context of entrepreneurship education.	Different levels at different universities	University strategy for collaboration with stakeholders
Hewitt-Dundas, 2012	158 universities across the UK	Stakeholder theory	Secondary data, Higher Education Business and Community Interaction Survey (HEBCIS)	K-means cluster analysis	Universities' approach to knowledge transfer is shaped by institutional and organisational resources, in particular their ethos and research quality, rather than the capability to undertake knowledge transfer through a technology transfer office.	Government, industry, university faculty, students, TTO, patenting office, science parks, business incubators, VCs	Institutional and organisational resources to support knowledge transfer

Author(s), publication year	Unit of analysis	Theoretical framework	Data	Methodology	Findings	Stakeholders covered	Research focus
Etzkowitz et al., 2019	Stanford University	Triple-Helix concept	Participant observation in the Office of Technology Licensing, archival research and interviews on university–industry relations	Case study	As innovation is institutionalised in novel organisational structures, as well as linked to teaching and research, the entrepreneurial university becomes a key element in the Triple Helix of university–industry–government interaction. Stanford developed university–industry and then university–government relationships as part of an increasingly explicit university–region co-development strategy. These double helices converged into a university–industry–government coalition, Joint Venture Silicon Valley, a public brainstorming initiative '… following a venture capital winnowing approach' that generated networking start-ups in response to the 1990s recession.	TTO, accelerator, incubator, coaching organisation, investors, industry, public and private funds, government, industry	University–government–industry relations and supportive stakeholders
Lazzeretti and Tavoletti, 2005	University of Twente	Entrepreneurial university (Clark, 1998)	15 interviews	Case study	Local economic relevance and international excellence are not incompatible objectives: they were not at the University of Twente; they can be reached even in a new-born and poor endowed university, located in a peripheral, depressed and not industrialised countryside.	Incubator, research centres (people), accelerators, business and science park, government, industry	Local economic relevance and international excellence

Author(s), publication year	Unit of analysis	Theoretical framework	Data	Methodology	Findings	Stakeholders covered	Research focus
Wong et al., 2007	University of Singapore	Entrepreneurial university	Documents analysis	Case study	University of Singapore was shifting from being primarily a manpower provider and knowledge creator to take on a more visible role in knowledge commercialisation through increased patenting, licensing to private industry and spinning-off new ventures.	Venture Support unit, incubator, patenting office, TTO, government	University's changing role in knowledge creation process.
Fuster et al., 2019	10 public universities in Spain	The knowledge spillover theory of entrepreneurship, social network approach	Interviews	Social network analysis, in-depth analysis	The entrepreneurial universities influence the development of regional entrepreneurial university ecosystems through the promotion of university spin-offs, as one of the knowledge transfer mechanisms. However, entrepreneurial universities should develop a more proactive role, through intermediaries like TTOs and university venture capitalists, collaborating with university spin-offs.	Science parks, business incubator, VC, industry, government, patenting office, TTO	University spin-offs as knowledge transfer mechanism in the ecosystem.
Bae et al., 2014	Korea Advanced Institute of Technologies	Human capital theory and entrepreneurial self-efficacy	Publications	A comprehensive review of the literature, meta-analysis	There is a significant correlation between entrepreneurship education and entrepreneurial intentions. This correlation is also greater than that of business education and entrepreneurial intentions. However, after controlling for pre-education entrepreneurial intentions, the relationship between entrepreneurship education and post-education entrepreneurial intentions was not significant.	Scientists, students, TTO, incubator, research centres/ institute for start-ups	Entrepreneurship education and entrepreneurial intentions

Author(s), publication year	Unit of analysis	Theoretical framework	Data	Methodology	Findings	Stakeholders covered	Research focus
Miller and Acs, 2017	University of Chicago	Turner's theory	Interviews, observation, document analysis, internet search/ analysis	Case study	The open, innovative American frontier that closed at the end of the twentieth century has re-emerged in the entrepreneurial economy on the US campus.	Alumnies, VCs, faculty, students, angel investors, government, business incubator	Entrepreneurial university as an ecosystem
Chrisman et al., 1995	Alberta, Canada	Entrepreneurship	Personnel interviews	Case study, in-depth analysis	Identification of administrative role, the impact of funds reduction and different types of entrepreneurial activities.	TTO, human capital, government, industry, patenting office	Administrators and their role in entrepreneurship
Bernasconi, 2005	Universidad Catholicde Chile	Entrepreneurial universities (the concept of Clark, 1998)	Secondary sources	Case study	The results suggest the orientation to market as a means of survival and growth under the pressure of privatisation, than a result of a Triple Helix strategy of university.	Government, human capital, industry	Entrepreneurship strategy of the university
de Zilwa, 2005	Australian universities		Secondary data from annual financial reports by Australian Higher Education	Descriptive analysis of the secondary data	Universities have used isomorphism tactics transforming themselves from being rigid bureaucracies to become more flexible network enterprises.	Industry, patenting office, government, human capital, investors, TTO	University strategy on entrepreneurship
Jacob et al., 2003	Chalmers University of Technology in Sweden	Entrepreneurial universities (Clark, 1998).	Interviews with the principal actors in the internal transformation process	Case study	One important element required for innovation is macro (vision and implementation) and micro (university organisation) level flexibility and diversity.	Patenting office, academic entrepreneurs, incubators, VCs	The factors for universities to become entrepreneurial

Author(s), publication year	Unit of analysis	Theoretical framework	Data	Methodology	Findings	Stakeholders covered	Research focus
Zhao, 2004	Australian universities	Academic entrepreneurship	Extensive interviews with academic entrepreneurs and commercialisation managers, survey	A comprehensive review of the literature on research commercialisation, in-depth analysis	Identified and discussed the key issues in the study and proposed a series of recommendations to enhance the overall performance of university research commercialisation.	Academic entrepreneurs and commercialisation managers	Issues related to research commercialisation
Schmoch, 1999	Germany and USA	Knowledge transfers	Description about the interaction	Comprehensive literature review	Identification of similes and differences related with the formalisation.	Patenting office, industry, government	University–industry relations formalisation
Klofsten and Jones-Evans, 2000	Ireland and Sweden universities	Academic entrepreneurship	10 case studies, 1857 structured questionnaires to all academics	Case study	Impact of previous entrepreneurial experiences among academics in both countries and their practical application in activities such as consultancy and contract research.	Industry, government, patenting office, TTO, academic entrepreneurs	Practical experience of academics
Ryu,1998	Yonsei University of Korea	Entrepreneurial scholarship	Semi-structured interviews with male full professors	Case study, in-depth analysis	Identification of strategic planning and the development of the academic services.	Government, academic entrepreneurs, industry, science/ technology park	Role of strategy in entrepreneurship

PART II

Financing for entrepreneurship

7. The invention and diffusion of venture capital: when knowledge married capital

Henry Etzkowitz, Chunyan Zhou, and Rosa Caiazza

INTRODUCTION

Firm formation based on new technology became a systematic process with the invention of venture capital. Investment capital focused on the early and presumably more risky stages of firm formation is justified, on the one hand, by the prospect of a higher rate of return, and on the other by spreading risk among a broad range of investments, with the huge success of a few investments expected to cover losses of unsuccessful investments and produce a higher rate of profits than normal banking activities. Instead of judging creditworthiness and evaluating collateral worth, the venture capitalist analyzes the potential of an investment as a balance between technical advance, human capital quality of the founders, and future market potential of the envisioned product.

Heretofore, firm founders were dependent upon individual investors and family funds. Whether focused on early or later stage ventures, new technologies or new business models, venture capital is the converse of the traditional banking approach with its focus on identifying choices perceived as low risk. The essence of venture capital is the management of high risk, not by increasing demands upon the seekers of capital to reduce risk but by the venture capitalists assuming it themselves.

In the following we shall outline the development of a university-based start-up strategy for regional development, prior to the passage of the Bayh–Dole Act of 1980 that legitimized this strategy and prepared the way for its spread to a broader range of academic institutions. Rather than taking the US Act or its analogues in other countries as the inception of the process of university-sourced economic development, we view it as its culmination.

Several elements came together to produce the regular output of spin-offs from academic research with practical application. First the university took moral responsibility for seeing that commercializable outcomes of its research activities were ethically utilized.

The invention of a milk testing device at the University of Wisconsin and the discovery of a diabetes treatment at the University of Toronto brought to the forefront of attention the need to protect the university from adverse consequences if the devices or treatments were freely disseminated and faulty products deliberately or carelessly marketed. The concern over adverse publicity alone impelled universities to seek the protection of the patent system to control and monitor the dissemination of these advances. On the other hand, at the Massachusetts Institute of Technology (MIT), interest in shaping a policy towards university inventions developed in response to instances of persons hanging around the campus for the purpose of picking up intellectual property (IP) that they could represent as their own, with no recompense to either the inventor or the university (Etzkowitz, 2002). Thus, organized university technology transfer arose from a combination of pecuniary, eleemosynary, and institutional protection motivations.

The creation of new economic activity, previously an indirect byproduct of academic research, is increasingly becoming a specific objective in tandem with the creation of new knowledge (Caiazza et al., 2021). The patent system has been adapted from its original intention to incentivize individual inventors to regulate the commercialization of academic discoveries with practical potential. The producer of useful knowledge has certain rights that it may choose to enforce. This was a lesson early learned both by universities, like MIT, interested in capitalizing their knowledge and by those that were not so inclined. When researchers at the University of Toronto invented insulin treatment for diabetes, the university found that it had to patent and license the technology in order to protect itself from potentially unethical manufacturers. The University of Wisconsin encountered a similar situation when a faculty member invented a device to test milk quality. Even before universities realized that they could earn income from inventions, they were impelled to create mechanisms for technology transfer in order to insure an orderly process of transfer and protect their reputations (Caiazza et al., 2020).

The paradox of university–industry relations, in the transition from an industrial society, is that the number and types of university–industry links increase as basic rather than applied research becomes more salient to economic development in a knowledge-based society (Belitski et al., 2020). Firm formation, based on new technology, involves a process of technical and business partners getting acquainted, building trust, and forming long-term alliances. Cross-fertilization between the two different perspectives of technical and business people is also the key to innovation. The building of creative relationships between technical and business people is an essential part of a firm-formation process that is much more than a simple investment of funds in exchange for a share of ownership in a start-up firm. A business partner may recognize some implications of a technology that have not been identified by the technical entrepreneur or, even if noted by them, may not have been viewed as feasible to follow-up until the suggestion came from the partner (Belitski et al., 2021).

Venture capital was originally organized in the United States as a corporation that made funds available for the early stages of firm formation in exchange for equity (Audretsch et al., 2021; Belitski et al., 2020).

More recently the definition of venture capital has been extended to buyouts and mergers. Since it typically takes as much time and effort to quantify a small or large investment, and since risk is expected to be lower in later stages, the private venture industry has been driven downstream, with the notable exception of the late 1990s Internet bubble. In the United States, public venture capital is typically considered an oxymoron, a contradiction in terms. Nevertheless, several federal and state government programs play the venture capitalist role, providing funds for firm formation, without taking equity. Government also played a significant role by changing the rules for investment in early-stage ventures. In Sweden, Israel, and Brazil, government jump-started the venture industry by setting up its own investment funds. Sweden also pioneered the role of foundations as quasi-public entities in venture capital.

Venture capital increases the likelihood of success in risky ventures by restructuring the relation between risk and reward in high-risk investing (Caiazza et al., 2021; Audretsch and Caiazza, 2016; Caiazza et al., 2020). On the one hand, by spreading the uncertainty of individual investments among various investors, the risk of catastrophic loss from any single new venture is reduced. On the other hand, by spreading an interest in the success that may arise from a few situations, or even one among a larger number of risky investments, the chance of gain from high-risk investing is improved. The venture capital firm introduced early-stage risky investing, with safeguards, to a broader constituency of universities, investment banks, and pension funds, traditionally oriented to lower-risk investing. Heretofore, only an extremely wealthy individual or family could provide some of the elements of the venture capital model, but even the Whitney and Rockefeller families soon chose to operate through professional venture capital entities.

The venture capital model also attempts to increase the chances of success in early-stage investing by professionalizing the search and selection process through an evaluation of the candidate firm's technology, management, and market prospects. In addition, once the selection process is completed, and if an investment is made, the venture firm seeks to increase the firm's chances of success through a "hands-on" involvement in its development by providing various kinds of advice and assistance, serving in effect as a "virtual incubator" for the nascent firm. The venture capital model also presumes an exit strategy within a reasonable time period with a clear idea for sale of the investment and distribution or reinvestment of the earnings, as opposed to a "holding company" that might seek to retain ownership in a group of companies.

THE REGIONAL RENEWAL ORIGINS OF THE VENTURE CAPITAL MODEL

The venture capital model was originally invented as a public/private format to achieve regional economic development objectives as well as financial returns (Etzkowitz, 2002). These dual objectives were formulated in the course of a regional economic development strategy formation process that took place during the 1930s within the New England Council, comprising the political, business, and academic leadership of the region.

The process began with attempts to implement traditional regional development strategies relying on tax policy, industry attraction, and reviving small and medium-sized enterprises (SMEs).

These strategies, relying on resources from a single institutional sphere, proved inadequate. They included (1) measures to lower taxes to "improve the business climate" undertaken by the political sphere, (2) initiatives on the part of local industrialists to persuade national automobile corporations to locate branch plants in the region, and (3) an attempt by MIT to establish a research unit to assist SMEs, an initiative that engendered insufficient support and interest and that the firms themselves were not in a condition to be able to effectively utilize.

When it was found that these strategies could not work, given the circumstances of the region, it was decided to focus upon the knowledge base of the region in its universities and colleges, which existed to a greater degree than in other parts of the United States. Several instances of high-tech firm formation from this academic base had already occurred by the 1920s, mostly from MIT.

However, to generalize these instances and systematize the capitalization of knowledge, gaps had to be filled such as providing business advice and seed capital to professors who might have commercializable technologies but lacked these other key elements that had heretofore been available only to a relatively few academics. This was the context in which a new organizational format was invented by academic, business, and governmental leaders, out of elements drawn from these institutional sources, in support of firm formation.

The very process of including actors from these various backgrounds in the strategy review and formulation process provided access to the resources required to implement the eventual plan. First, bringing the representatives of the three institutional spheres together in the Council provided an audience for Karl Compton, the president of MIT who, together with fellow MIT administrators, had formulated the concept of firm formation from academic research as an economic development strategy. This approach was based on extending an existing focus on "new products" as a possible basis of economic development, taking it one step further. By moving the "new product" approach from the industrial sphere and tying it to the academic research process, the MIT group, in effect, formulated a "linear model" of innovation.

Second, in addition to providing a receptive venue for the concept of firm formation from academia, the Council provided a venue for its specification as an organizational strategy. Compton had previously, and unsuccessfully, tried to introduce the general idea of science-based economic development at the national political level. However, it did not find a receptive audience due to prevailing views that too much new technology was possibly the cause of depression and unemployment. New England, with its history of industrial growth based on technological innovation, from at least the early 19th century provided an exception to the general rule of technological skepticism that was the prevailing ideology at the time.

Third, the New England Council provided a network to put the concept into effect. Several elements had to be brought together in order to invent the venture capital firm. These included changes in law to allow financial institutions to invest part of their capital in more risky ventures than previously allowed. Moreover, persons with technical expertise were needed to seek out and review candidate technologies for commercialization as well as individuals with business expertise to guide the firm-formation process. Finally, someone with an overview of all the elements of the process was required to knit these elements together into a coherent organization.

The individual elements were available in the region. The university–industry–government network created by the New England Council could call upon individuals such as Ralph Flanders, who had moved from the industrial sphere, as president of a Vermont tool company, to the political sphere, as Senator of Vermont, with an intervening stint as a member of the board of the Boston branch of the Federal Reserve Bank. Such persons were available to encourage the necessary legislation. MIT's senior faculty could be called upon as advisors to review candidate technologies and recent graduates could be hired as technology scouts. The Harvard Business School happened to have on its faculty a professor, Georges Doriot, who had taken an interest in new firm formation in contrast to the vast majority of the faculty who were focused on issues of existing, typically large, firms. Graduates, especially those who had taken his course in "manufacturing," could be recruited to work in an organization concerned with firm formation.

A university–industry–government network to promote regional development could be built on a substrate of academic institutions such as MIT that were already producing commercializable technologies and that already had experience in transferring technology to industry through consultation, patenting, and licensing. In addition, a business school, with a limited focus on entrepreneurship and entrepreneurial skills, was available. The necessary leadership to pull these elements together into a coherent organizational format was provided by Compton, operating within the context of the New England Council.

THE DIFFUSION OF VENTURE CAPITAL

The classic question of which came first, the chicken or the egg, can be answered with respect to the origins of venture capital in Silicon Valley. It was the start-up phenomenon that came first, in particular the emergence of the new firms from Fairchild Semiconductor in the 1960s. The original Draper firm was founded with the assistance of a federal Small Business Administration program to spread wide the New England phenomenon. Prospective firm founders also contacted sources of capital in New York City investment firms. When members of these firms, such as Arthur Rock, moved to northern California, to be close to the source of the new firms, a broad venture capital firm-formation process was initiated.

The early venture capital firm founders had a background in finance, although they soon became knowledgeable about the industries in which they were investing. The firm founders, on the other hand, started with a technical background, gaining business expertise as they developed their firms, typically bringing in persons with a business background to help grow the firm. Over time, a synthesis emerged with persons combining engineering and business skills becoming the prototypical Silicon Valley serial entrepreneur. More recently, some of these serial entrepreneurs have moved over to the financial side of the equation, joining venture capital firms as partners as well as entrepreneurs in residence, available to take leadership in a start-up funded by the venture firm (Etzkowitz and Leydesdorff, 1995).

Although there are notable exceptions, venture firms rarely provide funds at the so-called seed stage. Such funds are expected to come from associates of the firm founders, the so-called "FFF": friends, families, and fools. Even angel investors typically do not invest at the earliest stages of firm formation. They usually want to see a customer and revenues before they are willing to commit funds. They are business people and expect to use business, not technical, criteria in evaluating investment prospects. Business angels typically do not view universities as targets for investments and are not usually in touch with university technology transfer offices.

The business angel model works well for new firms that do not require a long technology development phase. Alternatively, the early stages of a firm may be informally incubated within a university research group. However, as with Google, this can cause tension between the open interchange of the group and the increasing wish of the proto-firm to keep its ideas to itself.

The tension is resolved as the firm moves outside of the university, but the transition period can be lengthened due to the pervasiveness of the informal process of firm formation, which works against establishing formal transition mechanisms such as incubator facilities that might speed the parturition process. Thus, even in regional environments like Silicon Valley, where informal processes work well from a business development perspective, formal transition mechanisms might be useful to manage conflicts of interest.

Lacking formal incubator facilities, firm formation from academia in Silicon Valley takes another route. The business angel gap in the early stages of creating a new firm from university-originated technology has been partially filled by a previous generation of academics who have earned funds from firm formation. These "university angels" are likely to have an excellent understanding of the technology and a good business sense of its potential given their previous experience. Thus, they are more likely to be willing to overlook the lack of revenues, customers, and even a clear business model that are the key requirements for the traditional angel community that, not surprisingly, requires clear business signals of potential success in order to invest.

Thus, with respect to Google, Andy Bechtolsheim – one of the founders of SUN, and a holder of a PhD from the Stanford Computer Science Department – became the university angel for its founders, at a point when their business model was not yet clear (Etzkowitz and Zhou, 2021).

Based on his commitment, the nascent firm was ready to negotiate for support from the venture capital community. The stamp of approval from a recognizable "brand name," whether a successful individual or firm, is crucial to gaining access to the networks that are such an important part of the firm-formation process in Silicon Valley (Etzkowitz and Zhou, 2018).

Such qualified introductions are crucial since time is a scarce commodity in a region where a multiplicity of potential firm founders are seeking access to capital and resources. The Silicon Valley paradox is that, at the same time it is widely considered there are too few good ideas available that are worth investing in, potential investors tend to focus on previously successful entrepreneurs and validated areas of activity. The learning process of a new area becoming validated for investment may be seen in the informal incubation process used by some angel groups in hosting nascent forms in an emerging field in their offices to become familiar with the new technology and its business model.

The venture capital industry is essentially an intermediary between several parties: sources of large blocks of funds such as pension funds, university endowments, insurance companies, and so on that have the capability to make large investments but not to break that investment decision down into smaller units. This is the role of the contemporary venture capital firm that is built into its structure, with its general and limited partners. The general partners provide the capital, in increasingly large amounts, while the limited partners provide the capabilities to judge and manage potential investments.

The search capabilities of the original venture capital model are less important, since so many opportunities are brought to the firm after undergoing an initial vetting process by angels. Indeed, the search function may be said to have been largely devolved to the other side of the equation since it is typically the firm founders who are searching for investments rather than the holders of funds actively seeking for investment opportunities. Nevertheless, in the division of labor between angels and venture capitalists, search functions persist, but they are increasingly formalized. For example, some angel groups require an introduction by one of their members for a nascent firm to be considered for review, while others require up-front payment of a fee to be entered into the review process of the group.

Symbiosis between Knowledge and Capital

A significant number of faculty members have adopted multiple objectives, "...to not only run a successful company ... and start a centre here [at the university that would become] internationally recognized but to retain their traditional role as 'individual investigator', directing a research group" (Etzkowitz, 2021, p. 30). An ideal-typical entrepreneurial scientist held that the "... interaction of constantly going back and forth from the field, to the university lab, to the industrial lab, has to happen all the time. These relationships involve different levels of commitment (financial and otherwise) by industrial sponsors, including the involvement of industrial sponsors in problem selection and research collaboration" (Etzkowitz, 2021, p. 30). As industrial sectors and universities move closer together, informal relationships and knowledge flows are increasingly overlaid by more intensive, formal institutional ties that arise from centers and joint projects (Etzkowitz, 2021). Firms formed by academics have been viewed in terms of their impact on the university, but they are also a "carrier" of academic values and practices into industry and, depending upon the arrangements agreed upon, a channel from industry back to the university. In these latter circumstances, traditional forms of academic–industry relations, such as consulting and liaison programs that encourage "knowledge flows" from academia to industry, become less important as an increasing number of large firms acquire academic start-ups for sources of new products. Many universities have built organizational capacities, aimed at venture creation and venture growth. Important to note before typifying and characterizing typical organizational functions is that successful venture creation environments, such as those around Stanford and MIT, today rely upon an entrepreneurial culture and network, rather than on formalized organizational capacities. In fact, apart from operating offices of technology licensing (OTLs) and entrepreneurship educational programs, these universities do not have operations, so much found at other places, such as incubators and science parks. As will be described in the Stanford case below, the OTL today actually operates with venture creation being the last alternative, once licensing the IP to established firms have been explored. Will younger entrepreneurial cultures, such as the ones nurtured in the two Swedish cases from Chalmers and Karolinska, also eventually evolve into such informal entrepreneurial networks – working next to and not within the university system? Or will the Stanford and MIT OTLs increasingly start to proactively manage venture creation, in order to utilize unexplored potentials in interrelating research and commercialization? Recent trends point at the latter alternative, making it important to also learn from cases not so proven as those of Stanford and MIT. In the last few years, a student group supported by Stanford's student government has expanded the informal start-up mentoring and coaching process into an experiential educational process that vets and mentors neophyte firms. The project was led by a recent graduate who had attempted to organize a firm as an undergraduate but realized that he lacked sufficient knowledge and skills. He found the entrepreneurial courses and assistance available on campus useful but insufficient to help him achieve his objective. The StartX initiative began from this premise and has developed from relatively modest beginnings as a student "lab" into a complex entrepreneurial support structure that has attracted significant resources, both human and financial. Filling a gap in a relatively strong support structure for spin-off activity in an already highly productive innovation system produced a significant increase in firm-formation activity at Stanford University in a short time (Etzkowitz, 2013). Within two years of its founding, 85% of the companies supported by StartX have successfully fundraised, representing over $88M in funding. StartX provides a Rolodex, if you will; it puts people in front of the right people and it's a great gateway for financing. Mentors also help by pointing investors to entrepreneurs and entrepreneurs to government grants. Indeed, StartX announced it is number two in the world in funding per start-up behind only Y Combinator. The student government originated StartX Accelerator showed that a significantly higher level of entrepreneurial activity was nascent in Stanford research groups and among students and faculty than was proceeding through the OTL process. However, to realize results from this underutilized capacity an explicit facilitative mentoring approach was required that is typically regularly available at aspiring entrepreneurial universities. Indeed, aspiring schools that have developed a variety of means to assist faculty and students' entrepreneurial and translational efforts may be an inspiration for Stanford's next steps. Thus, the University of California at San Francisco (UCSF) Mission Bay campus QB3 incubator may be a useful model for a similar project to fill Stanford's "wet lab" entrepreneurial support structure gap. It may be surprising to learn that there is a gap in entrepreneurial education at Stanford, the world's leading entrepreneurial university located in Silicon Valley, the world's leading entrepreneurial region. Indeed, Stanford administrators with responsibility for technology transfer believe that its unique location and the opportunities it offers makes it unnecessary for the university to take more explicit steps, commonplace at other universities, such as provision of an incubator facility. This laissez-faire attitude is encouraged by a pervasive empirical reality of serial faculty entrepreneurship, supported by the university's vast experience in technology transfer, through its OTL. A contemporary hands-off approach is paradoxically encouraged by a previous celebrated history of hands-on involvement by faculty members in facilitating technology start-ups. A "paradox of success" was hypothesized, but it is a phenomenon that is difficult to discern, let alone prove, since it posits the potential of a higher level of achievement in an already successful venue. The general attitude in the administration was that technology transfer at Stanford was working well, "it's not on our radar," and that, "if it is not broken don't fix it." Given the difficulty of proving a hypothetical, the question of whether Stanford's innovation system was sufficient or insufficient rested until 2010, when in the midst of the Great Recession, creating one's own job became an increasingly attractive employment strategy. While a direct relationship between economic conditions and "necessity entrepreneurship" is difficult to trace, it is perhaps not surprising that an increase in entrepreneurial activity occurs in academia during an era when degrees, especially the PhD, less often lead to academic employment. PhD students who are aware that the potential for future academic jobs, especially at a research-oriented university, has fallen into the single digits are also more open to an industrial career, including a start-up, even though they "... had not previously exhibited entrepreneurial inclinations" (Crawford, 2014). A program organized by the UCSF incubator facility, to coach PhD students in applying for Small Business Innovation Research (SBIR) grants, a funding source that can serve as the first step to firm formation, attracted larger numbers of students than expected and has become a regular source of firms for the incubator. Such student-originated firms often attract faculty members, who had not previously considered entrepreneurial ventures, to become involved, at least as advisors to the firms. Some faculty encourage their students to become involved in such entrepreneurship support programs as a way of "testing the waters" for their own involvement. A larger unrealized potential of US universities in contributing to economic development, going well beyond the Stanford case, may be hypothesized from the experience of the University of Utah. Operating from a much smaller funded research base than MIT and Stanford, Utah has the highest rate of firm formation in American universities. Utah views start-ups emanating from the university as part of its main mission, along with educating students and performing research, rather than as an accidental byproduct of these activities as is still commonplace at most universities. Participation in commercialization of research is credited in tenure and promotion proceedings, along with teaching and research. In contrast to schools where commercialization is de facto relegated to the post-tenure career stage, junior faculty are encouraged, rather than discouraged, to be entrepreneurial since it is part of the academic reward structure. Other faculty remain ambivalent, although the weight of opinion is shifting as holdouts in favorable fields like biotechnology follow their entrepreneurial colleagues at the University of California, San Diego in joining scientific advisory boards and taking further steps intrigued by the start-up experience which has become a new badge of scientific achievement and status. In the era of big data, opportunities are appearing across campus in the social sciences, where network analysis and social media analytics have opened up opportunities for firm formation. A French university incubator houses a start-up, spun-off from the performing arts department, that provides training in "improvisational theatre techniques" to organizations. Entrepreneurial activities have been undertaken by leading scientists who are viewed as role models. For example, a molecular biologist at a leading research university viewed his colleagues at Harvard who have formed firms with admiration and wished to emulate them. However, the willingness of a few "low-status" scientists to use findings for pecuniary advantage would likely have been taken as evidence of "deviance." If such normative infractions were negatively sanctioned, they would likely have served to strengthen the old normative pattern. However, participating in the formation of a firm has come to be positively defined as a new badge of scientific achievement.

CONCLUSION ON SMART SPECIALIZATION VERSUS INSIGHTFUL DIVERSIFICATION

There is continuing debate over the relative emphasis to be placed on renewal of existing industries versus creation of new ones as a regional economic and social development strategy. The former strategy tends to focus on firms, with the university as a subsidiary element, supplying existing knowledge; while in the latter strategy the university is the core providing advanced knowledge with commercial potential. The relative balance is dependent upon the potential of firms for renewal, on the one hand, and on the availability of universities with advanced commercializable knowledge, on the other. While some regions, given their overwhelming preponderance of resources or inertia, go in one direction or the other, many find a relative balance between the two fundamental strategies of specialization and diversification. A surrounding region filled with firms that have grown out of the university provides a significant impetus to future entrepreneurial activity.

REFERENCES

Audretsch, D., Belitski, M., and Caiazza, R. (2021). Start-ups, innovation and knowledge spill-overs, *Journal of Technology Transfer*, 46, 1995–2016.

Audretsch, D.B., and Caiazza, R. (2016). Technology transfer and entrepreneurship: Cross-national analysis, *Journal of Technology Transfer*, 41(6), 1247–1259.

Belitski, M., Caiazza, R., and Lehmann, E.E. (2021). Knowledge frontiers and boundaries in entrepreneurship research, *Small Business Economics*, 56, 521–531.

Belitski, M., Caiazza, R., and Rodionova, Y. (2020). Investment in training and skills for innovation within entrepreneurial start-ups firms and incumbents: Evidence from the United Kingdom, *International Entrepreneurship and Management Journal*, 16(2), 617–640.

Caiazza, R., Belitski, M., and Audretsch, D. (2020). From latent to emergent entrepreneurship: The knowledge spillover construction circle, *Journal of Technology Transfer*, 45, 694–704.

Caiazza, R., Phan, P., Lehman, H., and Etzcowitz, H. (2021). An absorptive capacity-based systems view of Covid-19 in the small business economy, *International Entrepreneurship and Management Journal*, 17, 1419–1439.

Crawford, C. (2014). Socio-economic differences in university outcomes in the UK: Drop-out, degree completion and degree class. IFS Working Papers No. W14/31.

Etzkowitz, H. (2002). *MIT and the Rise of Entrepreneurial Science*. London: Routledge.

Etzkowitz, H. (2013). StartX and the "paradox of success": Filling the gap in Stanford's entrepreneurial culture, *Social Science Information*, 52(4), 605–627.

Etzkowitz, H. (2021). The movement from incubator to incubation in the entrepreneurial university: Past, present and future. In S.A. Mian, M. Klofsten, and W. Lamine (eds.), *Handbook of Research on Business and Technology Incubation and Acceleration* (pp. 64–78). Cheltenham, UK and Northampton, MA, USA: Edward Elgar Publishing.

Etzkowitz, H., and Leydesdorff, L. (1995). The Triple Helix – university–industry–government relations: A laboratory for knowledge based economic development, *EASST Review*, 14(1), 14–19.

Etzkowitz, H., and Zhou, C. (2018). Innovation incommensurability and the science park, *R&D Management*, 48(1), 73–87.

Etzkowitz, H., and Zhou, C. (2021). Licensing life: The evolution of Stanford University's technology transfer practice, *Technological Forecasting and Social Change*, 168, 120764.

8. Public sector entrepreneurship, principal investigators, and entrepreneurial effectuation

James A. Cunningham, Matthias Menter, and Kayleigh Watson

1. INTRODUCTION

Publicly funded principal investigators (PIs) have been the focus of increasing empirical attention, as they are at the nexus of entrepreneurial ecosystems (see Cunningham et al., 2016; Mangematin et al., 2014; Menter, 2016). In being awarded large-scale research funding through public sector entrepreneurship (PSE) programs, scientists take on the PI role, which imposes additional managerial and leadership responsibilities as well as corresponding compliance with different governance mechanisms on these lead researchers (Cunningham et al., 2015b). Hence, funded PIs play crucial management roles in the governance, implementation, and realization of large-scale public research programs (Cunningham et al., 2015a, b; O'Kane et al., 2015; Romano et al., 2017). In formulating and delivering on PSE research programs that meet funders' requirements, PIs are becoming key agents of economic and social change (Carl, 2020).

In order to be successful in securing PSE funding, scientists in the PI role need to effectuate their own institutional environment and other entrepreneurial ecosystem stakeholders to shape their decision making and behaviors. PIs need to conceptualize value creation in developing a funding bid and to realize value in the delivery that can endure beyond the formal ending of a project. To be effective in delivering publicly funded PSE programs, PIs need to interact with key stakeholders internally and externally to their institutional setting to enhance their own resource and capital bases as well as to refine and shape delivery from scientific, knowledge transfer, and commercialization fronts. In effectuating, PIs are responding to value drivers in their own environment and the value creation expectation that they have to deliver for multiple stakeholders for their publicly funded entrepreneurship programs. Given the importance of PSE programs for the advancement of knowledge and the wider social, economic, and technological impacts that they can generate, there is a need to better understand at the micro level how PIs effectuate during a PSE project cycle. In a practical sense, the COVID-19 pandemic has highlighted the relevance of scientists responding to and participating in large-scale national and international research programs.

The purpose of this chapter is to develop an organizing conceptual framework of PI effectuation for PSE programs within an entrepreneurial ecosystem, considering that PIs effectuate their entrepreneurial ecosystem through all stages of a funded research project. Thus, PIs engage in notional co-creation during the conceptualization phase, then move towards actual value creation and actualization during the project implementation phase, and exploit and extract value during the project closure phase and beyond. As PIs may seek to commercially exploit new knowledge through further public funding mechanisms, we posit an iterative cycle, suggesting that the project closure phase might be followed by another project conceptualization phase. Based on our framework, we emphasize the interrelationships of PSE programs and derive policy recommendations on how to effectively set up respective programs.

The remainder of this chapter is organized as follows. Section 2 provides an overview on PSE programs and is followed by Section 3 that focuses on the emerging and growing literature on PIs. Section 4 details the concept of entrepreneurial effectuation. Section 5 develops our organizing conceptual framework. A final section concludes.

2.   PUBLIC SECTOR ENTREPRENEURSHIP PROGRAMS AND ENTREPRENEURIAL ECOSYSTEMS

Technological innovation constitutes a major force in economic growth, yet is based on entrepreneurial activities (Acs and Audretsch, 1988; Acs and Szerb, 2007; Wennekers and Thurik, 1999; Wong et al., 2005). Policy makers have therefore initiated PSE programs to encourage respective actions by creating a stimulating environment within which entrepreneurial behavior can arise (Leyden and Link, 2015). Leyden (2016: 557) describes PSE programs as public policy initiatives which "generate greater economic prosperity by transforming a status quo economic environment into one that is more conducive to individuals in either the public sector or the private sector engaging in greater innovative activities in the face of uncertainty".

Entrepreneurship policies try to facilitate knowledge spillovers and respective value creation by creating ecosystems which encourage entrepreneurial behavior, especially through financial subsidies, such as the US Small Business Technology Transfer (STTR) program or the US Small Business Innovation

Research (SBIR) program (Qian and Haynes, 2014), the Science Enterprise Challenge (SEC) and the University Challenge Fund (UCF) in the UK (Tomes, 2003), the French "Law on Innovation and Research to Promote the Creation of Innovative Technology Companies" (Mustar and Wright, 2010), the "Leading-Edge Cluster Competition" in Germany (Audretsch et al., 2016), or the German "Excellence Initiative" (Menter et al., 2018; Cunningham and Menter, 2021). In order to be effective, all entrepreneurship policies have to consider the respective context, as one-size-fits-all policies are likely to fail (Autio et al., 2014). Initiatives supporting scientific excellence and technological innovation should therefore consider the institutional context and provide targeted support to create and enhance respective conducive environments (Cunningham et al., 2019a).

The literature characterizes the respective ecosystems as national systems of innovation which are mainly driven by institutions (see Acs et al., 2017). However, this perspective does not take the actual value creation processes on the micro level into account, which recently led to a more appropriate concept, the national systems of entrepreneurship framework, with a main focus on individuals (see Acs et al., 2016). Some of the emerging literature on entrepreneurial ecosystems acknowledges the role that PIs play in both creating value and managing complex governance relationships (Cunningham et al., 2018; 2019b). It is the PI who bridges the gap between industry and academia and contributes to the exploitation of new knowledge that can be exploited by entrepreneurial ecosystem stakeholders. Ultimately, entrepreneurial ecosystems shall thereby exert positive externalities in terms of economic, technological, and societal impacts (Audretsch et al., 2019; Audretsch and Belitski, 2017).

3.   PRINCIPAL INVESTIGATORS

PIs are core and critical actors in transforming scientific, economic, and societal environments. PIs constitute the linchpin of the program-based organization as they are the individuals who are developing research projects to fit within programs (Mangematin et al., 2014) and thereby enact their environment, shape new organizations, and impact the technology transfer process (Boardman and Ponomariov, 2014; Cunningham et al., 2014). While producing scientific results, PIs shape new trajectories in their scientific domain, thus combining inputs from various actors within and beyond academia to finally enable the creation of value (Casati and Genet, 2014). Given their role, they can create strong linkages with industry whereby the country's culture also contributes to their entrepreneurial orientations (see Del Giudice et al., 2017). Furthermore, there are some gender differences in terms of publishing (Salerno et al., 2019), grant funding success (Oliveria et al., 2019), and technology transfer (Cunningham et al., 2017). Kidwell (2013) describes PIs as knowledge brokers that have to make strategic choices in relation to their workplace and the organization boundaries that they will span. Hence, Casati and Genet (2014) characterize PIs as scientific entrepreneurs who shape new paradigms and reshape existing boundaries.

Scientists are increasingly pressured by their institutions to acquire research funding through PSE programs. To achieve this, PIs create value for stakeholders through their boundary spanning and brokering activities (O'Kane et al., 2020b). At the micro level, PIs need to develop competencies in their role (Cunningham and Menter, 2020). Foncubierta-Rodríguez et al. (2020) identify these as research, innovation, and critical skills, research and performance ability, and research knowledge. Similarly, Cunningham and O'Reilly (2019) posit that scientists in the PI role have threshold responsibilities with respect to research leadership, innovation facilitator, boundary spanner, project coordinator, research allocator, and controller. They state that the PIs' role capabilities also encompass being an economic agent, technology transfer enabler, research strategist, value creation leader, manager, and governor.

Empirical studies to date highlight that, to be successful, publicly funded PIs need to effectuate different stakeholders and environments in order to meet the heightened expectations from funders, industry, and their own institutions as well as to realize their own envisioned scientific mission. Effectuation thereby relates to "a logic of entrepreneurial expertise, a dynamic and interactive process of creating new artifacts in the world" (Sarasvathy, 2008: 6). PIs thereby engage with actors outside academia to articulate scientific as well as societal and economic impact (Baglieri and Lorenzoni, 2014; Boehm and Hogan, 2014; Casati and Genet, 2014; Kidwell, 2013). Prior commercial experience of the PI can support their effectuating approaches when they are collaborating with industry partners (Cunningham et al., 2020). Moreover, such boundary spanning enables PIs to expand their opportunity recognition and identify potential opportunities that are relevant and important to industry in terms of enhancing firms' competitiveness (Cunningham, 2019). In doing this, scientists in the PI role experience role violation, and according to O'Kane et al. (2020a), their role identity comprises four roles: (1) science networker, (2) research contractor, (3) project manager, and (4) entrepreneur.

While previous studies have highlighted the positive benefits of close collaborations between universities and industry, some studies have emphasized that certain conditions need to be in place. For example, Leyden and Link (2015) posit that universities should structure their support programs so that the costs of collaborations are lower and firm revenues increase. The lack of access to universities' equipment can constitute barriers for firms in engaging with universities (see Cunningham and Link, 2014; Bozeman et al., 2013) and university involvement in intellectual property (IP) matters can be problematic

(Hertzfeld et al., 2006). From a university perspective, scientists in the PI role experience barriers in collaborating effectively with industry and other external partners as well as effectuating their environment (Cunningham et al., 2014). In particular, personal relationships, asset scarcity, and proximity issues are barriers for PIs' collaborations with small and medium-sized enterprises (SMEs; O'Reilly and Cunningham, 2017). Furthermore, O'Kane et al. (2017) find that funding bodies and commercialization support at the university are perceived barriers to commercialization among PIs. To overcome these perceived barriers within universities, technology transfer office (TTO) professionals are building stronger relationships with PIs to overcome some of the commercialization knowledge and expertise gaps they have (O'Kane, 2018; O'Kane et al., 2021). PIs' participation in a dedicated university research center/institute can thereby support technology transfer and research commercialization activities (Dolan et al., 2019). Such supports are critical as technology and knowledge transfer continues to be a barrier for scientists in the PI role (Cunningham et al., 2020). In summary, PIs learn the role on the job (Cunningham et al., 2014). Therefore, PIs need to effectuate within and outside their institutional environment to advance their research ambitions as well as to create value for the stakeholders involved in collaborating with them in these endeavors.

4.   ENTREPRENEURIAL EFFECTUATION

Effectuation privileges the iterative emergence rather than the predetermination of goals (Berends et al., 2014; Harmeling, 2008; Sarasvathy, 2001). It is strongly linked with the creation of opportunities utilizing personal resources (Maine et al., 2015; Sarasvathy, 2008). To this end, effectuation is traditionally presented as the inverse of the causation approach, whereby predetermined goals dictate the systematic selection of resources and pursuit of activities, which has commonly been used to explain entrepreneurial activity (Sarasvathy and Dew, 2005).

It has been deemed that effectuation offers a highly relevant explanation of entrepreneurial actions being undertaken by a range of entrepreneurial actors in a growing variety of contexts (Fisher, 2012; Watson, 2013). Namely, expert entrepreneurs (Dew et al., 2009; Sarasvathy, 2008) and novice entrepreneurs within new venture creation (Alsos et al., 2016; Björklund and Krueger, 2016; Gabrielsson and Politis, 2011) as well as those engaged in R&D (Brettel et al., 2012), new product innovation (Coviello and Joseph, 2012), and internationalization endeavors (Kalinic et al., 2014; Sarasvathy et al., 2014).

The behaviors which underpin an effectual approach are not as well understood as might be hoped (Fisher, 2012; Perry et al., 2012). However, there are several common strands of activity pursued by the entrepreneurial actors as

part of an effectual approach which can be observed within the extant literature. First, the consideration of means personally held; second, engagement in
experimentation; and third, pursuit of pre-commitments.

The entrepreneurial actor initially decides what is possible through active
assessment of the personal means they have readily available. An initial
appraisal of the means held is guided through answering three central questions: *"who am I?"*, *"what do I know?"*, and *"who do I know?"* (Sarasvathy,
2001). To answer the question *"who am I?"* entails the entrepreneurial actor
considering their identity (Watson, 2013) and aspects such as traits, attributes, tastes, values, preferences, passions, and interests (Sarasvathy, 2008).
Responding to the *"what do I know?"* question involves consideration of existing knowledge and skill-sets which have been gained through prior experience
and education and which might now be utilized (Berends et al., 2014; Maine
et al., 2015). Addressing the *"who do I know?"* question necessitates thought
be given to the professional and personal networks to which they belong and
in particular those contacts who they could draw from in terms of experience,
expertise, and further contacts, but also funding opportunities (Watson, 2013).

To progress the consideration of the means which are currently held entails
the entrepreneurial actor identifying aspects of these means which could be
mobilized to progress a new venture (Sarasvathy, 2008). For example, with
reference to using personal means held to access funding to progress a particular venture, this might involve the entrepreneurial actor utilizing prior
understanding of potential funding sources and knowledge about people who
might be able to help (Maine et al., 2015). The entrepreneurial actor creatively
recombines different aspects of their means; an example might be particular
knowledge of a sector with training previously undertaken, so as to develop
a distinctive offering (Fisher, 2012). Experimentation is a key facet of the
endeavor to find the best use for the means held (Chandler et al., 2011; Perry
et al., 2012). Such experimentation is a reoccurring behavior associated with
an effectuation approach, enabling the iterative development and refinement
of ideas as the entrepreneurial actors expand their repertoire of means through
action (Berends et al., 2014).

It is through experimental activity that the entrepreneurial actor finds a way
forward (Chandler et al., 2011). The results of experimentation are observed
carefully, with new insights gained used to inform the direction of subsequent
action (Chandler et al., 2011). It follows that continual learning is an important
endeavor associated with effectuation and allows flexibility, particularly in
the face of any frequently changing external demands (Sarasvathy, 2001)
and unforeseen events (Dew et al., 2009). Such is the experimental nature of
effectual endeavor that decisions around what course of action to take and
what resources to commit are made on the basis of what the entrepreneurial
actor is prepared to lose (Fisher, 2012). The courses of action pursued are those

which are not deemed resource intensive and the preference is usually to utilize external resources wherever possible (Berends et al., 2014). Activity which constrains the ability to be flexible and adaptable in response to unforeseen events and the generation of new knowledge is eschewed (Fisher, 2012). It is only through realizing results that further resources are committed (Chandler et al., 2011).

The co-creation of an opportunity in collaboration and partnership with others is an important dimension of effectual behavior (Chandler et al., 2011; Read et al., 2009; Sarasvathy, 2008). The entrepreneurial actor pursues pre-commitments to their emergent offering from other individuals and organizations in their broader community, forging alliances with those who they envisage they can work with and who might have an interest (Fisher, 2012). Examples might include potential competitors, customers, suppliers (Chandler et al., 2011), previous collaborators (Maine et al., 2015), and those in the broader entrepreneurial ecosystem (Björklund and Krueger, 2016), but also non-human actors (Murdock and Varnes, 2018). It follows that as new actors are brought on board the project evolves (Murdock and Varnes, 2018).

Interaction between the entrepreneurial actor and other parties directs action (Harmeling, 2008), makes a project tangible (Björklund and Krueger, 2016), enables the sharing, exchanging, and testing of ideas as well as the acquisition of feedback (Fisher, 2012), and facilitates the raising of funds to progress an opportunity further (Maine et al., 2015). The experience, abilities, knowledge, skills, and networks which are held by co-opted parties are also valuably used to expand the range of means which the entrepreneurial actor can subsequently draw upon to further refine and shape the offering (Björklund and Krueger, 2016; Wiltbank et al., 2009). Henceforth entrepreneurs re-evaluate their means as they interact with others that are stakeholders in a given project (Sarasvathy and Dew, 2005). Such behavior also serves to reduce the uncertainty of the project (Brettel et al., 2012; Fisher, 2012) through the sharing of responsibility (Chandler et al., 2011).

The antecedents of effectual behavior, although not very well elucidated (Perry et al., 2012), can be viewed as grounded in the entrepreneurial actors' need for pragmatism (Sarasvathy, 2001; Watson, 2013). Effectuation serves as an intuitive approach which responds to a need for flexibility (Chandler et al., 2011) in dynamic and non-linear environments when the immediate future is highly uncertain and precise objectives are unknown or ambiguous (Matalamäki, 2017; Sarasvathy, 2001; Sarasvathy and Dew, 2005; Wiltbank et al., 2006). In such situations, the strategic principles of prediction and control commonly associated with causation would be unfeasible and inappropriate (Read et al., 2009). Within resource-constrained environments, effectuation behaviors are considered less resource intensive than attempting to assemble what one does not already have ready access to (Whalen and Holloway, 2012).

5.   AN ORGANIZING CONCEPTUAL MODEL OF PI ENTREPRENEURIAL EFFECTUATION

Within the context of PSE programs, our conceptual framework brings together value drivers and resources, effectuation, as well as value creation, actualization, exploitation, and extraction from the *project conceptualization phase*, that is, the pre-funding stage, to the *project implementation phase*, that is, the funding stage of PSE programs, and the *project closure phase*, that is, the post-funding stage (see Figure 8.1).

At the *project conceptualization* stage of PSE programs, PIs are responding to value drivers that they are experiencing in their own institutional setting or in their scientific domain as well as values drivers that are being driven externally. This could be for example responding to new funding calls from funding bodies. Internal value drivers that PIs need to respond to include institutional norms with respect to individual annual funding, scientific outputs, and maintaining lab space and equipment as well as maintaining or growing scientific teams and collaborations with firms. These internal drivers may trigger scientists to consider their means as part of their own effectuation – the *"who am I?"*, *"what do I know?"*, and *"who do I know?"*. External value drivers may be derived from government policy and funding initiatives that are mandating and requiring greater interactions and engagement with industry partners – SMEs and multinational corporations (MNCs) or public sector bodies. Effectuation reflection focusing on means may focus more on *"who do I know?"* for the scientists in order to begin the process of configuring the optimal research team and partnership so as to secure the competitive funding. The assembling of the optimal research team may go beyond the scientists' own discipline domain. During the conceptualization phase of PSE programs, PIs have a duality of focus in responding to the most pressing value drivers and effectuating with respect to their own resources and that of collaborators that would create value through a PSE program proposal. In essence, their effectual approach at the project conceptualization phase will involve interactions with relevant triple helix stakeholders to create value, to maximize their chances of success, but also to reduce potential project uncertainties.

PIs are in essence harnessing their own resources, environments, and networks to respond to and shape PSE programs and to co-create value with relevant stakeholders to make project proposals relevant, effective, and attractive to reviewers and PSE funders and finally successful. This phase is less resource intensive and it involves commitments of relevant individual stakeholders to purse a common purpose that is articulated in a project proposal that is designed to address the requirements. PIs require an environment that enables them to leverage internal and external resources and create synergistic networks, to finally engage in notional co-creation. Thus, PIs cannot act independently from their environment but have to consider all the relevant actors of their entrepreneurial ecosystem.

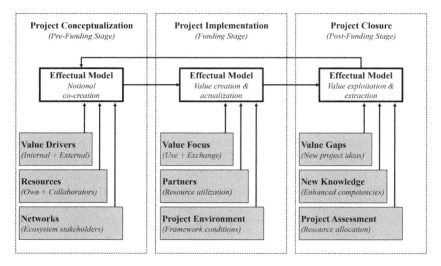

Figure 8.1   An organizing conceptual framework of PI effectuation for PSE programs

Once a PSE project has been funded, the effectual model that PIs adopt focuses on working with relevant partners to ensure value is actually created and actualized. This is the *project implementation* phase. The value focus may thereby be either on "use" or on "exchange", depending on the PSE project's purpose and objectives. This means that PIs are drawing on earlier effectuation approaches and partner-signaled involvement to expand their resource base in the project proposal phase to now ensure that those resources will be utilized in the delivery of the PSE-funded project. Due to the shift from conceptualization towards implementation, the PI's effectual model moves from notional co-created value at the project conceptualization phase to creating and actualizing value at the implementation phase to meet articulated project objectives. The value creation focus – "use" or "exchange" – is outlined and defined in the project proposal, but the emphasis may change as the project evolves and value drivers may change the value focus for the project, the team, and the PI. Of course, the project environment affects project implementation. Thus, framework conditions need to be constantly evaluated and shaped by PIs to ensure actual value creation. This project phase may also involve the combination of PIs' personal effectuation with some engagement with experimentation given the nature of the funded research being undertaken. If scientists have previously occupied the role of a PI, they can contribute to positive project dynamics. Moreover, it means that PIs can draw on their personal effectuation – the *"what do I know?"* – in order to lead a funded project from a scientific and research management perspective. Also, PIs can draw on other stakeholders within or outside the funded project in order to support their individual effectuation effects and that of the project.

In the course of *project closure* – the post-funding stage – PIs may be aware of value gaps that constitute the starting point for further project ideas to continue on their envisioned scientific trajectory. Initiating a new project further enhances their personal effectuation. In some instances, depending on the circumstances of the discipline and other considerations, the PI may initiate a new project during the project implementation phase, rather than waiting until the project closure stage. Depending on the motivations of the PI, the availability of financial resources, and local support, the PI may pursue a technology transfer mechanism to exploit and extract value from the new knowledge created. Their personal effectuation with respect to previous experience of research commercialization is a contributing factor as to whether value that has been potentially created in the project implementation phase can be exploited effectively. Moreover, the generated new knowledge complemented with enhanced competencies like industry experience may thereby support value exploitation and extraction and leverage the PI's personal effectuation. Reflecting on the last project may stimulate a more efficient resource allocation, more effective management, and better leadership behaviors and actions for subsequent projects. In other words, scientists, given their experience in the PI role, build their personal effectuation – the *"who am I?"* and *"what do I know?"*. They in essence become more effective serial PIs through building upon their own personal effectuation, which combined with enhanced networks bolsters the *"who do I know?"* that is necessary for the project conceptualization and implementation phases. Due to this iterative character, the project closure phase may end up in a new project conceptualization phase.

6.   CONCLUSION

The purpose of this chapter was to develop an organizing conceptual framework of PI effectuation for PSE programs that could be used as a basis for future empirical studies. Having an in-depth knowledge and understanding of the effectuating models of PIs is essential given the strategic importance of PSE programs in supporting economic, social, and technological developments. The chapter provides a conceptual frame for how universities, funding agencies, and other relevant stakeholders can plan and best support the formation and development of PIs to meet the growing expectations of entrepreneurial ecosystem stakeholders.

Our organizing conceptual framework provides two main policy considerations. First, in the operationalization of PSE programs, policy makers should take a holistic view of the various project stages and consider how scientists in the PI role effectuate to deliver their intended objectives. If there is for example a lack of financial support available to PIs at the project closure phase, their personal effectuation may not be sufficient to drive technology transfer and research commercialization. Therefore, policy makers need to ensure that policy instruments are appropriate and sufficient, addressing these types of issues that can constrain and inhibit PIs from realizing economic, social, and technological impacts.

Second, our conceptual model emphasizes how the design of PSE programs enhances the necessary effectuation activities of PIs. For example, from a practical perspective, policy makers need to ensure that PSE programs enhance PIs' effectuation in mobilizing the best configuration of ecosystem partners at the project conceptualization stage, that is, adding new partners and expertise during the project implementation phase from their entrepreneurial ecosystem. In essence, the PI is the agent for the policy maker/funder (see Cunningham et al., 2018). Therefore, such programs need to be designed to be as supportive as possible for PIs' effectuation throughout the project lifecycle.

For PIs, our conceptual model provides a means to reflect on their own effectual behaviors and actions through the project lifecycle of a PSE program. Through such a reflection, PIs can explore how they could further enhance their effectuation for PSE programs, but also for other aspects of their professional role. Furthermore, we posit that our conceptual model could be used to support the development of future PIs as part of their professional development activities. In this context, universities need to consider what tangible support they have in place to support PIs and enhance their effectuating behaviors (see Cunningham et al., 2021).

Our conceptual framework model may stimulate empirical investigations that provide insights into the effectuating behaviors and approaches of PIs that can be imitated by others, particularly those scientists that are early-career researchers. Future studies should focus on effectual approaches across different institutional settings and missions and across different domain areas and research centers/institutes, considering the project conceptualization phase, the project implementation phase, and the project closure phase. There is also scope to undertake further studies that examine the effectual approach from first grant holder PIs right through to serial PIs in different contexts and institutional settings – universities, public research organizations, private firms – and to take a gender and equality perspective to such empirical investigations into account.

REFERENCES

Acs, Z. J., and Audretsch, D. B. (1988). Innovation in large and small firms: an empirical analysis. *American Economic Review*, 78(4), 678–690.

Acs, Z. J., Audretsch, D. B., Lehmann, E. E., and Licht, G. (2016). National systems of entrepreneurship. *Small Business Economics*, 46(4), 527–535.

Acs, Z. J., Audretsch, D. B., Lehmann, E. E., and Licht, G. (2017). National systems of innovation. *Journal of Technology Transfer*, 42(5), 997–1008.

Acs, Z. J., and Szerb, L. (2007). Entrepreneurship, economic growth and public policy. *Small Business Economics*, 28(2–3), 109–122.

Alsos, G. A., Clausen, T. H., Hytti, U., and Solvoll, S. (2016). Entrepreneurs' social identity and the preference of causal and effectual behaviours in start-up processes. *Entrepreneurship and Regional Development*, 28(3/4), 234–258.

Audretsch, D. B., and Belitski, M. (2017). Entrepreneurial ecosystems in cities: establishing the framework conditions. *Journal of Technology Transfer*, 42(5), 1030–1051.

Audretsch, D. B., Cunningham, J. A., Kuratko, D. F., Lehmann, E. E., and Menter, M. (2019). Entrepreneurial ecosystems: economic, technological, and societal impacts. *Journal of Technology Transfer*, 44(2), 313–325.

Audretsch, D. B., Lehmann, E. E., and Menter, M. (2016). Public cluster policy and new venture creation. *Journal of International Business and Economy*, 43(4), 357–381.

Autio, E., Kenney, M., Mustar, P., Siegel, D., and Wright, M. (2014). Entrepreneurial innovation: the importance of context. *Research Policy*, 43(7), 1097–1108.

Baglieri, D., and Lorenzoni, G. (2014). Closing the distance between academia and market: experimentation and user entrepreneurial processes. *Journal of Technology Transfer*, 39(1) 52–74.

Berends, H., Jelinek, M., Reymen, I., and Stultiëns, R. (2014). Product innovation processes in small firms: combining entrepreneurial effectuation and managerial causation. *Journal of Product Innovation Management*, 31(3), 616–635.

Björklund, T. A., and Krueger, N. F. (2016). Generating resources through co-evolution of entrepreneurs and ecosystems. *Journal of Enterprising Communities*, 10(4), 477–498.

Boardman, C., and Ponomariov, B. (2014). Management knowledge and the organization of team science in university research centers. *Journal of Technology Transfer*, 39(1), 75–92.

Boehm, D. N., and Hogan, T. (2014). "A jack of all trades": the role of PIs in the establishment and management of collaborative networks in scientific knowledge commercialisation. *Journal of Technology Transfer*, 39(1), 134–149.

Bozeman, B., Fay, D., and Slade, C. P. (2013). Research collaboration in universities and academic entrepreneurship: the-state-of-the-art. *Journal of Technology Transfer*, 38(1), 1–67.

Brettel, M., Mauer, R., Engelen, A., and Küpper, D. (2012). Corporate effectuation: entrepreneurial action and its impact on R&D project performance. *Journal of Business Venturing*, 27(2), 167–184.

Carl, J. (2020). From technological to social innovation – the changing role of principal investigators within entrepreneurial ecosystems. *Journal of Management Development*, 39(5), 739–752.

Casati, A., and Genet, C. (2014). Principal investigators as scientific entrepreneurs. *Journal of Technology Transfer*, 39(1), 11–32.

Chandler, G. N., DeTienne, D. R., McKelvie, A., and Mumford, T. V. (2011). Causation and effectuation processes: a validation study. *Journal of Business Venturing, 26*(3), 375–390.

Coviello, N. E., and Joseph, R. M. (2012). Creating major innovations with customers: insights from small and young technology firms. *Journal of Marketing, 76*(6), 87–104.

Cunningham, J. A. (2019). Principal investigators and boundary spanning entrepreneurial opportunity recognition: a conceptual framework. In D. B. Audretsch, E. E. Lehmann, and A. N. Link (eds.), *A Research Agenda for Entrepreneurship and Innovation*, pp. 55–73. Cheltenham, UK and Northampton, MA, USA: Edward Elgar Publishing.

Cunningham, J. A., Dolan, B., Menter, M., O'Kane, C., and O'Reilly, P. (2020). How principal investigators' commercial experience influences technology transfer and market impacts. *Research-Technology Management, 63*(5), 49–58.

Cunningham, J. A., Lehmann, E. E., and Menter, M. (2021). The organizational architecture of entrepreneurial universities across the stages of entrepreneurship: a conceptual framework. *Small Business Economics*, 1–17. DOI:10.1007/s11187-021-00513-5

Cunningham, J. A., Lehmann, E. E., Menter, M., and Seitz, N. (2019a). The impact of university focused technology transfer policies on regional innovation and entrepreneurship. *Journal of Technology Transfer, 44*(5), 1451–1475.

Cunningham, J. A., and Link, A. N. (2014). Fostering university–industry R&D collaborations in European Union countries. *International Entrepreneurship and Management Journal, 11*(4), 849–860.

Cunningham, J. A., Mangematin, V., O'Kane, C., and O'Reilly, P. (2015a). At the frontiers of scientific advancement: the factors that influence scientists to become or choose to become publicly funded principal investigators. *Journal of Technology Transfer, 41*(1), 778–797.

Cunningham, J. A., and Menter, M. (2020). Micro-level academic entrepreneurship: a research agenda. *Journal of Management Development, 39*(5), 581–598.

Cunningham, J. A., and Menter, M. (2021). Transformative change in higher education: entrepreneurial universities and high-technology entrepreneurship. *Industry and Innovation, 28*(3), 343–364.

Cunningham, J. A., Menter, M., and O'Kane, C. (2018). Value creation in the quadruple helix: a micro level conceptual model of principal investigators as value creators. *R&D Management, 48*(1), 136–147.

Cunningham, J. A., Menter, M., and Wirsching, K. (2019b). Entrepreneurial ecosystem governance: a principal investigator-centered governance framework. *Small Business Economics, 52*(2), 545–562.

Cunningham, J. A., and O'Reilly, P. (2019). *Roles and Responsibilities of Project Coordinators: A Contingency Model for Project Coordinator Effectiveness.* JRC Technical Reports JRC117576. In V. Van Roy, and D. Nepelski (eds.), EUR 29869 EN, Publications Office of the European Union, Luxembourg, ISBN 978-92-76-11711-7 (online). DOI:10.2760/55062

Cunningham, J. A., O'Reilly, P., Dolan, B., O'Kane, C., and Mangematin, V. (2017). Gender differences and academic entrepreneurship: a study of scientists in the principal investigator role. In A. N. Link (ed.), *Gender and Entrepreneurial Activity*, pp. 221–251. Cheltenham, UK and Northampton, MA, USA: Edward Elgar Publishing.

Cunningham, J. A., O'Reilly, P., O'Kane, C., and Mangematin, V. (2014). The inhibiting factors that principal investigators experience in leading publicly funded research. *Journal of Technology Transfer*, *39*(1), 93–110.

Cunningham, J. A., O'Reilly, P., O'Kane, C., and Mangematin, V. (2015b). Managerial challenges of publicly funded principal investigators. *International Journal of Technology Management*, *68*(3–4), 176–202.

Cunningham, J. A., O'Reilly, P., O'Kane, C., and Mangematin, V. (2016). Publicly funded principal investigators as transformative agents of public sector entrepreneurship. In D. B. Audretsch, and A. N. Link (eds.), *Essays in Public Sector Entrepreneurship*, pp. 67–94. Heidelberg: Springer.

Del Giudice, M., Nicotra, M., Romano, M., and Schillaci, C. E. (2017). Entrepreneurial performance of principal investigators and country culture: relations and influences. *Journal of Technology Transfer*, *42*(2), 320–337.

Dew, N., Read, S., Sarasvathy, S. D., and Wiltbank, R. (2009). Effectual versus predictive logics in entrepreneurial decision-making: differences between experts and novices. *Journal of Business Venturing*, *24*(4), 287–309.

Dolan, B., Cunningham, J. A., Menter, M., and McGregor, C. (2019). The role and function of cooperative research centers in entrepreneurial universities. *Management Decision*, *57*(12), 3406–3425.

Fisher, G. (2012). Effectuation, causation, and bricolage: a behavioral comparison of emerging theories in entrepreneurship research. *Entrepreneurship Theory and Practice*, *36*(5), 1019–1051.

Foncubierta-Rodríguez, M. J., Martín-Alcázar, F., and Perea-Vicente, J. L. (2020). Measuring the human capital of scientists in the principal investigator role. *Journal of Management Development*, *39*(5), 777–790.

Gabrielsson, J., and Politis, D. (2011). Career motives and entrepreneurial decision-making: examining preferences for causal and effectual logics in the early stage of new ventures. *Small Business Economics*, *36*(3), 281–298.

Harmeling, S. S. (2008). That my neighbor's cow might live: effectuation and entrepreneurship education in Croatia. *International Journal of Entrepreneurship Education*, *6*, 23–42.

Hertzfeld, H. R., Link, A. N., and Vonortas, N. S. (2006). Intellectual property protection mechanisms in research partnerships. *Research Policy*, *35*(6), 825–838.

Kalinic, I., Sarasvathy, S., and Forza, C. (2014). Expect the unexpected: implications of effectual logic on the internationalization process. *International Business Review*, *23*(3), 635–647.

Kidwell, D. K. (2013). Principal investigators as knowledge brokers: a multiple case study of the creative actions of PIs in entrepreneurial science. *Technological Forecasting and Social Change*, *80*(2), 212–220.

Leyden, D. P. (2016). Public-sector entrepreneurship and the creation of a sustainable innovative economy. *Small Business Economics*, *46*(4), 553–564.

Leyden, D. P., and Link, A. N. (2015). *Public Sector Entrepreneurship: US Technology and Innovation Policy*. Oxford: Oxford University Press.

Maine, E., Soh, P., and Dos Santos, N. (2015). The role of entrepreneurial decision-making in opportunity creation and recognition. *Technovation*, *29/30*, 53–72.

Mangematin, V., O'Reilly, P., and Cunningham, J. A. (2014). PIs as boundary spanners, science and market shapers. *Journal of Technology Transfer*, *39*(1), 1–10.

Matalamäki, M. J. (2017). Effectuation, an emerging theory of entrepreneurship – towards a mature stage of the development. *Journal of Small Business and Enterprise Development, 24*(4), 928–949.

Menter, M. (2016). Principal investigators and the commercialization of knowledge. In D. B. Audretsch, E. E. Lehmann, M. Meoli, and S. Vismara (eds.), *University Evolution, Entrepreneurial Activity and Regional Competitiveness*, pp. 193–203. Heidelberg: Springer.

Menter, M., Lehmann, E. E., and Klarl, T. (2018). In search of excellence: a case study of the first excellence initiative of Germany. *Journal of Business Economics, 88*(9), 1105–1132.

Murdock, K., and Varnes, C. J. (2018). Beyond effectuation: analysing the transformation of business ideas into ventures using actor-network theory. *International Journal of Entrepreneurial Behavior and Research, 24*(1), 256–272.

Mustar, P., and Wright, M. (2010). Convergence or path dependency in policies to foster the creation of university spin-off firms? A comparison of France and the United Kingdom. *Journal of Technology Transfer, 35*(1), 42–65.

O'Kane, C. (2018). Technology transfer executives' backwards integration: an examination of interactions between university technology transfer executives and principal investigators. *Technovation, 76,* 64–77.

O'Kane, C., Cunningham, J. A., Mangematin, V., and O'Reilly, P. (2015). Underpinning strategic behaviours and posture of principal investigators in transition/uncertain environments, *Long Range Planning, 48*(3), 200–214.

O'Kane, C., Cunningham, J. A., Menter, M., and Walton, S. (2021). The brokering role of technology transfer offices within entrepreneurial ecosystems: an investigation of macro–meso–micro factors. *Journal of Technology Transfer, 46*(6), 1814–1844.

O'Kane, C., Mangematin, V., Zhang, J. A., and Cunningham, J. A. (2020a). How university-based principal investigators shape a hybrid role identity. *Technological Forecasting and Social Change, 159,* 120179.

O'Kane, C., Zhang, J. A., Cunningham, J. A., and Dooley, L. (2020b). Value capture mechanisms in publicly funded research. *Industrial Marketing Management, 90,* 400–416.

O'Kane, C., Zhang, J. A., Cunningham, J. A., and O'Reilly, P. (2017). What factors inhibit publicly funded principal investigators' commercialization activities? *Small Enterprise Research, 24*(3), 215–232.

Oliveira, D. F., Ma, Y., Woodruff, T. K., and Uzzi, B. (2019). Comparison of National Institutes of Health grant amounts to first-time male and female principal investigators. *Journal of the American Medical Association (JAMA), 321*(9), 898–900.

O'Reilly, P., and Cunningham, J. A. (2017). Enablers and barriers to university technology transfer engagements with small- and medium-sized enterprises: perspectives of principal investigators. *Small Enterprise Research, 24*(3), 274–289.

Perry, J. T., Chandler, G. N., and Markova, G. (2012). Entrepreneurial effectuation: a review and suggestions for future research. *Entrepreneurship Theory and Practice, 36*(4), 837–861.

Qian, H., and Haynes, K. E. (2014). Beyond innovation: the Small Business Innovation Research program as entrepreneurship policy. *Journal of Technology Transfer, 39*(4), 524–543.

Read, S., Dew, N., Sarasvathy, S. D., and Wiltbank, R. (2009). Marketing under uncertainty: the logic of an effectual approach. *Journal of Marketing, 73*(3), 1–18.

Romano, M., Elita Schillaci, C., and Nicotra, M. (2017). Principal investigators in entrepreneurial universities: a research framework. In D. Siegel (ed.), *The World*

Scientific Reference on Entrepreneurship: Volume 1: Entrepreneurial Universities: Technology and Knowledge Transfer, pp. 165–184. World Scientific Reference on Innovation.

Salerno, P. E., Páez-Vacas, M., Guayasamin, J. M., and Stynoski, J. L. (2019). Male principal investigators (almost) don't publish with women in ecology and zoology. *PloS ONE, 14*(6), e0218598.

Sarasvathy, S. D. (2001). Causation and effectuation: toward a theoretical shift from economic inevitability to entrepreneurial contingency. *Academy of Management Review, 26*(2), 243–263.

Sarasvathy, S. D. (2008). *Effectuation: Elements of Entrepreneurial Expertise.* Cheltenham, UK and Northampton, MA, USA: Edward Elgar Publishing.

Sarasvathy, S. D., and Dew, N. (2005). New market creation as transformation. *Journal of Evolutionary Economics, 15*(5), 533–565.

Sarasvathy, S., Kumar, K., York, J. G., and Bhagavatula, S. (2014). An effectual approach to international entrepreneurship: overlaps, challenges, and provocative possibilities. *Entrepreneurship Theory and Practice, 38*(1), 71–93.

Tomes, A. (2003). UK government science policy: the "enterprise deficit" fallacy. *Technovation, 23*(10), 785–792.

Watson, T. J. (2013). Entrepreneurship in action: bringing together the individual, organizational and institutional dimensions of entrepreneurial action. *Entrepreneurship and Regional Development, 25*(5–6), 404–422.

Wennekers, S., and Thurik, R. (1999). Linking entrepreneurship and economic growth. *Small Business Economics, 13*(1), 27–56.

Whalen, P. S., and Holloway, S. S. (2012). Effectual marketing planning for new ventures. *Academy of Marketing Science (AMS) Review, 2*, 34–43.

Wiltbank, R., Dew, N., Read, S., and Sarasvathy, S. D. (2006). What to do next? The case for non-predictive strategy. *Strategic Management Journal, 27*(10), 981–998.

Wiltbank, R., Sudek, R., and Read, S. (2009). The role of prediction in new venture investing. *Frontiers of Entrepreneurship Research, 29*(2), 1–12.

Wong, P. K., Ho, Y. P., and Autio, E. (2005). Entrepreneurship, innovation and economic growth: evidence from GEM data. *Small Business Economics, 24*(3), 335–350.

9. A systematic literature review of reward-based crowdfunding

Wendy Chen

INTRODUCTION

> Crowdfunding is an innovation in entrepreneurial finance that can fuel "the Rise of
> the Rest" globally. – World Bank, 2013

Entrepreneurship is a noteworthy source of innovation and economic development (Dees, 2012; Drucker, 1985; Schumpeter, 1934; Kirzner, 1973). One major challenge that almost all entrepreneurs and organizations face is the procurement of financial resources to implement their ideas (Bergamini et al., 2017; Chan and Parhankangas, 2017; Cosh et al., 2009; Crosetto and Regner, 2018; Dimov and Murray, 2008; Lehner, 2013). To address this issue, digital crowdfunding has emerged in the recent decade as a vital alternative financing source (Agrawal et al., 2015; Ordanini et al., 2011; Schwienbacher and Larralde, 2012). This new form of financing allows entrepreneurs to use the Internet to seek funds for their innovative projects, social initiatives, and other specific purposes directly from the public (the "crowd") (Gafni et al., 2019b; Meyskens and Bird, 2015; Mollick, 2014).

In contrast to traditional funding methods including bank loans, venture capital, donations, and so on, crowdfunding is widely praised for its democratic and decentralized features (Mollick and Robb, 2016; Sorenson et al., 2016; Stevenson et al., 2019). Through online crowdfunding platforms that connect entrepreneurs with potential backers, individual entrepreneurs can not only receive funds from their family, friends, and the general public but also solicit feedback from them (Agrawal et al., 2015; Belleflamme et al., 2014; Kuppuswamy and Bayus, 2013; Mollick, 2014; Scholz, 2015; Short et al., 2017). Crowdfunding allows entrepreneurs to have easier access to the funds necessary to fuel their ventures and assume lower financial risks and liability themselves (Berns et al., 2020). In addition, crowdfunding gives backers a way to mitigate their risk by investing small amounts for promising ideas so they can play the part of investors in the creation of new ventures that they would otherwise be unable to invest in (Kitchens and Torrence, 2012; Meric et al., 2015; Valanciene and Jegeleviciute, 2013). As a result, crowdfunding has gained growing attention from entrepreneurs, startups in particular, and researchers (Chan and Parhankangas, 2017; Mollick and Kuppuswamy, 2014).

The early crowdfunding platforms, such as ArtistShare and Kickstarter, were designed mainly to help artists finance their projects (Greenberg and Mollick, 2014). Subsequently, different types of crowdfunding platforms emerged that targeted different audiences, enabling more entrepreneurs to engage with their prospective backers across other domains.

There are four major types of crowdfunding, including reward-based crowdfunding, peer-to-peer lending, donation-based crowdfunding, and equity-based crowdfunding (Ahlers et al., 2015; Belleflamme et al., 2014; Kappel, 2009; Kuti and Madarász, 2014). Peer-to-peer lending such as Kiva focuses on lending small amounts of money for basic commodities to individuals who are oftentimes located in the Global South (Berns et al., 2020). Meanwhile, donation-based crowdfunding platforms such as GoFundMe focus primarily on providing support to individuals who are experiencing hardships of some sort or nonprofits seeking funds for their operations (Salido-Andres et al., 2019). Equity-based crowdfunding such as Crowdfunder is used exclusively for businesses who are seeking to use an alternative to traditional bank loans or venture capital investment to start or grow their business with an emphasis on profit maximization. Reward-based crowdfunding is unique in the sense that it embraces both social and commercial logics, making it the most versatile and popular of the four types of crowdfunding and, for these reasons, is the focus of this study (Alegre and Moleskis, 2019; Cholakova and Clarysse, 2015; Colgren, 2014; Cox and Nguyen, 2018; Profatilov et al., 2015). Through this type of crowdfunding, backers receive some kind of reward in exchange for their financial support for the project. This reward might be a discount for the purchase of the product/service which the project owner is raising money for or nonmonetary types of appreciation, like a thank-you note (Colombo et al., 2015; Liu and Liu, 2016; Schwienbacher and Larralde, 2010).

Because entrepreneurs are allowed to give their backers tangible or intangible rewards, entrepreneurs have more latitude to decide what types of rewards to give to backers instead of giving away equity or paying interest to investors, which makes reward-based crowdfunding more appealing to entrepreneurs (Gallemore et al., 2019; Liu, 2014; Mollick and Kuppuswamy, 2014).

Nevertheless, because reward-based crowdfunding can be used to support many different types of entrepreneurial projects, it is ambiguous and unclear to many. As a result, despite its popularity, reward-based crowdfunding is not very well understood (André et al., 2017; Colombo et al., 2015). Therefore, it is important to produce a structured systematic literature review on this topic.

This literature review differs from previous reviews on crowdfunding in several ways. First, prior reviews tend to focus on a very small number of high-impact and highly cited articles or do not differentiate among different types of crowdfunding. For instance, Short et al. (2017) focused on 21 papers and Lepola and Kärkkäinen (2017) reviewed 15. Alegre and Moleskis (2019) used journal impact factors to include only 63 crowdfunding papers for their examination. However, although crowdfunding is a relatively new phenomenon, it has been examined by researchers from a variety of perspectives. Therefore, reporting the general status of the crowdfunding literature based on only a small number of articles may not properly reflect the current status of crowdfunding research.

In addition, most reviews available on crowdfunding discuss crowdfunding research as a whole while disregarding the heterogeneity of different types of crowdfunding (e.g., Butticè et al., 2018a; Short et al., 2017). Nevertheless, as previously mentioned, each of the four major types of crowdfunding serves different purposes, and while they share the common trait of raising money from the crowd, their differences in structure and design attract different entrepreneurs and backers (Cumming and Hornuf, 2018; Scholz, 2015). Therefore, not considering the heterogeneity among crowdfunding types in literature reviews may prevent entrepreneurs and researchers from having a thorough understanding of the intricacies associated with specific types of crowdfunding.

Moreover, previous literature reviews focused only on select disciplines while omitting the findings from others. While many of the studies are from a business or economic perspective, there are still many other disciplines that explore it as well, including information science, public and nonprofit administration, the arts, and so on. However, so far, literature reviews on crowdfunding are mainly based on articles published in business journals.

Lastly, existing literature reviews on crowdfunding have only covered a short time span (e.g., Moritz and Block, 2016). Nevertheless, crowdfunding behavior is likely to have evolved over time. Therefore, a review of a short span of crowdfunding research might not be able to provide a holistic and developmental view of crowdfunding research.

To my knowledge, this is the first systematic literature review devoted solely to understanding reward-based crowdfunding. It covers the largest number of articles, the longest period of time, and the most industries and academic disciplines. This review seeks to aid future researchers who are interested in studying crowdfunding. However, it aims not only at benefiting scholars, who are interested in crowdfunding research in general, but also entrepreneurs, organizations, and policymakers, who can gain insights from the studies reviewed in this chapter that will help increase entrepreneurs' fundraising success and yield new policies to help venture financing.

This chapter starts with a discussion of the methodological approach used to build the database for this systematic literature review. This is followed by a summary of the findings from the articles reviewed including details about the number of reward-based crowdfunding studies over time classified by theoretical and empirical research, the disciplines of the crowdfunding researchers, the geographical settings of the research, the crowdfunding platforms used in the empirical studies, and the four research questions examined in reward-based crowdfunding. This literature review ends with a discussion of directions for future research and the challenges that future research may encounter.

METHODOLOGICAL APPROACH

A systematic literature review is a powerful tool to synthesize and report on evidence-based practice in a specific subject matter (Briner et al., 2009; Tranfield et al., 2003). To conduct a thorough literature review that reflects the most up-to-date status of the reward-based crowdfunding research, this chapter took several steps to locate the relevant existing literature and to develop a database of literature for this review.

First, research shows that crowdfunding involves multiple elements including (1) the definition of crowdfunding as an alternative financing and philanthropic mechanism; (2) entrepreneurs from different sectors that seek funds from the public; (3) crowdfunding backers who financially contribute to crowdfunding projects; and (4) crowdfunding platforms that act as multi-sided intermediaries to connect backers and entrepreneurs (Golić, 2014; Seghers et al., 2012; Schwienbacher and Larralde, 2012; Stemler, 2013). On these crowdfunding platforms, entrepreneurs post their crowdfunding campaigns that introduce their projects through a project title, description, target goal amount (i.e., the amount that the entrepreneur intends to raise from the crowd), rewards for backers, and other optional information that may attract backers (Butticè et al., 2018a). Although these are the key elements involved with crowdfunding, crowdfunding platforms and researchers use different terms to describe them. I therefore made a search term list with multiple possible key words for each of the four crowdfunding elements (Table 9.1). Using the key words in the list, I searched the major academic research databases including ProQuest, Sage, EBSCO, IEEE, Elsevier, AIM/Inform, ScienceDirect, Springer, PubMed, Taylor & Francis, Web of Science, and Wiley that cover journals in almost all subjects. The results from this search include academic journal articles, books, book chapters, and peer-reviewed conference proceedings from multiple disciplines including economics, business, computer science, environmental science, law, sociology, public and nonprofit management, and so on.

Next, I removed the duplicates from the first-round search and refined the search results to include only papers that were relevant to enhancing the understanding of reward-based crowdfunding. Put differently, papers exclusively

Table 9.1   Search terms by the reward-based crowdfunding elements

Crowdfunding elements	Search terms
Concept of crowdfunding	crowdfunding
	crowd funding
	crowdinvesting
	crowd + financing
	crowd-based financing
	crowd-based funding
	reward-based financing
	philanthropy + online
	philanthropy + platform
	online + giving
	giving + platform
	fintech
	entrepreneurial financing
	funding + startup
	funding + project
	funding + enterprise
	funding + nonprofit
	funding + public administration
	invest + online
	invest + platform
Entrepreneur	creator + platform
	project initiator + platform
	entrepreneur + platform
	online + fundraiser
Backer	crowdfunder
	backer
	online donor
	online contributor
	project supporters
	online funder
Crowdfunding platform	crowdsourcing platform
	platform economy
	online marketplace
	Kickstarter
	Indiegogo

studying equity-based crowdfunding, donation-based crowdfunding, or char-itable giving through traditional methods, and those about venture capital financing, were excluded from the analysis. Also, technical papers on the com-puter science and technical specifications of crowdfunding were not included in the database. Research published in languages other than English were also removed at this point, although they were used earlier to discover possible additional references in English.

Notably, due to the newness of crowdfunding, many research articles have not yet been published by academic journals. Therefore, I used Google Scholar and the Social Science Research Network (SSRN) as well as the National Bureau of Economic Research (NBER) to find additional unpublished but open-access articles with the same search terms.

After this round of search, I used the snowball strategy to locate the references cited in those articles that had not yet been included in this review and the articles that cited the sources already included in the review database. Finally, I included the conference proceedings and abstracts from the top academic conferences from different disciplines that may have interest in research on crowdfunding including the Academy of Management (AOM), Association for Research on Nonprofit Organizations and Voluntary Action (ARNOVA), American Economic Association (AEA), Academy of Entrepreneurial Finance (AEF), Institute of Electrical and Electronics Engineers (IEEE), and so on. After these searches, I read the entirety of the articles in the database and only kept the articles directly related to reward-based crowdfunding.

In total, these procedures yielded a final sample of 301 academic works, including 258 journal articles, 8 books, 14 book chapters, and 21 peer-reviewed conference proceedings. The publications reviewed in this paper span from the beginning of digital crowdfunding in 2009 up to March 2020. Through the aforementioned search methods, the results of the search serve as the foundation for this chapter.

Following recent systematic literature reviews like Rousseau et al. (2008), Maier et al. (2016), and Alegre and Moleskis (2019), I coded the publications in detail with the following items: (1) author(s); (2) title of the article; (3) name of the journal; (4) year of the publication; (5) discipline; (6) type of the publication (e.g., peer-reviewed journal article, book, book chapter, or conference proceedings); (7) characteristics of the article (e.g., empirical paper, literature review, or theoretical paper); (8) research question(s); (9) major theory/theories; (10) data sources, including the country, crowdfunding platform, year, and sample size; (11) research methods; and (12) key findings and contributions. The next section summarizes the findings from this systematic literature review.

FINDINGS FROM THE ARTICLES REVIEWED

This section reports on the findings from the 301 academic works reviewed pertaining to reward-based crowdfunding from 2009 to March 2020. The literature review studies reward-based crowdfunding from multiple perspectives including time, discipline, geographical setting, and the platforms used as the empirical setting. More specifically, it presents the overall trend of reward-based crowdfunding research over the years. After that, this review describes the reward-based crowdfunding research by discipline followed by the geographical settings as well as the crowdfunding platforms used for reward-based crowdfunding research. Next, this literature review identifies the four major research questions examined in the extant research and their findings.

Number of Reward-Based Crowdfunding Studies Over Time

With the largest collection of extant research on reward-based crowdfunding research, this literature review first clearly delineates the growing number of reward-based crowdfunding studies over the last decade (Figure 9.1). From one academic work in 2009 when the two largest reward-based crowdfunding platforms Kickstarter and Indiegogo were just launched to almost 60 papers on reward-based crowdfunding research in 2019, this research stream has experienced an exponential growth. Interestingly, when reward-based crowdfunding research just started, there were more conceptual or theoretical works. However, as the field has become more mature, in recent years there has been a growing number of empirical studies (Figure 9.2).

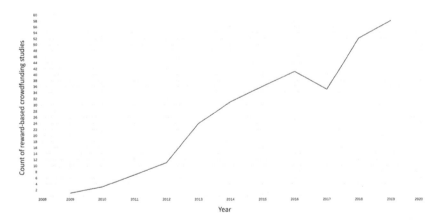

Figure 9.1   Reward-based crowdfunding research over time

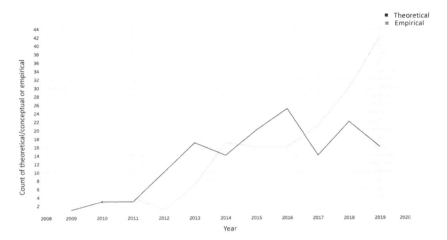

Figure 9.2   Theoretical vs. empirical crowdfunding research over time

Reward-Based Crowdfunding Research by Discipline and Type of Publication

Although crowdfunding research has drawn increased interest from academia, studies are predominantly concentrated in the business and entrepreneurship, information science, and economics and finance disciplines. Figure 9.3 presents the number of reward-based crowdfunding research papers by discipline. Of all the academic works reviewed, the largest percentage – about half – are from the business and entrepreneurship discipline followed by information science and economics and finance. Academic journals like the *Journal of Business Venturing*, *Entrepreneurship Theory and Practice*, and *Small Business Economics*, which target startup businesses, are some of the common outlets that publish crowdfunding research.

Geographical Settings for Crowdfunding Research

According to the Technavio Research Report, the crowdfunding market will see a growth of $89.72 billion with a 17 percent increase from 2018 to 2022 globally.[1] The World Bank (2013) has highlighted crowdfunding's potential for the developing world. As new technology provides developing areas with Internet connectivity, the small businesses and organizations in these areas stand to benefit in the form of external funding. Indeed, crowdfunding market reports in countries like Brazil, China, India, Poland, Russia, Switzerland, and Turkey exhibit an increasing number of crowdfunding campaigns (Chaston

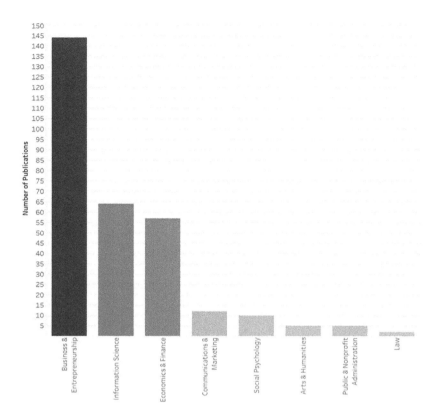

Figure 9.3   Reward-based crowdfunding research by discipline

and Scott, 2012; Demiray and Burnaz, 2019; Dietrich and Amrein, 2017; Motylska-Kuzma, 2018). However, although reward-based crowdfunding is a global phenomenon, a predominant number of extant studies have used the US as an empirical setting. Therefore, there is very limited understanding of crowdfunding in other countries. In other words, there is a lack of under-standing of the differences in crowdfunding practices between developing and developed countries (Makýšová and Vaceková, 2017).

While crowdfunding research may lack geographical diversity, Mourao et al. (2018) studied a Brazilian reward-based crowdfunding platform Kickante that targets the Latino market. In addition, Ilenkov and Kapustina (2018) discussed two of the largest crowdfunding platforms in Russia where they provided general descriptive statistics including the types of projects, the amount raised, the number of backers, and the success rate. Even so, very few

Table 9.2   *Geographical settings of reward-based crowdfunding research*

Country	Examples
Brazil	Mourao et al. (2018)
Czech Republic	Makýšová and Vaceková (2017)
China	Xie et al. (2019); Zheng et al. (2014)
France	André et al. (2017); Petitjean (2018)
Germany	Crosetto and Regner (2018)
Italy	Giudici et al. (2013)
Mexico	Madrazo-Lemarroy et al. (2019)
the Netherlands	Agrawal et al. (2015)
Poland	Motylska-Kuzma (2018)
Portugal	Bilau and Pires (2018)
Russia	Ilenkov and Kapustina (2018)
Spain	Rey-Martí et al. (2019)
UK	Cosh et al. (2009)
US	Kuppuswamy and Bayus (2017); Mollick (2014)

studies, including Dushnitsky and Fitza (2018) and Zheng et al. (2014), have really tried to link crowdfunding with an area's local culture or compare different crowdfunding practices across different cultural regions. Although most studies did not exclusively focus on a particular region, Table 9.2 presents the geographical settings of reward-based crowdfunding research that were explicitly studied with an example study or two for each country.

Crowdfunding Platforms Used in the Empirical Studies

The number of reward-based crowdfunding platforms has been growing all around the world (Massolution, 2015; The World Bank, 2013). Despite this diversity of reward-based platforms, this review finds that over 90 percent of the extant studies have used Kickstarter as their empirical setting for their studies. It is worth noting that reward-based crowdfunding platforms differ from each other in various aspects. For instance, Kickstarter is an all-or-nothing business model, meaning that if a crowdfunding campaign is not successful (i.e., does not reach its initial goal amount for the campaign fundraising), the entrepreneur will not receive anything. In contrast, if an entrepreneur starts a campaign on the Indiegogo platform, even if the campaign is not successful, he/she can still receive the collected funds from the crowd. Table 9.3 presents the leading reward-based crowdfunding platforms that have been

Table 9.3   *Leading crowdfunding platforms studied in the empirical studies*

Platform	Description	Examples
Kickstarter	Launched in 2009 in the US with an "All-or-Nothing" model. Heavily focuses on creative projects and other commercial projects.	Colombo et al. (2015); Mollick (2014); Kromidha and Robson (2016); Kuppuswamy and Bayus (2017); van de Rijt et al. (2014); Younkin and Kuppuswamy (2018)
Indiegogo	Launched in 2009 in the US. Entrepreneurs are allowed to keep the amount that they collect from the crowd regardless of whether the amount raised meets their initial target goal or not. Supports all types of projects.	Gallemore et al. (2019); Chen (2018)
Ulule	Headquartered in France in 2010, Ulule seeks to aid creators, citizens, nonprofits, and companies to help build a better society. Uses an "All-or-Nothing" model.	André et al. (2017)
Startnext	Launched in 2010 in Germany with an "All-or-Nothing" model, but project creators are allowed to openly donate to their own projects (self-funding). Supports all types of projects.	Crosetto and Regner (2018); Crosetto and Regner (2014)

empirically studied in academic journals, including Kickstarter, Indiegogo, Ulule, and Startnext.

Kickstarter was founded in New York in 2009 and has helped over 179,000 projects successfully raise funding for their idea.[2] Largely focused on creative works, Kickstarter's mission is to "help bring creative projects to life" and to democratize the art and entertainment world.[3] The company became a Public Benefit Corporation in 2015, meaning it seeks to provide societal benefit on top of shareholder value and company profits.[4] Kickstarter has served as the launching pad for highly successful projects such as Pebble, a smart watch company, which raised over $300 million and helped Kickstarter and crowdfunding gain popularity (Mitra and Gilbert, 2014).

Despite the strict rules of Kickstarter, it is the largest reward-based crowdfunding platform, and thus has attracted the most attention from crowdfunding researchers. Researchers have used Kickstarter as the empirical setting to examine the innovativeness of projects, donors' motivation, determinants of campaign success, and so on (Defazio et al., 2020; Elkhidir, 2017; Mollick, 2014).

Indiegogo is the second largest reward-based international crowdfunding platform based in the US. Started out of necessity by one of the founders who was trying to raise money to produce a play, Indiegogo helps a broad range of projects including technology-related, consumer goods, community-based, and socially oriented projects (Chen, 2020). Since 2008, the platform has helped "more than 800,000 projects get funded and has more than nine million backers in over 235 countries." As of 2019, Indiegogo averages roughly 19,000 campaign launches a month.[5] In contrast to Kickstarter's all-or-nothing business model, Indiegogo gives entrepreneurs the flexibility to choose to keep the amount that has been pledged by the public for their projects.[6] Also, compared to Kickstarter, which mainly focuses on creative and technology works, Indiegogo has specific categories devoted to projects that support community development and other social causes, which gives social entrepreneurs and nonprofit organizations more opportunity to raise their funds (Chen, 2018). Although Indiegogo is a very popular crowdfunding platform used by a large number of entrepreneurs, organizations, and backers, it is not well studied in academic research (Chen, 2018; Gallemore et al., 2019).

Ulule is one of Europe's leading reward-based crowdfunding platforms. Headquartered in France, Ulule seeks to aid creators, citizens, nonprofits, and companies to help build a better world that is "more diverse, more sustainable, and open to all."[7] To that end, many of the projects on the platform are social enterprises, operating as businesses with a social end in mind. Similar to other reward-based crowdfunding platforms, Ulule allows backers to review the details of a project and select which perk they would like to purchase. Using the Ulule crowdfunding platform as the empirical setting, studies found that users on this platform form relationships based on the "reciprocal giving" logic[8] (André et al., 2017).

Startnext, which was launched in 2010, is the largest crowdfunding platform in Germany (Crosetto and Regner, 2014, 2018). Similar to the Kickstarter business model, Startnext also follows an all-or-nothing model. However, although self-funding is allowed on other platforms as well, researchers were particularly interested in studying self-funded projects on this platform. Researchers found that about 9 percent of the total pledge amount for projects was actually provided by entrepreneurs themselves (Crosetto and Regner, 2018). In addition, research shows that communication between entrepreneurs and their backers especially matters toward the end of the campaign.

Other than the well-known platforms like Kickstarter and Indiegogo, there are many other reward-based crowdfunding platforms such as Crowdfunder in the UK, Pozible in Australia, Vision Bakery in Germany, RocketHub and Patreon in the US, and Thunderfund in South Africa. These platforms are largely similar to their well-known US counterparts, meaning studies of crowdfunding platforms such as Indiegogo are likely to be globally representative in many ways, especially considering project owners and backers can come from any country. However, the adoption rate and unique regional characteristics that may impact crowdfunding performance, backers' behavior, and so on in these other countries have yet to be examined.

Major Research Questions Examined in Reward-Based Crowdfunding

This systematic review reveals that the extant crowdfunding research has primarily focused on four research questions:

1. What are the factors that lead to a project's crowdfunding campaign success?
2. What motivates backers to financially support crowdfunding projects?
3. Why do entrepreneurs and organizations use crowdfunding?
4. How does crowdfunding affect ventures' entrepreneurial performance?

Of these questions, the first one investigating the success factors for a crowdfunding campaign has received the most scholarly interest. The main findings for each of these questions is reported below.

What are the factors that lead to a project's crowdfunding campaign success?

To date, most empirical research in reward-based crowdfunding has centered on investigating why some crowdfunding campaigns are more successful than others (André et al., 2017). Interestingly, since crowdfunding success has been defined differently by various theories, research on this question has yielded different results (Butticè et al., 2018a; Short et al., 2017).

The extant reward-based crowdfunding research has identified three major factors that lead to a crowdfunding project's success: (1) entrepreneurs' (i.e., project creators') social and territorial capital; (2) a crowdfunding campaign's narrative; and (3) entrepreneurs' personal traits or characteristics. Table 9.4 presents these factors with examples.

Table 9.4   Factors of crowdfunding success

Factors	Examples
Entrepreneurs' social and territorial capital	Agrawal et al. (2013); Colombo et al. (2015); Giudici et al. (2013); Josefy et al. (2017); Kang et al. (2017); Mollick (2014)
Crowdfunding campaign's narrative	Allison et al. (2017); Bi et al. (2017); Copeland (2015); Jancenelle et al. (2017); Kromidha and Robson (2016); Manning and Bejarano (2017); Marom and Sade (2013); Parhankangas and Renko (2017); Thies et al. (2016); Wessel et al. (2016)
Entrepreneurs' personal traits or characteristics	Anglin et al. (2018b); Gorbatai and Nelson (2015); Greenberg and Mollick (2017); Younkin and Kuppuswamy (2018)

Factor 1: Entrepreneurs' social and territorial capital

Multiple researchers have found that entrepreneurs' social capital is one of the key determinants of the success of a crowdfunding campaign (Colombo et al., 2015; Fan-Osuala et al., 2017; Mollick, 2014; Skirnevskiy et al., 2017). Social capital is a concept that originated in sociology (Coleman, 1998). It is defined as "the sum of the actual and potential resources embedded within, available through, and derived from the social structure that facilitates exchange and social interactions" (Dolfsma et al., 2009, p. 316).

In the extant crowdfunding literature, the effect of both internal and external social capital on crowdfunding success has been explored (Colombo et al., 2015; Saxton and Wang, 2014; Skirnevskiy et al., 2017). In terms of entrepreneurs' external social capital (family, friends, Facebook friends, etc.), researchers have found that an entrepreneur's existing social network plays a significant role if the backers are new to crowdfunding (Agrawal et al., 2015; Ordanini et al., 2011; Zheng et al., 2014). As Kuppuswamy and Bayus's (2013) research showed from the Kickstarter data, family members usually give to entrepreneurs during the first week a crowdfunding campaign is live. Similarly, Mollick (2014) found that the number of friends on an entrepreneur's Facebook page has a positive relationship with the amount of money that he/she raises in a crowdfunding campaign. Similar findings on external social capital and crowdfunding campaign success have been demonstrated in other cultural settings like China, Italy, and the Netherlands (Giudici et al., 2018; Song and van Boeschoten, 2015; Zhao and Vinig, 2020; Zheng et al., 2014).

Crowdfunding has a high degree of information asymmetry and uncertainty. Therefore, it is hard to predict whether a campaign will be successful and whether a backer will receive the reward or product that the entrepreneur or organization has promised to its backers, since backers are usually unfamiliar with the skillsets and trustworthiness of the entrepreneurs (André et al., 2017; Cordova et al., 2015; Mollick, 2014). Some reward-based crowdfunding platforms allow entrepreneurs to keep their full pledge amount raised from the crowd regardless of whether the campaign reached its funding goal. Although this type of business model can incentivize entrepreneurs and help them to implement their ideas, it does not provide a safety net for backers. As a result, entrepreneurs often first seek funds from their own social networks – including their family and friends – to generate a project's initial traction.

Different from external social capital, which represents individuals' existing social network, internal social capital is obtained through online interactions between entrepreneurs and their backers within crowdfunding platforms (Skirnevskiy et al., 2017). Research has shown that entrepreneurs who are backed by others on crowdfunding platforms are more likely to return the favor to those backers when they launch their own crowdfunding campaigns (Zheng et al., 2014). However, external and internal social capital intertwine with each other. In other words, there is a spillover effect of social capital on social media. Many crowdfunding backers become Facebook friends with entrepreneurs after they contribute to the latter's crowdfunding campaign and continue to support them afterwards (Ryu and Kim, 2016; Skirnevskiy et al., 2017).

Notably, social capital is not merely restricted to social relationships within a social network or online community. Rather, social capital exists at the regional level, also known as "localized social capital" (Laursen et al., 2012). Indeed, prior research has found that areas with high localized social capital are associated with high economic development (Giudici et al., 2013). The venture capital literature documents that investors tend to favor entrepreneurs who are located near them, as proximity reduces information asymmetry (Lerner, 1995). Although there is minimal literature on the effect of location on crowdfunding success, the few studies found that crowdfunding backers prefer investing in local ventures such as bands, which indicates the important role of geography (Agrawal et al., 2011; Giudici et al., 2018).

Factor 2: Crowdfunding campaign's narrative
One of the unique traits that differentiates digital crowdfunding from traditional financing methods is its capacity to connect entrepreneurs with a crowd of potentially complete strangers (Mollick, 2014). To combat information asymmetry due to the newness of projects and to win the trust of their backers, entrepreneurs rely on multiple strategies to send positive signals to the crowd (Kromidha and Robson, 2016; Jancenelle et al., 2017; Marom and Sade, 2013). Signaling theory, originating in economic literature, holds that one recipient party can receive signals from another sending party and make decisions based on the signals when the recipient party lacks information (Connelly et al., 2011; Spence, 1973). Crowdfunding relies largely on the project owner's communications within the online communities, which makes entrepreneurial narratives a key signaling strategy (Allison et al., 2015; Kim et al., 2016; Moss

et al., 2015; Short and Anglin, 2019). Research suggests that entrepreneurial narratives effectively assist entrepreneurs in garnering financial resources by introducing entrepreneurs' previous and current activities as well as their future plans for their projects (Garud et al., 2014). Entrepreneurs on crowdfunding platforms use their narratives to convey a compelling and trustworthy story about their projects and themselves – including their qualifications and past experience – to signal to their potential backers that their projects deserve to be funded and that they will be able to deliver on their promises.

In the reward-based crowdfunding literature, Anglin et al. (2018a) found that positive psychological language which indicates optimism and resilience links to a higher probability of crowdfunding success. In another study, seven types of narcissism narratives including "authority rhetoric" that exhibits leadership; "superiority rhetoric" indicating that the entrepreneur or his/her project is more superior than others; "exhibitionism rhetoric" by using words like "brilliant," "fantastic," "renowned," and so on; "vanity rhetoric" representing self-centeredness; "self-sufficiency rhetoric" indicating individualism; "exploitative rhetoric"; and "entitlement rhetoric" act as strong drivers of crowdfunding performance (Anglin et al., 2018b). Other than psychological language, projects that signal good quality are linked to stronger crowdfunding success, and backers who have supported high-quality projects are more likely to introduce these projects to other people (Bi et al., 2017).

In addition, research suggests that using a storytelling technique that describes a project's history and potential future and walks potential backers through the project's journey gives potential funders a feeling of being part of the entrepreneur's journey (Manning and Bejarano, 2017). Entrepreneurs employ different linguistic styles with language conveying positive, sympathetic, and inclusive effects to make their crowdfunding campaigns more understandable and more relatable to their potential backers (Chen et al., 2016; Parhankangas and Renko, 2017). Different from traditional fundraising methods, crowdfunding allows entrepreneurs to post videos and pictures to accompany their project descriptions. In this context, prior studies have found that entrepreneurs who use these features are more effective since they are able to exhibit entrepreneurs' passion and preparedness to their potential backers (Alegre and Moleskis, 2019; Davis et al., 2017; Wang et al., 2016).

While most research attention has been placed on the effects of positive signals, Wessel et al. (2016) pointed out that non-genuine social information could send negative signals to the crowdfunding community. By tracing the "unnatural peaks in the number of Facebook Likes" (p. 75), the authors observed that fake social activity that was presented by the campaign creators could lead to a short-term positive reaction from the crowd but was followed by a drop in the number of project backers afterwards.

Factor 3: Entrepreneurs' personal traits or characteristics
In terms of soliciting financial resources, beyond the two aforementioned factors, prior studies across many disciplines found that an entrepreneur's personal characteristics including his/her race and gender also play an important role in securing funding (Freeland and Keister, 2016; Fairlie and Robb, 2007; Pope and Sydnor, 2011). As Younkin and Kuppuswamy (2018) pointed out, potential backers use an entrepreneur's race, ethnicity, and gender "as a proxy for unobserved traits that are relevant to their investment or purchasing decision" (p. 3270). Multiple studies show that people are less likely to buy high-tech products from black sellers (Doleac and Stein, 2013) and that Blacks are less likely to procure adequate financing for their ventures (Freeland and Keister, 2016). Along the same lines, research on traditional funding methods have all reported that females receive lower amounts of venture funding than males (Greene et al., 2003).

Attempting to estimate the causal effect of entrepreneurs' race and ethnicity on their crowdfunding performance, Younkin and Kuppuswamy (2018) conducted a coarsened exact-matching strategy to compare crowdfunding outcomes of black and non-black entrepreneurs on Kickstarter. Their findings show that black entrepreneurs on average raise 86.1 percent less than their non-black counterparts on the same site. The results are similar when the authors used different dependent variables to measure crowdfunding performance, such as the number of backers and average amount funded.

Interestingly, unlike findings that women do not perform as well as men in other traditional fundraising domains, the crowdfunding literature has shown that female entrepreneurs fare better in crowdfunding. In order to test the causal effect of gender on crowdfunding performance, Greenberg and Mollick (2017) conducted a lab experiment by focusing on successfully funded projects that do not have a specific target group on Kickstarter, while disguising the names and genders of the project creators (i.e., the entrepreneurs). In order to have a fairer experiment, the authors used the photos of individuals with the same race and ethnicity. They also chose photos with similar attractiveness and age. The results suggest that women do better than men in achieving crowdfunding success. Gafni et al. (2019a) also found that females are more likely to participate in crowdfunding than other financial markets. The same study also reveals that female backers are more interested in backing female entrepreneurs. One explanation could be that females are risk averse and view crowdfunding as a safe funding mechanism for their projects (Radford, 2016). Furthermore, research has found that there is homophily among women to support other women, which could help drive the success of women (Gafni et al., 2019a; Greenberg and Mollick, 2017).

In addition to studying the impact of race and gender on crowdfunding campaign performance, prior research has examined the effect of personality traits on crowdfunding success. In the psychology literature, personality includes a dynamic set of characteristics that define an individual's thoughts and behavior (Barrick and Mount, 1991; McElroy et al., 2007). Davidson and Poor (2015) posit that since crowdfunding is similar to social media, individuals' personalities may play a role in their crowdfunding success. Employing the Big Five theory,[9] Thies et al. (2016) tested crowdfunding campaign performance on Kickstarter and found that entrepreneurs whose personalities are agreeable and open have a higher chance of achieving campaign success.

What motivates backers to financially support crowdfunding projects?
The question of why backers financially support crowdfunding projects has intrigued researchers for some time (Belleflamme et al., 2014; Gerber et al., 2012; Mollick and Kuppuswamy, 2014). Research findings reveal that most backers provide support for practical or moral reasons. Practically speaking, reward-based crowdfunding embodies reciprocal giving, which is an exchange between two parties that is neither purely selfish or purely altruistic (André et al., 2017; Cordova et al., 2015). This type of arrangement can be particularly attractive to backers who are interested in having early access to new products with lower prices or simply want to earn rewards, which is self-benefiting (Agrawal et al., 2013; Gerber et al., 2012; Kuppuswamy and Bayus, 2013; White and Peloza, 2009). A similar finding is echoed in Belleflamme et al.'s (2014) study, which finds that backers contribute to a crowdfunding campaign when they intend to become a future consumer of the product. Although some rewards may not be directly related to financial gains, they allow backers to get formal recognition in the crowdfunding campaign platform (André et al., 2017). Therefore, backers who support crowdfunding projects could be driven by an extrinsic motivation for recognition (Van Wingerden and Ryan, 2011).

Interestingly, a large number of backers who support crowdfunding for moral reasons are intrinsically motivated. First, some people view crowdfunding as a way to promote innovation while helping entrepreneurs through a democratic system. These individuals feel they are part of an online community in which project creators and the crowd work together to achieve a common goal, a phenomenon known as social participation (Colistra and Duvall, 2017; Ordanini et al., 2011). As one of the informants in a study by Gerber et al. (2012) revealed, he/she wanted to have a sense of belonging with the innovative community by contributing to other community members' projects. Therefore, instead of viewing themselves as customers for products, these backers perceive themselves as patrons who are supporting innovators (Kuti and Madarász, 2014).

According to the goal-gradient effect,[10] people tend to help others or show prosocial behavior when they believe a goal is about to be reached (Touré-Tillery and Fishbach, 2011). Applying this theory to the crowdfunding setting, researchers found that people are more likely to give money to a project when they see the project has almost reached its target funding goal even when there is no tangible reward for their support (Gerber et al., 2012; Kim and Hann, 2014; Kuppuswamy and Bayus, 2017).

In addition, crowdfunding supporters have a desire to help a group or cause because of altruism (Colombo et al., 2015; Steigenberger, 2017). According to the psychology literature, doing good is "psychologically rewarding" and has a "warm glow" effect (Henderson and Malani, 2009; Steigenberger, 2017). Specifically, people tend to fund crowdfunding projects to help their local communities, including nonprofits and businesses (Kitchens and Torrence, 2012). Based on participatory culture theory (Jenkin, 2006), Colistra and Duvall (2017) used an online survey with follow-up interviews to investigate how backers make decisions to give money to crowdfunding projects. One of the respondents revealed that the reason he/she backed an art project on Kickstarter was because "the arts aren't supported very well by our leadership and our government, so it's something that we have to do from the ground up" (p. 7), and another one believed that backing a crowdfunding project was similar to donating to a local charitable organization.

Finally, research has shown that "herding behavior" is also common in crowdfunding. Similar to peer influence in real life, herding behavior on crowdfunding is exhibited when backers consciously mimic their peers' behavior by giving money to a project (Borst et al., 2018; Chan et al., 2020; Gleasure and Feller, 2018). According to Gerber and Hui's (2013) interviews, when entrepreneurs disseminate their projects on social media such as YouTube and Facebook, they are more likely to pique the interests of their fans who follow other online community members' behaviors and support these projects. Similarly, Agrawal et al. (2011) reported that contributors are more interested in investing in entrepreneurs who had reached 80 percent of their goal amount on the Sellaband platform.

However, social media does not only play a positive role in helping entrepreneurs raise more money on crowdfunding due to the crowd's herding behavior. Social media can also introduce a "bystander effect" (Agrawal et al., 2013; Borst et al., 2018). This theory holds that when potential backers see the popularity of a crowdfunding project, they assume that their peers on social media have already financially contributed to the project. As a result, they themselves do not necessarily feel the need to contribute (Burtch et al., 2013; Mollick, 2014). Table 9.5 presents the backers' motivations for contributing to crowdfunding campaigns with examples.

Why do entrepreneurs and organizations use crowdfunding?
While much research has been conducted to understand what motivates an individual to back a crowdfunding campaign, considerably less research has

Table 9.5   *Backers' motivations for contributing to crowdfunding campaigns*

Motivations	Examples
Early access to new products for personal gain	Agrawal et al. (2013); André et al. (2017); Kuppuswamy and Bayus (2013); Ryu and Kim (2016)
Support the online entrepreneurial community	Belleflamme et al. (2014); Gerber et al. (2012); Lin et al. (2014); Pitschner and Pitschner-Finn (2014)
Help the local community philanthropically	Colistra and Duvall (2017); Steigenberger (2017)
Herding behavior	Gerber and Hui (2013); Mollick (2014)

explored why entrepreneurs use crowdfunding to fund their projects. Some studies argue that crowdfunding provides a lower cost of entry compared to traditional means of raising funds, and is especially suitable for those who have no other means to collect the funds necessary to develop their ideas (Fleming and Sorenson, 2016; Mollick, 2014).

Crowdfunding also removes many barriers that often exist in traditional financing mechanisms. For instance, entrepreneurs who marshal financial resources from a large number of backers making small contributions can avoid prolonged negotiations with their backers, which increases fundraising efficiency (Kuti and Madarász, 2014). Also, by operating in an online setting, crowdfunding allows entrepreneurs to expand beyond their geographical location and social networks that might otherwise have limited their solicitation range (Agrawal et al., 2013). This reason to use crowdfunding is especially important for entrepreneurs who have limited social networks or for those looking to streamline their funding process by bypassing traditional gatekeepers (Mollick, 2016).

In addition to using crowdfunding to raise initial capital for startups, entrepreneurs may also rely on crowdfunding to market and pre-sell their new products and thereby increase awareness of their products (Crosetto and Regner, 2018; Scholz, 2015). By using crowdfunding to pre-sell their products or services, entrepreneurs entice customers to buy early at a lower price than the full price that future customers will have to pay (Belleflamme et al., 2014). For instance, the British rock band Marillion successfully sold 12,674 copies of its album *Anoraknophobia* to fans via crowdfunding before the album was even recorded (Gerber et al., 2012).

At the same time, many entrepreneurs post their projects on crowdfunding platforms for nonmonetary reasons. Gerber et al. (2012) conducted interviews with 11 individuals who have used crowdfunding platforms, and found that some entrepreneurs use crowdfunding as a market-testing tool to improve their products or services through people's feedback and comments.

Table 9.6   Reasons that entrepreneurs use crowdfunding

Reasons	Examples
Lower cost of entry	Agrawal et al. (2013); Fleming and Sorenson (2016); Mollick (2016)
Product pre-sale and marketing	Belleflamme et al. (2014); Crosetto and Regner (2018); Scholz (2015)
Receive public feedback/market validation	Gerber et al. (2012); Roma et al. (2017)
Build long-term relationship with their future customers	Gerber et al. (2012); Kuti and Madarász (2014)

Similarly, Formlabs, a 3D-printing startup, used its crowdfunding campaign on Kickstarter as a test ground to gauge the market reception to its product (Roma et al., 2017). Entrepreneurs rely on initial market feedback to improve their projects to be more marketable (Belleflamme et al., 2014). Many agree that entrepreneurs are particularly attracted to the openness and democratic practice of crowdfunding, where they can receive feedback and additional ideas from the crowd to boost their innovation (Gleasure and Feller, 2016; Mollick and Robb, 2016; Stanko and Henard, 2017).

Moreover, many entrepreneurs recognize that crowdfunding platforms are essentially another form of social media (Kuti and Madarász, 2014). Therefore, they use these platforms to connect with their users, both backers and non-backers, and to form a supportive social network that will provide encouragement. Consequently, users may become emotionally attached to entrepreneurs and their projects and become future backers (Kuti and Madarász, 2014). Gerber et al.'s (2012) study shows that some entrepreneurs take advantage of the large user base of a crowdfunding platform to establish long-term relationships with their potential buyers. This dynamic motivates entrepreneurs to deliver their products and services to their crowdfunding community (Gerber and Hui, 2013; Mollick, 2016). Table 9.6 summarizes the major reasons for entrepreneurs to use crowdfunding.

How does crowdfunding affect ventures' entrepreneurial performance?
A number of startups have turned into multi-billion-dollar companies after receiving funds from their crowdfunding campaigns (Agrawal et al., 2013). One of the most successful projects is a virtual reality startup Oculus. The startup was ignored by traditional financiers, but it was enthusiastically supported by virtual reality hobbyists on Kickstarter and raised millions of dollars. After its big success on crowdfunding, Oculus received a great deal of attention in the field and was later bought by Facebook (Gleasure and Feller, 2016; Mollick, 2016). Successful crowdfunding campaigns such as this one

were what helped push crowdfunding into the spotlight and spike the interests of researchers to understand the outcomes of crowdfunding campaigns.

Mollick and Kuppuswamy's (2014) research shows that successfully crowdfunded ventures have a high chance of staying in business (Mollick and Kuppuswamy, 2014). In their study on Kickstarter, the authors found that over 90 percent of the crowdfunded projects remained in business. By looking at the music industry, Gamble et al. (2017) found that reward-based crowdfunding substantially helps independent artists obtain direct funding and enhances their stability. However, another study shows that the amount raised during crowdfunding does not necessarily help market performance afterwards. Rather, the number of backers a project receives in a crowdfunding campaign is a stronger determinant of future success (Stanko and Henard, 2017).

Studies also found that projects which received higher pledge amounts from the crowd have a higher probability of attracting the attention of professional investors who may provide subsequent funding for the project, especially when the project has a patent to show its technological advantages (Roma et al., 2017). In the venture capital literature, professional venture capitalists make their investment decision based heavily on the startup's prior funding success (Agrawal et al., 2013).

Entrepreneurs who launch a crowdfunding campaign have a strong tendency to launch multiple crowdfunding campaigns, making them serial crowdfunders. After winning trust from and developing reliable social relationships with their prior campaign backers, the entrepreneurs take advantage of this established social capital to launch new crowdfunding campaigns and are typically more successful than novice campaigners (Butticè et al., 2017; Skirnevskiy et al., 2017). Using a large Kickstarter dataset, Butticè et al. (2018b) found that each crowdfunding campaign reduces information asymmetry, which then helps increase the entrepreneurs' performance in their subsequent crowdfunding campaign.

In addition, just as with other startups that receive financial support, the funding collected through crowdfunding helps ventures grow and scale. In turn, it allows ventures to hire more employees and contribute to economic growth. According to the Kickstarter research, 32 percent of crowdfunded projects received more than $100,000 in revenue per year and created 2.2 jobs to meet the venture's expanding demands (Mollick and Kuppuswamy, 2014).

Nevertheless, this question about how crowdfunding affects performance can still be answered more thoroughly. For instance, so far, research on post-crowdfunding outcomes has focused mainly on the ventures and organizations that have successfully reached their crowdfunding goals. However, questions remain regarding how crowdfunding affects ventures that were not successful in reaching their target goals. Table 9.7 presents the

Table 9.7   Post-crowdfunding outcomes

Main outcomes	Examples
Gain customers to maintain their business	Gamble et al. (2017); Mollick and Kuppuswamy (2014)
Receive more external funding from traditional financing mechanisms	Agrawal et al. (2013); Roma et al. (2017)
Launch another crowdfunding campaign	Butticè et al. (2017); Butticè et al. (2018b); Skirnevskiy et al. (2017)
Scale their businesses and organizations	Mollick and Kuppuswamy (2014)

post-crowdfunding outcomes that have been examined and examples of the research which has been conducted on this topic.

CHALLENGES AND OPPORTUNITIES FOR FUTURE RESEARCH

This systematic literature review of over 300 academic works on reward-based crowdfunding indeed demonstrates an upward trend for crowdfunding research over the last decade. While it shows some positive developments in the reward-based crowdfunding research domain, including an increasing number of empirical studies from different disciplines and nations, crowdfunding research is still in its infancy and there are multiple gaps and opportunities for future research in this space.

First, as stated in the previous section, crowdfunding research is most commonly found in the business and entrepreneurship disciplines followed by information science and economics and finance. Admittedly, crowdfunding is an alternative financing mechanism for entrepreneurs (Bruton et al., 2015; Golić, 2014; Schwienbacher and Larralde, 2012; Seghers et al., 2012), so it is understandable why these disciplines are more interested in studying crowdfunding. However, as mentioned earlier, crowdfunding is a multi-faceted process that involves multiple fields and sectors including public policy, law, culture, nonprofit organizations, and so on. Therefore, future research could look into crowdfunding from various disciplinary perspectives using different theories. For instance, the public policy discipline might provide additional insights on how countries can learn about successful crowdfunding regulations that have been implemented by other countries.

In addition, so far, most empirical studies have focused on answering the following questions: (1) What are the factors that lead to a project's crowdfunding campaign success? (2) What motivates backers to financially support crowdfunding projects? (3) Why do entrepreneurs and organizations use crowdfunding? (4) How does crowdfunding affect ventures' entrepreneurial performance? Other than these questions, many questions remain unexamined including why are some crowdfunding platforms more popular than others, what are the ethical issues surrounding crowdfunding campaigns, how does the crowding performance of organizations compare to that of individuals, and what are the legal constraints for organizations involved in crowdfunding? Therefore, future research could explore these questions further to provide a clearer understanding of the different entities involved in crowdfunding.

Also, most of the extant research has been exploratory due to the newness of the crowdfunding concept and the limitations of data access. So far, of all the studies in the reward-based crowdfunding research, the success of individual project campaigns is the most studied topic and is the best understood. Future research should explore whether regional characteristics also play a role in project success considering that crowdfunding is supposed to be decentralized and democratic (Mollick, 2014). Similarly, most of the studies examining entrepreneurs' intentions to use crowdfunding have focused on the conceptual or small-scale empirical level. More empirical studies are needed to dig deeper into the additional motivations that propel entrepreneurs to participate in crowdfunding: why they choose one type of crowdfunding (reward-based, equity-based, donation-based, or peer-to-peer lending) over another, why they prefer one crowdfunding platform over another, and so on. Similarly, studies looking into crowdfunding campaign creators have neglected the study of small organizations and nonprofits that seek additional funds from crowdfunding platforms. The incentives for all these entities to participate in crowdfunding that are provided by platforms or governments could be explored as well.

The current crowdfunding research field could benefit from greater methodological diversity, which could provide more conclusive findings with a more holistic view. Some of the extant research on reward-based crowdfunding takes a quantitative approach to study a small set of data from a crowdfunding platform (e.g., Belleflamme et al., 2013; Liu and Liu, 2016), with results that may not be representative or generalizable. Other studies that attempt to provide more generalizable findings with a larger dataset are not able to analyze the data in great detail (Kuppuswamy and Bayus, 2017; Pitschner and Pitschner-Finn, 2014). Only a few studies use survey methods, lab experiments, or interviews (Colistra and Duvall, 2017; Greenberg and Mollick, 2017), but they are not without limitations. Future research could seek to remedy these shortcomings by incorporating larger sample sizes along with more robust datasets that contain more variables. In addition, future research projects could also combine different research methods. For instance, they could employ both textual analyses of news reports and quantitative analyses of the crowdfunding data to study the ethical issues arising from crowdfunding.

Additionally, of the quantitative studies, the extant crowdfunding research projects have mainly employed Ordinary Least Square (OLS) modeling and logistic regression modeling because a crowdfunding project's success is often defined as whether the project reaches its original target amount or not (Crosetto and Regner, 2014; Pitschner and Pitschner-Finn, 2014). As some observed, "This measure is very convenient to determine success and failure empirically, but it involves several limitations: time is not taken into account, nor the number of backers, or the number of qualitative feedback written by backers (feedback which could help the founder to improve the project)" (André et al., 2017, p. 318). Therefore, future research might consider using alternative variables to measure a project's success with crowdfunding and to generate more robust results that can be applicable for practitioners. Furthermore, more diverse modeling strategies including multi-level modeling, geospatial analysis, and so on could be explored in future research on crowdfunding.

Due to the multi-sided nature of crowdfunding platforms that connects project owners with backers and the severe information asymmetry issues present in crowdfunding, using one method may not be sufficient to answer all possible questions. For instance, although extant research has revealed some of the intentions of backers, many puzzles still remain, such as do backers who donate a small amount share the same motivation as those who donate a large amount? Also, the current research has labeled crowdfunding users as either entrepreneurs or backers. But if a crowdfunding user has been an entrepreneur for his/her own campaign as well as a backer for others' projects, does that individual have the same motivation as other crowdfunding users? These questions cannot be addressed by using only one method. Very little research on crowdfunding is based on interviews, and the studies that do use interviews sometimes suffer from a small sample size (Gerber et al., 2012). Therefore, future research could take a mixed-methods research approach and increase the sample size to examine questions like the motivations of backers and entrepreneurs who use crowdfunding.

Over 90 percent of the research is based on one crowdfunding platform: Kickstarter. Nevertheless, as introduced earlier, each crowdfunding platform has its own purposes and rules designed for different users. For instance, Kickstarter mainly attracts artists and technological innovators to request funds, while Indiegogo appeals to a broader audience including inventors, activists, and so on (Gerber and Hui, 2013). Kickstarter and Indiegogo also have different business models, with the former taking an "all-or-nothing" approach while the latter allows entrepreneurs to keep everything that they have collected from the crowd. In order for us to have a better understanding of crowdfunding, researchers should consider different crowdfunding platforms in different empirical settings, including emerging economies. Moreover, future research on crowdfunding should include more comparative studies. Comparing two or more crowdfunding platforms will not only increase the robustness of existing findings but also provide more actionable and clearer managerial implications for ventures.

Notably, the majority of the extant academic works on crowdfunding target commercial businesses. However, nonprofit organizations and hybrid social enterprises, which mix nonprofit and for-profit values, also stand to benefit from crowdfunding as a new funding source (Bergamini et al., 2017; Dees, 1998, 2012; Presenza et al., 2019). As other research has discussed, compared to commercial ventures, nonprofits and social enterprises are having a much harder time securing funding as philanthropic donations and government grants have become more and more competitive (Lehner and Nicholls, 2014; Moore et al., 2012). Therefore, crowdfunding could be a viable alternative financial source for nonprofits and social enterprises that allows them to solicit funds from a larger number of contributors and enables nonprofits and social enterprises to achieve their missions more efficiently (Schwienbacher and Larralde, 2012; Saxton and Wang, 2014; Seghers et al., 2012; Zhou and Ye, 2019). However, while more and more crowdfunding platforms like Indiegogo and Ulule have been striving to include or prioritize social projects, not much research has examined the effect of crowdfunding on social entrepreneurship and fewer studies have compared crowdfunding strategies for commercial versus social ventures (Bergamini et al., 2017; Chen, 2018; Lehner, 2013). Although some attempt to use Kickstarter to compare nonprofit and for-profit projects, this is not appropriate since this platform has very few nonprofit projects (Pitschner and Pitschner-Finn, 2014). Future research should consider using other data sources than Kickstarter to examine whether and to what extent crowdfunding helps fundraising for nonprofit organizations and social enterprises.

Finally, governments around the world are increasingly aware of the potential of crowdfunding as $34 billion has been raised up to 2020 through crowdfunding globally and 270,000 jobs have been created through crowdfunding. Moreover, crowdfunding is projected to "grow to over $300 billion by 2025."[11] In this context, some governments like that of the US have reduced legal barriers for crowdfunding, but very few articles study the policy environment for crowdfunding (Kitchens and Torrence, 2012; Lehner and Nicholls, 2014). In fact, the extant research has not examined the role that government plays in the crowdfunding market. This void presents a great opportunity for future research to investigate the effectiveness of different public policies on crowdfunding around the world. More research is needed to inform policymakers and managers and improve crowdfunding performance in different types of economies.

CONCLUSION

Over the last decade, the world has witnessed the growing popularity of crowdfunding – especially reward-based crowdfunding – for both business and philanthropic purposes. Meanwhile, the novel phenomenon of crowdfunding has also drawn interest from researchers across many disciplines. Since crowdfunding research is rather young and there is a dearth of reliable and robust data, our understanding of crowdfunding remains limited and scattered. In this context, this large systematic review is timely in that "consolidation and integration of existing research findings is vitally important in a field in which tremendous research interest has been created in a short period of time" (Ritz et al., 2016, p. 424).

This chapter reviewed 301 academic works from different disciplines and countries that are related to reward-based crowdfunding, making it the first systematic literature review focused on reward-based crowdfunding and one that covers a long time span and a large number of sources. By examining prior works systematically, this chapter presents the state of the art in reward-based crowdfunding research, reveals the gaps in existing research, and identifies directions for and challenges facing future research. Researchers in the crowdfunding or entrepreneurial financing field who are interested in either commercial or social ventures can benefit from this comprehensive review to gain a more thorough understanding of this burgeoning literature. More importantly, this review provides a solid foundation for practitioners including policymakers, nonprofit managers, and entrepreneurs to have a better knowledge of crowdfunding so that they can utilize it to advance their economic and social missions.

NOTES

1. Bloomberg News, 2019. Crowdfunding market is witnessed to grow USD 89.72 billion from 2018–2022. Technavio. https://www.bloomberg.com/press -releases/2019-06-26/crowdfunding-market-is-witnessed-to-grow-usd-89-72 -billion-from-2018-2022-technavio.
2. Kickstarter About Us: https://www.kickstarter.com/about?ref=global-footer.
3. Ibid.
4. Ibid.
5. Indiegogo mission statement: https://www.indiegogo.com/about/our-story.
6. Indiegogo: https://support.indiegogo.com/hc/en-us/articles/205138007-Choose -Your-Funding-Type-Can-I-Keep-My-Money-.
7. Ulule mission statement: https://www.ulule.com/about/ulule/.
8. Reciprocal giving refers to the notion that we return favors to those "who have previously done for us" (Gouldner, 1960, p. 171).

9. Big Five theory holds that there are five dimensions of human personality: "Openness to experience, conscientiousness, extroversion, agreeableness, and neuroticism" (Barrick and Mount, 1991, p. 1).
10. The "goal-gradient effect" suggests that "motivation to reach a goal's end state increases as distance to the goal decreases" (Touré-Tillery and Fishbach, 2011, p. 415).
11. Fundly, 2020. The crowdfunding industry is projected to grow to over $300 billion by 2025. https://blog.fundly.com/crowdfunding-statistics/.

REFERENCES

Agrawal, A., Catalini, C., and Goldfarb, A. (2011). The geography of crowdfunding. NBER Working Paper No. 16820.

Agrawal, A., Catalini, C., and Goldfarb, A. (2013). Some simple economics of crowdfunding. NBER Working Paper No. 19133.

Agrawal, A., Catalini, C., and Goldfarb, A. (2015). Crowdfunding, geography, social networks, and the timing of decision. *Journal of Economics and Management Strategy*, *24*, 253–274.

Ahlers, G. K. C., Cumming, D., Günther, C., and Schweizer, D. (2015). Signaling in equity crowdfunding. *Entrepreneurship Theory and Practice*, *39*, 955–980.

Alegre, I., and Moleskis, M. (2019). Beyond financial motivations in crowdfunding: A systematic literature review of donations and rewards. *VOLUNTAS: International Journal of Voluntary and Nonprofit Organizations*, 1–12.

Allison, T. H., Davis, B. C., Short, J. C., and Webb, J. W. (2015). Crowdfunding in a prosocial microlending environment: Examining the role of intrinsic versus extrinsic cues. *Entrepreneurship Theory and Practice*, *39*(1), 53–73.

Allison, T. H., Davis, B. C., Webb, J. W., and Short, J. C. (2017). Persuasion in crowdfunding: An elaboration likelihood model of crowdfunding performance. *Journal of Business Venturing*, *32*(6), 707–725.

André, K., Bureau, S., Gautier, A., and Rubel, O. (2017). Beyond the opposition between altruism and self-interest: Reciprocal giving in reward-based crowdfunding. *Journal of Business Ethics*, *146*(2), 313–332.

Anglin, A. H., Short, J. C., Drover, W., Stevenson, R. M., McKenny, A. F., and Allison, T. H. (2018a). The power of positivity? The influence of positive psychological capital language on crowdfunding performance. *Journal of Business Venturing*, *33*(4), 470–492.

Anglin, A. H., Wolfe, M., Short, J., Mckenny, A., and Pidduck, R. (2018b). Narcissistic rhetoric and crowdfunding performance: A social role theory perspective. *Journal of Business Venturing*, *33*(6), 780–812.

Barrick, M. R., and Mount, M. K. (1991). The big five personality dimensions and job performance: A meta-analysis. *Personnel Psychology*, *44*(1), 1–26.

Belleflamme, P., Lambert, T., and Schwienbacher, A. (2013). Individual crowdfunding practices. *Venture Capital*, *15*(4), 313–333.

Belleflamme, P., Lambert, T., and Schwienbacher, A. (2014). Crowdfunding: Tapping the right crowd. *Journal of Business Venturing*, *29*(5), 585–609.

Bergamini, T., Navarro, C., and Hilliard, I. (2017). Is crowdfunding an appropriate financial model for social entrepreneurship? *Academy of Entrepreneurship Journal*, *23*(1), 44–57.

Berns, J. P., Figueroa-Armijos, M., Da Motta Veiga, S. P., and Dunne, T. C. (2020). Dynamics of lending-based prosocial crowdfunding: Using a social responsibility lens. *Journal of Business Ethics, 161,* 169–185.

Bi, S., Liu, Z., and Usman, K. (2017). The influence of online information on investing decisions of reward-based crowdfunding. *Journal of Business Research, 71,* 10–18.

Bilau, J., and Pires, J. (2018). What drives the funding success of reward-based crowd-funding campaigns? *Business Excellence, 12*(2), 27–40.

Borst, I., Moser, C., and Ferguson, J. (2018). From friendfunding to crowdfunding: Relevance of relationships, social media, and platform activities to crowdfunding performance. *New Media and Society, 20*(4), 1396–1414.

Briner, R. B., Denyer, D., and Rousseau, D. M. (2009). Evidence-based management: Concept clean-up time? *Academy of Management Perspectives, 23,* 19–32.

Bruton, G., Khavul, S., Siegel, D., and Wright, M. (2015). New financial alternatives in seeding entrepreneurship: Microfinance, crowdfunding, and peer-to-peer innova-tions. *Entrepreneurship Theory and Practice, 39*(1), 9–26.

Burtch, G., Ghose, A., and Wattal, S. (2013). An empirical examination of the antecedents and consequences of contribution patterns in crowd-funded markets. *Information Systems Research, 24*(3), 499–519.

Buttice, V., Colombo, M., and Wright, M. (2017). Serial crowdfunding, social capital, and project success. *Entrepreneurship Theory and Practice, 41*(2), 183–207.

Buttice, V., Franzoni, C., Rossi-Lamastra, C., and Rovelli, P. (2018a). The road to crowdfunding success: A review of the extant literature. In C. L. Tucci, A. Afuah, and G. Viscusi (eds), *Creating and Capturing Value through Crowdsourcing* (pp. 97–126). Oxford: Oxford University Press.

Buttice, V., Orsenigo, C., and Wright, M. (2018b). The effect of information asym-metries on serial crowdfunding and campaign success. *Economia e Politica Industriale, 45*(2), 143–173.

Chan, C., and Parhankangas, A. (2017). Crowdfunding innovative ideas: How incre-mental and radical innovativeness influence funding outcomes. *Entrepreneurship Theory and Practice, 41*(2), 237–263.

Chan, C. R., Parhankangas, A., Sahaym, A., and Oo, P. (2020). Bellwether and the herd? Unpacking the u-shaped relationship between prior funding and subsequent contributions in reward-based crowdfunding. *Journal of Business Venturing, 35*(2), 105934.

Chaston, I., and Scott, G. (2012). Entrepreneurship and open innovation in an emerging economy. *Management Decision, 50*(7), 1161–1177.

Chen, S., Thomas, S., and Kohli, C. (2016). What really makes a promotional campaign succeed on a crowdfunding platform? *Journal of Advertising Research, 56*(1), 81–94.

Chen, W. (2018). Does crowdfunding benefit social entrepreneurship? Manuscript prepared for the ARNOVA Annual Conference.

Chen, W. (2020). Crowdfunding. In H. Anheier, R. List, and S. Toepler (eds), *International Encyclopedia of Civil Society.* Heidelberg: Springer.

Cholakova, M., and Clarysse, B. (2015). Does the possibility to make equity investments in crowdfunding projects crowd out reward-based investments? *Entrepreneurship Theory and Practice, 39,* 145–172.

Coleman, J. S. (1998). Social capital in the creation of human capital. *American Journal of Sociology, 94,* 95–120.

Colgren, D. (2014). The rise of crowdfunding: Social media, big data, cloud technolo-gies. *Strategic Finance, 96*(4), 56–57.

Colistra, R., and Duvall, K. (2017). Show me the money: Importance of crowdfunding factors on backers' decisions to financially support Kickstarter campaigns. *Social Media + Society*, 1–12.

Colombo, M. G., Franzoni, C., and Rossi-Lamastra, C. (2015). Internal social capital and the attraction of early contributions in crowdfunding. *Entrepreneurship Theory and Practice*, *39*(1), 75–100.

Connelly, B. L., Certo, S. T., Ireland, R. D., and Reutzel, C. R. (2011). Signaling theory: A review and assessment. *Journal of Management*, *37*(1), 39–67.

Copeland, A. J. (2015). A multimodal analysis of faith-related giving rhetoric on Indiegogo. *Heidelberg Journal of Religions on the Internet*, *9*, 1–18.

Cordova, A., Dolci, J., and Gianfrate, G. (2015). The determinants of crowdfunding success: Evidence from technology projects. *Procedia – Social and Behavioral Sciences*, *181*, 115–124.

Cosh, A., Cumming, D., and Hughes, A. (2009). Outside entrepreneurial capital. *The Economic Journal*, *119*(540), 1494–1533.

Cox, J., and Nguyen, T. (2018). Does the crowd mean business? An analysis of rewards-based crowdfunding as a source of finance for start-ups and small businesses. *Journal of Small Business and Enterprise Development*, *25*(1), 147–162.

Crosetto, P., and Regner, T. (2014). Crowdfunding: Determinants of success and funding dynamics. Jena Economics Research Papers No. 2014-035.

Crosetto, P., and Regner, T. (2018). It's never too late: Funding dynamics and self pledges in reward-based crowdfunding. *Research Policy*, *47*(8), 1463–1477.

Cumming, D., and Hornuf, L. (2018). *The Economics of Crowdfunding: Startups, Portals and Investor Behavior*. Cham, Switzerland: Palgrave.

Davidson, R., and Poor, N. (2015). The barriers facing artists' use of crowdfunding platforms: Personality, emotional labor, and going to the well one too many times. *New Media and Society*, *17*(2), 289–307.

Davis, B. C., Hmieleski, K. M., Webb, J. W., and Coombs, J. E. (2017). Funders' positive affective reactions to entrepreneurs' crowdfunding pitches: The influence of perceived product creativity and entrepreneurial passion. *Journal of Business Venturing*, *32*(1), 90–106.

Dees, J. G. (1998). Enterprising nonprofits: What do you do when traditional sources of funding fall short. *Harvard Business Review*, *76*(1), 55–67.

Dees, J. G. (2012). A tale of two cultures: Charity, problem solving, and the future of social entrepreneurship. *Journal of Business Ethics*, *111*(3), 321–334.

Defazio, D., Franzoni, C., and Rossi-Lamastra, C. (2020). How pro-social framing affects the success of crowdfunding projects: The role of emphasis and information crowdedness. *Journal of Business Ethics*, 1–22.

Demiray, M., and Burnaz, S. (2019). Positioning of crowdfunding platforms: Turkey as an emerging market case. *Journal of Management Marketing and Logistics*, *6*(2), 84–94.

Dietrich, A., and Amrein, S. (2017). *Crowdfunding Monitoring Switzerland*. Institute of Financial Services Zug IFZ.

Dimov, D., and Murray, G. (2008). Determinants of the incidence and scale of seed capital investments by venture capital firms. *Small Business Economics*, *30*, 127–152.

Doleac, J. L., and Stein, L. (2013). The visible hand: Race and online market outcomes. *Economics Journal*, *123*(572), F469–F492.

Dolfsma, W., van der Eijk, R., and Jolink, A. (2009). On a source of social capital: Gift exchange. *Journal of Business Ethics*, *89*(3), 315–329.

Drucker, P. F. (1985). *Innovation and Entrepreneurship: Practice and Principles*. New York: HarperCollins.

Dushnitsky, G., and Fitza, M. (2018). Are we missing the platforms for the crowd? Comparing investment drivers across multiple crowdfunding platforms. *Journal of Business Venturing Insights*, *10*, e00100.

Elkhidir, K. M. F. (2017). Reward-based crowdfunding technological projects determinants of success: A quantitative study. *Journal of Entrepreneurial Finance*, *19*(2), 1–25.

Fairlie, R. W., and Robb, A. (2007). Why are black-owned businesses less successful than white-owned businesses? The role of families, inheritances, and business human capital. *Journal of Labor Economics*, *25*(2), 289–323.

Fan-Osuala, O., Zantedeschi, D., and Jank, W. (2017). Using past contribution patterns to forecast fundraising outcomes in crowdfunding. *International Journal of Forecasting*, *34*(1), 30–44.

Fleming, L., and Sorenson, O. (2016). Financing by and for the masses: An introduction to the special issue on crowdfunding. *California Management Review*, *58*(2), 5–19.

Freeland, R. E., and Keister, L. A. (2016). How does race and ethnicity affect persistence in immature ventures? *Journal of Small Business Management*, *54*(1), 210–228.

Gafni, H., Marom, D., Robb, A., and Sade, O. (2019a). Gender dynamics in crowdfunding (Kickstarter): Evidence on entrepreneurs, investors, deals and taste based discrimination. SSRN Working Paper.

Gafni, H., Marom, D., and Sade, O. (2019b). Are the life and death of an early-stage venture indeed in the power of the tongue? Lessons from online crowdfunding pitches. *Strategic Entrepreneurship Journal*, *13*(1), 3–23.

Gallemore, C., Nielsen, K., and Jespersen, K. (2019). The uneven geography of crowdfunding success: Spatial capital on Indiegogo. *Environment and Planning A: Economy and Space*, *51*(6), 1389–1406.

Gamble, J. R., Brennan, M., and McAdam, R. (2017). A rewarding experience? Exploring how crowdfunding is affecting music industry business models. *Journal of Business Research*, *70*, 25–36.

Garud, R., Gehman, J., and Giuliani, A. P. (2014). Contextualizing entrepreneurial innovation: A narrative perspective. *Research Policy*, *43*, 1177–1188.

Gerber, E. M., and Hui, J. (2013). Crowdfunding: Motivations and deterrents for participation. *ACM Transactions on Computer–Human Interaction (TOCHI)*, *20*(6), 1–32.

Gerber, E. M., Hui, J. S., and Kuo, P. (2012). Crowdfunding: Why people are motivated to post and fund projects on crowdfunding platforms. *Proceedings of the International Workshop on Design, Influence, and Social Technologies: Techniques, Impacts and Ethics*, *2*, 11–21.

Giudici, G., Guerini, M., and Rossi-Lamastra, C. (2013). Why crowdfunding projects can succeed: The role of proponents' individual and territorial social capital. SSRN Working Paper.

Giudici, G., Guerini, M., and Rossi-Lamastra, C. (2018). Reward-based crowdfunding of entrepreneurial projects: The effect of local altruism and localized social capital on proponents' success. *Small Business Economics*, *50*(2), 307–324.

Gleasure, R., and Feller, J. (2016). A rift in the ground: Theorizing the evolution of anchor values in crowdfunding communities through the Oculus Rift case study. *Journal of the Association for Information Systems*, *17*(10), 708–736.

Gleasure, R., and Feller, J. (2018). What kind of cause unites a crowd? Understanding crowdfunding as collective action. *Journal of Electronic Commerce Research*, *19*(3), 223–236.

Golić, Z. (2014). Advantages of crowdfunding as an alternative source of financing of small and medium-sized enterprises. *Proceedings of the Faculty of Economics in East Sarajevo*, (8), 39–48.

Gorbatai, A., and Nelson, L. (2015). Gender and the language of crowdfunding. SSRN Working Paper.

Gouldner, A. W. (1960). The norm of reciprocity: A preliminary statement. *American Sociological Review*, *25*(2), 161–178.

Greenberg, J., and Mollick, E. (2014). Leaning in or leaning on? Gender, homophily, and activism in crowdfunding. SSRN Working Paper.

Greenberg, J., and Mollick, E. (2017). Activist choice homophily and the crowdfunding of female founders. *Administrative Science Quarterly*, *62*(2), 341–374.

Greene, P. G., Hart, M. M., Gatewood, E. J., Brush, C. G., and Carter, N. M. (2003). Women entrepreneurs: Moving front and center: An overview of research and theory. Coleman White Paper Series.

Henderson, M. T., and Malani, A. (2009). Corporate philanthropy and the market for altruism. *Columbia Law Review*, *109*(3), 571–627.

Ilenkov, D., and Kapustina, V. (2018). Crowdfunding in Russia: An empirical study. *European Research Studies*, *21*(2), 401–410.

Jancenelle, V. E., Javalgi, R. G., and Cavusgil, E. (2017). The role of economic and normative signals in international prosocial crowdfunding: An illustration using market orientation and psychological capital. *International Business Review*, *27*, 208–212.

Jenkins, H. (2006). *Convergence Culture: Where Old and New Media Collide*. New York: New York University Press.

Josefy, M., Dean, T. J., Albert, L. S., and Fitza, M. A. (2017). The role of community in crowdfunding success: Evidence on cultural attributes in funding campaigns to "save the local theater". *Entrepreneurship Theory and Practice*, *41*(2), 161–182.

Kang, L., Jiang, Q., and Tan, C. (2017). Remarkable advocates: An investigation of geographic distance and social capital for crowdfunding. *Information and Management*, *54*(3), 336–348.

Kappel, T. (2009). Ex ante crowdfunding and the recording industry: A model for the US. *Loyola LA Entertainment Law Review*, *29*, 375–385.

Kim, K., and Hann, I. H. (2014). Crowdfunding and the democratization of access to capital: A geographical analysis. SSRN Working Paper.

Kim, P. H., Buffart, M., and Croidieu, G. (2016). TMI: Signaling credible claims in crowdfunding campaign narratives. *Group and Organization Management*, *41*(6), 717–750.

Kirzner, I. M. (1973). *Competition and Entrepreneurship*. Chicago, IL: University of Chicago Press.

Kitchens, R., and Torrence, P. D. (2012). The jobs act – crowdfunding and beyond. *Economic Development Journal*, *11*(4), 42–47.

Kromidha, E., and Robson, P. (2016). Social identity and signaling success factors in online crowdfunding. *Entrepreneurship and Regional Development*, *28*(9), 605–629.

Kuppuswamy, V., and Bayus, B. L. (2013). Crowdfunding creative ideas: The dynamics of project backers in Kickstarter. UNC Kenan-Flagler Research Paper No. 2013-15.

Kuppuswamy, V., and Bayus, B. L. (2017). Does my contribution to your crowdfunding project matter? *Journal of Business Venturing*, *32*(1), 72–89.

Kuti, M., and Madarász, G. (2014). Crowdfunding. *Public Finance Quarterly*, *59*(3), 355–366.

Laursen, K., Masciarelli, F., and Prencipe, A. (2012). Regions matters: How localized social capital affects innovation and external knowledge acquisition. *Organization Science*, *23*(1), 177–193.

Lehner, O. (2013). Crowdfunding social ventures: A model and research agenda. *Venture Capital*, *15*, 289–311.

Lehner, O., and Nicholls, A. (2014). Social finance and crowdfunding for social enterprises: A public–private case study providing legitimacy and leverage. *Venture Capital*, *16*(3), 271–286.

Lepola, A. and Kärkkäinen, H. (2017). Using crowdfunding for extracting feedback: Literature review. In *AcademicMindtrek '17: Proceedings of the 21st International Academic Mindtrek Conference* (pp. 194–202). New York: ACM. https://doi.org/10 .1145/3131085.3131125

Lerner, J. (1995). Venture capitalists and the oversight of private firms. *Journal of Finance*, *50*(1), 301–318.

Lin, Y., Boh, F., and Goh, K. (2014). How different are crowdfunders? Examining archetypes of crowdfunders and their choice of projects. SSRN Working Paper.

Liu, C., and Liu, J. (2016). Antecedents of success rate of award-based crowdfunding: The case of the "Kickstarter". *Modern Economy*, *7*, 250–261.

Liu, W. H. (2014). The influence of Kickstarter in China. *21st Century Business Review*, *16*, 64–65.

Madrazo-Lemarroy, P., Barajas-Portas, K., and Tovar, M. E. L. (2019). Analyzing campaign's outcome in reward-based crowdfunding. *Internet Research*, *29*(5), 1171–1189.

Maier, F., Meyer, M., and Steinbereithner, M. (2016). Nonprofit organizations becoming business-like: A systematic review. *Nonprofit and Voluntary Sector Quarterly*, *45*(1), 64–86.

Makýšová, L., and Vaceková, G. (2017). Profitable nonprofits? Reward-based crowdfunding in the Czech Republic. *NISPAcee Journal of Public Administration and Policy*, *10*(2), 203–227.

Manning, S., and Bejarano, T. A. (2017). Convincing the crowd: Entrepreneurial storytelling in crowdfunding campaigns. *Strategic Organization*, *15*(2), 194–219.

Marom, D., and Sade, O. (2013). Are the life and death of an early stage venture indeed in the power of the tongue? Lessons from online crowdfunding pitches. SSRN Working Paper.

Massolution. (2015). *The Crowdfunding Industry Report.* http://www.smv.gob.pe/ Biblioteca/temp/catalogacion/C8789.pdf

McElroy, J. C., Hendrickson, A. R., Townsend, A. M., and DeMarie, S. M. (2007). Dispositional factors in internet use: Personality versus cognitive style. *MIS Quarterly*, *31*(4), 809–820.

Meric, J., Bouiass, K., and Maque, I. (2015). More than three's a crowd … in the best interest of companies! *Society and Business Review*, *10*, 23–39.

Meyskens, M., and Bird, L. (2015). Crowdfunding and value creation. *Entrepreneurship Research Journal*, *5*(2), 155–166.

Mitra, T., and Gilbert, E. (2014). The language that gets people to give: Phrases that predict success on Kickstarter. In *Proceedings of the 17th ACM Conference on Computer Supported Cooperative Work and Social Computing, CSCW '14* (pp. 49–61). New York: ACM.

Mollick, E. (2014). The dynamics of crowdfunding: An exploratory study. *Journal of Business Venturing*, *29*(1), 1–16.

Mollick, E. (2016). The unique value of crowdfunding is not money – it's community. *Harvard Business Review*, 21 April.

Mollick, E. R., and Kuppuswamy, V. (2014). After the campaign: Outcomes of crowdfunding. UNC Kenan-Flagler Research Paper No. 2376997.

Mollick, E., and Robb, A. (2016). Democratizing innovation and capital access: The role of crowdfunding. *California Management Review*, *58*(2), 72–87.

Moore, M. L., Westley, F. R., and Nicholls, A. (2012). The social finance and social innovation nexus. *Journal of Social Entrepreneurship*, *3*(2), 115–132.

Moritz, A. and Block, J. H. (2016). Crowdfunding: A literature review and research directions. In D. Brüntje, and O. Gajda (eds), *Crowdfunding in Europe: State of the Art in Theory and Practice* (pp. 25–53). FGF Studies in Small Business and Entrepreneurship. Cham, Switzerland: Springer.

Moss, T. W., Neubaum, D. O., and Meyskens, M. (2015). The effect of virtuous and entrepreneurial orientations on microfinance lending and repayment: A signaling theory perspective. *Entrepreneurship Theory and Practice*, *39*, 27–52.

Motylska-Kuzma, A. (2018). Crowdfunding and sustainable development. *Sustainability*, *10*(12), 4650.

Mourao, P., Silveira, M. A. P., and De Melo, R. S. (2018). Many are never too many: An analysis of crowdfunding projects in Brazil. *International Journal of Financial Studies*, *6*(4), 95.

Ordanini, A., Miceli, L., Pizzetti, M., and Parasuraman, A. (2011). Crowd-funding: Transforming customers into investors through innovative service platforms. *Journal of Service Management*, *22*, 443–470.

Parhankangas, A., and Renko, M. (2017). Linguistic style and crowdfunding success among social and commercial entrepreneurs. *Journal of Business Venturing*, *32*(2), 215–236.

Petitjean, M. (2018). What explains the success of reward-based crowdfunding campaigns as they unfold? Evidence from the French crowdfunding platform KissKissBankBank. *Finance Research Letters*, *26*, 9–14.

Pitschner, S., and Pitschner-Finn, S. (2014). Non-profit differentials in crowd-based financing: Evidence from 50,000 campaigns. *Economics Letters*, *123*(3), 391–394.

Pope, D. G., and Sydnor, J. R. (2011). What's in a picture?: Evidence of discrimination from prosper.com. *Journal of Human Resources*, *46*(1), 53–92.

Presenza, A., Abbate, T., Cesaroni, F., and Appio, F. (2019). Enacting social crowdfunding business ecosystems: The case of the platform Meridonare. *Technological Forecasting and Social Change*, *143*, 190–201.

Profatilov, D. A., Bykova, O. N., and Olkhovskaya, M. O. (2015). Crowdfunding: Online charity or a modern tool for innovative projects implementation? *Asian Social Science*, *11*(3), 146–151.

Radford, J. S. (2016). The emergence of gender inequality in a crowdfunding market: An experimental test of gender system theory. SSRN Working Paper.

Rey-Martí, A., Mohedano-Suanes, A., and Virginia, S. (2019). Crowdfunding and social entrepreneurship: Spotlight on intermediaries. *Sustainability*, *11*(4), 1175.

Ritz, A., Brewer, G., and Neumann, O. (2016). Public service motivation: A systematic literature review and outlook. *Public Administration Review*, *76*(3), 414–426.

Roma, P., Messeni Petruzzelli, A., and Perrone, G. (2017). From the crowd to the market: The role of reward-based crowdfunding performance in attracting professional investors. *Research Policy*, *46*, 1606–1628.

Rousseau, D. M., Manning, J., and Denyer, D. (2008). Evidence in management and organizational science: Assembling the field's full weight of scientific knowledge through syntheses. *Academy of Management Annals*, *2*(1), 475–515.

Ryu, S., and Kim, Y. G. (2016). A typology of crowdfunding sponsors: Birds of a feather flock together? *Electronic Commerce Research and Applications*, *16*, 43–54.

Salido-Andres, N., Rey-Garcia, M., Álvarez-González, L. I., and Vázquez-Casielles, R. (2019). Determinants of success of donation-based crowdfunding through digital platforms: The influence of offline factors. *CIRIEC-España*, *95*, 119–141.

Saxton, G. D., and Wang, L. (2014). The social network effect: The determinants of giving through social media. *Nonprofit and Voluntary Sector Quarterly*, *43*(5), 850–868.

Scholz, N. (2015). *The Relevance of Crowdfunding: The Impact on the Innovation Process of Small Entrepreneurial Firms*. Wiesbaden: Springer.

Schumpeter, J. A. (1934). *The Theory of Economic Development*. Cambridge, MA: Harvard University Press.

Schwienbacher, A., and Larralde, B. (2010). Crowdfunding of small entrepreneurial ventures. SSRN Working Paper.

Schwienbacher, A., and Larralde, B. (2012). Crowdfunding of entrepreneurial ventures. In D. Cumming (ed.), *The Oxford Handbook of Entrepreneurial Finance* (pp. 369–391). Oxford: Oxford University Press.

Seghers, A., Manigart, S., and Vanacker, T. (2012). The impact of human and social capital on entrepreneurs' knowledge of finance alternatives. *Journal of Small Business Management*, *50*, 63–86.

Short, J. C., and Anglin, A. (2019). Is leadership language "rewarded" in crowdfunding? Replicating social entrepreneurship research in a rewards-based context. *Journal of Business Venturing Insights*, *11*, e00121.

Short, J. C., Ketchen, D. J., McKenny, A. F., Allison, T. H., and Ireland, R. D. (2017). Research on crowdfunding: Reviewing the (very recent) past and celebrating the present. *Entrepreneurship Theory and Practice*, *41*(2), 149–160.

Skirnevskiy, V., Bendig, D., and Brettel, M. (2017). The influence of internal social capital on serial creators' success in crowdfunding. *Entrepreneurship Theory and Practice*, *41*(2), 209–236.

Song, Y., and van Boeschoten, R. (2015). Success factors for crowdfunding founders and funders. Paper presented at the *5th International Conference on Collaborative Innovation Networks COINs15*, Tokyo, Japan.

Sorenson, O., Assenova, V., Li, G.-C., Boada, J., and Fleming, L. (2016). Expand innovation finance via crowdfunding. *Science*, *354*(6319), 1526–1528.

Spence, M. (1973). Job market signaling. *Quarterly Journal of Economics*, *87*, 355–374.

Stanko, M. A., and Henard, D. (2017). Toward a better understanding of crowdfunding, openness and the consequences for innovation. *Research Policy*, *46*(4), 784–798.

Steigenberger, N. (2017). Why supporters contribute to reward-based crowdfunding. *International Journal of Entrepreneurial Behavior and Research*, *23*(2), 336–353.

Stemler, A. (2013). The JOBS Act and crowdfunding: Harnessing the power and money of the masses. *Business Horizons*, *56*, 271–275.

Stevenson, R., Kuratko, D., and Eustler, J. (2019). Unleashing main street entrepreneurship: Crowdfunding, venture capital, and the democratization of new venture investments. *Small Business Economics*, *52*(2), 375–393.

The World Bank. (2013). *Crowdfunding's Potential for the Developing World*.

Thies, F., Wessel, M., Rudolph, J., and Benlian, A. (2016). Personality matters: How signaling personality traits can influence the adoption and diffusion of crowdfunding campaigns. *24th ECIS Conference Proceedings*, Istanbul, Turkey.

Touré-Tillery, M., and Fishbach, A. (2011). The course of motivation. *Journal of Consumer Psychology*, *21*(4), 414–423.

Tranfield, D., Denyer, D., and Smart, P. (2003). Towards a methodology for developing evidence-informed management knowledge by means of systematic review. *British Journal of Management, 14*, 207–222.

Valanciene, L., and Jegeleviciute, S. (2013). Valuation of crowdfunding: Benefits and drawbacks. *Economics and Management, 18*(1), 39–48.

van de Rijt, A., Kang, S., Restivo, M., and Patil, A. (2014). Field experiments of success-breeds-success dynamics. *Proceedings of the National Academy of Sciences of the United States of America, 111*(19), 6934–6939.

Van Wingerden, R., and Ryan, J. (2011). Fighting for funds: An exploratory study into the field of crowdfunding. Lund University School of Economics and Management.

Wang, Z., Mao, H., Li, Y. J., and Liu, F. (2016). Smile big or not? Effects of smile intensity on perceptions of warmth and competence. *Journal of Consumer Research, 43*(5), 787–805.

Wessel, M., Thies, F., and Benlian, A. (2016). The emergence and effects of fake social information: Evidence from crowdfunding. *Decision Support Systems, 90*, 75–85.

White, K., and Peloza, J. (2009). Self-benefit versus other-benefit marketing appeals: Their effectiveness in generating charitable support. *Journal of Marketing, 73*(4), 109–124.

Xie, K., Liu, Z., Chen, L., Zhang, W., Liu, S., and Chaudhry, S. (2019). Success factors and complex dynamics of crowdfunding: An empirical research on Taobao platform in China. *Electronic Markets, 29*(2), 187–199.

Younkin, P., and Kuppuswamy, V. (2018). The colorblind crowd? Founder race and performance in crowdfunding, *Management Science, 64*(7), 3269–3287.

Zhao, L., and Vinig, T. (2020). Guanxi, trust and reward-based crowdfunding success: A Chinese case. *Chinese Management Studies, 14*(2), 455–472.

Zheng, H., Li, D., Wu, J., and Xu, Y. (2014). The role of multidimensional social capital in crowdfunding: A comparative study in China and US. *Information and Management, 51*, 488–496.

Zhou, H., and Ye, S. (2019). Legitimacy, worthiness, and social network: An empirical study of the key factors influencing crowdfunding outcomes for nonprofit projects. *Voluntas, 30*(4), 849–864.

10. Business angels' ties with entrepreneurs

Mahsa Samsami, Hoda El Kolaly, and Thomas Schøtt

1.   INTRODUCTION

Entrepreneurial finance and technology is a theme that children become acquainted with through the universe of Donald Duck, whose rich uncle Scrooge McDuck financed the inventions by Gyro Gearloose. Gyro Gearloose did not come to Scrooge McDuck as a stranger pitching a good idea. Actually, his ideas were often not technologically sound. Nevertheless, Scrooge McDuck often financed his entrepreneurial endeavors. The financing was apparently based on their friendship.

Friendship and other ties are influencing business angels' decisions on financing entrepreneurs. Business angels often fund entrepreneurs they have a particular tie with, such as close family, relatives, coworkers, neighbors, or friends (Ding et al., 2014, 2015; Sudek, 2006). Sometimes, though, business angels finance entrepreneurs without having a particular tie, but who are strangers presenting a promising idea.

Institutional context also matters for financing. Financing is influenced by regulative, normative, and cognitive pillars (Scott, 2013). The regulative pillar denotes the formal institutional arrangements such as laws and their enforcement, which influence financing under contract. The normative pillar refers to the values and norms, here especially values and norms concerning the family, which influence whom the business angel feels a moral obligation to finance. The cognitive pillar represents the taken-for-granted beliefs, here especially the radius of trust. The common belief in a society may be that only family can be trusted; whereas in another society, the basic belief may be that even strangers can be trusted.

National context also matters. Family and relatives are selected more often in Iran, Egypt, and China than in Norway and Germany (Samsami, 2021). Conversely, strangers are selected more frequently in Norway and Germany than in Iran, Egypt, and China (ibid.). This may be interpreted as a consequence of culture. A family-oriented culture prevails in Iran, Egypt, and China, more so than it does in Norway and Germany. This may be interpreted more generally. Iran, Egypt, and China have a traditional culture that values family and obligations toward family, whereas Norway and Germany have a modern or secular-rational culture that deemphasizes family and values universalism and generalized trust in strangers, bolstered by laws and their enforcement (Ding et al., 2014; Freitag and Traunmüller, 2009).

This frames our research question: *how is traditional versus secular-rational culture affecting business angels' selection of ties for funding?*

In answering this question we make two contributions to the understanding of entrepreneurial financing. First, we provide an account of the importance of different types of business angels' ties with entrepreneurs around the world, ties that can be based on trust, cultural positions, entrepreneurship, and trade relations. Second, we contextualize financing by understanding the embeddedness of business angels' selection of ties in culture, specifically in traditional versus modern culture.

In the current study, the most important finding is that traditional culture enhances angels' likelihood of funding family. Conversely, funding strangers is more common in secular-rational cultures than in traditional cultures.

The following reviews the theoretical background and specifies hypotheses, describes our research design with a globally representative survey of business angels, reports analyses, and concludes with a discussion.

2.   THEORETICAL PERSPECTIVE AND HYPOTHESES

Business angels invest their financial resources in new ventures led by others (Ramadani, 2009). Having business angels on board enhances access to other sources of funding (Maxwell et al., 2011). Many new ventures would not have existed without business angel funding or would have failed at an early stage before attracting formal investments (Bonini et al., 2018; White and Dumay, 2017). The value that business angels bring to businesses goes beyond financing. Typically, they become actively involved at the strategic and operational level, and thus enter the entrepreneurial team (Mason and Harrison, 2000; Paul et al., 2007; Sørheim, 2003). They make use of their experience, mentoring less experienced entrepreneurs by offering strategic advice, and capitalize on their networking (Maxwell et al., 2011; Ramadani, 2009). Moreover, they facilitate financing by increasing the attractiveness of the business (Madill et al., 2005).

2.1   The Factors Influencing Business Angels' Investment Decision

Based on the financial and non-financial benefits business angels add to businesses, entrepreneurs are typically keen on attracting business angel investments. Therefore, scholars wish to understand the investment decision process of business angels and what influences it. Cardon et al. (2009) consider the entrepreneur's displayed passion as an important factor that affects business angels' decisions. Mason and Harrison (2000) emphasize the importance of the entrepreneur's impression management skills for gaining the business angels' confidence. The importance of personal factors and confidence in the founder entrepreneur to business angels' decision making is repeatedly highlighted (Paul et al., 2007; Mason and Stark, 2004; Sudek, 2006). Furthermore, Haines et al. (2003) consider the people in the start-up to be the most important factor influencing business angels' investment decisions, since the business angels would typically be spending a lot of time with them; hence the business angels search for people who are not only right for the job, but also with whom they would like to spend time. Moreover, Au and Kwan (2009) stress the importance of social settings and the significant effect of networks on the financing of entrepreneurial ventures. Similarly, Sørheim (2003) emphasizes business angels' concern to establish common ground with entrepreneurs as a prerequisite for long-term reliable relationships. Furthermore, Paul et al. (2007) argue that business angels give more weight in their decision making to softer factors, due to the limited data on which investment decisions can be based. Another major factor that affects business angels' investment decisions is trust (Ding et al., 2015), which will be discussed in the following section.

2.2   The Effect of Trust on Business Angels' Decisions

Trust is considered a prerequisite for prosperity and business success. Evidence suggests that it shapes people's investment behavior and affects business angels' investment decisions (Ding et al., 2015). In contrast to other investment forms, business angels rely less on formal procedures and depend more on empathy, personal relationships, and trust in selecting projects (Ding et al., 2014; Sudek, 2006). The business angels' decision making seems influenced by two dimensions of trust, namely radius and level. Freitag and Traunmüller (2009) identified two types of trust. The first is particularized trust, which is an intimate type directed to people in the close circle, and which depends on personal and familial relationships. The second is generalized trust that is universal, extending beyond the familial sphere to include strangers, and is reinforced by institutions to control contacts with strangers by imposing credible sanctions in case of trust breaching. Scrutinizing the classification of trust by Freitag and Traunmüller (2009), it is evident that the type of tie is of the essence. As Granovetter (1985) elaborates, behavior and economic transactions are embedded in social ties. Specifically, business angels' ties with entrepreneurs affect their investment decision, and are embedded in context (Samsami, 2021). Therefore, for understanding the effect of ties on the decision process, we should consider the context.

2.3   The Effect of Context

Context is a wide concept which includes political, economic, and cultural facets (Liñán et al., 2020). It provides valuable insights to entrepreneurship research, and hence has attracted the attention of several scholars (Welter, 2011). A relevant research stream focused on the effect of context on funding and investment decisions. Li and Zahra (2012) explored the effect of formal institutional context across countries on venture capital activity, which was found to be encouraged by the existence of more developed institutions. Other studies explored the impact of context on business angel funding (Ding et al., 2014, 2015; Samsami, 2021). Organizations and individuals are embedded in institutional contexts, which in turn affect their investment decisions (Baker et al., 2005). Ding et al. (2014) further explain that business angels are more embedded in local institutions, hence the effect of context on their decision making is even stronger. However, the effect of the cultural context on business angels' decision making remains under-studied despite its significance, hence the focus of this study is to fill this gap.

The culture of a society – the values, norms, and taken-for-granted beliefs prevailing among the people – provides a guide to life (Hofstede, 2001), including business life and entrepreneurial behavior (Li and Zahra, 2012; Freytag and Thurik, 2007; Hechavarría, 2016).

2.4   Traditionality versus Modernity

Among the many dimensions of culture, it seems most relevant and promising to focus here on a dimension reflecting orientation toward family versus strangers. Such a conceptualization is elaborated by Inglehart and Welzel (2005). They find that many of the basic values within culture are closely correlated and are explained by the traditional versus secular-rational dimension. This dimension is used to draw the World Values Survey cultural map, which is based on all the major areas of human values including religion, politics, economy, and social life. Every country is positioned based on people's values instead of geographical location, hence neighbor countries are cultural neighbors sharing values (Inglehart and Welzel, 2010). In traditional societies, family and family values are central, and the respect and obedience of authority is paramount. By contrast, in modern or secular-rational societies, people have the opposite priorities, and emphasize individualism and liberation from authority. Traditional countries tend to rely on informal relationships, networks, and connections, whereas secular-rational countries depend on exchange relations and transactions that are based on generalized trust and contract (Tiessen, 1997; Li and Zahra, 2012). Secular-rational culture entails rather individualist societies, characterized by loose ties between its individuals, and relies mostly on formal institutions to preserve order. In contrast, traditional culture brings more collectivist societies in which people are joined into cohesive communities governed primarily by informal institutions based on shared norms and values, and collective goals (Li and Zahra, 2012). Traditional and secular-rational societies differ in terms of the type of trust prevailing in each. Particularized trust is more common in the former (Fukuyama, 1995; Huff and Kelley, 2003; Ma et al., 2011), whereas generalized trust prevails in the latter, along with trusted formal institutions (Delhey et al., 2011; Ding et al., 2015).

2.5   The Cultural Dimensions and Entrepreneurship

The national value system in which entrepreneurs are embedded affects their choices and decisions (Hechavarría, 2016). Furthermore, the traditional versus secular-rational cultural dimension provides insights about business behavior (Hill, 2000). It also predicts entrepreneurial activity and explains differences across countries (Uhlaner and Thurik, 2010; Pinillos and Reyes, 2011). Ashourizadeh and Schøtt (2016) found that exporting is encouraged by secular-rational culture where the benefits of transnational networking are higher than in traditional culture. Hechavarría (2016) suggested that traditional societies foster commercial entrepreneurship, whereas secular-rational societies encourage social entrepreneurship. Most relevant here, Samsami (2021) suggested that ties between business angels and entrepreneurs are embedded in the cultural context, which affects the salience of various types of ties across societies. In the following section, we hypothesize about the effect of such ties on business angels' decisions from the perspective of traditional versus secular-rational culture.

2.6   A Cultural Perspective on the Effect of Ties on Business Angels' Decisions

Business angels' ties with entrepreneurs can range from strong family ties when funding a family member to no prior ties in the case of funding a stranger pitching a business idea. Literature suggests that ties affect business angel's investment propensity (Wong and Ho, 2007). Family relations are considered the typical form of strong ties (Aldrich and Cliff, 2003; Kramarz and Skans, 2014). Family is both a source and user of social capital (Arregle et al., 2007; Dyer et al., 2014). Bird and Wennberg (2014) show that family start-ups overcome the scarcity of resources by drawing on their social capital. Evidence suggests that family ties play a vital role in new venture creation, and that family is the primary source of informal investment in many countries (Bygrave and Hunt, 2007; Au and Kwan, 2009; Pistrui et al., 2001).

Ding et al. (2014) offer valuable initial insights regarding the effect of ties on business angels' decisions. By comparing business angels' selection criteria in China and Denmark, they found that Chinese business angels depend on relational reliability and trust in strong ties as protection from the uncertainty and risks associated with a weak legal protection. The priority of strong ties for Chinese business angels was further highlighted by Li et al. (2014). Similarly, Peng and Zhou (2005) and Ma et al. (2011) emphasize the importance of strong ties in recognizing and exploiting opportunities in relationship-based contexts.

A relevant study is that of Samsami (2021), who investigates the ties between business angels and entrepreneurs in three traditional countries (China, Egypt, and Iran) and two secular-rational countries (Germany and Norway). The findings suggest that culture affects ties through two mechanisms: trust and obligations. In traditional societies, trust is strong in family and weak in strangers (Freitag and Traunmüller, 2009; Lever-Tracy, 1992; Li et al., 2014). Moreover, traditional culture imposes family obligations in the form of support and solidarity (Samara, 2021). Ding et al. (2014) further explain the positive "cushion effect" of strong ties in relationship-based contexts, where family members intervene to help those facing losses (Au et al., 2013). Samsami (2021) suggests that in traditional culture, funding those with strong ties (family, relatives, and friends) is encouraged, while financing strangers is avoided. Based on these arguments and the characteristics of traditional culture, where family and family obligations are central and the level of generalized trust is low, we hypothesize:

Hypothesis 1. Culture affects funding for close family, in that traditionality in culture enhances business angels' likelihood of funding close family rather than others.

Hofstede (2001) highlights the differences in the complexity of family units in which people live in various societies, where some live in nuclear families while others live in extended families. The latter is more common in traditional societies, and hence affects the entrepreneurial decisions in traditional countries (Samara, 2021). Pistrui et al. (2001) explain that due to the high marginal cost associated with developing new relationships in the traditional society of China, extended family is a main source of start-up capital, since it is only logical to consider the extended family right after the close family when doing business. Lever-Tracy (1992) found that migrant entrepreneurs of Indian descent further relied on the participation of extended family in their businesses. Samsami (2021) highlights that in traditional cultures, trust is strong not only in close family but also in relatives. Her findings also suggest that it is more common for business angels to fund relatives in traditional culture than in secular-rational culture. Therefore, to further account for the significance of the extended family and relatives in traditional societies, we specify,

Hypothesis 2. Culture affects funding for relatives, in that traditionality in culture enhances business angels' likelihood of funding relatives rather than others.

Having considered one extreme of the spectrum of business angels' ties with entrepreneurs, namely family ties (both close and extended), the other end of the spectrum is considered next by exploring funding strangers. Evidence suggests that in traditional societies, where non-family members are considered outsiders (Lever-Tracy, 1992), strangers have less chance of being funded by business angels (Li et al., 2014; Pistrui et al., 2001). Similarly, Samsami (2021) suggests that funding strangers is less common in traditional cultures compared to secular-rational cultures. This may be explained by trust as previously discussed. Trusting and cooperating with out-group members and strangers are more encouraged in individualist societies than in collectivist societies (Schøtt and Jensen, 2016; Freitag and Traunmüller, 2009). This can be attributed to the high level of generalized trust in secular-rational societies, fostered by the presence of strong legal systems and enforcement mechanisms that decrease the uncertainty of engaging in exchange relationships with strangers (Fukuyama, 1995; Ding et al., 2014). Therefore, in secular-rational societies, weak ties can be leveraged to identify investment opportunities (Ma et al., 2011; Peng and Zhou, 2005). Ding et al. (2015) explain that strong ties can lead business angels to choose inferior options out of love. However, business angels in individualist societies are liberated from such obligations, and hence are free to choose any good pitch, even from strangers. Interestingly, Bygrave and Hunt (2007) suggest that as the ties between the entrepreneur and the business angel become weaker, the expected returns on informal investments increase. Furthermore, the explicit investment contracts governed by the formal institutions in secular-rational societies greatly decrease business angels' risks by protecting their interests and equity, and hence motivate business angels to fund strangers (Ding et al., 2014; Poppo and Zenger, 2002). Therefore, we propose,

Hypothesis 3. Culture affects funding for strangers with a good idea, in that secular-rational culture enhances business angels' likelihood of funding strangers rather than others.

3. RESEARCH DESIGN

Our ideas concern business angels in the context of societies. We consider the "population" of business angels and the "population" of societies, forming a two-level hierarchy with business angels nested within societies. Business angels have been surveyed by the Global Entrepreneurship Monitor (GEM). The data are freely available at the GEM website, www.gemconsortium.org.

3.1 Sampling

GEM samples in two stages. In the first stage, countries are sampled, essentially by self-selection when a national team of researchers joins GEM and conducts the survey in their country. Since 2001, the survey has asked about financing in 115 countries around the world, covering more than 90 percent of the population and far more than 90 percent of the GDP in the world, entailing a high degree of representativeness.

In the second stage of sampling, adults (age 18 to 64 years old) are sampled randomly within each selected country. Business angels are identified as those adults answering affirmatively to the question: *Have you, in the past three years, personally provided funds for a new business started by someone else, excluding any purchases of stocks or mutual funds?* Thereby the survey has yielded a sample of 133,553 business angels. Representativeness implies that findings can be generalized to the world's business angels.

3.2 Measurements

3.2.1 Ties
Business angels' ties with entrepreneurs have been measured by asking each business angel:

What was your relationship with the person who received your most recent personal investment?
Was this ...

* *a close family member, such as a spouse, brother, child, parent, or grandchild;*
* *some other relative, kin, or blood relation;*
* *a work colleague;*
* *a friend or neighbor; or*
* *a stranger with a good business idea?*

This categorical variable is transformed into five dichotomous variables measuring presence or absence of a tie with each of the five: family, relative, colleague, friend, stranger.

3.2.2   Culture
Culture is measured in the dimension of traditional culture versus secular-rational or modern culture (Inglehart and Welzel, 2005). This culture has been measured in the World Values Survey by asking people about their human values (www.worldvaluessurvey.org). The primary dimension of culture has traditional culture at one end and secular-rational culture at the other, with a numerical measure for each country (some countries have missing values, so we imputed values based on measured neighboring or similar countries). The measure is standardized, negative where secular-rational culture dominates and positive where traditional culture prevails.

3.2.3   Control variables
The GEM survey enables us to control for characteristics of business angels which are related to investing,

- gender, coded 0 for females and 1 for males;
- age, coded in years;
- education, coded in years of schooling to highest completed degree; and
- income, coded 1 for lowest third of family incomes, 2 for middle third, and 3 for highest third of family incomes reported by the adults in the country.

3.2.4   Techniques for analyzing the data
With two-level hierarchical data, we use two-level hierarchical linear modeling (Snijders and Bosker, 2012). This is similar to regression, but takes into consideration that the data are hierarchical, with business angels nested within countries.

4.   RESULTS

4.1   Background of the Business Angels

The background of the business angels is briefly described by the means and frequencies of their characteristics (Table 10.1). Business angels are most often males, and somewhat older, more educated, and wealthier than the typical adult.

The business angels are described further by the correlations between the variables used in the analysis (Table 10.2).

Table 10.1   Means and frequencies of characteristics of business angels

Sample	Number of business angels	133,553 business angels
	Number of countries	115 countries
Gender: Male	Percent males among business angels	61%
Age	Mean years of age of the business angels	39.4 years
Education	Mean years of schooling of the business angels	12.4 years
Income	Mean, on a 1 to 3 scale, of the business angels	2.28

Table 10.2   Correlations among variables

	Traditionality	Family	Relative	Coworker	Friend	Stranger	Gender	Age	Education
Traditionality									
Tie: Family	0.00								
Tie: Relative	0.09	−0.34							
Tie: Coworker	0.01	−0.26	−0.10						
Tie: Friend	−0.03	−0.60	−0.23	−0.17					
Tie: Stranger	−0.09	−0.23	−0.09	−0.07	−0.16				
Gender: Male	0.03	−0.16	−0.01	0.06	0.12	0.04			
Age	−0.16	0.11	−0.03	−0.03	−0.11	0.03	−0.04		
Education	−0.16	−0.06	−0.04	0.04	0.03	0.07	0.02	0.00	
Income	−0.04	−0.01	−0.01	0.01	0.00	0.02	0.08	0.05	0.21

The correlations are rather weak, indicating that no problem of multicollinearity will arise in the analyses.

4.2   Ties between Business Angel and Entrepreneur

Which ties are frequent and which ties are sparse between business angels and entrepreneurs? Family ties and friendship ties are frequent (Table 10.3). Ties with coworkers and strangers are sparse.

4.3   Culture Affecting Ties

Our research question is: how is traditional versus secular-rational culture affecting business angels' selection of ties for funding? For each type of tie, a hierarchical linear model (Table 10.4), controlling for other conditions, ascertains the effect of culture.

Table 10.3   Frequency of each tie between business angel and entrepreneur

	Frequency
Family	47%
Relative	12%
Coworker	7%
Friend	29%
Stranger	6%
Sum	100%
N business angels	133,553 business angels

Hypothesis 1 posits that culture affects funding for close family, in that traditional culture enhances business angels' likelihood of funding close family rather than others. This hypothesis is tested in model 1 in Table 10.4. The positive coefficient shows that traditionality promotes funding close family, thus supporting hypothesis 1.

Hypothesis 2 holds that culture affects funding for relatives, in that traditional culture enhances business angels' likelihood of funding relatives rather than others. This hypothesis is tested in model 2 in Table 10.4. The positive coefficient shows that traditionality promotes funding relatives, thus supporting hypothesis 2.

Hypothesis 3 claims that culture affects funding for strangers with a good idea, in that secular-rational culture enhances business angels' likelihood of funding strangers rather than others. This hypothesis is tested in model 5 in Table 10.4. The negative coefficient shows that traditionality attenuates funding strangers, that is, secular-rational culture promotes funding strangers, thus supporting hypothesis 3.

5.   DISCUSSION

In this section, the main findings are presented, the academic and theoretical contributions are elaborated, the limitations are acknowledged, and an agenda for future research is proposed.

5.1   Findings

The objective of this study is to analyze the effect of traditionality versus modernity on the ties that business angels select for funding. Our findings confirm that traditional culture enhances angels' likelihood of funding family (both close family and relatives). This is consistent with Ding et al. (2014)

Table 10.4   *Business angels' selection of ties for financing*

	Family	Relative	Coworker	Friend	Stranger
	Model 1	Model 2	Model 3	Model 4	Model 5
Traditionality	0.015†	0.036***	−0.005*	−0.022**	−0.023***
Gender: Male	−0.138***	−0.004*	0.027***	0.101***	−0.014***
Age	0.051***	−0.001	−0.005***	−0.046***	0.001†
Education	−0.008***	−0.005***	0.005***	0.003*	0.006***
Income	0.002	0.000	0.000	−0.002†	0.003***
Intercept	0.542***	0.133***	0.053***	0.221***	0.052***
Country	Yes	Yes	Yes	Yes	Yes
N countries	115	115	115	115	115
N business angels	109,446	109,446	109,446	109,446	109,446

Notes: Hierarchical linear models, with random effect of country.
Dichotomous variables are coded as 0–1 dummies.
Macro-level numerical independent variable is standardized.
Micro-level numerical independent variables are standardized and centered within country.
The number of cases in the analysis is less than the full sample size because of missing values.
† $p<0.01$; * $p<0.0$; ** $p<0.01$; *** $p<0.001$.

and Samsami (2021) whose interpretations are based on a few countries, but we here extend the idea globally. Our findings further support previous studies identifying family as the main source of informal investment in traditional countries (Au and Kwan, 2009; Pistrui et al., 2001). Moreover, our results agree with prior research that highlights the importance of strong ties in recognizing and exploiting opportunities in relationship-based contexts (Peng and Zhou, 2005; Ma et al., 2011; Li et al., 2014). This can be attributed to two main factors. The first is family commitment in the form of support and solidarity imposed by traditional societies (Samara, 2021). Second, the particularized trust prevailing in traditional societies fosters trust in family and not in strangers (Freitag and Traunmüller, 2009). While traditional societies attenuate the chance of strangers being funded, secular-rational culture encourages funding strangers (Li et al., 2014; Samsami, 2021). Our findings further support this argument by showing that funding strangers is more common in secular-rational cultures than in traditional cultures. This confirms that trusting and cooperating with strangers are more encouraged in modern than in traditional culture (Schøtt and Jensen, 2016; Freitag and Traunmüller, 2009). This can be attributed to the high generalized trust present in secular-rational countries, reinforced by strong legal and contractual frameworks (Fukuyama, 1995; Ding et al., 2014).

5.2   Theoretical Contributions

This study contributes to the under-researched areas of business entrepreneurial finance and connectivity (Ding et al., 2015) by exploring business angels' selection of ties for funding across the world.

It answers recent calls to adopt culture as a country-level contextual condition (Gimenez-Jimenez et al., 2020) and to study its effect on angels' funding (Ding et al., 2015; Samsami, 2021).

We achieved this finding by combining the individual-level data with national-level measures of culture from the World Values Survey; hence we contextualized angels' financing by accounting for the embeddedness of investors' selection of relationships in traditional versus modern culture.

Furthermore, we answered the call of Ding et al. (2014) to investigate the role of strong versus weak ties in angels' decision making by exploring the effect of ties on angels' funding from a cultural perspective (traditional versus secular-rational culture).

5.3   Practical Implications

From a practical standpoint, policy makers, entrepreneurs, and business angels can benefit from this study. It could drive governments to develop more effective policies to encourage business angels, by examining the salient ties in various countries based on culture, which greatly affects the development or limitation of entrepreneurship and trade relations, especially in the international arena. The study sheds light on the changes occurring in people's value system worldwide, emphasizing the need for governments to not only understand their country's current cultural position, but also to monitor changes. Moreover, governments in traditional countries should prioritize improving their formal institutions to help increase the generalized trust level, since lack of effective systems weakens trust, which in turn limits relationships and reduces entrepreneurial opportunities. Furthermore, this research helps entrepreneurs by providing insights regarding angels' decision making in terms of selection of ties in various countries, hence can increase their chances of obtaining funds. Finally, culture seems to play a role in the growth or failure of promising ideas. Our findings suggest that business angels in traditional cultures may need to learn to better utilize weak ties for more opportunities, since close relationships may not always lead to business success and can greatly limit opportunity recognition.

5.4   Limitations and Future Research Avenues

This research offers a platform for undergoing further research. For instance, business angels' selection of a tie for financing has been considered dichotomously, that is, the business angel either funds the tie or not, hence further research can dig deeper and examine amounts of financing. This study sheds initial light on the effect of the two types of trust (particularized and generalized) on business angels' selection of ties. Future research can further measure the two types in different countries. While we included business angels' attributes (gender, age, education, and income) as control variables, it would be informative to examine how the effects of attributes depend on culture. Furthermore, research on angel investments from a cultural perspective can be advanced along various avenues. For instance, an interesting research area would be to explore angel–entrepreneur conflicts in different cultures. Another useful endeavor would be to adopt a gendered lens and to explicitly study the effect of culture on women business angels. While this study considered gender (as a control variable), and our findings confirmed that female business angels are more likely than male business angels to fund family, it would be interesting to examine whether this gendering is more pervasive in traditional culture than in secular-rational culture. Finally, examining changes in business angels' financing following disruption (e.g., COVID-19) would be timely research that could further our understanding of selection of ties in different cultures.

REFERENCES

Aldrich, H.E., and Cliff, J.E. (2003). The pervasive effects of family on entrepreneurship: Toward a family embeddedness perspective. *Journal of Business Venturing, 18*(5), 573–596.

Arregle, J.L., Hitt, M.A., Sirmon, D.G., and Very, P. (2007). The development of organizational social capital: Attributes of family firms. *Journal of Management Studies, 44*(1), 73–95.

Ashourizadeh, S., and Schøtt, T. (2016). Exporting embedded in culture and transnational networks around entrepreneurs: A global study. *International Journal of Business and Globalisation, 16*(3), 314–334.

Au, K., Chiang, F., Birtch, T., and Ding, Z.J. (2013). Incubating the next generation to venture: The case of a family business in Hong Kong. *Asia Pacific Journal of Management, 30*(3), 749–767.

Au, K., and Kwan, H.K. (2009). Start-up capital and Chinese entrepreneurs: The role of family. *Entrepreneurship Theory and Practice, 33*(4), 889–908.

Baker, T., Gedajlovic, E., and Lubatkin, M. (2005). A framework for comparing entrepreneurship processes across nations. *Journal of International Business Studies, 36*(5), 492–504.

Bird, M., and Wennberg, K. (2014). Regional influences on the prevalence of family versus non-family start-ups. *Journal of Business Venturing, 29*(3), 421–436.

Bonini, S., Capizzi, V., Valletta, M., and Zocchi, P. (2018). Angel network affiliation and business angels' investment practices. *Journal of Corporate Finance*, *50*(6), 592–608.

Bygrave, W., and Hunt, S. (2007). For love or money? A study of financial returns on informal investments in businesses owned by relatives, friends and strangers. In L.M. Gillin (ed.), *Regional Frontiers of Entrepreneurship Research*. Melbourne: Swinburne University, 33–57.

Cardon, M.S., Sudek, R., and Mitteness, C. (2009). The impact of perceived entrepreneurial passion on angel investing. *Frontiers of Entrepreneurship Research*, *29*(2), 1.

Delhey, J., Newton, K., and Welzel, C. (2011). How general is trust in "most people"? Solving the radius of trust problem. *American Sociological Review*, *76*(5), 786–807.

Ding, Z., Au, K., and Chiang, F. (2015). Social trust and angel investors' decisions: A multilevel analysis across nations. *Journal of Business Venturing*, *30*(2), 307–321.

Ding, Z., Sun, S.L., and Au, K. (2014). Angel investors' selection criteria: A comparative institutional perspective. *Asia Pacific Journal of Management*, *31*(3), 705–731.

Dyer, W., Nenque, E., and Hill, E.J. (2014). Toward a theory of family capital and entrepreneurship: Antecedents and outcomes. *Journal of Small Business Management*, *52*(2), 266–285.

Freitag, M., and Traunmüller, R. (2009). Spheres of trust: An empirical analysis of the foundations of particularised and generalised trust. *European Journal of Political Research*, *48*(6), 782–803.

Freytag, A., and Thurik, R. (2007). Entrepreneurship and its determinants in a cross-country setting. *Journal of Evolutionary Economics*, *17*(2), 117–131.

Fukuyama, F. (1995). *Trust: The Social Virtues and the Creation of Prosperity*. New York: Free Press.

Gimenez-Jimenez, D., Edelman, L.F., Dawson, A., and Calabrò, A. (2020). Women entrepreneurs' progress in the venturing process: The impact of risk aversion and culture. *Small Business Economics*, 1–21. https://doi.org/10.1007/s11187-020-00435-8

Granovetter, M. (1985). Economic action and social structure: The problem of embeddedness. *American Journal of Sociology*, *91*(3), 481–510.

Haines, G.H., Madill, J.J., and Riding, A.L. (2003). Informal investment in Canada: Financing small business growth. *Journal of Small Business and Entrepreneurship*, *16*(3–4), 13–40.

Hechavarría, D.M. (2016). The impact of culture on national prevalence rates of social and commercial entrepreneurship. *International Entrepreneurship and Management Journal*, *12*(4), 1025–1052.

Hill, J.S. (2000). Modern-traditional behaviors: Anthropological insights into global business behaviors. *Journal of Transnational Management Development*, *5*(3), 3–21.

Hofstede, G. (2001). *Culture's Consequences*. London: Sage.

Huff, L., and Kelley, L. (2003). Levels of organizational trust in individualist versus collectivist societies: A seven nation study. *Organization Science*, *14*, 81–90.

Inglehart, R., and Welzel, C. (2005). *Modernization, Cultural Change, and Democracy: The Human Development Sequence*. Cambridge: Cambridge University Press.

Inglehart, R., and Welzel, C. (2010). The WVS cultural map of the world. World Values Survey. https://www.worldvaluessurvey.org/WVSContents.jsp?CMSID=Findings

Kramarz, F., and Skans, O. (2014). When strong ties are strong: Networks and youth labour market entry. *Review of Economic Studies*, *81*(3), 1164–1200.

Lever-Tracy, C. (1992). Interpersonal trust in ethnic business – traditional, modern or postmodern? *Policy, Organisation and Society, 5*(1), 50–63.

Li, Y., Jiang, S., Long, D., Tang, H., and Wu, J. (2014). An exploratory study of business angels in China: A research note. *Venture Capital, 16*(1), 69–83.

Li, Y., and Zahra, S. (2012). Formal institutions, culture, and venture capital activity: A cross-country analysis. *Journal of Business Venturing, 27*(1), 95–111.

Liñán, F., Jaén, I., and Martín, D. (2020). Does entrepreneurship fit her? Women entrepreneurs, gender-role orientation, and entrepreneurial culture. *Small Business Economics*. https://doi.org/10.1007/s11187-020-00433-w

Ma, R., Huang, Y.C., and Shenkar, O. (2011). Social networks and opportunity recognition: A cultural comparison between Taiwan and the United States. *Strategic Management Journal, 32*, 1183–1205.

Madill, J.J., Haines, J., George, H., and Riding, A.L. (2005). The role of angels in technology SMEs: A link to venture capital. *Venture Capital, 7*(2), 107–129.

Mason, C., and Harrison, R. (2000). The size of the informal venture capital market in the United Kingdom. *Small Business Economics, 15*(2), 137–148.

Mason, C., and Stark, M. (2004). What do investors look for in a business plan? A comparison of the investment criteria of bankers, venture capitalists and business angels. *International Small Business Journal, 22*(3), 227–248.

Maxwell, A.L., Jeffrey, S.A., and Lévesque, M. (2011). Business angel early stage decision making. *Journal of Business Venturing, 26*(2), 212–225.

Paul, S., Whittam, G., and Wyper, J. (2007). Towards a model of the business angel investment process. *Venture Capital, 9*(2), 107–125.

Peng, M.W., and Zhou, J.Q. (2005). How network strategies and institutional transitions evolve in Asia. *Asia Pacific Journal of Management, 22*(4), 321–336.

Pinillos, M., and Reyes, L. (2011). Relationship between individualist-collectivist culture and entrepreneurial activity: Evidence from global entrepreneurship monitor data. *Small Business Economics, 37*(1), 23–37.

Pistrui, D., Huang, W., Oksoy, D., Jing, Z., and Welsch, H. (2001). Entrepreneurship in China: Characteristics, attributes, and family forces shaping the emerging private sector. *Family Business Review, 14*(2), 141–152.

Poppo, L., and Zenger, T. (2002). Do formal contracts and relational governance function as substitutes or complements? *Strategic Management Journal, 23*, 707–725.

Ramadani, V. (2009). Business angels: Who they really are. *Strategic Change: Briefings in Entrepreneurial Finance, 18*(7–8), 249–258.

Samara, G. (2021). Family businesses in the Arab Middle East: What do we know and where should we go. *Journal of Family Business Strategy, 12*(3), 100359. https://doi.org/10.1016/j.jfbs.2020.100359

Samsami, M. (2021). Business angels' ties with entrepreneurs in traditional and secular-rational societies: China, Egypt and Iran contrasted with Germany and Norway. *European Journal of International Management* (in press).

Schøtt, T., and Jensen, K.W. (2016). Firms' innovation benefiting from networking and institutional support: A global analysis of national and firm effects. *Research Policy, 45*, 1233–1246.

Scott, W.R. (2013). *Institutions and Organizations: Ideas, Interests, and Identities.* London: Sage.

Snijders, T.A.B., and Bosker, R. (2012). *Multilevel Modeling.* London: Sage.

Sørheim, R. (2003). The pre-investment behaviour of business angels: A social capital approach. *Venture Capital, 5*(4), 337–364.

Sudek, R. (2006). Angel investment criteria. *Journal of Small Business Strategy*, *17*, 89–103.

Tiessen, J. (1997). Individualism, collectivism, and entrepreneurship: A framework for international comparative research. *Journal of Business Venturing*, *12*(5), 367–384.

Uhlaner, L., and Thurik, R. (2010). Postmaterialism influencing total entrepreneurial activity across nations. In A. Freytag, and R. Thurik (eds), *Entrepreneurship and Culture*. Berlin: Springer, 301–328. https://doi.org/10.1007/978-3-540-87910-7_14

Welter, F. (2011). Contextualizing entrepreneurship – conceptual challenges and ways forward. *Entrepreneurship Theory and Practice*, *35*(1), 65–184.

White, B., and Dumay, J. (2017). Business angels: A research review and new agenda. *Venture Capital*, *19*, 183–216.

Wong, P.K., and Ho, Y.P. (2007). Characteristics and determinants of informal investment in Singapore. *Venture Capital*, *9*(1), 43–70.

11. Exploring the landscape of corporate venture capital and corporate accelerators in Germany

Nikolaus Seitz and Patrick Haslanger

1. INTRODUCTION

In an era of rapid change, corporations need to innovate constantly to survive. Therefore, companies explore different organizational modes to absorb innovations from both inside and outside company boundaries. Over the past years, corporations have discovered the benefits of collaborating with young entrepreneurial firms, for multiple reasons. By working with start-ups they gain perspective on new opportunities (Benson and Ziedonis, 2009), screen potential innovations, recruit new talents, and/or rejuvenate their corporate culture. However, this engagement is for the sake of both parties, as start-ups, in turn, also benefit from having an experienced corporate partner. They gain access to complementary resources, including entrepreneurial funding, R&D, business networks, and advice, which may help start-ups to accelerate their new venture creation.

Today, external corporate venturing activity is cited as a key success factor for vibrant entrepreneurship ecosystems (Colombo et al., 2018); hence, promoting exchange and spillovers between established corporations and start-ups is top priority on almost every innovation policy agenda across the globe. Practical examples show that start-ups and corporations engage with each other via different channels and use various organizational arrangements, with corporate venture capital (CVC) investments and the growing phenomenon of corporate accelerators (CAs) as the most prominent forms. In 2019, more than 25 percent of all venture capital investments worldwide were made by corporations (PwC and CBInsights, 2019; CBInsights, 2019). Additionally, among the Fortune 500, well-known firms like AT&T, Microsoft, Allianz, and Walt Disney either invest in or manage their own start-up accelerator programs.

Although the proliferation of CVC and corporate-led accelerator programs is evident, we still know little about the different forms of investments and program types, nor how they really work or what outcomes they produce across various organizational settings and contexts. While scholars are quite optimistic about the positive impact of CVC and CA programs on start-ups, their impact on billion-dollar companies is still open for debate (Steiber and Alänge, 2020). Moreover, research has stressed that there are not only advantages to these arrangements, and managing the collaborations between such unequal partners is a challenging task involving issues of governance, cultural differences, and match-making competence (Hutter et al., 2021). A large strand of research has also highlighted that the preferred types of external corporate venturing, strategies, and outcomes differ across countries and institutional contexts (Lerner and Tåg, 2013; Li and Zahra, 2012; Belderbos et al., 2018; Dushnitsky and Shapira, 2010). For example, while US corporations often use their CVC vehicles for majority stake investments in the early seed stages of venture development, European CVC units prefer to invest in later rounds and avoid majority stake investments. Considering the nature of CA programs, European-based programs seem to be more strategically driven and often specialized with a narrow industry-focus, whereas programs sponsored by US-based firms are often generic, selecting start-ups from diverse technological and industry backgrounds (e.g. Jeng and Wells, 2000; Bertoni et al., 2015; Bonini and Alkan, 2012).

Nevertheless, our understanding about these differences remains fragemented. Most prior studies are US based or case-study driven, considering only best practices. A systematic review and report on the landscape of external corporate venturing across other countries and regions, for example Europe or East Asia, is yet missing. However, this gap in the literature is unfortunate, as both regions are constantly catching up. Taking the volume of CVC investments as a proxy for external corporate venturing, the global share of all CVC deals closed in North America decreased from 60 percent in 2013 to 40 percent in 2019. With a 38 percent share, East Asia is close behind (CBInsights, 2019), while central Europe (17 percent share in 2019), as the third largest market, is gaining more importance (Röhm, 2018).

It is the main purpose of this chapter to broaden our understanding of external corporate venturing activity across countries. We therefore draw a detailed map of the external corporate venturing landscape of Germany, the largest market for corporate venturing in Europe. In doing so, we focus on the two most popular types of external corporate venturing: CVC activity and CA programs. Based on a hand-collected dataset, combining data from 29 corporations, 36 corporate venturing units, and 765 start-ups, we aim to provide novel insights into corporate venturing in Germany, which is suggested to "differ quite markedly" (Weber and Weber, 2003, p. 22) from that in other countries in several aspects.

The chapter is structured as follows: in the second section, we review the literature on external corporate venturing and define the nature of CVC and CAs. In the third and fourth sections, we present descriptive statistics and map the corporate venturing market in Germany. The last section summarizes key insights and concludes with practical and future research implications.

2.   THE LITERATURE ON EXTERNAL CORPORATE VENTURING

As an integral part of their innovation strategies, established firms have discovered the advantages of seeking innovation capacities outside the organization (e.g. Covin and Miles, 2007). By going beyond the boundaries of a firm, corporations hope to gain access to complementary capabilities and overcome organizational barriers to innovation (Agarwal and Helfat, 2009; Eisenhardt and Martin, 2000). Besides mergers and acquisitions (M&As), the engagement with young, entrepreneurial firms has especially become a major trend in external corporate venturing (Schildt et al., 2005).

For collaborating with start-ups, established firms choose various channels and organizational forms. These could involve more loosely coupled arrangements such as joint-ventures or R&D alliances, or include equity investments or acquisitions. CVC as well as the rapidly growing phenomenon of CA programs have become quite popular for corporations seeking innovation growth outside the firm (Dushnitsky and Lavie, 2010; Keil et al., 2008; Van De Vrande and Vanhaverbeke, 2013).The main idea behind both CVC and CAs is to create a win–win scenario. Both parties lack some specific resources that the other partner is able to complementarily fill (Alvarez-Garrido and Dushnitsky, 2016; Anokhin et al., 2016; Chemmanur et al., 2014; Park and Steensma, 2012; Van De Vrande and Vanhaverbeke, 2013). Thus, while corporations get access to innovations and new trends, learn future strategic options, and meet new entrepreneurial talents to hire, start-ups benefit from "smart" entrepreneurial financing, thus gaining access to corporate resources and advice (Sauermann, 2018; Anokhin et al., 2016; Dushnitsky and Lenox, 2006; Wadhwa and Kotha, 2006).

However, while the principal purpose of CVC is quite similar to that of CAs, they are distinct institutional forms of external corporate venturing which differ regarding central aspects and main objectives, and have both advantages and disadvantages for both parties.

Corporate Venture Capital

CVC investments are minority stake equity investments from large corporations in rather new, privately held start-ups (Bertoni et al., 2013; Christofidis and Debande, 2001; Colombo and Murtinu, 2017; Gompers and Lerner, 1998; Röhm, 2018). As a vehicle for managing their start-up investments, corporations often choose specialized and autonomous business units (Bielesch et al., 2012; Keil, 2004; Chua et al., 1999). These "corporate venture capitalists" act as intermediaries, matching and balancing the resources and interests of the corporation and their portfolio of start-ups (Dushnitsky and Lenox, 2006; Ernst et al., 2005). Today, CVC accounts for more than 25 percent of all venture capital deals made globally (PwC and CBInsights, 2019; CBInsights, 2019).

Historically, financial returns were the primary objective of CVC investments (Siegel et al., 1988). Over time, however, the importance of strategic considerations for corporations increased, such as gaining insight on new technology, opening up to different markets, getting access to talent, and starting a cultural rejuvenation within their own organization (Anokhin et al., 2016; Dushnitsky and Lenox, 2006; Wadhwa and Kotha, 2006). Start-ups, besides funding, gain access to complementary resources and business networks that only an experienced corporate partner can offer (Asel et al., 2015; Gans and Stern, 2003; Ivanov and Xie, 2010; Park and Bae, 2018). Despite its financial and strategic objective, it remains unclear whether CVC is value-enhancing for both of the involved parties (e.g. Röhm, 2018; Seitz et al., 2020).

The empirical literature reflects the trade-off between benefits and costs. The results are not as convincing as is often assumed. While a broad consensus exists on the overall positive effects of CVC (e.g. Colombo and Murtinu, 2017; Dushnitsky and Lenox, 2005), a few studies doubt the generous incentives of corporations supporting start-ups, stating for example that "CVC programs as an investor class were value destroyers" (Allen and Hevert, 2007, p. 273) and concluding that "CVC-backed start-ups do not outperform" their control group (Park and Bae, 2018, p. 332). They even warn start-ups of the potential downsides of CVC programs that may threaten their future market value. Yet it remains unclear whether these inconsistencies in the literature stem from methodological differences among the studies' design, or whether it is because of conceptual rigor. Recent research concludes that reported effects may be considerably affected by the objective of investments and whether strategic or financial returns are considered (e.g. Seitz et al., 2020). Other studies highlighted that while start-ups always benefit from CVC, the effect on corporations' performance is mostly poor and over-estimated (Dushnitsky and Shapira, 2010). Likewise, the context is also considered to be a crucial factor for understanding the contrasting findings. Specifically, the country and institutional context and the timing of investments also matters when evaluating the existing findings.

Corporate Accelerators

CA programs differ from CVC in several ways. A CA is a type of start-up accelerator that has a form of direct sponsorship from an established corporation (Hallen et al., 2017; Cohen et al., 2019). Similar with all types of start-up accelerators (public, private, investor-sponsored, university, etc.), corporate-led accelerators invite and select promising new start-ups and entrepreneurial teams to work side-by-side during a short-term bootcamp program of about two to three months. The start-ups are organized in cohorts, so-called "batches." Every start-up in a batch receives the same amount of funding, which is meant to cover the basic expenses for experimentation during the program, but not enough to allow substantial development afterwards (Cohen et al., 2019). During the program start-ups have access to professional coaching, mentors, and network partners to develop their ventures and business innovations (Drori and Wright, 2018). The program usually ends with a "demo day" event, where the accelerated start-ups pitch their business ideas in front of a jury and potential investors. New, promising start-ups may leave the program with a follow-up investment.

Thereby, CA programs are innovation intermediaries between start-ups and their corporate sponsors (e.g. Hallen et al., 2017). In a very early "seed" stage of venture development, they help discover potential new innovations (Yu, 2020) while filtering the "bad" entrepreneurs from the "good" ones (Kupp et al., 2017). Start-ups, in turn, benefit from industry-related advice, access to corporate resources, and usually their first entrepreneurial financing. The major advantage of this type of external corporate venturing is in its speed and flexibility for both parties. Whereas CVC is primarily a long-term investment, CAs normally just cover a start-up's costs during the two to three months of the program. After this short timeframe, start-ups either receive the next stage of funding or come away empty-handed (e.g. Moschner et al., 2019). Thus, corporations get a relatively risk-free opportunity to screen new trends and ideas without being tied up in costly equity investments. Start-up teams, on the other hand, have the chance to experiment and provide a first proof-of-concept for their business idea.

However, while the impact of a "few" start-ups on the performance of a multi-billion-dollar corporation is difficult to demonstrate empirically (e.g. Steiber and Alänge, 2020; Cohen et al., 2019), researchers are quite optimistic about the value of CAs for start-ups. However, consistent empirical evidence remains missing. Initial studies that controlled for some sort of corporate sponsorship report mixed findings. Yu (2020) found that accelerated start-ups need more time and are less likely to achieve key milestones than their non-accelerated peers. Cohen et al. (2019) report that investor-led accelerators outperform CAs in boosting the market valuation of accelerated start-ups. Cohen (2013), Dempwolf et al. (2014), and Hochberg (2016) raise general concerns about the impact of these programs. Thus, given the short timeframe of training, just a matter of weeks, the effect of acceleration on start-ups' future growth prospects is questionable. Other articles highlight that it is more context-specific, and whether start-ups benefit or not depends on the background of the founder (Cohen et al., 2019), the prospective outcomes (Vandeweghe and Fu, 2018), and the accelerators' program design and services (Pauwels et al., 2016). Stayton and Mangematin (2019), for instance, outline the importance of the accelerators' proximity to start-up hubs and industrial clusters. Cohen et al. (2019) stress the important role of accelerators' external mentors and partner network for speeding up market access of the portfolio of start-ups. Seitz et al. (2019) report that whether start-ups benefit from CA programs is related to the design and governance of these programs (industry specialization, batch sizes, relationship to the parent company, etc.).

To summarize, while the literature on CVC is already well-established (e.g. Röhm et al., 2018), research on CAs is still in its developmental stages (Crişan et al., 2021; Colombo et al., 2018; Kanbach and Stubner, 2016). For future research possibilities, scholars identify several blind spots in the literature on CAs and CVC. Thus, only a limited set of studies discusses governance aspects (e.g. Dokko and Gaba, 2012; Dushnitsky and Shapira, 2010; Hill and Birkinshaw, 2014; Souitaris et al., 2012), like the organizational set-up or human capital of the CVC unit. Anokhin et al. (2016) highlight the need to incorporate governance factors in CVC studies. Moreover, more work has to be done on the infrastructural and service factors, for example coaching, networks, and structure and design of programs (e.g. Alvarez-Garrido and Dushnitsky, 2016; Park and Steensma, 2012). Colombo et al. (2018) stress the need for further research on the organization and design of CAs, specifically whether it is better to have generalist programs or specialized programs with a specific industry-focus. Thus, the present chapter aims to provide insights into the practice of external venturing in Germany. In the following section, we offer anectodical evidence and descriptive statistics on the nature and characteristics of German-based CVC and CA programs.

3. EXTERNAL CORPORATE VENTURING IN GERMANY

Most studies on corporate venturing refer to the US. Being the largest entrepreneurship market, sufficient data is available (Harrison and Fitza, 2014). In contrast, European data is poorly covered by the popular databases (Colombo and Murtinu, 2017). The success of any form of venturing is highly contextual and influenced by a complex ecosystem, including fiscal (e.g. taxes), regulatory (e.g. labor market and company laws), infrastructural (e.g. research centers and technology parks), and cultural dimensions, in addition to the peculiarities of each financial system (Acs et al., 2017; Audretsch and Belitski, 2020). For example, equity-oriented countries like the US, the UK, and the Netherlands show more developed CVC markets than debt-oriented countries like Germany, Italy, and France (Christofidis and Debande, 2001; Shah et al., 2019). Numerous research studies report that the financial system in Germany presents a hurdle to venture capital investments, especially due to it being bank-based (e.g. Röhm, 2018; Sunley et al., 2005), its insufficient investor protection (Becker and Hellmann, 2003), and an inadequately active stock market (Black and Gilson, 1998). In Germany, silent partnerships or private limited partnerships with a restricted use of debt and equity instruments, such as no mechanism for convertible debt (Bascha and Walz, 2002), further limit investments. Economically, Germany differs from other countries due to its strong group of innovative hidden champions, the German "Mittelstand" (Lehmann et al., 2019; Audretsch et al., 2018). Despite its long history of successful innovations that are mainly driven by the economy's engineering capabilities, Germany's innovations tend to be rather incremental and exploitative, rather than being radical, breathtaking, explorative innovations (e.g. Woschke et al., 2017; Becker and Hellmann, 2003). In the last decade, the relatively good German economy resulted in low unemployment and, consequently, a steady decline in the founder ratio to only 1.3 percent in 2016 (Metzger, 2017). In contrast to the overall economy, which is historically focused on manufacturing industries and engineering, 70 percent of start-ups in Germany are in the service sector (Metzger, 2017).

The frequency and intensity of CVC is also dependent on the entrepreneurial culture and spirit of a country (e.g. Fritsch et al., 2019; Lehmann and Seitz, 2017). Innovativeness, availability of good scientists, motivation, and skill sets are equally as important as failure tolerance, a supporting infrastructure, and an accommodating legal framework (Christofidis and Debande, 2001; National Venture Capital Association, 2015). Regional culture influences firm culture (Hofstede, 2001, p. 373; Fritsch et al., 2019), which in turn influences the behavior and mental models of individuals (Herbig and Dunphy, 1998; Hofstede et al., 2010, p. 4). The German culture is not necessarily supportive to entrepreneurship. The "German Angst" produces risk aversion and the low public perception of being self-employed contributes to a modest founding rate in Germany (Jokela et al., 2017). In addition, German entrepreneurs prefer strong control over their firm, making third-party equity investments difficult (Bascha and Walz, 2002, p. 18). Lastly, founder role models are important in giving support, serving as an inspirational example and strengthening entrepreneurial confidence (Rocha and Van Praag, 2020; Röhl, 2016). Clearly, Germany lacks great inspiring founders and start-up unicorns, such as Google, Facebook, or Amazon, that may act as role models (e.g. Block, 2011).

The policy context also matters to corporate venture activity. In Germany, entrepreneurship has gained political interest since the late 1990s, resulting in the setting up of public policy initiatives, including programs to foster research and technology transfer, accelerators, incubators, and venture subsidiaries for high-tech start-ups (Audretsch et al., 2019). Nonetheless, the "German norms on contracting and corporate governance provided insufficient investor protection, especially for the financing of early stage, high-risk ventures" (Becker and Hellmann, 2003, p. 37). This resulted in a relatively under-developed market for venture capital on the one hand (Avnimelech et al., 2010), but on the other hand, it shaped Germany's rich supply of alternative start-up support structures, including a vibrant CVC scene, corporate innovation labs and incubators, and a variety of accelerator programs. In the following, we provide descriptive facts about the organizational design and current trends and developments of CVC and CAs in Germany.

4.   THE LANDSCAPE OF CVC AND CAs IN GERMANY

In order to shed light on the CVC and CA landscape in Germany, we collected and synthesized firm data from multiple sources and at multiple levels (corporations, start-ups, and external corporate venturing units). To identify CVC units and CA programs we searched the globally known funding database *PitchBook* for venture investments. *PitchBook* collects data on ventures, start-ups, investors, mergers and acquisitions, funds, advisors, start-up coaches, founders, and people across the entrepreneurship community (PitchBook, 2021).

We found that during the time of data collection (2017–2019) in Germany, 29 corporations are actively engaged in 36 external corporate venturing units, 15 CAs and 21 CVC units. Table 11.1 gives a complete overview of the included units and programs.

Up to the end of 2019, 765 start-ups in total have been under the management of those external venture units (n=223 in CAs; n=542 in CVC units). Several start-ups are included multiple times in the table as they are under the management of two or even three corporate ventures in parallel. Next, we combine the start-up data from *PitchBook* with our own hand-collected CA characteristics and information on the sponsoring corporate firm. Therefore, we used information from various sources, including corporate websites, annual reports, and social media profiles (LinkedIn, Facebook).

Table 11.1   Overview of all sampled CVC units and CA programs

Corporate Venturing Unit	Type	Location	Establishment	Industry	Parent company	Headquarters	Start-ups under Management
Agile Accelerator	CA	Berlin	2013	Energy	E.ON SE	Essen	62
Airbus BizLab	CA	Hamburg	2016	Industrial & Material	Airbus S.A.S	Toulouse (FRA)	10
Audi Electronics Venture	CVC	Ingolstadt	2001	Consumer Discretionary	Audi AG	Ingolstadt	7
Axel Springer Digital Ventures	CVC	Berlin	2014	Multiple Industries	Axel Springer SE	Berlin	8
Axel Springer Plug and Play Accelerator	CA	Berlin	2013	Multiple Industries	Axel Springer SE	Berlin	75
BASF Venture Capital	CVC	Ludwigshafen	2001	Industrial & Material	BASF SE	Ludwigshafen	23
Beyond1435	CA	Berlin	2017	Industrial & Material	Deutsche Bahn AG	Berlin	3
BMW i Ventures	CVC	Munich	2011	Multiple Industries	BMW AG	Munich	28
Boehringer Ingelheim Venture Fund	CVC	Mainz	2010	Health Care	Boehringer Ingelheim AG & Co. KG	Ingelheim	20
CommerzVentures	CVC	Frankfurt am Main	2014	Multiple Industries	Commerzbank AG	Frankfurt am Main	11
Deutsche Telekom Capital Partners	CVC	Hamburg	2014	Information and Communications Technology (ICT)	Deutsche Telekom AG	Bonn	87
Dieter von Holzbrinck Ventures	CVC	Munich	2000	Consumer Discretionary	Verlagsgruppe Georg von Holzbrinck	Stuttgart	16
DuMont Venture Holding	CVC	Cologne, Bonn	2007	Consumer Discretionary	M. DuMont Schauberg	Cologne	10
E.ON Strategic Co-Investments	CVC	Dusseldorf	2013	Energy	E.ON SE	Essen	12
EnBW New Ventures	CVC	Karlsruhe	2015	Energy	EnBW Energie Baden-Wurtemberg AG	Karlsruhe	4
Evonik Venture Capital	CVC	Frankfurt am Main	2012	Industrial & Material	Evonik Industries AG	Essen	10
Fresenius Medical Care Ventures	CVC	Frankfurt am Main	2015	Health Care	Fresenius SE & Co KGaA	Bad Homburg	1
Grants4Apps	CA	Berlin	2014	Health Care	Bayer AG	Leverkusen	32
Henkel Ventures	CVC	Dusseldorf	2017	Multiple Industries	Henkel AG & Co. KGaA	Dusseldorf	4
Hubraum	CA	Berlin	2012	Multiple Industries	Deutsche Telekom	Bonn	74
Innogy Innovation Hub	CA	Essen	2015	Multiple Industries	Innogy SE	Essen	4
K – Invest	CVC	Berlin	2009	Consumer Discretionary	K – Mail Order GmbH & Co. KG (Klingel Group)	Pforzheim	13
Main Incubator	CA	Frankfurt am Main	2014	Financials	Commerzbank AG	Frankfurt am Main	14
Merck Accelerator	CA	Darmstadt	2015	Health Care	Merck KGaA	Darmstadt	23
Merck Ventures	CVC	Darmstadt	2009	Health Care	Merck KGaA	Darmstadt	29
Mobile Ventures (Frankfurt)	CVC	Frankfurt am Main	2013	Information and Communications Technology (ICT)	Drillisch AG	Maintal	2
Next Media Accelerator	CA	Hamburg	2015	Consumer Discretionary	dpa Deutsche Presse Agentur	Hamburg	16
Next47	CVC	Munich	2016	Multiple Industries	Siemens AG	Berlin, Munich	58
ProSiebenSat.1 Accelerator	CA	Munich	2013	Consumer Discretionary	ProSiebenSat.1 Media SE	Munich	31
Retailtech Hub	CA	Munich	2017	Consumer Discretionary	Media Saturn Holding, Plug and Play	Munich	8
Robert Bosch Venture Capital	CVC	Stuttgart	2007	Multiple Industries	Robert Bosch GmbH	Stuttgart	30
Seven Ventures	CVC	Munich	2009	Multiple Industries	ProSiebenSat.1 Media SE	Munich	19
Siemens Technology Accelerator	CA	Munich	2001	Information and Communications Technology (ICT)	Siemens AG	Berlin, Munich	5
Startup Autobahn	CA	Stuttgart	2016	Information and Communications Technology (ICT)	Daimler AG (Mercedes-Benz AG)	Stuttgart	40
Techstars METRO Accelerator	CA	Berlin	2015	Consumer Discretionary	Metro AG	Dusseldorf	9
Vogel Ventures	CVC	Berlin	2013	Multiple Industries	Vogel Communications Group GmbH & Co. KG	Wurzburg	10

Most of these companies are large, well-established global players and have their headquarters in Germany. Almost half of the sponsoring corporations are active in consumer industries. Nonetheless, the data also covers sectors like industrial & material (17 percent), health care (14 percent), energy (10 percent), ICT (7 percent), and financial (3 percent). Several corporations, Siemens being one example, are active in multiple industries. The sponsoring corporations differ widely in age. Some of the oldest companies, like Siemens (Next47 and Siemens Technology Accelerator) and DuMont Schauberg (DuMont Venture Holding), were founded in the first half of the 19th century. The majority of corporations have their headquarters in Germany, where only Merck (US) and Airbus (France) are exceptions. As expected, there is some local concentration around metropolitan areas like Munich, Stuttgart, Berlin, Cologne, and Essen. However, some companies are located in smaller cities due to their heritage, like BASF (BASF Venture Capital) in Ludwigshafen or Klingel (K – Invest) in Pforzheim. As corporate venturing is a costly endeavor, most of the corporations are of a larger size. For example, Siemens and Bosch (Robert Bosch Venture Capital) are the largest companies, having generated revenues above 300bn€ in 2017. In terms of the number of employees, the car manufacturers Daimler (Startup Autobahn) and BMW (BMW iVentures) are on the top of the list. Nonetheless, smaller players are also included, such as Drillisch AG (Mobile Ventures), with revenues only slightly above 3bn€ and around 3,000 employees. Corporate venturing is an avenue for corporate innovation. As expected, the corporations with the highest R&D spending all operate in the health care industry. Boehringer Ingelheim (17 percent), Merck (14 percent), and Bayer (13 percent) all spend more than 10 percent of their annual revenue on R&D. However, the dataset shows that it is not limited to corporations in technology- and research-intensive sectors. For example, the energy providers E.ON (E.ON Strategic Co-Investments) and EnBW (EnBW Venture Capital) spend relatively little on R&D but still operate CVC units.

The Development of CVC and CAs in Germany

Figure 11.1 outlines the development of CVC and CAs in Germany. The data shows a lagging behavior for German-based CAs, with the majority being incorporated from 2013 onwards. The skewness towards CVC units can especially be explained by a look back in history. As CVC units are the older phenomenon, it is not surprising that they comprise the larger share. In the US (the leading market), CVC units can be traced back to shortly after the Second World War, experiencing a strong boost in the 1970s (Christofidis and Debande, 2001). Selected business analysts even consider the chemicals company DuPont's 1914 investment in six-year-old car manufacturer General Motors as the first corporate venturing activity (Jafar, 2018).

Although the first European CVC units were founded in the 1980s, the fast spread of the internet in the 2000s changed the way corporate innovation occurred and thereby increased the importance of corporation venturing (Christofidis and Debande, 2001). A key turning point happened in 2009 when the CVC market was growing even though the overall economy was on the decline. According to Radcliffe and Lehot (2018), this signals the increased strategic importance of corporate venturing. Since the early days, CVC investments have had a cyclical nature with the most recent wave having started in early 2000 (Dushnitsky and Lenox, 2006). Since the financial crisis in 2007 and 2008, CVC units have remained an attractive tool for corporations to source external innovations. Most recently, Henkel Ventures was founded in 2017.

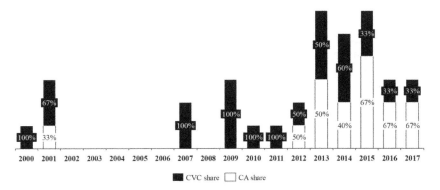

Figure 11.1   Share of CVC units vs. CAs by date of establishment

The establishment of CAs in general, and specifically in Germany, is a more recent trend, with Siemens Technology Accelerator being an exception. This particular accelerator was founded in 2001 with the goal of detecting and commercializing external non-core innovative technologies. Although Siemens Technology Accelerator follows the definition of a CA, it also provides CVC investments.

However, the rapid uptick of CVC and CAs since 2013 is driven by the digitization agendas of German corporations and the emergence of a vibrant German start-up scene. Thus, firms accept and appreciate the disrupting nature of new technological advances. Moreover, the German start-up ecosystem is more healthy nowadays than it was during the internet bubble, accelerating the set-up of CVC units and CAs, especially for the companies of the German Mittelstand (VentureCapital Magazin, 2017).

The Geography of CVC Units and CAs in Germany

A large strand of entrepreneurship literature has highlighted the importance of location and spatial proximity for start-up growth and innovation spillovers (e.g. Audretsch and Feldman, 1996; Audretsch and Belitski, 2017). Cultural amenities, the clustering of talents, and a close distance to research institutes and universities stimulates creativity and innovation spillovers, thereby boosting start-up success (e.g. Audretsch et al., 2021; Belderbos et al., 2018). Hence, it is not surprising that most external corporate venturing units are based in large cities, for example Munich, Cologne, and Berlin, Germany's largest start-up hub. A main promised advantage for start-ups selecting a corporate venturing unit is the possibility of desired spillovers through corporate partnership. However, since "great ideas have to pass through doorways not halls" (Audretsch and Feldman, 1996), spatial proximity and a close distance between the sponsoring corporation and the start-ups could be beneficial for spillover effects and the sharing of complementary resources. Considering the two different types of corporate venturing activity in our dataset, we observe an interesting geographical pattern (see Figure 11.2). CVC units are closely located to the headquarters of the sponsoring firm. This can be in vibrant metropolitan areas, as is the case for Siemens in Munich, but also in more rural, industrial areas such as Ludwigshafen where BASF is located. CAs operate exclusively in start-up hotspots and are not necessarily located closely to the corporation running these programs.

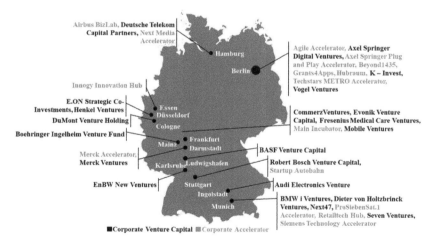

Figure 11.2   Location of CVC units and CAs

This underlines the distinct objectives, working styles, and requirements of CVC units compared to CAs. CVC units primarily share an investment objective, without a need to provide vibrant spaces to coach and train a portfolio of start-ups, while CAs are platforms for start-ups, providing space and "playgrounds" for experimentation and creativity spillovers. Therefore, an entire ecosystem is needed for CAs, including amenities, functions, and other infrastructures where start-ups can exchange with each other.

Industry Specialization of CVC Units and CAs in Germany

Across industries, start-ups and corporations use CVC units and CA programs primarily as innovation vehicles. Whether potential spillovers may be exploited is a question of the investment strategy and focus of the program (Colombo et al., 2018, p. 195). Specifically, there has been ongoing research into whether specialized programs selecting and investing in start-ups with a clear industry-focus are better, or whether diversity is best to boost synergies and the acceleration of start-ups (e.g. Cohen et al., 2019). For our sample, we use Standard Industrial Classification (SIC) codings to compare the industry affiliations. Figure 11.3 gives an overview of the industry patterns among CVC and CA programs in Germany.

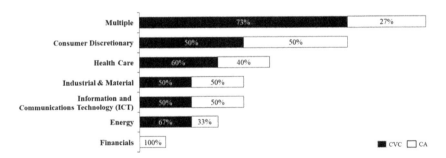

Figure 11.3   Split of CVC units and CAs by industry

Although there are some slight differences between the sectors (e.g. energy sector), CVC units and CAs are similarly popular among industries. In Germany, 73 percent of the CVC units invest in portfolio start-ups with diverse industry backgrounds, whereas the majority of CA programs are industry-specific, focusing on the core industry of the sponsoring firm. However, this supports the main intuition that CA programs are primarily designed to create spillovers due to corporate mentorship, where the industry-fit is essential for exploiting synergies. CVC units, however, are often

*Table 11.2   Summary of selected design features and services of CVC
units and CAs*

Variable	Obs.	Mean	Std. Dev.	Min.	Max.
Employees	**30**	**24.0**	**29.2**	**3**	**131**
Employees (CVC)	18	24.6	35.1	3	131
Employees (CA)	12	23.0	18.4	5	62
Start-ups under management	**36**	**22.4**	**22.4**	**1**	**87**
Start-ups under management (CVC)	21	19.1	20.2	1	87
Start-ups under management (CA)	15	27.1	25.1	3	75
Corporate partners	**36**	**3.3**	**4.5**	**0**	**17**
Corporate partners (CVC)	21	1.5	2.2	0	11
Corporate partners (CA)	15	5.9	5.5	1	17
Independent business unit	**35**	**0.9**	**0.4**	**0**	**1**
Independent business unit (CVC)	21	0.9	0.3	0	1
Independent business unit (CA)	14	0.8	0.4	0	1
Number of mentors	**6**	**98.2**	**84.2**	**21**	**238**
Number of mentors (CVC)	-	-	-	-	-
Number of mentors (CA)	6	98.2	84.2	21	238
Provision of co-working space	**36**	**0.3**	**0.5**	**0**	**1**
Provision of co-working space (CVC)	21	0.0	0.0	0	0
Provision of co-working space (CA)	15	0.8	0.4	0	1

used for acquiring complementary resources and new technologies, or other
investment objectives. In this context, diverse backgrounds better complement
existing resources.

Design and Management of CVC Units and CAs in Germany

Program design, the accessibility and availability of resources, and organ-
izational/operational management of the corporate venturing units are also
essential for exploiting spillovers (e.g. Pauwels et al., 2016). Within this
context, research outlines the importance of portfolio and batch sizes, the role
of management, accessibility to mentors and network partners, and the organizational embeddedness of the corporate venturing unit. Table 11.2 presents
the sample of relevant design features and services for the CVC units and CAs
activity in Germany.

CVC units and CA programs are relatively similar regarding their size, considering the number of employees. However, the results are heavily impacted
by the outliers of Audi (n=131) and Siemens' Next47 (n=100). With regard

to start-ups under management, differences between CVC units and CAs are larger. Although the CVC Deutsche Telekom Capital Partners has almost 90 start-ups under management, CVC units tend to be more focused, managing 19 start-ups on average.

Surprisingly, CVC units tend to have a broader corporate network than CA programs. However, these findings could be also biased by several outliers. For instance, the Deutsche Telekom Capital Partners name 11 corporate partners, whereas Seven Ventures reports no corporate partnerships at all. Moreover, several CAs, for example the Siemens Technology Accelerator or Bayer's Grants4Apps, only report one corporate partner. In contrast, Daimlers Startup Autobahn is a joint program hosted together with the University of Stuttgart while Axel Springer's Plug and Play is in a project-based partnership with either BASF or Siemens at any given time.

The majority of CVC units and CAs are managed independently and separated from the sponsoring corporation and its operations. However, only a few programs are integrated in corporate units, for example managed as a sub-department of R&D. In line with Weiblen and Chesbrough (2015), Kohler (2016), and Hallen et al. (2017), this study finds that CVC units and CAs differ in their offerings. CAs are much closer to the start-up through the offer of specific mentoring, whereas CVC units do not explicitly report any mentoring activities. Moreover, CAs often supply office space to start-ups, allowing for co-working possibilities with the peer start-ups in the batch in order to promote spillovers.

The Selection and Portfolio of Start-Ups in German CVC and CAs

Our sample encompasses 765 distinct start-ups that are under the management of German CVC units or CAs.[1] Some variables like revenue are, however, not available for all start-ups.[2] Figure 11.4 shows the establishment year of the start-ups. As expected, the majority are between two and ten years old. Some start-ups are young and were established only in 2017. One can see that CVC units manage more seasoned start-ups, whereas younger start-ups tend to be under CA management, which is in line with expectations. Interestingly, some of the start-ups were established more than 30 years ago, for example Dalim Software and Locanis in 1985 or Transparent Energy Systems in 1986. Transparent Energy Systems, for example, is an India-based provider of systems designed for power cogeneration, waste heat recovery, effluent water recycling, and ammonia absorption refrigeration. Although the company was established in 1986, they received their first financing from Next47 in 2009. Having only around 50 employees, they still operate in a start-up-like manner.

The example of Transparent Energy Systems shows that the age of a start-up alone is not a sufficient indicator for its lifecycle stage. Therefore, start-ups

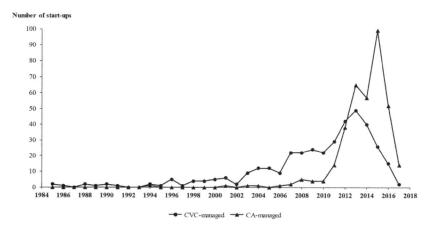

Number of start-ups

Figure 11.4   Number of start-ups by establishment date

are clustered according to their stage of venture development, as shown in Figure 11.5. As expected, CVC units tend to invest in early and later stage start-ups, whereas CAs focus on start-ups in the seed and start-up phases. This is fully in line with the different missions of the corporate venturing vehicles. Surprisingly, hardly any of the start-ups are reported as being in the expansion stage. Despite thorough analysis and discussions with other scholars, no compelling explanation for this phenomenon has been found.

Although the sample focuses on Germany-based corporate venturing vehicles only, the accelerated start-ups are geographically headquartered all around the world. Figure 11.6 presents the location of the start-ups. The start-ups are founded in 41 different countries, with a large number coming from either Europe, the US, or Canada. Corporations and especially corporate venturing units that are based in Germany know the European market much better and have closer links to the local start-up environment. The large number of start-ups from the US, especially from Silicon Valley and the Boston area, is due to the high number of (especially tech-driven) start-ups that are situated in these hubs. Outside of Europe and North America, the country with the largest number of start-ups is Israel. Although this might be surprising to some, the knowledgeable reader will be aware of Israel's entrepreneurial potential, especially in Tel Aviv. The city is often seen as one of the major start-up hubs outside the US, mainly due to its open culture, the strong talent pool, and the fact that English proficiency is high. In contrast, several countries are the location of only one start-up in the sample. For example, ES Media, the provider of an online news platform, is the only start-up from Egypt. Furthermore, mainland China and Hong Kong are underrepresented with only one start-up each.

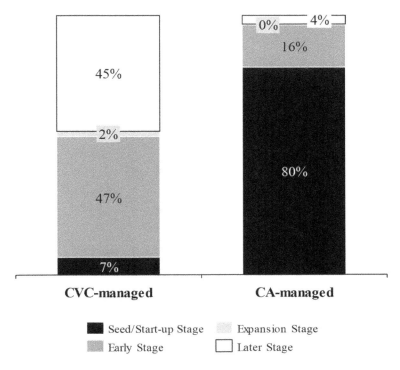

Figure 11.5   Share of start-ups by lifecycle stage

Although start-ups come from different parts of the world, there is a clear tendency with regard to the industry they operate in (see Figure 11.7). Around half of all start-ups are active in the Information and Communications Technology (ICT) industry. This finding can be traced to the fact that all corporations, independent of their own industry, follow the trend of digitization. Especially with regard to state-of-the-art innovation, ICT capabilities, for example big-data analytics, are required. The ICT start-ups range from Bio Check Technologies, a cloud-based food distribution software for retailers, to Easycheck, a platform for comparing energy costs of electric devices, to Watt Works, a grid optimization software, to JustPark, a provider of car-parking applications. No big differences between CVC units and CAs seem to exist with regard to the industries of start-ups under management. The low share of energy and financial sector start-ups can be explained by the low number of respective corporate venturing units under consideration.

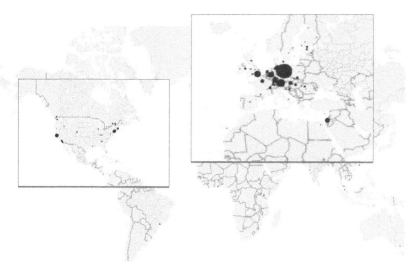

Figure 11.6   Location of start-ups (bubble size represents number of start-ups)

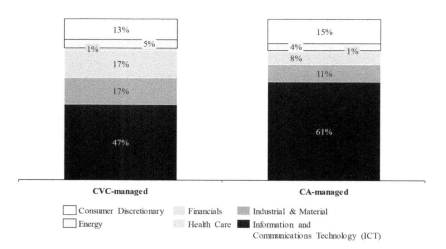

Figure 11.7   Industry split of start-ups by CVC vs. CA

Table 11.3 provides insights on the size, financials, and social media activities of start-ups and reports the minimum, maximum, and averages for each of the respective indicators. On average, CVC-backed start-ups have 288 employees,

Table 11.3   *Summary statistics on selected start-up variables*

Variable	Obs.	Mean	Std. Dev.	Min.	Max.
Employees	**579**	**170.7**	**2,137.6**	**1**	**50,000**
Employees (CVC-managed)	332	288.3	2,818.8	2	50,000
Employees (CA-managed)	247	12.6	25.1	1	290
Revenue	**90**	**42.5**	**139.7**	**0.01**	**1,047.1**
Revenue (CVC-managed)	74	51.6	152.8	0.01	1,047.1
Revenue (CA-managed)	16	0.6	0.6	0.01	1.84
Total raised	**603**	**29.5**	**99.9**	**0.01**	**1,008.0**
Total raised (CVC-managed)	325	52.8	131.6	0.02	1,008.0
Total raised (CA-managed)	278	2.3	8.4	0.01	70.18
Facebook likes[a]	**538**	**10,741.7**	**88,504.0**	**1**	**1,708,117**
Facebook likes (CVC-managed)	260	21,939.8	126,477.0	1	1,708,117
Facebook likes (CA-managed)	278	268.7	685.2	1	10,298
Twitter followers[b]	**597**	**5,121.4**	**90,002.2**	**1**	**2,193,656**
Twitter followers (CVC-managed)	294	10,155.9	128,167.3	1	2,193,656
Twitter followers (CA-managed)	303	236.5	528.7	1	7,729

Notes: [a] Excluding start-ups without Facebook presence; [b] Excluding start-ups without Twitter presence.

whereas CA-backed start-ups only have 13. The extreme outlier with 50,000 employees (the second biggest start-up only has 9,100 employees) is the Merck Venture-backed Alcan Systems, a provider of smart antenna technology. The largest CA-backed start-up is N26, a well-known mobile banking provider backed by the Axel Springer Plug and Play Accelerator. Hardly any information is available in regard to revenue, as many start-ups either fail to generate a revenue or do not report the revenue that they make.

Nonetheless, CVC-backed start-ups are larger in size, thus are more likely to generate and report revenues than CA-backed start-ups. One key financial indicator of start-up success is the total venture capital start-ups have raised in financing rounds. First, CVC-managed start-ups raise, as expected, more money than CA-managed start-ups. Second, the average amount raised is surprisingly similar to the average revenue. However, one cannot derive a 1× revenue valuation multiple from that. First, the number of observations for revenue is too small. Second, and more important, the total raised does not refer to a 100 percent equity stake, but to lower shares. Therefore, the revenue multiple of the start-ups is clearly higher than 1×. In fact, a back-of-the-envelope calculation of revenue multiples, based on the last financing information available, leads to multiples of around 4×–5× for CVC-managed start-ups and 7× for CA-backed enterprises.

Lastly, a brief glance of the start-ups' social media activities is provided. CVC-managed start-ups have both more Facebook likes and more Twitter followers than CA-managed ventures. Interestingly, CVC-managed start-ups have more than 80 times as many Facebook likes than CA-managed start-ups on average, whereas they only have around 40 times as many Twitter followers.

5.   SUMMARY AND DISCUSSION

This study complements prior research by providing a regional focus on Germany, a comparison of different corporate venturing forms, and a discussion of all three layers involved in corporate venturing – namely corporate venturing units, start-ups, and corporations. Based on a novel, hand-collected sample of 21 German CVC units and 15 CAs managing 765 distinct start-ups, the results corroborate that the two forms of corporate venturing differ with regard to their missions, organization designs, governance models, and networks. Moreover, the start-ups under management differ, with CVC units supporting larger and more established start-ups than CAs.

Through offering first insights and descriptive statistics, this study adds to the literature in several ways. Most research on corporate venturing is focused on the US (Harrison and Fitza, 2014). This skewedness is due to the fact that the US is seen as the leading venturing market (Christofidis and Debande, 2001). The European market is only poorly covered (Colombo and Murtinu, 2017). By bringing in a German perspective, this chapter contributes to the development of more generalizable findings and conclusions through giving a perspective on corporate venturing units in a market that differs from the US in many regards.

Recently, the topic of corporate venturing received great attention from both scholars and practitioners. In particular, the topic of CAs has only been discussed for a few years. From a scholarly perspective, this study sheds light on multiple research problems as both CVC units and CAs are considered in more detail. Another contribution of this study is the multi-level data structure, as recommended by Colombo et al. (2018, p. 188). Thus, our dataset includes information on three levels, namely the sponsoring corporation, the corporate venturing vehicle, and the start-ups under management.

Although this study offers novel insights on external corporate venturing activity in Germany, it comes with several limitations and implications for future research. Of course, while the country-focus helps to mitigate the effect of differences in legal or tax regimes, culture, or specifics of the economy, like a large share of small- and medium-sized companies, it also restricts the possibility to compare derived findings across countries. Therefore, the generalizability of findings derived from this dataset to other countries is limited. The novel, hand-collected, multi-level dataset is based on various public sources and start-up-specific databases. Although this serves as a strong foundation for meticulous analytical research, further insights on corporate venturing could be drawn from a combination of quantitative and qualitative research. For example, one could enhance the data by performing surveys and interviews with experts from both the corporate and start-up worlds. Such an approach could unveil insights regarding non-published information, for example the pay and incentive structure of the corporate venturing unit managers or the corporate objectives for engaging in corporate venturing activities. This dataset is limited to corporate venturing units, their start-ups under management, and their parent corporation. In line with existing literature on venture capital, a comparison of corporate venturing, that is, CVC units and CAs, with venturing done by non-corporate players, for example independent venture capital funds or stand-alone accelerators, would enable the identification of the advantages and drawbacks corporate venturing has in comparison to other players in the start-up support ecosystem. Moreover, start-ups that do not enjoy the merits of corporate support could be used as a control group to highlight differences. In our opinion, the most unfortunate limitation comes from not having time-series data. This limitation is heavily driven by the newness of CAs, limiting the available data to only a few years. Therefore, the long-term effects of corporate venturing on both the corporation and the start-up sides cannot be determined yet.

Nevertheless, despite its shortcomings, this study should be a first step and a door-opener for a future research agenda. First, deep-dives on both types individually will help to answer questions such as whether accelerators really accelerate start-ups and whether corporations perform venturing for altruistic motives or their own advantage. Moreover, the collected dataset can be used to differentiate CVC units and CAs more specifically. Owing to their different objectives, one can hypothesize that different structures, personnel, and network characteristics are required for a superior performance. Second, well-established theories in management science can be reviewed analytically for a specific area. Foremost, topics of corporate governance should be reviewed and the impact of varying degrees of autonomy or integration of both the corporate venturing unit towards the corporation and the start-up towards the corporate venturing unit should be explored. Third, and in accordance with Colombo et al. (2018, p. 188), this study urges scholars to take a multi-level lifecycle approach and differentiate CAs from adjacent players like business angels or venture capitalists. Future research should examine whether CAs serve as pre-selection tools for CVC units, how the two different forms collaborate or compete within one corporation, and whether different forms of corporate venturing will successfully co-exist in the long run. Scholars ought to detect whether corporations first use CAs as a broad funnel to screen multiple start-ups in their batches and then later invest in the most promising cases through their CVC units.

NOTES

1.	As alluded to earlier several start-ups are included multiple times as they are under the management of two or even three corporate ventures in parallel.
2.	If no N is reported specifically, N = 765, that is, information on all start-ups is available.

REFERENCES

Acs, Z. J., Stam, E., Audretsch, D. B., and O'Connor, A. (2017). The lineages of the entrepreneurial ecosystem approach. *Small Business Economics*, *49*(1), 1–10.

Agarwal, R., and Helfat, C. E. (2009). Strategic renewal of organizations. *Organization Science*, *20*(2), 281–293. https://doi.org/10.1287/orsc.1090.0423

Allen, S. A., and Hevert, K. T. (2007). Venture capital investing by information technology companies: Did it pay? *Journal of Business Venturing*, *22*(2), 262–282.

Alvarez-Garrido, E., and Dushnitsky, G. (2016). Are entrepreneurial venture's innovation rates sensitive to investor complementary assets? Comparing biotech ventures backed by corporate and independent VCs. *Strategic Management Journal*, *37*(5), 819–834. https://doi.org/10.1002/smj.2359

Anokhin, S., Peck, S., and Wincent, J. (2016). Corporate venture capital: The role of governance factors. *Journal of Business Research*, *69*(11), 4744–4749. https://doi.org/10.1016/j.jbusres.2016.04.024

Asel, P., Park, H. D., and Velamuri, S. R. (2015). Creating values through corporate venture capital programs: The choice between internal and external fund structures. *Journal of Private Equity*, *19*(1), 63–72. https://doi.org/10.3905/jpe.2015.2015.1.047

Audretsch, D. B., and Belitski, M. (2017). Entrepreneurial ecosystems in cities: Establishing the framework conditions. *Journal of Technology Transfer*, *42*(5), 1030–1051.

Audretsch, D. B., and Belitski, M. (2020). Towards an entrepreneurial ecosystem typology for regional economic development: The role of creative class and entrepreneurship. *Regional Studies*, 1–22.

Audretsch, D. B., and Feldman, M. P. (1996). R&D spillovers and the geography of innovation and production. *American Economic Review*, *86*(3), 630–640.

Audretsch, D. B., Lehmann, E. E., Menter, M., and Seitz, N. (2019). Public cluster policy and firm performance: Evaluating spillover effects across industries. *Entrepreneurship and Regional Development*, *31*(1–2), 150–165.

Audretsch, D. B., Lehmann, E. E., and Schenkenhofer, J. (2018). Internationalization strategies of hidden champions: Lessons from Germany. *Multinational Business Review*, *26*(1), 2–24.

Audretsch, D. B., Lehmann, E. E., and Seitz, N. (2021). Amenities, subcultures, and entrepreneurship. *Small Business Economics*, *56*(2), 571–591.

Avnimelech, G., Rosiello, A., and Teubal, M. (2010). Evolutionary interpretation of venture capital policy in Israel, Germany, UK and Scotland. *Science and Public Policy*, *37*(2), 101–112.

Bascha, A., and Walz, U. (2002). Financing practices in the German venture capital industry – an empirical assessment. CFS Working Paper, 08. Retrieved from https:// ideas.repec.org/p/zbw/cfswop/200208.html

Becker, R., and Hellmann, T. (2003). The genesis of venture capital – lessons from the German experience. CESifo Working Paper.

Belderbos, R., Jacob, J., and Lokshin, B. (2018). Corporate venture capital (CVC) investments and technological performance: Geographic diversity and the interplay with technology alliances. *Journal of Business Venturing*, *33*, 20–34. https://doi.org/ 10.1016/j.jbusvent.2017.10.003

Benson, D., and Ziedonis, R. H. (2009). Corporate Venture capital as a window on new technologies: Implications for the performance of corporate investors when acquiring startups. *Organization Science*, *20*(2), 329–351. https://doi.org/10.1287/ orsc.1080.0386

Bertoni, F., Colombo, M. G., and Grilli, L. (2013). Venture capital investor type and the growth mode of new technology-based firms. *Small Business Economics*, *40*(3), 527–552.

Bertoni, F., Colombo, M. G., and Quas, A. (2015). The patterns of venture capital investment in Europe. *Small Business Economics*, *45*(3), 543–560.

Bielesch, F., Brigl, M., Khanna, D., Roos, A., and Schmieg, F. (2012, October 31). Corporate venture capital: Avoid the risk, miss the rewards. bcg.perspectives by the Boston Consulting Group. Retrieved from https://www.bcgperspectives .com/content/articles/innovation_growth_mergers_acquisitions_corporate_venture _capital/

Black, B. S., and Gilson, R. J. (1998). Venture capital and the structure of capital markets: Banks versus stock markets. *Journal of Financial Economics*, *47*, 243–277. https://doi.org/10.1016/S0304-405X(97)00045-7

Block, J. H. (2011). Entrepreneurship culture in Germany: German person-ality as a barrier to entrepreneurship? (Zur Gründungskultur in Deutschland: Persönlichkeitseigenschaften als Gründungshemmnis?) (in German). In N. Irsch and P. Witt (Eds.), *Gründungsförderung in Theorie und Praxis* (pp. 131–144). Frankfurt am Main: KfW-Bankengruppe.

Bonini, S., and Alkan, S. (2012). The political and legal determinants of venture capital investments around the world. *Small Business Economics*, *39*(4), 997–1016.

CBInsights. (2019). *The 2018 Global CVC Report*. New York. Retrieved from https:// www.cbinsights.com/research/report/corporate-venture-capital-trends-2018/

Chemmanur, T. J., Loutskina, E., and Tian, X. (2014). Corporate venture capital, value creation, and innovation. *Review of Financial Studies*, *27*(8), 2434–2473.

Christofidis, C., and Debande, O. (2001). Financing innovative firms through venture capital. EIB Sector Papers (February). Retrieved from http://www.eib.org/ attachments/pj/vencap.pdf

Chua, J. H., Chrisman, J. J., and Sharma, P. (1999). Defining the family business by behavior. *Entrepreneurship Theory and Practice*, *23*(4), 19–29. https://doi.org/10 .1177/104225879902300402

Cohen, S. (2013). What do accelerators do? Insights from incubators and angels. *Innovations*, *8*(3), 19–25. https://doi.org/10.1162/INOV_a_00184

Cohen, S., Fehder, D. C., Hochberg, Y. V., and Murray, F. (2019). The design of startup accelerators. *Research Policy*, *48*(7), 1781–1797.

Colombo, M. G., and Murtinu, S. (2017). Venture capital investments in Europe and firm productivity: Independent versus corporate investors. *Journal of Economics and Management Strategy*, *26*(1), 35–66. https://doi.org/10.2139/ssrn.2384816

Colombo, M. G., Rossi-Lamastra, C., and Wright, M. (2018). Accelerators: Insights for a research agenda. In M. Wright and I. Drori (Eds.), *Accelerators: Successful Venture Creation and Growth* (pp. 188–203). Cheltenham, UK and Northampton, MA, USA: Edward Elgar Publishing.

Covin, J. G., and Miles, M. (2007). Strategic use of corporate venturing. *Entrepreneurship Theory and Practice*, *31*(2), 183–207. https://doi.org/10.1111/j.1540-6520.2007.00169.x

Crişan, E. L., Salanţă, I. I., Beleiu, I. N., Bordean, O. N., and Bunduchi, R. (2021). A systematic literature review on accelerators. *Journal of Technology Transfer*, *46*, 62–89.

Dempwolf, C. S., Auer, J., and D'Ippolito, M. (2014). *Innovation Accelerators: Defining Characteristics among Startup Assistance Organizations*. Report prepared for the Small Business Administration, October. https://doi.org/10.13140/RG.2.2.36244.09602

Dokko, G., and Gaba, V. (2012). Venturing into new territory: Career experiences of corporate venture capital managers and practice variation. *Academy of Management Journal*, *55*(3), 563–583. https://doi.org/10.5465/amj.2009.0909

Drori, I., and Wright, M. (2018). Accelerators: Characteristics, trends and the new entrepreneurial ecosystem. In M. Wright and I. Drori (Eds.), *Accelerators: Successful Venture Creation and Growth* (pp. 1–20). Cheltenham, UK and Northampton, MA, USA: Edward Elgar Publishing.

Dushnitsky, G., and Lavie, D. (2010). How alliance formation shapes corporate venture capital investment in the software industry: A resource-based perspective. *Strategic Entrepreneurship Journal*, *4*(1), 22–48. https://doi.org/10.1002/sej.81

Dushnitsky, G., and Lenox, M. J. (2005). When do incumbents learn from entrepreneurial ventures? Corporate venture capital and investing firm innovation rates. *Research Policy*, *34*(5), 615–639. https://doi.org/10.1016/j.respol.2005.01.017

Dushnitsky, G., and Lenox, M. J. (2006). When does corporate venture capital investment create firm value? *Journal of Business Venturing*, *21*(6), 753–772. https://doi.org/10.1016/j.jbusvent.2005.04.012

Dushnitsky, G., and Shapira, Z. (2010). Entrepreneurial finance meets organizational reality: Comparing investment practices and performance of corporate and independent venture capitalists. *Strategic Management Journal*, *31*, 990–1017. https://doi.org/10.1002/smj.851

Eisenhardt, K. M., and Martin, J. A. (2000). Dynamic capabilities: What are they? *Strategic Management Journal*, *21*, 1105–1112. https://doi.org/10.1002/smj.233

Ernst, H., Witt, P., and Brachtendorf, G. (2005). Corporate venture capital as a strategy for external innovation: An exploratory empirical study. *R&D Management*, *35*(3), 233–242. https://doi.org/10.1111/j.1467-9310.2005.00386.x

Fritsch, M., Obschonka, M., and Wyrwich, M. (2019). Historical roots of entrepreneurship-facilitating culture and innovation activity: An analysis for German regions. *Regional Studies*, *53*(9), 1296–1307.

Gans, J. S., and Stern, S. (2003). The product market and the market for "ideas": Commercialization strategies for technology entrepreneurs. *Research Policy, 32*(2), 333–350.

Gompers, P., and Lerner, J. (1998). The determinants of corporate venture capital success: Organizational structure, incentives, and complementarities. In R. K. Morck (Ed.), *Concentrated Corporate Ownership* (pp. 17–54). Chicago: University of Chicago Press.

Hallen, B. L., Bingham, C. B., and Cohen, S. (2017). Do accelerators accelerate? If so, how? The impact of intensive learning from others on new venture development. *SSRN Electronic Journal.* https://doi.org/10.2139/ssrn.2719810

Harrison, J. S., and Fitza, M. A. (2014). Heterogeneity of corporate parents and the paradox of corporate venture capital: A social capital approach. *Frontiers of Entrepreneurship Research, 34*(2), 3.

Herbig, P., and Dunphy, S. (1998). Culture and innovation. *Cross Cultural Management: An International Journal, 5*(4), 13–21. https://doi.org/10.1108/13527609810796844

Hill, S. A., and Birkinshaw, J. (2014). Ambidexterity and survival in corporate venture units. *Journal of Management, 40*(7), 1899–1931. https://doi.org/10.1177/0149206312445925

Hochberg, Y. V. (2016). Accelerating entrepreneurs and ecosystems: The seed accelerator model. *Innovation Policy and the Economy, 16*(1), 25–51. https://doi.org/10.1086/684985

Hofstede, G. (2001). *Culture's Consequences: Comparing Values, Behaviors, Institutions, and Organizations across Nations* (2nd ed.). London: Sage Publications.

Hofstede, G. J., Hofstede, G., and Minkov, M. (2010). *Cultures and Organizations: Software of the Mind* (3rd ed.). New York: McGraw-Hill.

Hutter, K., Gfrerer, A., and Lindner, B. (2021). From popular to profitable: Incumbents' experiences and challenges with external corporate accelerators. *International Journal of Innovation Management, 25*(3), 2150035.

Ivanov, V. I., and Xie, F. (2010). Do corporate venture capitalists add value to start-up firms? Evidence from IPOs and acquisitions of VC-backed companies. *Financial Management Association International, 39*(1), 129–152. https://doi.org/10.1111/j.1755-053X.2009.01068.x

Jafar, B. (2018). Mideast corporates need to get into venture capital. Retrieved from https://gulfnews.com/business/analysis/mideast-corporates-need-to-get-into-venture-capital-1.2218192

Jeng, L. A., and Wells, P. C. (2000). The determinants of venture capital funding: Evidence across countries. *Journal of Corporate Finance, 6*(3), 241–289.

Jokela, M., Obschonka, M., Stuetzer, M., Rentfrow, P. J., Potter, J., and Gosling, S. D. (2017). Did strategic bombing in the Second World War lead to "German angst"? A large-scale empirical test across 89 German cities. *European Journal of Personality, 31*(3), 234–257.

Kanbach, D. K., and Stubner, S. (2016). Corporate accelerators as recent form of startup engagement: The what, the why, and the how. *Journal of Applied Business Research, 32*(6), 1761–1776. https://doi.org/10.19030/jabr.v32i6.9822

Keil, T. (2004). Building external corporate venturing capability. *Journal of Management Studies, 41*(5), 799–825. https://doi.org/10.1111/j.1467-6486.2004.00454.x

Keil, T., Maula, M., Schildt, H., and Zahra, S. A. (2008). The effect of governance modes and relatedness of external business development activities on innovation performance. *Strategic Management Journal, 29*, 895–907. https://doi.org/10.1002/smj.672

Kohler, T. (2016). Corporate accelerators: Building bridges between corporations and startups. *Business Horizons, 59*(3), 347–357. https://doi.org/10.1016/j.bushor.2016.01.008

Kupp, M., Marval, M., and Borchers, P. (2017). Corporate accelerators: Fostering innovation while bringing together startups and large firms. *Journal of Business Strategy, 38*(6), 47–53.

Lehmann, E. E., Schenkenhofer, J., and Wirsching, K. (2019). Hidden champions and unicorns: A question of the context of human capital investment. *Small Business Economics, 52*(2), 359–374.

Lehmann, E. E., and Seitz, N. (2017). Freedom and innovation: A country and state level analysis. *Journal of Technology Transfer, 42*(5), 1009–1029.

Lerner, J., and Tåg, J. (2013). Institutions and venture capital. *Industrial and Corporate Change, 22*(1), 153–182.

Li, Y., and Zahra, S. A. (2012). Formal institutions, culture, and venture capital activity: A cross-country analysis. *Journal of Business Venturing, 27*(1), 95–111.

Metzger, G. (2017). *KfW-Gründungsmonitor 2017*. Retrieved from https://www.kfw.de/PDF/Download-Center/Konzernthemen/Research/PDF-Dokumente-Gründungsmonitor/KfW-Gründungsmonitor-2017.pdf

Moschner, S. L., Fink, A. A., Kurpjuweit, S., Wagner, S. M., and Herstatt, C. (2019). Toward a better understanding of corporate accelerator models. *Business Horizons, 62*(5), 637–647.

National Venture Capital Association. (2015). *2015 National Venture Capital Association Yearbook*. Retrieved from https://mthightech.org/wp-content/uploads/2015/11/NVCA-Yearbook-2015.pdf

Park, H. D., and Steensma, H. K. (2012). When does corporate venture capital add value for new ventures. *Strategic Management Journal, 33*(1), 1–22. https://doi.org/10.1002/smj.937

Park, J. H., and Bae, Z. T. (2018). When are "sharks" beneficial? Corporate venture capital investment and startup innovation performance. *Technology Analysis and Strategic Management, 30*(3), 324–336. https://doi.org/10.1080/09537325.2017.1310376

Pauwels, C., Clarysse, B., Wright, M., and van Hove, J. (2016). Understanding a new generation incubation model: The accelerator. *Technovation, 50–51*, 13–24. https://doi.org/10.1016/j.technovation.2015.09.003

PitchBook. (2021). About. Retrieved from https://pitchbook.com/about

PwC, and CBInsights. (2019). *MoneyTree™ Report Q4 2018*. New York. Retrieved from https://www.pwc.com/us/en/industries/technology/moneytree.html

Radcliffe, M., and Lehot, L. (2018). Corporate venturing hitting record highs, intensifying global innovation. Retrieved from https://www.dlapiper.com/en/us/insights/publications/2018/03/corporate-venturing-hitting-record-highs-intensifying-global-innovation/

Rocha, V., and Van Praag, M. (2020). Mind the gap: The role of gender in entrepreneurial career choice and social influence by founders. *Strategic Management Journal, 41*(5), 841–866.

Röhl, K. R. (2016). Entrepreneurial culture and start-ups – Could a cultural shift in favour of entrepreneurship lead to more innovative start-ups? IW Policy Paper, *2*, 38.

Röhm, P. (2018). Exploring the landscape of corporate venture capital: A systematic review of the entrepreneurial and finance literature. *Management Review Quarterly*, *68*(3), 279–319. https://doi.org/10.1007/s11301-018-0140-z

Röhm, P., Köhn, A., Kuckertz, A., and Dehnen, H. S. (2018). A world of difference? The impact of corporate venture capitalists' investment motivation on startup valuation. *Journal of Business Economics*, *88*(3–4), 531–557. https://doi.org/10.1007/s11573-017-0857-5

Sauermann, H. (2018). Fire in the belly? Employee motives and innovative performance in start-ups versus established firms. *Strategic Entrepreneurship Journal*, *12*, 423–454. https://doi.org/10.1002/sej.1267

Schildt, H., Maula, M., and Keil, T. (2005). Explorative and exploitative learning from external corporate ventures. *Entrepreneurship Theory and Practice*, *29*(4), 493–515. https://doi.org/10.1111/j.1540-6520.2005.00095.x

Seitz, N., Lehmann, E., and Haslanger, P. (2019). Corporate accelerators and start-up performance: Evidence from Germany. *Academy of Management Proceedings*, *2019*(1).

Seitz, N., Lehmann, E., and Haslanger, P. (2020). Does corporate venture capital deliver performance? A meta-analysis. *Academy of Management Proceedings*, *2020*(1).

Shah, S. M., Abdul-Majid, M., and Karim, Z. A. (2019). Debt-oriented capital structure and economic growth: Panel evidence for OECD countries. *European Review*, *27*(4), 519–542.

Siegel, R., Siegel, E., and MacMillan, I. C. (1988). Corporate venture capitalists: Autonomy, obstacles, and performance. *Journal of Business Venturing*, *3*(3), 233–247.

Souitaris, V., Zerbinati, S., and Liu, G. (2012). Which iron cage? Endo- and exomorphism in corporate venture capital programs. *Academy of Management Journal*, *55*(2), 477–505. https://doi.org/10.5465/amj.2009.0709

Stayton, J., and Mangematin, V. (2019). Seed accelerators and the speed of new venture creation. *Journal of Technology Transfer*, *44*(4), 1163n1187.

Steiber, A., and Alänge, S. (2020). Corporate–startup collaboration: Effects on large firms' business transformation. *European Journal of Innovation Management*. https://doi.org/10.1108/EJIM-10-2019-0312

Sunley, P., Klagge, B., Berndt, C., and Martin, R. (2005). Venture capital programmes in the UK and Germany: In what sense regional policies? *Regional Studies*, *39*(2), 255–273.

Van De Vrande, V., and Vanhaverbeke, W. (2013). How prior corporate venture capital investments shape technological alliances: A real options approach. *Entrepreneurship Theory and Practice*, *37*(5), 1019–1043. https://doi.org/10.1111/j.1540-6520.2012.00526.x

Vandeweghe, L., and Fu, J. Y. T. (2018). Business accelerator governance. In M. Wright and I, Drori (Eds.), *Accelerators: Successful Venture Creation and Growth* (pp. 37–57). Cheltenham, UK and Northampton, MA, USA: Edward Elgar Publishing.

VentureCapital Magazin. (2017). *Start-Up 2018: Auf dem Weg zum Gipfel* (*Start-Up 2018: On the Way to the Summit*). Munich: Going Public Media.

Wadhwa, A., and Kotha, S. (2006). Knowledge creation through external venturing: Evidence from the telecommunications equipment manufacturing industry. *Academy of Management Journal*, *49*(4), 819–835. https://doi.org/10.2307/20159800

Weber, C., and Weber, B. (2003). Corporate venture capital organizations in Germany: A comparison. Discussion Paper SP III 2003-113 Wissenschaftszentrum. Retrieved from papers2://publication/uuid/6A402240-E4E0-4D33-865E-24346B730A12

Weiblen, T., and Chesbrough, H. W. (2015). Engaging with startups to enhance corporate innovation. *California Management Review*, *57*(2), 66–90. https://doi.org/10 .1525/cmr.2015.57.2.66

Woschke, T., Haase, H., and Kratzer, J. (2017). Resource scarcity in SMEs: Effects on incremental and radical innovations. *Management Research Review*, *40*(2), 195–217.

Yu, S. (2020). How do accelerators impact the performance of high-technology ventures? *Management Science*, *66*(2), 530–552.

12. Non-accounting drivers of start-up valuation by early-stage equity investors: literature review and future research agenda

Daniel Agyare, Davide Hahn, Tommaso Minola, and Silvio Vismara

1.   INTRODUCTION

Innovative start-ups are a driving force for most developed economic systems. Audretsch et al. (2020) suggest that innovative start-ups can be defined based on the features that influence their development and outcome. Accordingly, we define innovative start-ups as "start-ups that are knowledge-intensive and research-based, young and independent and devote significant resources to research and development (R&D) and innovation" (Colombelli et al., 2020, p. 1). Innovative start-ups typically present these features (Colombelli et al., 2016): lack of tangible resources and financial information, illiquidity of investment, high level of economic and technological uncertainty, high cash burn rates, and, most importantly, high level of asymmetric information.

When innovative start-ups require equity financing from early-stage equity investors such as Venture Capitalists (VCs) or Business Angels (BAs), the issue of valuation becomes critical (Sievers et al., 2013). The corporate finance literature proposes financial accounting methods such as the discounted cash flow (DCF), asset-based, and earnings multiple approaches. These approaches, however, are problematic when it comes to innovative start-ups (Miloud et al., 2012; Sievers et al., 2013; Sanders and Boivie, 2004). For example, in the DCF approach, due to the uncertainty surrounding the commercialization of the new products or services developed by innovative start-ups, it is challenging to estimate the appropriate discount rate and determine the future cash flows. The net assets approach does not adequately consider the economic value of growth opportunities, while the earnings multiple approach is based on earnings which an innovative start-up often does not have until it reaches later financing stages. To address this, Ge et al. (2005, p. 3) state that "when it is difficult to value a subject based on output (e.g., future cash flows), pricing it based on inputs (e.g., entrepreneur, industry attractiveness) might be an alternative solution". Non-financial information, non-accounting information, and beyond financial-report information have been used in the valuation literature to describe input variables related to – among others – management and shareholders, background information about the firm, and human and intellectual capital (Amir and Lev, 1996; Amir et al., 2003; Robb et al., 2001; Cinquini et al., 2012; Orens and Lybaert, 2007; Orens and Lybaert, 2010; Sievers et al., 2013).

Throughout this chapter, we embrace this perspective and adopt the term "non-accounting", defined as "information drawn from outside the financial statement" (Barker and Imam, 2008, p. 313). Some recent examples show a surge in the use of non-accounting information in valuation research (Wyatt, 2008; Wessendorf et al., 2019; Moghaddam et al., 2016; Block et al., 2014; Zheng et al., 2010). Yet, we do not know to what extent, and how, the literature has recognized the role of non-accounting drivers of innovative start-up valuation by early-stage equity investors. Hence, by means of a scoping study, we review 24 studies to detect and depict the most significant shortcomings in the literature. Additionally, by proposing *university* as the context of origin and distinctiveness of many innovative start-ups, we offer a set of *University-Based Dimensions* (UBDs) to be incorporated in valuation studies and practice. We refer to UBDs as features of innovative start-ups which capture distinctive characteristics related to the university context from which they are originated. Given the diversity of the theoretical backgrounds in this field, this chapter emphasizes the relevance of a cross-fertilization between different research disciplines as a way to help advance knowledge on non-accounting drivers of start-up valuation by early-stage investors.

2.   THEORETICAL BACKGROUND

Firm valuation is a fundamental necessity for business investments to occur (Bose and Thomas, 2007). It builds on the firm's resources, its competitive position within its sector, and its future financial expectations. Early-stage investments are meant to support the pre-launch, launch, and early-stage development phases of a start-up (Davila et al., 2003). As such, venture capital firms serve as an important financial intermediary in financial markets and they raise funds from individuals and institutions for investment in early-stage start-ups that offer high potential but high-risk returns (Sahlman, 1990; Gompers, 1995). Next to VCs, BAs are wealthy individuals who invest their own money to acquire shares of innovative start-ups. BAs typically take a less structured approach to valuation than VCs; they rely on intuition, heuristics, personal enjoyment, and gut instinct (Drover et al., 2017).

BAs and VCs invest in innovative start-ups and their investments usually concern R&D expenses related to design and marketing of the new product and disbursement for new capital equipment (Hall, 2002). In the venture capital market, firm valuations are determined through a face-to-face negotiation between management and equity investors. These investors usually adopt a multistage decision-making process and are structured in a way that deals with information asymmetries. Such activities – board positions, frequent interactions with and monitoring of management, and so on – allow VCs to extract management's private information and thus reduce information asymmetries.

Research into non-accounting drivers that impact early-stage venture valuation of innovative start-ups has developed over the past decade. In terms of start-ups' characteristics, industry relevance and geographical location (Houlihan Valuation Advisors, 1998), early adoption of management accounting systems and management control systems (Davila et al., 2015; Davila and Foster, 2005), and firm age (Armstrong et al., 2006) are believed to be decisive factors that determine start-up valuation by early-stage equity investors. Founder and team characteristics such as number of founders, management team, prior start-up, management and relevant industry experience, and level of education have been empirically proven to be valuable resources of a start-up, thereby informing its valuation (Hsu, 2007; Miloud et al., 2012; Sievers et al., 2013; Wasserman, 2017). These studies indicate that non-accounting drivers are receiving growing attention. However, existing literature is fragmented and lacks a theoretical rigor integrating research on such drivers for innovative start-ups (Cumming and Vismara, 2017). Also, previous reviews in this field either do not focus specifically on innovative start-ups and non-accounting drivers (Köhn, 2018) or do not offer a theory-informed taxonomy of non-accounting drivers (Wessendorf et al., 2019).

3.   METHODOLOGY

3.1   Planning the Review

Following the definitions of Arksey and O'Malley (2005), we have developed a *scoping study* of the literature. Our choice of this methodological approach is underpinned by two important considerations: first, a scoping study is particularly useful because it aims to map rapidly the key concepts underlying a research area and the main sources and types of evidence available, especially where an area is complex or has not been reviewed comprehensively (Mays et al., 2001). Second, it allows to develop a framework that addresses

Table 12.1   Paper selection criteria

The valuation object	The valuation perspective	The valuating entity
Start*	Valuation	VC*
Ventur*	Valu*	BA*
Firm*	Evalu*	Venture capital*
Spin*		Business angel*
Compan*		Invest*
Enterp*		
Entrep*		
Business*		

a specific topic (i.e. the non-accounting drivers of innovative start-up valuation), by taking a systematic albeit inclusive approach and ensuring rigorous and transparent execution throughout its different structured stages (Pham et al., 2014).

3.2   Identifying the Research Question

The first step in a scoping study is to identify the research question to be addressed so as to build a solid search strategy (Centre for Reviews and Dissemination, 2001). Our guiding research question is the following: "To what extent, and how, has the literature recognized the role of non-accounting drivers of innovative start-up valuation by early-stage equity investors?" Conscious of the fact that scholars use different terms to describe "innovative start-ups", we consulted prior literature studies and reviews to mitigate the threat of variety in relation to terminology (Luger and Koo, 2005; Hsu, 2006; Colombelli et al., 2016; Köhn, 2018; Wessendorf et al., 2019; Audretsch et al., 2020). These studies were particularly useful because they provided the appropriate concepts and terminology in the area of study; they also helped us in identifying relevant keywords for use in the search for papers (listed in Table 12.1).

3.3   Identifying Relevant Studies

The primary focus when scoping the field is to be as systematic as possible in identifying studies for answering a research question. To achieve this, we employed a strategy that required searching for potential papers through different sources: electronic databases, existing networks, and reference lists. Figure 12.1 offers a summary of the search process.

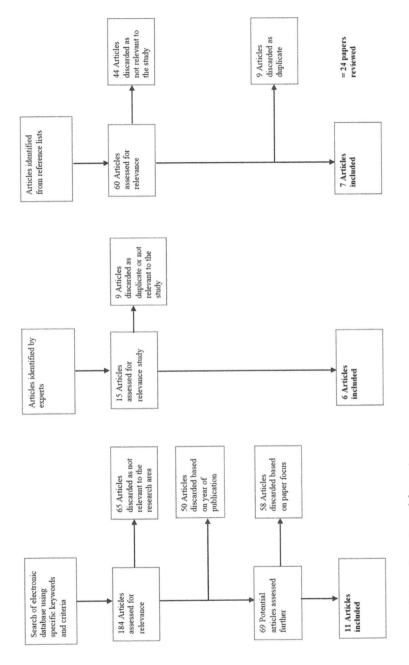

Figure 12.1   Overview of the review process

3.3.1   Electronic database

Electronic databases are the primary source of bibliographic contents and abstracts of published material. We developed a baseline search strategy for the articles to be inserted in the review. The strategy involved three categories of keywords. The categories were used in Elsevier's Scopus database by combining them as search algorithms using the Boolean search operator "AND" alongside the search operator "OR" for keywords within each category. The focus of the search was within "article title, abstract, or keywords" fields. The following describes each category (details in Table 12.1):

- The valuation object: refers to the different terminologies used to describe innovative start-ups.
- The valuation perspective: refers to the scope of the papers analyzed. Here, we included the terms "valuation" and "evaluation", as they are sometimes used interchangeably.
- The valuating entity: as different investors might have different approaches to valuation, we include the investor performing the valuation of the start-up in our search strategy.

Next, the Scopus database was used for an extensive literature search. Only studies published in the post-dot-com period (i.e. after 2004) were included in the study. The starting date of 2004 was chosen because empirical literature on start-up valuations published before the dot-com period is too distant from the current reality (Köhn, 2018). Only English language articles were considered, as they are viewed in the academic literature as an established body of knowledge. To eliminate studies that did not address our central research question, we included only papers satisfying the following criteria:

1. The unit of analysis has to be the firm (i.e. the innovative start-ups).
2. The research topic has to concern non-accounting drivers related to valuation in the context of early-stage equity investors.
3. The field of research falls within the area of business management, accounting, economics, econometrics, finance, and decision sciences.

A manual assessment was conducted on the 184 potential papers generated by the Scopus database, by reading each paper thoroughly to determine its eligibility (mainly by verifying criteria (1) and (2) above). At the end of this process, we identified 11 relevant papers to be included in our final sample. As noted above, the relatively high number of papers excluded within the overall study selection process is mainly driven by the rigorous inclusion criteria applied and the very specific research question guiding the study.

3.3.2   VC interviews

Since practitioners can contribute to improve the selection of papers included in scoping studies (Newbronner and Hare, 2002), we interviewed three VC investors from our network. In the structured interviews displayed in Table 12.2 we asked them about the non-accounting drivers they use to evaluate innovative start-ups. Interviews were conducted online using either Microsoft teams or Zoom as the platform for our video conferencing and the time devoted for each interview was approximately 45 minutes. Respondents were also invited to suggest empirical studies from which they draw information regarding non-accounting drivers when dealing with innovative start-ups. This provided 15 additional studies, of which 9 were discarded as duplicates and/or not relevant to the study.

3.3.3   Reference lists

To improve completeness, we also checked the bibliographies of 17 studies. We performed a "snowballing" investigation technique using backward and forward citation on the references of the identified articles. This process generated 60 papers, which were subsequently assessed in terms of focus and eligibility. Out of these 60 papers, 7 additional articles were included in our final sample.

3.4   Charting, Collating, and Summarizing the Information

We "charted" key items of information obtained from the 24 papers being reviewed. Ritchie and Spencer (1993) describe the term "charting" as a technique for synthesizing and interpreting qualitative data by screening, extracting data, and sorting material according to key issues and themes. In our case, we focused on author(s), paper title, journal name, theory used, sample and data source, research method, non-accounting criteria covered, and fit with our research question. The data that we charted were then stored using a spreadsheet (details in Table 12.3). This enabled us to depict the main areas of interest and highlight significant academic voids.

4.   OVERVIEW OF THE SELECTED PAPERS

This section presents an overview of the 24 identified papers. As highlighted in Figure 12.2, the number of published research papers on non-accounting drivers of start-up valuation is quite steady. Seven papers were published between 2004 and 2007 (excluding the working paper), seven papers between 2010 and 2014, and nine papers between 2016 and 2020.

Table 12.2   VC interviews – data collection protocol

Introduction (5 minutes)	Thank you for agreeing to meet with us. I'm _____ from the University of Bergamo and a member of the Center for Young and Family Enterprise (CYFE). I also have two of my colleagues _____ present to take notes for us. We are interviewing a small group of VC investors to get information about the valuation of innovative start-ups. The study is being funded by e-Novia. As a VC investor, we are particularly interested in talking with you about the role of non-accounting drivers (i.e. information drawn from outside the financial statement) and their influence on the valuation of innovative start-ups. What we learn from today's discussion will help us improve our study, given the paucity of research in this domain. We will treat your answers as confidential. We will not include your names or any other information that could identify you in any reports we write. We will destroy the notes and video recordings after we complete our study and publish the results. Do you have any questions about the study?

Part A
(10 minutes)
	Part A: Inclusion and exclusion criteria
	
	1. To begin, please tell me about your company, as well as a brief description about the kind of activities you are usually involved in?
	    a. PROBE: Does your company invest or intend to invest in an innovative start-up?
	    b. PROBE: Why do you think that it is important to invest in this type of start-up?
	    c. PROBE: How long have you worked in this industry?
	
	If VC investor is involved in the valuation process and question #1a is yes, then proceed. Otherwise, terminate interview and ask him/her to put you in contact with a VC investor within his/her contact network.

Part B (25 minutes)	Part B: Assessing the importance of non-accounting drivers
	Now, we'd like to discuss the valuation of innovative start-ups
	2. What words would you use to describe the valuation of innovative start-ups?
	3. How does your company meet the needs of innovative start-ups?
	4. From a financial standpoint, what are some of the drivers that have an influence on the valuation of innovative start-ups?
	5. What about non-accounting drivers (i.e. information drawn from outside the financial statement), are they equally important?
	a. PROBE: How accessible is information regarding non-accounting drivers?
	b. PROBE: Tell me about which non-accounting drivers matter most to your company during the valuation process?
	c. PROBE: Is this set of non-accounting drivers supported by empirical evidence?
	d. Could you please suggest to us some of the empirical studies from which you draw your information regarding non-accounting drivers?
Final thoughts (5 minutes)	Those were the questions that we wanted to ask.
	6. Do you have any final thoughts about non-accounting drivers that you would like to share?
	Thank you for your time.

As shown in Figure 12.3, most of the papers are empirical (19) while three papers are conceptual and two other studies are review papers. Sixteen articles in our sample primarily use quantitative methods. Two papers adopt qualitative methods whereas only a single paper employs a mixed method approach (the use of both qualitative and quantitative methods). All the empirical quantitative studies employ the use of a firm's pre-money[1] or post-money[2] valuation as the dependent variable and the start-up's non-accounting value drivers as the main independent variables. Considering the somewhat nascent developmental stage of the literature on the valuation of innovative start-ups, more papers based on qualitative or mixed methods could offer a valuable contribution by inductively adding more nuanced knowledge about contexts, processes, and mechanisms of innovative start-ups' valuation (Yin, 2015; George and Bennett, 2005).

The selected papers have been published in 13 journals highly ranked in the Chartered Association of Business Schools' Academic Journal Guide 2018 (ABS – AJG 2018) (CABS, n.d.). Four of them are ranked 4*: *The Accounting*

Table 12.3   *Selected articles on non-accounting drivers of innovative start-up valuation*

Paper	Author(s)	Title	Journal	Theory	Sample and data source	Method	Criteria covered	Fit with research
1	Dittmann, Maug, and Kemper (2004)	How fundamental are fundamental values? Valuation methods and their impact on the performance of German venture capitalists	*European Financial Management*	N/A	53 VCs; German Venture Capital Association (BVK)	Quantitative	Quality of management; Novelty of the product; Barriers to entry; Market and technological feasibility	This paper shows that a small portion of VCs use the technology evaluation and the valuation of financing requirements valuation methodologies, which consider non-accounting drivers.
2	Ge, Mahoney, and Mahoney (2005)	New venture valuation by venture capitalists: An integrative approach	*Urban Champaign Working Paper*	Structure–Conduct–Performance (SCP) paradigm; Resource-based theory; The network theory	210 new business ventures; Thomson Financial Securities Data (TFSD)	Quantitative	Product differentiation; Industry demand growth; Founders' industry experience; Founders' managerial experience; Founders' start-up experience; Founding team vs. solo founder; Completeness of management team; Network size	This paper examines whether VCs' valuation of a new venture can be explained by variables identified in the strategy literature as important to predicting firm-level economic performance.
3	Hand (2005)	The value relevance of financial statements in the venture capital market	*The Accounting Review*	N/A	204 US-based biotechnology firms; Recombinant capital (a US consulting firm)	Quantitative	Firm age; Patent; Strategic alliances; Development stage; Degree of equity dilution	This paper also studies the value relevance of non-financial statement information within and across the pre-IPO venture capital market.

Paper	Author(s)	Title	Theory	Journal	Sample and data source	Method	Criteria covered	Fit with research
4	Armstrong, Davila, and Foster (2006)	Venture-backed private equity valuation and financial statement information	N/A	*Review of Accounting Studies*	502 venture-backed firms; VentureOne	Quantitative	Firm age; Round of financing; Degree of equity dilution; Patent application	This study investigates the association between financial and non-financial statement information and private equity values.
5	Hand (2007)	Determinants of the round-to-round returns to pre-IPO venture capital investments in US biotechnology companies	N/A	*Journal of Business Venturing*	193 US biotech companies; Market report data	Quantitative	Firm age; Degree of equity dilution; Patent; Strategic alliances; Firm size; Investor type	This paper investigates whether the returns earned by venture investors in a pre-IPO setting can be explained by the size of the firm and its book-to-market ratio, while controlling for other non-accounting variables.
6	Sander and Kõomägi (2007)	Valuation of private companies by Estonian private equity and venture capitalists	N/A	*Baltic Journal of Management*	N/A	Conceptual	Founders' human capital	In this paper equity investors' required internal rate of return (IRR) is determined by intuition and positioning. This is facilitated by considering the existence of human capital as a prerequisite for future growth potential.
7	Bose and Thomas (2007)	Valuation of intellectual capital in knowledge-based firms: The need for new methods in a changing economic paradigm	N/A	*Management Decision*	N/A	Conceptual	Management ability; Quality of intellectual property (IP)	This paper attempts to address the intricacy of valuing intellectual capital by identifying the critical underlying value drivers of intellectual assets and establishing their relationships to value creation.

Paper	Author(s)	Title	Journal	Theory	Sample and data source	Method	Criteria covered	Fit with research
8	Hsu (2007)	Experienced entrepreneurial founders, organizational capital, and venture capital funding	*Research Policy*	N/A	149 early-stage start-ups; E-Lab (MIT)	Quantitative	Network; Prior start-up founding experience; Founders' level of education	This study examines not only the correlates of varied sourcing and valuation of venture capital funding among entrepreneurs with disparate backgrounds, but also investigates the comparative roles of prior founding experience, academic training, and social capital in venture capital funding.
9	Zheng, Liu, and George (2010)	The dynamic impact of innovative capability and inter-firm network on firm valuation: A longitudinal study of biotechnology start-ups	*Journal of Business Venturing*	N/A	170 biotechnology firms; Bioscan (biotechnology industry directory)	Quantitative	Patent; Network size; Firm age	This study sheds light on the age-related effects of innovative capability and inter-firm networks on firm valuation.
10	Miloud, Aspelund, and Cabrol (2012)	Startup valuation by venture capitalists: An empirical study	*Venture Capital*	Structure–Conduct–Performance (SCP) paradigm; Network theory; Resource-based theory	102 new ventures; Thomson Financial Securities Data (TFSD)	Quantitative	Industry type; Founders' industry experience; Founders' managerial experience; Founders' prior start-up experience; Management team completeness; Network size	This article investigates whether VCs' valuation of a new venture can be explained by factors identified in the strategy theories as important to firm performance.

Paper	Author(s)	Title	Journal	Theory	Sample and data source	Method	Criteria covered	Fit with research
11	Heughebaert and Manigart (2012)	Firm valuation in venture capital financing rounds: The role of investor bargaining power	*Journal of Business Finance and Accounting*	N/A	180 different firms; Multiple sources	Quantitative	Patent; Firm age; Industry type; Firm size	This paper empirically examines the effects of VC type on valuations while controlling for investee firm characteristics, venture capital firm characteristics and market conditions.
12	Sievers, Mokwa, and Keienburg (2013)	The relevance of financial versus non-financial information for the valuation of venture capital-backed firms	*European Accounting Review*	N/A	127 innovative firms; KfW Bankengruppe (KfW)	Quantitative	Management team completeness; Management level of education; Market validation (customers); Patents	This study extends the value relevance results of prior accounting studies by further considering the relationship between key non-financial metrics and their ability to provide reliable pre-money value predictions.
13	Festel, Wuermseher, and Cattaneo (2013)	Valuation of early stage high-tech start-up companies	*International Journal of Business*	N/A	16 high-tech start-ups; N/A	Conceptual	Reputation of scientist; Maturity of technology; Patent protection; Unique Selling Proposition (USP); Competition; Scalability; Geographical location; Competence of advisory board; Competences of top management team; Business development plan	This paper develops a standardized scheme for the adjustment of the beta coefficient based on various categories such as technological, organizational, financial, and other characteristics.

Paper	Author(s)	Title	Journal	Theory	Sample and data source	Method	Criteria covered	Fit with research
14	Greenberg (2013)	Small firms, big patents? Estimating patent value using data on Israeli start-ups' financing rounds	*European Management Review*	Signaling theory	317 companies; Israel Venture Capital (IVC)	Quantitative	Patents	This study estimates whether patent grant, which reduces uncertainty about the scope of the IP rights conferred, enhances start-ups' valuations by VCs.
15	Block, De Vries, Schumann, and Sandner (2014)	Trademarks and venture capital valuation	*Journal of Business Venturing*	Signaling theory	2,671 start-ups; VentureXpert, PATSTAT, and USPTO	Quantitative	Trademark	This study seeks to analyze the role of trademarks in VCs' valuations of start-ups based on the number and breadth of a start-up's trademark applications.
16	Hellmann and Wasserman (2016)	The first deal: The division of founder equity in new ventures	*Management Science*	Theory of costly bargaining	1,761 private technology ventures; CompStudy survey	Quantitative	Founders' equity division	This article provides empirical evidence that explains under what circumstances founders choose to split their shares equally, the process of how they reach that decision, and how this decision may be related to subsequent outcomes (e.g. team performance).
17	Moghaddam, Bosse, and Provance (2016)	Strategic alliances of entrepreneurial firms: Value enhancing then value destroying	*Strategic Entrepreneurship Journal*	Resource-Based View (RBV); The dynamic capability theory	151 small entrepreneurial firms; VentureXpert database; SDC Platinum database	Quantitative	Strategic alliance	This study explains the relationship between resources accessed and capabilities developed through alliancing in pursuit of an entrepreneurial firm's chosen opportunity and how they signal greater value creation potential to their VCs.

Paper	Author(s)	Title	Journal	Theory	Sample and data source	Method	Criteria covered	Fit with research
18	Wasserman (2017)	The throne vs. the kingdom: Founder control and value creation in startups	*Strategic Management Journal*	Agency theory and ownership structure	6,130 private technology start-ups; CompStudy survey	Quantitative	Founders' control and equity division	This article investigates the degree to which start-up founders' control can affect the value of the new venture.
19	Köhn (2018)	The determinants of startup valuation in the venture capital context: A systematic review and avenues for future research	*Management Review Quarterly*	N/A	N/A	Review	Industry type; Geographical location; Management control system; Headcount growth; Firm age; Founder team vs. solo founder; Management team completeness; Management industry experience; Founders' level of education; Patents; Trademarks; Strategic alliances	This paper compiles relevant empirical research on the determinants of start-up valuations in the venture capital context and highlights the complexity involved, given that start-up valuation involves the interplay and dynamics of different factors.
20	Pisoni and Onetti (2018)	When startups exit: Comparing strategies in Europe and the USA	*Journal of Business Strategy*	N/A	5,744 start-ups; CrunchBase	Quantitative	Firm age; Geographical location	This paper examines the idea of exits with a specific focus on those involving start-ups and provides descriptive statistics based on – among many things – firm age and geographical location (EU vs. USA).

Paper	Author(s)	Title	Journal	Theory	Sample and data source	Method	Criteria covered	Fit with research
21	Wessendorf, Kegelmann, and Terzidis (2019)	Determinants of early-stage technology venture valuation by business angels and venture capitalists	*International Journal of Entrepreneurial Venturing*	N/A	N/A	Review	Strategic alliances; Patents and applications; Market; Founders' personality; Team completeness; Firm age; Industry experience; Investor reputation; Management experience; Market growth; Product status; Prior start-up experience; USP	This review offers a holistic view of the determinants that influence venture valuation in general and technology-venture valuation in particular.
22	Dhochak and Doliya (2020)	Valuation of a startup: Moving towards strategic approaches	*Journal of Multi-Criteria Decision Analysis*	Internal-based theory; Industry-based theory; Network-based theory	25 venture capital firms; Survey	Qualitative	Network size; Entrepreneurs track record; Product differentiation	This article examines the link between VCs' economic valuation of a new venture and established strategic management theories.

Paper	Author(s)	Title	Journal	Theory	Sample and data source	Method	Criteria covered	Fit with research
23	Isaksson and Fredriksen (2020)	Venture capital firms valuation in bull and bear markets: Evidence from Sweden	*International Journal of Entrepreneurship and Innovation Management*	N/A	13 managers of Swedish venture capital firms; Survey	Qualitative	Management team; Business idea; Intellectual property rights (IPR); Products; Business plan; Customers; Employees; Strategic alliance	This paper proposes the results of a survey that asked a group of Swedish VCs to rank in order of priority the factors considered when investing during different development phases of growth companies.
24	Wessendorf, Schneider, Gresch, and Terzidis (2020)	What matters most in technology venture valuation? Importance and impact of non-financial determinants for early-stage venture valuation	*International Journal of Entrepreneurial Venturing*	N/A	35 investors from German-speaking Europe; Survey	Quantitative and Qualitative	Entrepreneurial spirit; USP; Patents and applications; Management experience; Industry experience; Market growth; Prior start-up experience; Strategic alliance; Founders' education and expertise	This paper analyzes relevant non-financial valuation determinants of early-stage venture valuation, their relative importance among each other, and their impact on valuation.

Note: The reviewed papers are organized in a chronological order.

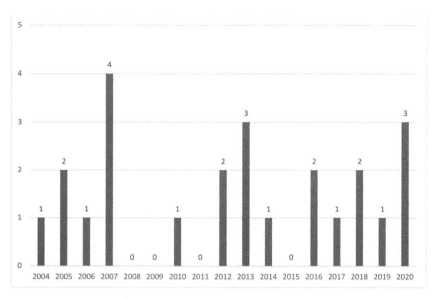

Figure 12.2   Number of papers by year of publication

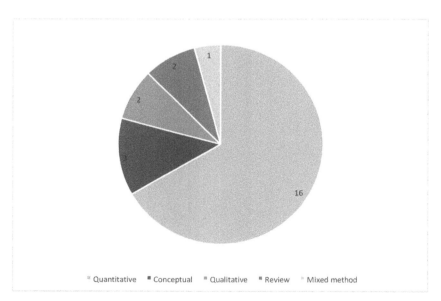

Figure 12.3   Number of papers by methodology type

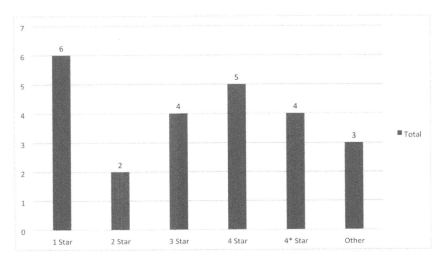

Figure 12.4   Number of papers by ABS – AJG 2018 ranking

Review (1 paper), *Research Policy* (1), *Management Science* (1), *Strategic Management Journal* (1). Five journals are rated 4 stars: *Review of Accounting Studies* (1), *Journal of Business Venturing* (3), *Strategic Entrepreneurship Journal* (1). The remaining four journals are ranked 3 stars: *European Financial Management* (1), *Journal of Business Finance and Accounting* (1), *European Accounting Review* (1), *European Management Review* (1). Together, these journals represent 54 percent of the final database (see Figure 12.4). Overall, the papers in the sample stem from 20 different journals.

As shown in Figure 12.5, most of the papers identified stem from the field of *Entrepreneurship and Small Business Management* (8), *Accounting* (4), and *General Management* (3). Collectively, they represent 62.5 percent of the final sample. The remainder emerge from the fields of *Strategy* (2), *Operations Research and Management Science* (2), *Innovation* (2), *Finance* (1), and *International Business and Area Studies* (1). The journal and subject diversity seem to suggest that the field and the scholarly dialogue is still rather fragmented.

5.   TOWARDS A THEORY-INFORMED TAXONOMY OF NON-ACCOUNTING DRIVERS

In Table 12.4, we summarize the common theories used in the identified papers and the various non-accounting drivers that the authors investigated,

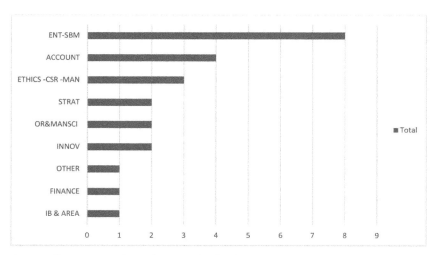

Figure 12.5   Number of papers by field of study

clustered around the primary focus of such theories, which are also used to organize the taxonomy.

5.1   Structure–Conduct–Performance Paradigm

According to the Structure–Conduct–Performance (SCP) paradigm of industrial organization economics (Bain, 1968), the conditions of supply and demand in an industry will determine its structure. The competitive conditions that result from this industry structure shape the conduct of companies, thereby influencing performance. Conduct refers to a variety of individual actions taken by a firm, which encompasses product differentiation, tacit collusion, price-taking, and exploitation of market power (Berry et al., 2019). Similarly, the performance of the firm can be appraised by looking at several indicators such as productive efficiency, profitability, and allocative efficiency (Lelissa and Kuhil, 2018). Hereafter, we present the key non-accounting drivers relative to the SCP paradigm that emerged in the review, namely industry type, product differentiation within the industry, and industry demand growth. It should be noted that these features are related to the structure of the industry.

5.1.1   Industry type

Industry characteristics are vital in the valuation of a new venture because start-ups in different industries may have different risk profiles (Ruhnka and Young, 1991). Eisenmann (2020) explored the relationship between

Table 12.4   *Integrating theories from selected articles*

Theory	Focus	Criteria covered	Description	Example
Structure–Conduct–Performance (SCP) paradigm (Ge et al., 2005; Miloud et al., 2012; Dhochak and Doliya, 2020)	Market and Industry Structure	Industry type	Sector in which the new firm competes	High-tech industry vs. low-tech industry
		Industry demand growth	Current and potential growth of aggregate demand within the industry	Percentage change of revenue in industry
		Product differentiation	Uniqueness of the new product	Advertising intensity ratio / R&D intensity
Resource-Based View (RBV) (Ge et al., 2005; Miloud et al., 2012; Dhochak and Doliya, 2020)	Resources and capabilities	Founders' experience	Knowledge of how to operate a business in a certain sector	Relevant number of years in a particular industry
		Founding team vs. solo founder	Founding team or individual founders with overall responsibility for the firm	Number of founders
		Management team completeness	Team covering all key managerial positions	CEO/president, vice president (VP) of marketing, engineering, finance, and manufacturing
		Network size	External relationships through which founders channel resource flow and shape their strategies	Number of alliance partners
Signaling theory (Greenberg, 2013; Block et al., 2014)	Signals of quality	Patents	Number of patents granted and patent applications, and respective scope	Number of patent applications and number of patents granted
		Trademark	Number of trademarks granted and trademark applications, and respective scope	Number of trademark applications filed by start-up
Agency theory and ownership structure (Wasserman, 2017)	Ownership and control	Founder control and equity division	Percentage of venture ownership	Equal splitting vs. unequal splitting

a start-up's industry sector and valuation outcomes and found that information technology had the strongest relationship with valuation outcomes. Specifically, information technology start-ups, representing 53 percent of the sample, were less likely to have low valuations and more likely to have high valuations (8 percent low and 66 percent high), compared to counterparts offering consumer products and services (17 percent low and 58 percent high, representing 19 percent of the sample) or business services (10 percent low and 65 percent high, representing 13 percent of the sample). This is because industries with higher aggregate levels of R&D intensity are linked to higher rates of firm-level innovation, which in turn impact on revenue growth (Thornhill, 2006).

5.1.2   Product differentiation

Industries characterized by product differentiation present higher margins and economic profitability (Porter, 1985). Accordingly, Miloud et al. (2012), studying 102 new French ventures from 18 industries, found that new ventures in highly differentiated industries receive a higher valuation from VCs. Ge et al. (2005) obtained similar results by analyzing a sample of 210 US-based new business ventures in 48 different industries. In the same vein, Dhochak and Doliya (2020) investigated VCs' opinions about the relative importance of strategic theories in the venture valuation literature. After conducting a survey of 18 Indian venture capital funds and 7 foreign-based venture capital funds, they found that product differentiation is considered among the most important valuation criteria since product differentiation might enable start-ups to quickly gain traction.

5.1.3   Industry demand growth

The demand growth rate of an industry is a key indicator of its market attractiveness for both new ventures and established firms (Porter, 1985). Since early-stage equity investors usually focus their investments on innovative start-ups with high growth potential (Zider, 1998), a high demand growth rate typically results in a higher valuation (Miloud et al., 2012; Ge et al., 2005).

5.2   Resource-Based View

Understanding sources of sustained competitive advantage is of the utmost importance, not only to entrepreneurs who wish to build the "next big thing", but also to investors who allocate resources to these firms. Consequently, the Resource-Based View (RBV) has become one of the most influential and cited theories in strategic management. The work of Barney (1991) entitled "Firm resources and sustained competitive advantage" is widely acknowledged as focal to the development of this theory. In analyzing sources of competitive advantage, the author focused on the link between a firm's internal characteristics and its performance. The fundamentals of this theory are based on two important assumptions. First, firms within an industry (or group) are heterogeneous in relation to the strategic resources that they control, and second, such heterogeneity persists over time, since resources are not perfectly mobile across firms. Firm resources, such as physical and financial assets, capabilities, technologies, knowledge, organizational processes, employees, and social networks, enable firms to implement value-creating strategies. Firms achieve competitive advantage when their value-creating strategy is not being introduced concurrently by other existing or potential future competitors. When other firms are also unable to replicate the benefits of that value-creating strategy, the competitive advantage is sustainable. Below, we present a set of firm resources that, according to the extant literature, affect the valuation of innovative start-ups because they contribute to firm competitive advantage.

5.2.1 Founders' experience

Founders' prior industry experience is associated with a better understanding of customer demand within the industry and provides social ties to suppliers and distributors of the sector in which the new firm operates (Delmar and Shane, 2006). These advantages are reflected in the valuation of start-ups. For example, Ge et al. (2005) found that, *ceteris paribus*, founders' prior industry experience positively affects the valuation of new ventures by VCs.

Since management experience is associated with knowledge about strategies and organizational structures required to manage the growth and development of new firms, it leads to higher start-up valuation by equity investors (Dhochak and Doliya, 2020; Ge et al., 2005; Miloud et al., 2012).

Extant literature suggests that a founder's start-up experience provides valuable entrepreneurial skills, a business reputation, and extensive network contacts, which serve as strategic resources that can be exploited in the future of the business. Such experience also allows founders to accumulate the wealth, power, and legitimacy that can be used to overcome the liability of newness (Starr and Bygrave, 1991). In line with these arguments, Ge et al. (2005) and Miloud et al. (2012) found that a new venture is valued higher if its founder has previous start-up experience.

5.2.2 Founding team vs. solo founder

Extant literature has emphasized the key role of teams in the context of technological entrepreneurship, because, compared to a single founder, teams are more likely to possess the broad set of skills and capabilities needed to achieve a fit between technology and market (Visintin and Pittino, 2014) and to commercialize first breakthrough innovations (Tushman and Anderson, 1986). This is reflected in the valuation assigned by equity investors, which is higher for start-ups founded by teams rather than individual entrepreneurs (Ge et al., 2005; Miloud et al., 2012).

5.2.3   Management team completeness

Recent research points out the importance of having a complete management team as it determines how well and how fast work can be done (Ge et al., 2005). More specifically, a complete team is one where essential business functions such as finance, R&D, production, and marketing are fully covered by the entrepreneurial team (Roure and Keeley, 1990). Management team completeness has a positive impact on the valuation of the new venture by VCs because it reduces the need for investors to address the risks caused by gaps in a start-up's management (Miloud et al., 2012).

5.2.4   Network size

Liabilities of newness and smallness (Freeman et al., 1993) can be somewhat mitigated by new ventures' network size, defined by Ge et al. (2005) as the number of alliance partners. For Hansen (1995), network size captures the extent to which resources can be accessed by the entrepreneur and the organization. Alliances between organizations therefore facilitate the achievement of strategically significant objectives (Elmuti and Kathawala, 2001). Network size also helps to mitigate the uncertainty surrounding young companies, because alliances can certify the quality of new ventures to third parties (Stuart et al., 1999). Consistently with these arguments, empirical studies show that the size of a venture's network is significantly and positively related to its valuation by VCs (Ge et al., 2005; Miloud et al., 2012). Moreover, in examining the direct effects of strategic alliances on the valuation of 166 US venture-backed software firms, Moghaddam et al. (2016) found that alliances formation positively and significantly affects firm valuations in the software industry.

5.3   Signaling Theory

Signaling theory is useful for describing behavior when two parties (individuals or organizations) have access to different information. Spence's (1973) seminal work on labor markets showed how a job applicant might engage in behaviors to reduce information asymmetry that hinders the selection ability of potential employers. As an example, Spence described how high-quality prospective employees distinguish themselves from low-quality candidates through the costly signal of rigorous higher education. Signaling theory is frequently used in entrepreneurship literature as well as in management literature to explain the influence of information asymmetry in different strands of research (Connelly et al., 2011). The key concept of the signaling theory involves two actors – the signaler and receiver – as well as the signal itself. Spence describes signalers as insiders (e.g. executives or managers) who have private information about an individual, the product, or the organization that is not available to outsiders. The information obtained can be either positive or negative and could include early-stage R&D results, later-stage news regarding preliminary sales results, or pending lawsuits (Connelly et al., 2011). Upon receipt of the information, insiders must then decide whether to communicate this information to outsiders. Here, signaling theory suggests that insiders will deliberately communicate only positive information to outsiders, with the hope of conveying positive organization attributes. However, insiders may also send negative signals, but this is often an unintentional consequence of their actions. The signals sent to outsiders must be observable (i.e. outsiders are able to notice the signal); the signaler must be able to bear the costs of launching the signal. Lastly, receivers refers to outsiders who lack information about the organization in question but would like to receive this information.

5.3.1 Patents

The availability of formal intellectual property rights (IPR) protection may help reduce information asymmetries by allowing new ventures to demonstrate their future potential to external investors. Accordingly, technology start-ups patent to obtain funds and reputation (Graham et al., 2009). Studying Israeli technology start-ups, Greenberg (2013) demonstrates the importance of patents in the valuation of young technology-based ventures. They found a positive relationship between patent applications and firm valuations for non-software-based ventures. The positive impact of patents on valuation was stronger for start-ups that were younger, in their pre-revenue stages, and during early financing rounds.

5.3.2 Trademarks

Another important component of a firm's IP asset is its trademarks, which offer protection to the firm's brands and marketing assets (Wood, 2000). Trademarks grant their holders the right to exclude others from the use of protected words, signs, or symbols (Besen and Raskind, 1991).

Filing of trademarks also signals a start-up's degree of market and growth orientation and willingness to protect its current and future marketing efforts from the infringement of others (Sandner and Block, 2011). In investigating the influence of the number and breadth of a start-up's trademark applications on VCs' financial valuation of the start-up as well as the effect of trademark applications in later funding rounds, Block et al. (2014) showed that trademarks are strong predictors of VCs' valuation of start-ups. In particular, they found that the number of trademarks and the breadth of their applications provide additional information about the scope and direction of start-ups' marketing strategies. Their findings also indicate that the signaling value of trademarks decreases as the venture progresses into different stages of development.

5.4   Agency Theory

Agency theory is related to the conflicting interests of principals and agents. The work of Jensen and Meckling (1976) on agency costs and ownership structure holds a cardinal role in the corporate governance literature. The focal point of Jensen and Meckling's model is that there is a conflict of interest between firm managers and owners, since both parties seek to maximize their own utility. The mismatch of interests between owners and managers generates agency costs, such as monitoring costs (i.e. principal's activities intended to limit agents' detrimental actions). In the context of entrepreneurial finance, agency theory has been used to describe frictions between founders and resources providers (Wasserman, 2017).

5.4.1   Equity ownership and control

To acquire resources for their start-ups, founders often have to sacrifice ownership stakes and decision-making control, as the providers of those resources – cofounders, hires, and investors – often trade their capital for equity stakes. Such decisions can create agency costs, which impair start-up value. In line with these arguments, Wasserman (2017) found that such changes of a founder's ownership stakes negatively affect the start-up's valuation. Also, splitting equity equally among founding members negatively affects valuation because it can foster free-riding opportunistic behavior of some founders (Hellmann and Wasserman, 2016).

6.   DISCUSSION OF THE LITERATURE ON NON-ACCOUNTING DRIVERS

The literature discussed in the previous section offers at least three areas to extend our knowledge about valuation of innovative start-ups by early-stage equity investors.

Heterogeneity appraisal. A significant shortcoming of the existing studies stems from the lack of elaboration on the heterogeneity in the entrepreneurial opportunities exploited by innovative start-ups and in the actions whereby such opportunities are developed from ideas to actual products or services (cf. Berglund et al., 2020). Innovative start-ups differ substantially, for example in terms of business model, products and services, and technology base (Audretsch et al., 2020). They also differ in terms of entrepreneurial strategies, style, and skills, as well as organizational characteristics (Chan et al., 2006). The direct and indirect effect of these heterogeneity dimensions on the valuation process is rather neglected, thereby reducing the interpretative and explanatory power of these studies.

Origin. In their quest for solutions to complex problems, innovative firms obtain knowledge from different sources (Agarwal and Shah, 2014; Caiazza et al., 2020; Minola et al., 2019). These sources are also known as knowledge contexts. Since knowledge contexts determine the initial performance advantage (or disadvantage) of innovative start-ups (Hahn et al., 2019), they are likely to determine their valuation (Tether and Tajar, 2008). Despite the importance of originating knowledge contexts for innovative start-ups being well acknowledged in the literature (Bose and Thomas, 2007), in the identified papers, we found no empirical study investigating equity investors' approach to valuation based on (or, at least, controlling for) the contexts originating the innovative start-ups. According to Minola et al. (2019), the origin of innovative start-ups is particularly important because it affects the characteristics of the firms' technological knowledge in terms of scope and newness, due to the fact that these firms take advantage of the knowledge spillovers from their knowledge providers (universities, research centers, science parks, corporations, etc.). A clear example of how innovative start-ups' take advantage of the context from which they originate can be provided by looking at start-ups founded by scientists, that is, individuals involved in research and scientific work in academia and other research institutions (Stephan, 2014). During their scientific careers, scientists internalize attitudes towards experimentation (Van Maanen and Schein, 1977) and exchanging knowledge (Jain et al., 2009); in turn, such a mindset assists scientists in the commercialization process (Hahn et al., 2019). Founders with prior experience in an established corporation can also take advantage of the market- and industry-related knowledge acquired during employment to develop and commercialize new products or services and achieve higher growth rates (Wennberg et al., 2011). Despite the role of innovative start-ups' origin in determining their competitive advantage, innovative behavior, and growth prospect (Hahn et al., 2019), this dimension is still neglected in extant literature.

Narrow scope of theories. In order to address the limitations highlighted above (i.e. lack of heterogeneity appraisal and of empirical investigation of the origin dimension), non-accounting drivers should be informed by a broader set of management and entrepreneurship theories. For example, to explain the link between origin and valuation, imprinting theory represents an exemplar case, where the biography of organizations and their founders are taken into account. Imprinting theory assumes that the founding conditions of new ventures have a long-lasting imprint on their performance (Bamford et al., 2000), particularly in high-technology sectors (Gimmon and Levie, 2020). Imprinting theory also highlights the importance of founders' prior career experiences (Marquis and Tilcsik, 2013). The knowledge, skills, and values internalized by founders during their careers shape the behavior, development, and subsequent performance of their start-ups (Bryant, 2014; Simsek et al., 2015; Burton et al., 2016), thereby affecting their value. Scholars could also take advantage of theoretical perspectives concerned with the design of entrepreneurial opportunities and the actions undertaken by new ventures to transform ideas into marketable new products or services, such as effectuation (Sarasvathy, 2001), entrepreneurial judgment (Foss et al., 2019), and entrepreneurship as design (Berglund et al., 2020). By focusing on how entrepreneurs uniquely manage the uncertainty surrounding the innovation process and the acquisition of resources, these theories help scholars to identify actions undertaken by start-ups (e.g. landing pages, co-creation communities, beta versions, proto-typing) that could contribute to their valuation.

In view of the limitations stated above, we propose that recognizing the university as a context of origin of innovative start-ups represents a valuable direction to advance our knowledge on the valuation of innovative start-ups based on non-accounting drivers. Universities play a key role in the generation of innovative start-ups, not only by facilitating the formation of firms founded by faculty members to commercialize research results, but also in providing valuable technological and entrepreneurial knowledge to students and graduates to help them found their own ventures (Shah and Pahnke, 2014).

In the following section, we propose a set of UBDs that could inform research on valuation. We define UBDs as characteristics describing the university context from which innovative start-ups are originated. First, since UBDs illustrate the unique challenges associated with science commercialization (Fini et al., 2019), they help us to appraise the heterogeneity of the innovation processes undertaken by innovative start-ups. Second, since UBDs capture the distinctiveness of innovative start-ups' originating context (Hahn et al., 2019), they allow researchers to incorporate origin in the valuation literature. Finally, by describing the transition between the university and business worlds, UBDs offer the opportunity to use a broad set of management theories (Fini et al., 2019).

7.   THE UNIVERSITY-BASED DIMENSIONS OF INNOVATIVE START-UPS

The key role of universities in driving innovation and entrepreneurship through science commercialization has been widely acknowledged by scholars and is central in the agenda of policymakers (Agarwal and Shah, 2014; Audretsch and Belitski, 2013; Fini et al., 2019). Based on a wide variety of activities, universities are able to generate knowledge spillovers and enable the transfer of technologies from research labs to the market (Bekkers and Freitas, 2008; Belitski et al., 2019). Prior studies suggest that firms consider more formal activities based on intellectual property – patenting and licensing – as the most important form of accessible knowledge that is being developed by the university (D'Este and Patel, 2007). Other studies indicate that less formal as well as informal and non-commercial activities are equally or even more important forms of knowledge transfer (Abreu and Grinevich, 2013; Caldera and Debande, 2010). Additionally, other third-mission elements, such as collaboration of university researchers with incumbent firms, collaborative research, contracts with industry, contracts with public bodies, and the formation of university spinoffs or student start-ups, represent means to transfer knowledge from the university to the industry (Colombo and Piva, 2020; D'Este and Patel, 2007; Wennberg et al., 2011).

Despite the central role played by universities in the generation of innovative start-ups, we do not know much about its implications for start-up valuation. Only a few studies have analyzed the attractiveness of UBDs to potential investors, probably due to a paucity of data. Previous researchers have analyzed a small number of universities, relied on case studies, or drawn on small-scale surveys to acquire their data. This gap is surprising, since the valuation of innovative start-ups by early-stage equity investors could benefit from signals of scientific quality as well as the substantive benefits associated with university affiliation. For example, affiliation with a prestigious university also provides substantive benefits to affiliated firms. Indeed, previous studies have shown that biotech firms generally maintain close links with universities (Audretsch and Stephan, 1996). Affiliation with a university places the affiliated firm in an ideal position to leverage the state-of-the-art scientific knowledge produced by the university, because of the social links of its upper echelons. In turn, biotech firms that in-license advanced scientific knowledge from universities are more likely to craft revenue-generating commercial alliances with pharmaceutical firms (Stuart et al., 1999). Affiliated firms also have easier access to the state-of-the-art laboratories of the university and can benefit from the effective administrative and legal support that the university offers to affiliated firms.

From an empirical standpoint, so far scholars have studied initial public offerings (IPOs) of university-affiliated firms in order to document the positive impact of affiliation with a university on the valuation of innovative start-ups. In particular, two studies stand out. First, Bonardo et al. (2011) investigate the valuation of university-based companies and their ability to translate the potential benefits of academic affiliation into long-term performance gains. Among the 499 high-tech small and medium-sized enterprises (SMEs) that went public in Europe between 1995 and 2003, they find that 131 were university-based firms. For firms who publicize the fact that they are university-based and have chosen to go public, affiliation with a university is recognized as beneficial by investors. Second, Colombo et al. (2019) study the combined effect of affiliation with prestigious universities, underwriters, and VCs on the valuation of biotech ventures at IPO and their post-IPO performance. They argue that affiliation to a prestigious university provides the affiliated firm with a quality signal in the scientific domain. The pure quality signaling effect of the affiliation is isolated from the substantive benefits it provides by performing a difference-in-difference approach based on the scientific reputation of scientists in firms' upper echelons. The signal is stronger the weaker is the scientific reputation of scientists of the focal IPO firm and is additive to those provided by prestigious VCs and underwriters.

Despite this evidence, to date research is relatively silent on how the peculiar elements of university context affect the valuation of innovative start-ups specifically. Innovative start-ups originated by universities present some unique "genetic" (Colombo and Piva, 2012) features, which can be categorized along three basic dimensions of "university-based distinctiveness". These three UBDs are resources, governance, and goals (Lockett and Wright, 2005; Sciarelli et al., 2021; Fernández-Alles et al., 2015; Nikiforou et al., 2018; Meoli and Vismara, 2016; Chesbrough, 2003). In the next subsections, we introduce and describe these UBDs and provide some possible exemplary research questions to advance the literature on innovative start-ups valuation (see Table 12.5).

7.1   Resources and Related UBDs

The academic setting provides unique resources to innovative start-ups, which distinguish them from other new ventures (Colombo and Piva, 2012). In terms of human resources, innovative start-ups originated from universities present unique human capital, rooted in the academic profile and career of academic entrepreneurs (Bonardo et al., 2011). University education can also provide to students and graduates unique knowledge about technological opportunities and the skills required to exploit them through venture creation (Eesley and Lee, 2020; Shah and Pahnke, 2014), as well as useful contacts and networks that can support the development of new ventures. Despite the unique contribution of founders' university background to commercialization (Hahn et al., 2019), valuation literature has largely overlooked this aspect. For example, Knockaert et al. (2011) found that the presence of a larger proportion of the original research team in the venture can enhance the transfer of tacit knowledge, which consequently affects the probability of reaching sufficient post-founding speed to successfully launch a first product. Scientists in the founding team are more likely to possess start-of-the-art technological knowledge (Colombo and Piva, 2012), leading to breakthrough innovations (Minola et al., 2019). Future research, thus, could look into how the scientific or university background of the founding team affects the valuation of the

Table 12.5   *The University-Based Dimensions (UBDs) of innovative*
start-ups

Dimension	Theme	Description	Examples
Resources	Human	Skills, knowledge, and experience possessed by the founder	Presence of original research team, their technical and scientific skills
	Social	Social relationships and social structures	Size of team and cohesion
	Technological	The stock of firm's unique know-how	IPR, publications
	Symbolical	Recognitions and considerations that the founder holds	Reputation/h-index
Governance	Scientist and non-scientist founders	Team diversity	Scientist and non-scientist founders
	Surrogate entrepreneurs	Entrepreneurs from outside the university assuming the role of entrepreneur	External entrepreneurs
	Corporate governance	How the new venture is directed and controlled	Composition of the board
	University formal involvement	Participation of the university	Presence of faculty members on the board
Goals	University-oriented goals	Desired results over the short and long term	Placement of young scholars without academic career
	University-oriented non-economic goals	Desired results over the short and long term	Prestige, publication, advancement of science
	Innovation strategy	Approach to innovation	Basic research vs. applied research

start-up. Moreover, even though entrepreneurs' social capital is crucial to firm valuation (Hsu, 2007) and scientists are embedded in a network of contacts providing valuable scientific knowledge and advice (Colombo and Piva, 2012; Stuart and Ding, 2006), the university-originated part of this social capital has not received scholarly attention.

In addition, team size in innovative start-ups that originated from universities is particularly important, as science commercialization requires a different set of capabilities that a single person usually does not possess. Larger teams signal quality (Clarysse and Moray, 2004) and higher growth (Czarnitzki et al., 2014) as team members combine their capabilities to successfully bring new technology to market. Studies of the founding teams of innovative start-ups that originated from university have also revealed some unique dynamics, such as trust and team cohesion, driving the performance of new ventures, even though they have not been considered as non-accounting drivers of start-up valuation. According to Chen and Wang (2008), trust facilitates the exchange of information within a team whereas it suppresses the free flow of external information, as teams with high levels of trust tend to place more value on internally generated ideas than on ideas coming from outsiders. The cohesion of founding teams appears to have a positive association with team effectiveness (Bjornali et al., 2016) and the financial performance of innovative start-ups (Ensley and Hmieleski, 2005). Trust and cohesion may be affected by the shared educational background of the entrepreneurial team members, in terms of shared experience and ease of communication. In view of this, future research could examine how the unique internal team dynamics of start-ups originated from the academic setting (Ensley and Hmieleski, 2005) affect valuation.

Finally, innovative start-ups can benefit from the academic status of their founders. Zucker et al. (2007) note that "star" scientists from higher-quality academic institutions create innovative firms to capture the rents generated by their intellectual capital. Similarly, Di Gregorio and Shane (2003) conclude that it may be easier for scientists from top-tier universities to assemble resources to create start-ups due to their increased credibility. Scientist entrepreneurs' credibility and reputation stem from the number of academic papers published in top-ranked journals or the number of citations of these papers. In contrast, the reputation of non-scientist entrepreneurs is rooted in the number of successful start-ups that they have contributed to creating. We maintain it would be interesting to investigate the effect of founders' scientific reputation on the valuation of their start-ups.

7.2   Corporate Governance and Related UBDs

The ownership and control of innovative start-ups by university and faculty members generate some unique features in the governance of firms that originated in the academic setting. For example, these ventures may appoint surrogate entrepreneurs (i.e. entrepreneurs from outside the academic institution) to compensate for the lack of market-related knowledge, which often characterizes academic founders (Lockett et al., 2003). Research suggests that innovative start-ups that involve surrogate entrepreneurs perform better than those that do not (Lundqvist, 2014). Yet we do not know to what extent the appointing of surrogate entrepreneurs affects the valuation of start-ups. Concerning university involvement in start-ups' governance, Ferretti et al. (2019) employ a quantitative method to investigate the engagement of universities in different roles on the boards of directors and in the ownership structures of 194 Italian innovative start-ups. In particular, they found that the involvement of the university affects the performance of innovative start-ups, but a strategy of "neither absent nor too present" is the optimal way for them to support the growth of start-ups. In addition, they find a positive association between the presence of academics on the board and sales growth, as well as a positive association with time to break even. Scientist entrepreneurs may attract experienced and well-connected directors to their boards who can play an important role in accessing critical external resources (Lynall et al., 2003). Studying a sample of 140 high-tech start-ups, Clarysse et al. (2007) found that high-tech start-ups with a public research organization as an external equity shareholder are more likely to include outside board members with complementary skills to the founding team than innovative start-ups with VCs or founders as the main stakeholders. Even though such evidence shows that university involvement in the governance of innovative start-ups matters, the way in which the quality of the public research organization and the extent of its involvement affect the valuation of the start-up has not been investigated so far.

7.3   Goals and Related UBDs

Different theories, so far neglected in the valuation literature, have been used to shed light on the relationship between the innovative start-up and the university environment in which founders have worked or been trained: imprinting theory (Hahn et al., 2019), identity theories (Jain et al., 2009), institutional theory (Fini and Toschi, 2016), and social embeddedness (Stuart and Ding, 2006) are some examples. These theories converge to the idea that exposure to academic logics influences scientist founders' priorities. In particular, they are often motivated by passion-driven and socio-emotional achievements or reputation in the scientific community and society (Hayter, 2011). Prior research also suggests that innovative entrepreneurs' drivers differ depending on their attachment to the traditional norms of science (Huyghe et al., 2016). The motivation to advance research and gain a strong reputation and prestige within the scientific community drives some scientists to initiate entrepreneurial activities (Lam, 2011). In turn, the extent to which such drivers are emphasized by innovative start-ups has an impact on the firm commercialization strategies and performance. For example, the extent to which innovative start-ups search for knowledge from external sources is affected by the career imprints of academic founders and the emphasis they put on non-commercial goals (Hahn et al., 2019). Despite the influence of academic logics on the commercialization activities undertaken by innovative start-ups, and on the outcomes of these activities, valuation literature is relatively silent in this respect. Therefore, future research could look at the extent to which academic logics and norms of science permeating innovative start-ups affect their valuation by early-stage equity investors.

8.   CONCLUSION

The scoping review of this chapter offers three main contributions to literature on start-up valuation. First, we present a theory-informed taxonomy of the non-accounting drivers used by early-stage equity investors in the valuation of innovative start-ups. While to date extant research on non-accounting drivers has been fairly fragmented, our taxonomy could represent a starting point for scholars to theoretically advance this vibrant research stream. In particular, given the variety of theoretical perspectives shown in the review, researchers would greatly benefit from cross-fertilization among disciplines. Second, our review revealed three areas for future improvement: (i) appraisal of start-ups' heterogeneity; (ii) consideration of start-ups' originating context; and (iii) extending the scope of theories. Third, to address the aforementioned opportunities and advance research on and the practice of valuation, the chapter proposes a focus on *university* as the context of origin and distinctiveness of many innovative start-ups. In doing so, it offers a set of UBDs to be incorporated in valuation studies.

These contributions also provide implications of interest to those involved in technology transfer at universities. In particular, managers of technology transfer offices should be aware that the distinctive characteristics connected to UBDs could be crucial in determining the valuation of start-ups generated by universities. The chapter also provides interesting insights for investors as it gives evidence on non-accounting drivers of start-up valuation. The chapter also offers some insights on how to approach the valuation of start-ups affiliated with a university, whose technological potential can be particularly appealing for VCs and BAs. Our contributions are also significant for actual academic entrepreneurs who would like to shape the valuation process to their advantage.

ACKNOWLEDGMENTS

We would like to express our very great appreciation to e-Novia for their financial support. Our appreciation also goes to Prof. Karl Wennberg (Linköping University) and Prof. Francis Hoy (Worcester Polytechnic Institute) for their insights and useful discussions.

NOTES

1. Pre-money valuation indicates the value of the start-up before the investment; it is obtained by deducting the money invested at the financing round from the firm's announced worth (Ge et al., 2005).
2. Post-money valuation is the value of the start-up after the investment has been made; it is obtained by summing the pre-money valuation of the start-up and the amount of funds invested (Block et al., 2014).

REFERENCES

Abreu, M., and Grinevich, V. (2013). The nature of academic entrepreneurship in the UK: Widening the focus on entrepreneurial activities. *Research Policy*, 42(2), 408–422.

Agarwal, R., and Shah, S. K. (2014). Knowledge sources of entrepreneurship: Firm formation by academic, user and employee innovators. *Research Policy*, 43(7), 1109–1133.

Amir, E., and Lev, B. (1996). Value-relevance of nonfinancial information: The wireless communications industry. *Journal of Accounting and Economics*, 22(1–3), 3–30.

Amir, E., Lev, B., and Sougiannis, T. (2003). Do financial analysts get intangibles? *European Accounting Review*, 12(4), 635–659.

Arksey, H., and O'Malley, L. (2005). Scoping studies: Towards a methodological framework. *International Journal of Social Research Methodology*, 8(1), 19–32.

Armstrong, C., Davila, A., and Foster, G. (2006). Venture-backed private equity valuation and financial statement information. *Review of Accounting Studies*, 11(1), 119–154.

Audretsch, D. B., and Belitski, M. (2013). The missing pillar: The creativity theory of knowledge spillover entrepreneurship. *Small Business Economics*, 41(4), 819–836.

Audretsch, D., Colombelli, A., Grilli, L., Minola, T., and Rasmussen, E. (2020). Innovative startups and policy initiatives. *Research Policy*, 49(10), 104027.

Audretsch, D. B., and Stephan, P. (1996). Company–scientist locational links: The case of biotechnology. *American Economic Review*, 86, 641–652.

Bain, J. S. (1968). *Industrial Organization*. 2nd Ed. New York: John Wiley & Sons.

Bamford, C. E., Dean, T. J., and McDougall, P. P. (2000). An examination of the impact of initial founding conditions and decisions upon the performance of new bank start-ups. *Journal of Business Venturing*, 15(3), 253–277.

Barker, R., and Imam, S. (2008). Analysts' perceptions of "earnings quality". *Accounting and Business Research*, 38(4), 313–329.

Barney, J. (1991). Firm resources and sustained competitive advantage. *Journal of Management*, 17(1), 99–120.

Bekkers, R., and Freitas, I. M. B. (2008). Analysing knowledge transfer channels between universities and industry: To what degree do sectors also matter? *Research Policy*, 37(10), 1837–1853.

Belitski, M., Aginskaja, A., and Marozau, R. (2019). Commercializing university research in transition economies: Technology transfer offices or direct industrial funding? *Research Policy*, 48(3), 601–615.

Berglund, H., Bousfiha, M., and Mansoori, Y. (2020). Opportunities as artifacts and entrepreneurship as design. *Academy of Management Review*, 45(4), 825–846.

Berry, S., Gaynor, M., and Scott Morton, F. (2019). Do increasing markups matter? Lessons from empirical industrial organization. *Journal of Economic Perspectives*, 33(3), 44–68.

Besen, S. M., and Raskind, L. J. (1991). An introduction to the law and economics of intellectual property. *Journal of Economic Perspectives*, 5(1), 3–27.

Bjornali, E., Knockaert, M., and Erikson, T. (2016). The impact of top management team characteristics and board service involvement on team effectiveness in high-tech startups. *Long Range Planning*, 49(4), 447–463.

Block, J. H., De Vries, G., Schumann, J. H., and Sandner, P. (2014). Trademarks and venture capital valuation. *Journal of Business Venturing*, 29, 525–542.

Bonardo, D., Paleari, S., and Vismara, S. (2011). Valuing university-based firms: The effects of academic affiliation on IPO performance. *Entrepreneurship Theory and Practice*, 35, 755–776.

Bose, S., and Thomas, K. (2007). Valuation of intellectual capital in knowledge-based firms: The need for new methods in a changing economic paradigm. *Management Decision*, 45(9), 1484–1496.

Bryant, P. T. (2014). Imprinting by design: The microfoundations of entrepreneurial adaptation. *Entrepreneurship Theory and Practice*, 38, 1081–1102.

Burton, M. D., Sørensen, J. B., and Dobrev, S. D. (2016). A careers perspective on entrepreneurship. *Entrepreneurship Theory and Practice*, 40, 237–247.

Caiazza, R., Belitski, M., and Audretsch, D. B. (2020). From latent to emergent entrepreneurship: The knowledge spillover construction circle. *Journal of Technology Transfer*, 45(3), 694–704.

Caldera, A., and Debande, O. (2010). Performance of Spanish universities in technology transfer: An empirical analysis. *Research Policy*, 39(9), 1160–1173.

Centre for Reviews and Dissemination (CRD). (2001). *Undertaking Systematic Reviews of Research on Effectiveness: CRD's Guidance for Those Carrying Out or Commissioning Reviews*, CRD Report 4 (2nd Ed.). York: NHS Centre for Reviews and Dissemination, University of York.

Chan, Y. E., Bhargava, N., and Street, C. T. (2006). Having arrived: The homogeneity of high growth small firms. *Journal of Small Business Management*, 44(3), 426–440.

Chartered Association of Business Schools (CABS). (n.d.). *Academic Journal Guide 2018*. Retrieved February 2020 from https://charteredabs.org/academic-journal-guide-2018/

Chen, M., and Wang, M. (2008). Social networks and a new venture's innovative capability: The role of trust within entrepreneurial teams. *R&D Management*, 38(3), 253–264.

Chesbrough, H. (2003). The governance and performance of Xerox's technology spin-off companies. *Research Policy*, 32(3), 403–421.

Cinquini, L., Passetti, E., Tenucci, A., and Frey, M. (2012). Analyzing intellectual capital information in sustainability reports: Some empirical evidence. *Journal of Intellectual Capital*, 13(4), 531–561.

Clarysse, B., Knockaert, M., and Lockett, A. (2007). Outside board members in high tech startups. *Small Business Economics*, 29, 243–259.

Clarysse, B., and Moray, N. (2004). A process study of entrepreneurial team formation: The case of a research-based spin-off. *Journal of Business Venturing*, 19(1), 55–79.

Colombelli, A., Grilli, L., Minola, T., and Mrkajic, B. (2020). To what extent do young innovative companies take advantage of policy support to enact innovation appropriation mechanisms? *Research Policy*, 49(10), 103797.

Colombelli, A., Krafft, J., and Vivarelli, M. (2016). To be born is not enough: The key role of innovative start-ups. *Small Business Economics*, 47(2), 277–291.

Colombo, M. G., Meoli, M., and Vismara, S. (2019). Signaling in science-based IPOs: The combined effect of affiliation with prestigious universities, underwriters, and venture capitalists. *Journal of Business Venturing*, 34(1), 141–177.

Colombo, M., and Piva, E. (2012). Firms' genetic characteristics and competence-enlarging strategies: A comparison between academic and non-academic high-tech start-ups. *Research Policy*, 41(1), 79–92.

Colombo, M. G., and Piva, E. (2020). Start-ups launched by recent STEM university graduates: The impact of university education on entrepreneurial entry. *Research Policy*, 49(6), 103993.

Connelly, B. L., Certo, T. S., Ireland, D. R., and Reutzel, C. R. (2011). Signaling theory: A review and assessment. *Journal of Management*, 37(1), 39–67.

Cumming, D. J., and Vismara, S. (2017). De-segmenting research in entrepreneurial finance. *Venture Capital*, 19(1–2), 17–27.

Czarnitzki, D., Rammer, C., and Toole, A. A. (2014). University spin-offs and the "performance premium". *Small Business Economics*, 43, 309–326.

Davila, A., and Foster, G. (2005). Management accounting systems adoption decisions: Evidence and performance implications from startup companies. *The Accounting Review*, 80, 1039–1068.

Davila, A., Foster, G., and Gupta, M. (2003). Venture capital financing and the growth of startup firms. *Journal of Business Venturing*, 18(6), 689–708.

Davila, A., Foster, G., and Jia, N. (2015). The valuation of management control systems in startup companies: International field-based evidence. *European Accounting Review*, 24(2), 207–239.

Delmar, F., and Shane, S. (2006). Does experience matter? The effect of founding team experience on the survival and sales of newly founded ventures. *Strategic Organization*, 4(3), 215–247.

D'Este, P., and Patel, P. (2007). University–industry linkages in the UK: What are the factors underlying the variety of interactions with industry? *Research Policy*, 36(9), 1295–1313.

Dhochak, M., and Doliya, P. (2020). Valuation of a startup: Moving towards strategic approaches. *Journal of Multi-Criteria Decision Analysis*, 27(1–2), 39–49.

Di Gregorio, D., and Shane, S. (2003). Why do some universities generate more start-ups than others? *Research Policy*, 32(2), 209–227.

Dittmann, I., Maug, E., and Kemper, J. (2004). How fundamental are fundamental values? Valuation methods and their impact on the performance of German venture capitalists. *European Financial Management*, 10(4), 609–638.

Drover, W., Busenitz, L., Matusik, S., Townsend, D., Anglin, A., and Dushnitsky, G. (2017). A review and road map of entrepreneurial equity financing research: Venture capital, corporate venture capital, angel investment, crowdfunding, and accelerators. *Journal of Management*, 43(6), 1820–1853.

Eesley, C. E., and Lee, Y. S. (2020). Do university entrepreneurship programs promote entrepreneurship? *Strategic Management Journal*, 42(4), 833–861.

Eisenmann, T. (2020). Determinants of early-stage startup performance: Survey results. Harvard Business School Entrepreneurial Management Working Paper, 2157.

Elmuti, D., and Kathawala, Y. (2001). An overview of strategic alliances. *Management Decision*, 39(3), 205–218.

Ensley, M. D., and Hmieleski, K. M. (2005). A comparative study of new venture top management team composition, dynamics and performance between university-based and independent start-ups. *Research Policy*, 34(7), 1091–1105.

Fernández-Alles, M., Camelo-Ordaz, C., and Franco-Leal, N. (2015). Key resources and actors for the evolution of academic spin-offs. *Journal of Technology Transfer*, 40(6), 976–1002.

Ferretti, M., Ferri, S., Fiorentino, R., Parmentola, A., and Sapio, A. (2019). Neither absent nor too present: The effects of the engagement of parent universities on the performance of academic spin-offs. *Small Business Economics*, 52(1), 153–173.

Festel, G., Wuermseher, M., and Cattaneo, G. (2013). Valuation of early stage high-tech start-up companies. *International Journal of Business*, 18(3), 216–231.

Fini, R., Rasmussen, E., Wiklund, J., and Wright, M. (2019). Theories from the lab: How research on science commercialization can contribute to management studies. *Journal of Management Studies*, 56(5), 865–894.

Fini, R., and Toschi, L. (2016). Academic logic and corporate entrepreneurial intentions: A study of the interaction between cognitive and institutional factors in new firms. *International Small Business Journal*, 34(5), 637–659.

Foss, N. J., Klein, P. G., and Bjørnskov, C. (2019). The context of entrepreneurial judgment: Organizations, markets, and institutions. *Journal of Management Studies*, 56(6), 1197–1213.

Freeman, J., Carroll, G. R., and Hannan, M. T. (1993). The liability of newness: Age dependence in organizational death rates. *American Sociological Review*, 48(5), 692–710.

Ge, D., Mahoney, J. M., and Mahoney, J. T. (2005). New venture valuation by venture capitalists: An integrative approach. Urban Champaign Working Paper.

George, A. L., and Bennett, A. (2005). *Case Studies and Theory Development in the Social Sciences*. Cambridge, MA: MIT Press.

Gimmon, E., and Levie, J. (2020). Early indicators of very long-term venture performance: A 20-year panel study. *Academy of Management Discoveries*, 7(2), 203–224.

Gompers, P. A. (1995). Optimal investment, monitoring, and the staging of venture capital. *Journal of Finance*, 50(5), 1461–1489.

Graham, S. J., Merges, R. P., Samuelson, P., and Sichelman, T. (2009). High technology entrepreneurs and the patent system: Results of the 2008 Berkeley Patent Survey. *Berkeley Technology Law Journal*, 24(4), 1255–1327.

Greenberg, G. (2013). Small firms, big patents? Estimating patent value using data on Israeli start-ups' financing rounds. *European Management Review*, 10, 183–196.

Hahn, D., Minola, T., and Eddleston, K. A. (2019). How do scientists contribute to the performance of innovative start-ups? An imprinting perspective on open innovation. *Journal of Management Studies*, 56(5), 895–928.

Hall, B. H. (2002). The financing of research and development. *Oxford Review of Economic Policy*, 18(1), 35–51.

Hand, J. R. (2005). The value relevance of financial statements in the venture capital market. *The Accounting Review*, 80(2), 613–648.

Hand, J. R. (2007). Determinants of the round-to-round returns to pre-IPO venture capital investments in US biotechnology companies. *Journal of Business Venturing*, 22(1), 1–28.

Hansen, E. (1995). Entrepreneurial network and new organization growth. *Entrepreneurship Theory and Practice*, 19, 395–412.

Hayter, C. S. (2011). In search of the profit-maximizing actor: Motivations and definitions of success from nascent academic entrepreneurs. *Journal of Technology Transfer*, 36, 340–352.

Hellmann, T., and Wasserman, N. (2016). The first deal: The division of founder equity in new ventures. *Management Science*, 63(8), 2647–2666.

Heughebaert, A., and Manigart, S. (2012). Firm valuation in venture capital financing rounds: The role of investor bargaining power. *Journal of Business Finance and Accounting*, 39(3–4), 500–530.

Houlihan Valuation Advisors. (1998). The pricing of successful venture capital backed high tech and life sciences companies. *Journal of Business Venturing*, 13(5), 333–351.

Hsu, D. H. (2006). Venture capitalists and cooperative start-up commercialization strategy. *Management Science*, 52(2), 204–219.

Hsu, D. H. (2007). Experienced entrepreneurial founders, organizational capital, and venture capital funding. *Research Policy*, 36, 722–741.

Huyghe, A., Knockaert, M., and Obschonka, M. (2016). Unraveling the "passion orchestra" in academia. *Journal of Business Venturing*, 31, 344–364.

Isaksson, A., and Fredriksen, Ö. (2020). Venture capital firms valuation in bull and bear markets: Evidence from Sweden. *International Journal of Entrepreneurship and Innovation Management*, 24(2–3), 97–115.

Jain, S., George, G., and Maltarich, M. (2009). Academics or entrepreneurs? Investigating role identity modification of university scientists involved in commercialization activity. *Research Policy*, 38, 922–935.

Jensen, M. C., and Meckling, W. H. (1976). Theory of the firm: Managerial behavior, agency costs and ownership structure. *Journal of Financial Economics*, 3(4), 305–360.

Knockaert, M., Ucbasaran, D., Wright, M., and Clarysse, B. (2011). The relationship between knowledge transfer, top management team composition, and performance: The case of science-based entrepreneurial firms. *Entrepreneurship Theory and Practice*, 35(4), 777–803.

Köhn, A. (2018). The determinants of startup valuation in the venture capital context: A systematic review and avenues for future research. *Management Review Quarterly*, 68(1), 1–34.

Lam, A. (2011). What motivates academic scientists to engage in research commercialization: "Gold", "ribbon" or "puzzle"? *Research Policy*, 40(10), 1354–1368.

Lelissa, T. B., and Kuhil, A. M. (2018). The Structure Conduct Performance model and competing hypothesis – a review of literature. *Research Journal of Finance and Accounting*, 9(1), 76–89.

Lockett, A., and Wright, M. (2005). Resources, capabilities, risk capital and the creation of university spin-out companies. *Research Policy*, 34(7), 1043–1057.

Lockett, A., Wright, M., and Franklin, S. (2003). Technology transfer and universities' spinout strategies. *Small Business Economics*, 20, 185–200.

Luger, M. I., and Koo, J. (2005). Defining and tracking business start-ups. *Small Business Economics*, 24(1), 17–28.

Lundqvist, M. A. (2014). The importance of surrogate entrepreneurship for incubated Swedish technology ventures. *Technovation*, 34(2), 93–100.

Lynall, M. D., Golden, B. R., and Hillman, A. J. (2003). Board composition from adolescence to maturity: A multitheoretic view. *Academy of Management Review*, 28(3), 416–421.

Marquis, C., and Tilcsik, A. (2013). Imprinting: Toward a multilevel theory. *Academy of Management Annals*, 7(1), 195–245.

Mays, N., Roberts, E., and Popay, J. (2001). Synthesising research evidence. In N. Fulop, P. Allen, A. Clarke, and N. Black (eds.), *Studying the Organisation and Delivery of Health Services: Research Methods*. London: Routledge, pp. 188–220.

Meoli, M., and Vismara, S. (2016). University support and the creation of technology and nontechnology academic spin-offs. *Small Business Economics*, 47(2), 345–362.

Miloud, T., Aspelund, A., and Cabrol, M. (2012). Startup valuation by venture capitalists: An empirical study. *Venture Capital*, 14(2–3), 151–174.

Minola, T., Hahn, D., and Cassia, L. (2019). The relationship between origin and performance of innovative start-ups: The role of technological knowledge at founding. *Small Business Economics*, 56(2), 553–569.

Moghaddam, K., Bosse, D. A., and Provance, M. (2016). Strategic alliances of entrepreneurial firms: Value enhancing then value destroying. *Strategic Entrepreneurship Journal*, 10(2), 153–168.

Newbronner, E., and Hare, P. (2002). *Services to Support Carers of People with Mental Health Problems: Consultation Report*. York: Social Policy Research Unit, University of York.

Nikiforou, A., Gruber, M., Zabara, T., and Clarysse, B. (2018). The role of teams in academic spin-offs. *Academy of Management Perspectives*, 31(1), 78–103.

Orens, R., and Lybaert, N. (2007). Does the financial analysts' usage of non-financial information influence the analysts' forecast accuracy? Some evidence from the Belgian sell-side financial analyst. *International Journal of Accounting*, 42, 237–271.

Orens, R., and Lybaert, N. (2010). Determinants of sell-side financial analysts' use of nonfinancial information. *Accounting and Business Research*, 40(1), 39–53.

Pham, M. T., Rajić, A., Greig, J. D., Sargeant, J. M., Papadopoulos, A., and McEwen, S. A. (2014). A scoping review of scoping reviews: Advancing the approach and enhancing the consistency. *Research Synthesis Methods*, 5(4), 371–385.

Pisoni, A., and Onetti, A. (2018). When startups exit: Comparing strategies in Europe and the USA. *Journal of Business Strategy*, 39(3), 26–33.

Porter, M. E. (1985). Competitive strategy: The core concepts. In *Competitive Advantage*. New York: Free Press.

Ritchie, J., and Spencer, L. (1993). Qualitative data analysis for applied policy research. In A. Bryman and R. Burgess (eds.), *Analysing Qualitative Data*. London: Routledge, pp. 173–194.

Robb, S. W. G., Single, L. E., and Zarzeski, M. T. (2001). Nonfinancial disclosures across Anglo-American countries. *Journal of International Accounting, Auditing and Taxation*, 10(1), 71–83.

Roure, J. B., and Keeley, R. H. (1990). Predictors of success in new technology-based ventures. *Journal of Business Venturing*, 5(4), 201–220.

Ruhnka, J. C., and Young, J. E. (1991). Some hypotheses about risk in venture capital investing. *Journal of Business Venturing*, 6(2), 115–133.

Sahlman, W. (1990). The structure and governance of venture-capital organizations. *Journal of Financial Economics*, 27(2), 473–521.

Sander, P., and Kõomägi, M. (2007). Valuation of private companies by Estonian private equity and venture capitalists. *Baltic Journal of Management*, 2(1), 6–19.

Sanders, W. G., and Boivie, S. (2004). Sorting things out: Valuation of new firms in uncertain markets. *Strategic Management Journal*, 25(2), 167–186.

Sandner, P. G., and Block, J. (2011). The market value of R&D, patents, and trademarks. *Research Policy*, 40(7), 969–985.

Sarasvathy, S. D. (2001). Causation and effectuation: Toward a theoretical shift from economic inevitability to entrepreneurial contingency. *Academy of Management Review*, 26(2), 243–263.

Sciarelli, M., Landi, G. C., Turriziani, L., and Tani, M. (2021). Academic entrepreneurship: Founding and governance determinants in university spin-off ventures. *Journal of Technology Transfer*, 46, 1083–1107.

Shah, S. K., and Pahnke, E. C. (2014). Parting the ivory curtain: Understanding how universities support a diverse set of startups. *Journal of Technology Transfer*, 39(5), 780–792.

Sievers, S., Mokwa, C. F., and Keienburg, G. (2013). The relevance of financial versus non-financial information for the valuation of venture capital-backed firms. *European Accounting Review*, 22(3), 465–511.

Simsek, Z., Fox, B. C., and Heavey, C. (2015). What's past is prologue: A framework, review, and future directions for organizational research on imprinting. *Journal of Management*, 41, 288–317.

Spence, M. (1973). Job market signaling. *Quarterly Journal of Economics*, 87, 355–374.

Starr, J., and Bygrave, W. (1991). The assets and liabilities of prior startup experience: An exploratory study of multiple venture entrepreneurs. *Frontiers of Entrepreneurship Research*, 11, 213–227.

Stephan, A. (2014). Are public research spin-offs more innovative? *Small Business Economics*, 43, 353–368.

Stuart, T. E., and Ding, W. W. (2006). When do scientists become entrepreneurs? The social structural antecedents of commercial activity in the academic life sciences. *American Journal of Sociology*, 112(1), 97–144.

Stuart, T. E., Hoang, H., and Hybels, R. C. (1999). Interorganizational endorsements and the performance of entrepreneurial ventures. *Administrative Science Quarterly*, 44(2), 315–349.

Tether, B. S., and Tajar, A. (2008). Beyond industry–university links: Sourcing knowledge for innovation from consultants, private research organizations and the public science base. *Research Policy*, 37(6–7), 1079–1095.

Thornhill, S. (2006). Knowledge, innovation and firm performance in high- and low-technology regimes. *Journal of Business Venturing*, 21(5), 687–703.

Tushman, M. L., and Anderson, P. (1986). Technological discontinuities and organizational environments. *Administrative Science Quarterly*, 31(3), 439–465.

Van Maanen, J. E., and Schein, E. H. (1977). Toward a theory of organizational socialization. MIT Working Paper, 960–977.

Visintin, F., and Pittino, D. (2014). Founding team composition and early performance of university-based spin-off companies. *Technovation*, 34(1), 1–43.

Wasserman, N. (2017). The throne vs. the kingdom: Founder control and value creation in startups. *Strategic Management Journal*, 38, 255–277.

Wennberg, K., Wiklund, J., and Wright, M. (2011). The effectiveness of university knowledge spillovers: Performance differences between university spinoffs and corporate spinoffs. *Research Policy*, 40(8), 1128–1143.

Wessendorf, C. P., Kegelmann, J., and Terzidis, O. (2019). Determinants of early-stage technology venture valuation by business angels and venture capitalists. *International Journal of Entrepreneurial Venturing*, 11(5), 489–520.

Wessendorf, C. P., Schneider, J., Gresch, M. A., and Terzidis, O. (2020). What matters most in technology venture valuation? Importance and impact of non-financial determinants for early-stage venture valuation. *International Journal of Entrepreneurial Venturing*, 12(5), 490–521.

Wood, L. (2000). Brands and brand equity: Definition and management. *Management Decision*, 38(9), 662–669.

Wyatt, A. (2008). What financial and non-financial information on intangibles is value-relevant? A review of the evidence. *Accounting and Business Research*, 38(3), 217–256.

Yin, R. K. (2015). Causality, generalizability, and the future of mixed methods research. In S. Hesse-Biber and R. B. Johnson (eds.), *The Oxford Handbook of Multimethod and Mixed Methods Research Inquiry*. Oxford: Oxford University Press, pp. 652–664.

Zheng, Y., Liu, J., and George, G. (2010). The dynamic impact of innovative capability and inter-firm network on firm valuation: A longitudinal study of biotechnology start-ups. *Journal of Business Venturing*, 25(6), 593–609.

Zider, B. (1998). How venture capital works. *Harvard Business Review*, 76, 131–139.

Zucker, L. G., Darby, M. R., and Armstrong, J. (2007). Geographically localized knowledge: Spillovers or markets? *Economic Inquiry*, 36(1), 65–86.

Index

academic and scientific entrepreneurs
 characteristics of 83
 industry partnerships 125–8
 in innovative startups 253, 256–8, 259
 knowledge transfer 97
 see also entrepreneurial activity; entrepreneurship; principal investigators (PIs); universities
academic spin-offs *see* spin-offs
actor-network theory (ANT) 13–16, 17
agency theory 252
Agrawal, A. 164
Agyare, Daniel xxiii–xxiv
Ahl, H. 56
Alegre, I. 148
Alharthi, A. 68, 69
Amankwah-Amoah, J. 48
Amaral, A. 49
Amit, R. 91
Anglin, A. H. 161
Anokhin, S. 204
Arksey, H. 229
Aronica, Martina xxi–xxii
Ashourizadeh, S. 186
Au, K. 184
Audretsch, David B. 227
Autio, Erkko 84

Balachandra, L. 50
Barney, J. 248–9
Bartell, M. 91
Baù, M. 49
Bayh–Dole Act (1980) 95, 118
Bayus, B. L. 159
Bechtolsheim, Andy 124
Belitski, Maksim 97
Belleflamme, P. 163
Bengtsson, O. 48
big data

characteristics of 69
consulting firms 68, 70–71, 78
defined 68–9
internal and external firm resources 71–2, 75, 77, 78
international e-commerce 68, 69–71, 72, 75, 78
Porter's value chain 69
technological barriers 70
types of approaches 68
Bijker, W. E. 10
Bimber, B. 7
Bird, M. 187
Block, J. H. 251–2
Bonardo, D. 255
Bulliet, R. W. 6–7
Burns, T. 6
Burrows, P. 91
business angels (BAs)
 approach to valuation of startups 228–9
 demographics of 190–191
 firm formation model 123–4
 funding strangers 188, 192, 193
 and gender 190–191, 195
 impact of context on entrepreneurial ties 185
 institutional context for financing 182
 investment decision factors 184, 186–7
 investment propensity and personal ties 186–7
 personal ties 182–3, 186–8, 191–3
 role overview 183
 in secular-rational cultures 183, 188, 190, 192, 193, 194
 in traditional cultures 183, 187–8, 190, 192–3, 194
 traditional vs secular-rational culture 185–6, 190, 194
 and trust 184–5, 186, 187, 188, 193